COLIN POWELL

COLIN POWELL

★   ★   ★   ★

IMPERFECT

PATRIOT

JEFFREY J. MATTHEWS

University of Notre Dame Press

Notre Dame, Indiana

University of Notre Dame Press
Notre Dame, Indiana 46556
undpress.nd.edu

Published in the United States of America

Library of Congress Cataloging-in-Publication Data

Names: Matthews, Jeffrey J., 1965– author.
Title: Colin Powell : imperfect patriot / Jeffrey J. Matthews.
Description: Notre Dame, Indiana : University of Notre Dame Press, [2019] |
Includes bibliographical references and index. |
Identifiers: LCCN 2018055514 (print) | LCCN 2018057014 (ebook) |
ISBN 9780268105112 (pdf) | ISBN 9780268105129 (epub) |
ISBN 9780268105099 (hardback : alk. paper) | ISBN 026810509X
(hardback : alk. paper)
Subjects: LCSH: Powell, Colin L. | African American generals—Biography. |
Generals—United States—Biography. | United States. Army—Officers—
Biography. | Statesmen—United States—Biography. | Cabinet officers—
United States—Biography. | Iraq War, 2003–2011—Causes. | Leadership—
United States. | Followership. | United State—Politics and
government—2001–2009.
Classification: LCC E840.5.P68 (ebook) | LCC E840.5.P68 M38   2019
(print) | DDC 327.730092 [B] —dc23
LC record available at https://lccn.loc.gov/2018055514

∞This paper meets the requirements of ANSI/NISO Z39.48-1992
(Permanence of Paper).

To Emily and Kate,
carpe diem

Every statement I make today is backed up by sources, solid sources. These are not assertions. What we are giving you are facts and conclusions based on solid evidence.

—COLIN L. POWELL

Certitude is not the test of certainty. We have been cocksure of many things that were not so.

—OLIVER WENDELL HOLMES JR.

CONTENTS

CONTENTS

PREFACE

By early spring 2017, I had completed a draft of this Colin Powell biography and was planning to contact the general to request an interview. Before I did, he reached out to me. On the evening of March 26, I was on my way to a birthday dinner with my daughters when I received an email from "Colin Powell" with the subject line "Re: Colin Powell." I was surprised and enormously suspicious of the email's authenticity. Years earlier, through his assistant, Powell had granted me permission to examine his personal papers, which are archived at the library of the National Defense University (NDU), but we had never communicated directly. Here is our first email exchange:

CP: *Dear Professor Matthews, is this a good email address for you? I'd like to send a message. Colin Powell*

JM: *General Powell, although I doubt you would be emailing me, feel free to send any message. Jeff*

CP: *Thanks, I really am. Thought your book on Command was quite good. Will be back to you in a day or so. It relates to the piece you had in the HuffPost about HR and me. cp*

JM: *Thank you, General. Looking forward to it. Jeff*

The book he referred to is *The Art of Command: Military Leadership from George Washington to Colin Powell*, which includes a chapter I wrote about the general's "exemplary followership" in the U.S. Army. The "HuffPost" piece was actually a March 14, 2017, article I wrote for *The Hill*, a political newspaper in Washington, DC.

The Hill op-ed, titled "How H. R. McMaster can win on the political battlefield of Washington," identified lessons that McMaster, Donald Trump's new national security adviser, could learn from Powell's experience. While the article was largely positive about Powell's performance as a public servant, it also criticized him for not cultivating a closer relationship with President George W. Bush and for failing to exercise sufficient independent judgment regarding the supposed threat of weapons of mass destruction in Iraq. These criticisms, not the substantive compliments, had prompted Powell to contact me.

On March 27 the general emailed again to offer a vigorous self-defense. Nothing he wrote was surprising to me, and having no desire to debate a former secretary of state and chairman of the Joint Chiefs of Staff via email, I maneuvered for a personal interview. Here is our exchange:

CP: *Dear Professor Matthews,*

I thought your article in The Hill was quite good, but I take exception to your glancing paragraph about my "failures."

You have no idea about my relationship with President Bush. I am amused how you tied "close, and thus more open and influential" together as a failure. On 5 August 2002 I met privately with him in his WH residence. After a relaxing dinner, I told him I was not comfortable with the political and diplomatic considerations relevant to a potential conflict with Iraq. I told him it would probably suction all the air out of his presidency and that he needed to understand that when you take out a government, you become the government. "If you break it, you own it." He asked what he should do. My answer was to take it to the UN, they are the offended party and see if we could get what we needed from Iraq on WMD [weapons of mass destruction] to avoid a war. I also asked him if he was prepared to accept Saddam in place if there were no WMD. He said, "yes." We sold that position to the rest of the reluctant NSC members. That is what the president did in his famous 12 Sept UN speech. It took me six weeks of intense negotiations to get a unanimous resolution that gave Hussein a "get out of jail card." Pretty open.

Hussein failed the test and in January 2003 the President decided on military action. On 4 days' notice I gave my famous UN speech on 5 Feb to present our case to the world. Since I set the President on this diplomatic path I told him if he chose war I would support. You said I did not give enough "independent and critical thought" to the WMD issue. Independent of what? Sixteen intelligence agencies, to include my INR, concurred in the intel, 376 members of Congress had access to the NIE they requested and voted for a resolution that opened the path to war. The President, the VP, the Cabinet, the CJCS, JCS, Cinc, NS Adviser all bought into it. Most of the serious charges in my speech were in the State of Union speech a few weeks earlier. Hillary, Kerry, et al were full-throated in support. Do they all deserve the same hit you place on me? Every word in the speech was approved by the DCI. What "sufficient independence" do you think I should have had? In my recent book and in interviews I express my regret and regret my instincts failed me. Maybe I failed myself, but please don't lecture me that I failed the President and Country. If I did we all did.

By the way, if you read General Tommy Franks' memoir you will find a page discussing my phone call to him when I suggested he didn't have enough troops for the unknowns that might occur. Keep writing! All the best, Colin Powell

JM: *Dear General Powell,*

First, let me extend my sincere appreciation for your emails and expressed concerns. Certainly, my objective as a

*historian is to be accurate and fair, and I will take into ac-
count everything that you have written here and elsewhere.
After many years of research and writing, I am finishing my
book on your professional career this summer. I benefited
immensely from reading your papers at NDU, so thank you
for that access as well. Susan and the staff were exceedingly
helpful.*

*To better understand your perspective on multiple is-
sues, would it be possible to set up an interview(s) sometime
between April and August? I am a frequent visitor to DC for
research, plus my brother (Maj. Gen. Earl Matthews, USAF
Ret.) lives in Alexandria. I know for sure I will be there in
latter June. I would be more than happy to provide questions in advance.*

*General, I do realize that you get hundreds of interview
requests, but I have purposely waited to ask until I was at
the tail end of the biography, which, in large part, focuses on
the idea of what makes for an exemplary subordinate. As
you have said, "Leadership is all about followership." Re-
spectfully, Jeff*

Powell ultimately agreed to an interview, which occurred at
his home in June 2017. I began our meeting by explaining the
book's premise, and when I stated that even America's greatest
presidents were flawed human beings who made consequential
mistakes, the general smiled broadly and pointed to himself with
both hands. Although we did not set a time limit for the meeting,
I suspect that the four hours we spent together were much more
time than he had anticipated. The general had originally asked
that the interview be conducted "on background," but afterward he gave me permission to cite the meeting and to para-
phrase his responses. In brief, the interview directly or indirectly
confirmed the principal arguments and assertions I make herein.

ACKNOWLEDGMENTS

Although the process of researching and writing is often conducted in quiet solitude, my work has depended on the generous contributions of others. Above all, military historian Harry S. Laver helped to bring this book to fruition. During its decade-long gestation, he thoroughly and effectively challenged my thinking, my evidence, and my prose. Thank you, my friend. Equally inspiring were my gentlemen mentors, historians Joseph A. Fry and George C. Herring, who continue to provide stalwart support and wise counsel. The culmination of this project is but another small return on their significant investment in me.

I want to thank Professor Howard Jones for reviewing my chapter on Powell's Vietnam War experience, Malcolm Byrne for reading the Iran-Contra chapter, and the Leadership and Military History faculty of the U.S. Army Command and General Staff College for our vibrant discussion of Powell's "followership" and his 2003 presentation to the U.N. Security Council. Thanks also to Karen DeYoung, senior national security and foreign policy correspondent of the *Washington Post*, for agreeing to discuss Powell with me. Her 2006 Powell biography, *Soldier*, is simply superb.

Many people at the University of Puget Sound have backed this project, and none more so than Professor Priti Joshi, who, for two years, acted as my primary local interlocutor on all things Powell. Thank you, Priti, for your munificence and

ACKNOWLEDGMENTS

thoughtful interrogations, which honed my arguments and fortified my confidence. I also want to thank my colleagues in the School of Business and Leadership, Provost Kris Bartanen, President Isiaah Crawford, Professors Doug Goodman, Bruce Mann, Eric Orlin, Nick Kontogeorgopoulos, and my many students, especially those who have endured the Paradigms of Leadership and Leadership in American History courses. I also must acknowledge the generous financial support of the Jewett family, whose endowment continues to underwrite my research, and the ever-generous George and Susan Matelich for providing me the opportunity to mentor our incredible group of Matelich Scholars.

Thanks to my loving family—Kate, Emily, Mom, Andy, Earl, Linda, and Nadia, all my nieces and nephews, and my late father, Lieutenant Colonel Cleve E. Matthews. Thanks also to my dear friends Liz Collins and Rebecca Harrison. Clearly, angels do exist. Libby, you have captured and inspired my heart. It is indeed a long road to Yakima, but we made it. Ohio!

Finally, I must thank both Colin Powell and the staff at the University of Notre Dame Press, especially my champions Stephen Wrinn and Eli Bortz, my superb copy editor Kellie M. Hultgren, and two anonymous peer reviewers. Thanks to General Powell himself for inspiring me to write this biography, for giving me unfettered access to his papers at the NDU, and for opening up his home for an extended interview. At our meeting, I informed Powell that there would be sections of the book he would not like. To his credit, he encouraged me to "write what I think is right," and I have.

Leadership is all about followership.

—COLIN L. POWELL

Introduction

On the morning of February 5, 2003, Colin Powell took his seat at the large, curved table of the United Nations Security Council. He had been tasked by President George W. Bush to prosecute Iraqi dictator Saddam Hussein in the court of world opinion. "This is an important day," Powell announced, "for us all."[1] The American secretary of state's highly anticipated presentation marked the zenith of his extraordinary forty-year career in government service; it was as if he had been preparing for the moment all of his life.

According to the Bush administration, Saddam Hussein represented a clear and present danger to the security of the United States, a danger so ominous that it warranted an internationally televised evidentiary hearing. The president had allotted Powell less than a week to prepare a comprehensive case meant to justify preventive warfare and the overthrow a foreign government. Powell was up to Bush's challenge.

The secretary was the perfect person to assemble and present the case against Iraq. Effective prosecutors must have credibility and ability, and the retired four-star army general possessed both, in spades. Having served successfully as the senior military assistant to Defense Secretary Caspar Weinberger, as national security adviser to President Ronald Reagan, and as chairman of the Joint Chiefs of Staff for presidents George H. W. Bush and Bill Clinton, Powell's experience in international security affairs was exceptional. Moreover, by 2003, the secretary of state's reputation for trustworthiness at home and abroad was unparalleled, far exceeding that of President Bush and all other senior advisers, including Dick Cheney, Donald Rumsfeld, and Condoleezza Rice. Powell's stature and popularity had been forged during the 1990–1991 Persian Gulf War when, as chairman of the Joint Chiefs of Staff, he earned a reputation as an articulate, trustworthy, and decisive warrior-leader. A decade later, in the aftermath of the terrorist attacks of September 11, 2001, Secretary of State Powell, more than any other principal of a hawkish National Security Council, was perceived as the least likely to exaggerate the threat posed by Saddam Hussein. In January 2003, when Bush instructed Powell to prepare the brief against Iraq at the United Nations, he told the secretary, "We've really got to make the case, and I want you to make it. You have the credibility to do this. Maybe they'll believe you."[2]

Powell's sterling reputation was matched by his capacity to construct and deliver persuasive and compelling briefings. Acutely aware that his and the president's credibility would be at stake, the secretary and his staff worked assiduously with the Central Intelligence Agency (CIA) and the White House to craft a cogent, nonpoliticized, fact-based presentation that exposed the Iraqi danger. Inherently cautious, Powell sought to draw only incontrovertible conclusions from "solid evidence" and to discard questionable intelligence "that seemed a stretch or wasn't multisourced."[3]

Powell's first decision was to reject a White House proposal for a three-day U.N. presentation that dissected Iraq's nexus with terrorists, its record of human rights violations, and its weapons of mass destruction (WMD) programs. Instead, Powell insisted on a succinct ninety-minute presentation that focused predominately on WMD. He and CIA Director George Tenet also rejected a WMD report prepared by Vice President

Cheney's office. Powell and Tenet concluded that Cheney's contrived document contained numerous unsubstantiated claims that rendered it "a disaster," "worthless," "incoherent," and "unusable."[4] In the end, Powell's presentation relied extensively on the October 2002 National Intelligence Estimate (NIE) regarding "Iraq's Continuing Programs for Weapons of Mass Destruction."[5] CIA officer Michael Morell, who assisted Powell in the intelligence vetting process, marveled at the secretary's rigorous, systematic approach to building the prosecutorial case against Iraq. With each iteration of the U.N. speech, Powell challenged every sentence and renewed his questioning about the quality of the intelligence. "Point by point," Morell later wrote, the secretary "would ask us for backup information on the assertions, and as we dug into them, many seemed to fall apart before my eyes. . . . What was collapsing was some of the facts used in the NIE."[6] After four days and nights of meticulous labor, Powell, Tenet, Rice, and Deputy CIA Director John McLaughlin were satisfied that they had constructed a highly credible, "airtight" briefing that proved the president's contention that Iraq was an evident and immediate danger to the United States and others.[7]

At the United Nations, before a worldwide television audience, Powell, with Tenet visible in a seat behind him, delivered a formidable case against Iraq. The secretary of state spoke soberly, methodically, and confidently for seventy-five minutes. "Every statement I make today," he proclaimed, "is backed up by sources, solid sources. These are not assertions. What we are giving you are facts and conclusions based on solid evidence."[8] Powell's prosecution, which purportedly gave proof of Iraq's active WMD programs and its nefarious association with terrorist groups, was a multimedia affair that featured a vial of fake anthrax, satellite imagery, audiotapes, photographs, and renderings of mobile biological weapons laboratories. In his closing statement, the secretary concluded that Saddam Hussein was either on the brink of launching WMD or sharing them with terrorist organizations. As a consequence, Powell, the trusted and beloved hero of the Persian Gulf War, announced to the world that the United States "will not and cannot run that risk." The Bush administration, he vowed, "will not shirk" from eliminating the Iraqi menace.[9]

Foreign reactions to Powell's performance were mixed at best, but the response at home was decidedly favorable. Like many Americans, the secretary believed that he had made a powerful casus belli argument against Iraq. "My feeling," Powell later wrote, "was that the presentation went well. . . . On balance, we seemed to have made a powerful case."[10] Tenet thought that Powell gave "an extraordinary performance."[11] Bush and Rice concurred. The latter described the presentation as a "tour de force."[12] The president characterized it as an "exhaustive, eloquent, and persuasive" briefing, and he ultimately concluded that it had "profound impact on the public debate."[13] Indeed, Powell's line of argumentation converted many skeptics across the nation, assuring Republicans and Democrats alike.[14] Both the *Washington Post* and *New York Times* editorialized that the secretary had made an earnest and convincing case.[15] Forty-three days after Powell's presentation, the United States invaded Iraq with the support of a majority of American citizens and with a formal authorization from Congress.

At the time of the invasion, before it was known that Iraq no longer possessed WMD, Powell's performance in the preparation and delivery of the U.N. speech seemed a model of excellent followership in service to the president and country. Bush had assigned Powell an important and challenging mission, one that tested his abilities and leveraged his enormous prestige. The secretary responded with considerable competence, composure, and dedication. Moreover, he demonstrated characteristic initiative and resourcefulness and exercised his capacity for independent critical judgment. Above all, perhaps, Powell acted honorably; he believed what he said. In building the U.N. briefing, he rejected information that he considered spurious and included only intelligence that he or the CIA leadership appraised as credible and reliable. That President Bush and so many Americans thought so highly of Powell's conduct was completely understandable.

The thesis of this book is that Powell's decades-long development as an *exemplary subordinate* was crucial to his extraordinary rise from a working-class immigrant neighborhood in the South Bronx to the highest echelons of American military and political power. Although once an aimless teenager, Powell joined the U.S. Army in 1958 with unbridled enthusiasm and a commitment to cultivating his professional skills and serving his superiors. He succeeded brilliantly. During thirty-five years in the military, Powell earned the respect and fidelity of numerous bosses and mentors who intervened regularly to advance his career. Early on, his superiors judged him as having unlimited potential and unswerving loyalty. They described Powell as "a young ambitious officer" who "immediately responds to suggestion and correction" and who "is completely dedicated to the service."[16] While Powell was stationed in South Vietnam as a junior officer, his commanders extolled his virtues as a model subordinate who "has demonstrated constantly his complete competence, levelheadedness, and dependability."[17] One major general even characterized Powell as "the most outstanding staff officer that I have seen in 32 years of service."[18]

Similarly, Powell's conduct as a senior army officer garnered profuse praise from civilian superiors. National Security Adviser Frank Carlucci characterized him as "totally dedicated," "unfailingly loyal to me," and "indefatigable in ensuring that I have been properly supported."[19] Defense Secretary Weinberger assessed Powell as being "categorically superlative," writing that the major general's performance as his senior military assistant "only confirms my belief that I could not have chosen a more loyal, capable, or dependable officer to fill this position of special trust and confidence."[20] By the time Powell was appointed as President George H. W. Bush's chairman of the Joint Chiefs of Staff, he had become the consummate subordinate: a highly experienced professional who personified competence, commitment, thoughtfulness, agreeableness, composure, independence, and integrity.

Powell's exemplary followership notwithstanding, there can be little doubt that he also exercised effective leadership, both during his military career and thereafter at the State Department. Subordinates, superiors, and outside observers regularly assessed Powell as a capable, ethical, and inspirational leader.[21] As early as 1961, when he was a twenty-four-year-old first lieutenant, his army evaluator wrote, "[Powell is] a truly outstanding officer in every aspect and attribute of leadership. . . . This young lieutenant has the professional knowledge equivalent to an officer of higher rank and greater experience."[22] A decade later, after Powell successfully led a once-troubled American battalion in South Korea, his boss, the colorful and exacting Major General Henry E. Emerson, concluded, "Goddamn, this son of a bitch can command soldiers. He was charismatic. He really raised the morale, especially the *esprit* of that unit. . . . He sure as shit showed me what he could do as a commander."[23]

By 1991, in the afterglow of decisive U.S. military victories in Panama and the Persian Gulf, Republican senator John McCain boldly proclaimed that General Powell was "the greatest military leader this country has produced since World War II."[24] After his retirement from the army, Powell continued to demonstrate able leadership during the first term of the George W. Bush administration, at the helm of the State Department. According to John Naland, former president of the American Foreign Service Association, "Powell [was] easily the best leader and manager State has seen since George Shultz. . . . As far as the Foreign Service is concerned, Powell has been an absolute standout."[25]

While acknowledging Powell's praiseworthy leadership, this book's primary focus is on his development and performance as a follower. Throughout his forty-year public career, Powell was *always* somebody's subordinate. Even if one excludes Powell's Army Reserve Officer Training Corps experience at City College of New York, he spent more than 10 percent of his active-duty army career as a full-time student, a definitive follower role. Furthermore, as a senior military officer—serving at the rank of colonel and higher—most of Powell's job titles reflected not his expanding leadership authority but rather the persistence of his follower status: executive *assistant* to the special assistant to the secretary and the deputy secretary of defense, military *assistant* to the deputy secretary of defense, executive *assistant* to the secretary of energy, senior military *assistant* to the deputy secretary of defense, deputy senior military *assistant* to the secretary of defense, deputy *assistant* to the president for national security affairs, and *assistant* to the president for national security affairs. Moreover, even after securing the exalted positions of national security adviser, chairman of the Joint Chiefs of Staff, and secretary of state, Powell's principal duty was to serve as a chief counselor to four presidents and three secretaries of defense.

Powell's performance as a subordinate reveals not only core elements of superior followership, but also human fallibility and central characteristics of bad followership. Too often successful and patriotic military officers such as Powell have prioritized career ambition, excessive obedience, and blind loyalty over independent critical reasoning and ethical principles. The U.S. Army's cover-up of atrocities committed against Vietnamese civilians in Vietnam, in which Powell played a minor role, and later, the Reagan administration's Iran-Contra scandal, in which he played a substantive role, exemplified the degrading nature and dangerous consequences of unethical followership. And while Powell's subsequent tenure as chairman of the Joint Chiefs of Staff marked a high point in his evolution as an exceptionally effective and ethical subordinate, his followership skills were tested mightily after he became George W. Bush's senior foreign policy adviser. In fact, many critics of the Bush administration characterize Powell's performance, as represented by his influential yet fallacious 2003 U.N. speech, as the epitome of bad followership.[26] Powell himself has acknowledged some dire career mistakes and has written that his presentation advocating a second war with Iraq "was one of my most momentous failures" because it "had enormous impact and influence in this country and worldwide. It convinced many people that we were on the right course."[27]

From a broad perspective, this book examines and promotes the often pivotal, if relatively unsung, role of effective and ethical followership in the leadership process. Only in recent decades did scholars begin to seriously investigate the nature and influence of good and bad followers.[28] Unlike prior research on followership, this book takes a biographical approach, offering a fresh examination of Colin Powell's distinguished, though ultimately controversial, public career. Powell's story is instructive on many levels. During various periods of his life, he personified the qualities associated with both good and bad followership. Moreover, Powell's government service shows that ethical and effective followership, as with good leadership, is developed over time and is dependent on the influence of others, especially superiors, mentors, and role models. Powell's career further demonstrates the tremendous power that followers can exert on leaders and organizations, and also exemplifies the reality that most people in positions of leadership serve concurrently in positions of followership.

In the end, this biography provides a critical perspective on the nature of good and bad followership and thus on the broader phenomenon of the leadership process. "Some may wonder why so much is made of just where leadership and followership begin and end," writes Pulitzer Prize winner James MacGregor Burns. "But this question lies at the heart of the core issue—the relationship of leadership and followership not only to each other but to social change and historical causation."[29]

PART I

The Military Years

In my family, especially,
you did what your parents expected of you.
— COLIN L. POWELL

CHAPTER ONE

Obedient Son

(1937–1957)

There is little in Colin Powell's youth that foreshadowed his becoming the most powerful and admired American military leader of his generation. Raised by immigrant parents in a working-class neighborhood of New York's South Bronx, Powell never excelled in academics or athletics, nor did he display the extroverted qualities so often associated with burgeoning young leaders. Powell, in fact, was frequently seen by family members as lacking direction, motivation, and commitment. There were "no sightings of greatness," his older sister Marilyn later recalled. "I guess he was a late bloomer."[1] In his 1995 autobiography, Powell aptly described his young self as "amenable, amicable, and aimless."[2] Nevertheless, a close examination of his childhood reveals the emergence of traits and behaviors, including deference, cautiousness, affability, and loyalty, that ultimately contributed to his remarkably successful career in the U.S. Army and beyond. By the age of eighteen, after he had entered City College of New York, he had begun a radical transformation into a focused, intelligent, skillful, and tireless follower and leader.

Powell's Jamaican-born parents were part of a post–World War I exodus of Caribbean immigrants seeking economic opportunity in America. They proved influential role models whose lived values shaped and guided their son's life. Powell's father, Luther Theophilus Powell, was born at the time of Spanish-Cuban-American War to a large, poor, and uneducated family. He immigrated to America aboard a United Fruit Company steamboat in 1920. Luther worked a variety of menial jobs before settling into Manhattan's garment district, where he embarked on a lengthy career with Ginsburg's, a clothing company later known as the Gaines Company. There, Luther rose from stock boy to shipping department foreman, proudly touting the latter as a position in "management."[3] In 1929 Luther married Maud Ariel "Arie" McKoy, who had come ashore at Ellis Island six years prior. She too was from a sizable family, but unlike her husband, Arie had completed high school before emigrating. The couple lived first in Harlem and then relocated to a fourth-story walk-up apartment in the Hunts Point section of the Bronx. Arie, a member of the International Ladies' Garment Workers' Union, labored as a seamstress, managed the household, and cared for the children: Marilyn, born in 1931, and Colin Luther, born five and half years later.

The influence of Colin's parents on the development of his personality, ethics, and goals, cannot be exaggerated. As was common in immigrant families from the West Indies, the Powells took immense pride in work, personal integrity, and self-improvement.[4] Luther and Arie had both become U.S. citizens by 1940, and they, like many of their émigré relatives from Jamaica, made higher education and upward socioeconomic mobility top priorities for their children. Colin, his sister, and their cousins were made to "feel that education was the way to pull yourself up," that there was a "tradition of hard work being the

way to succeed. And there was simply an expectation that existed in the family—you were supposed to do better. And it was
a bloody disappointment to the family if you didn't."[5]

Luther and Arie worked long hours and set high standards
for personal comportment. As parents, they taught their children by modeling best behaviors, not by lecturing or engaging in
earnest conversation. "It was nothing they ever said that taught
us," Colin remembered. "I had been shaped not by preaching,
but by example, by moral osmosis."[6] He continued, "It wasn't
a matter of spending a great deal of time with my parents discussing things. We didn't sit down at night like the Brady Bunch
and review the work of the day. It was just the way they lived
their lives."[7]

Arie Powell was a diminutive dynamo who garnered much
love and respect from her children. Her devotion had a lasting
effect on her son. "When I picture Mom," Powell later wrote,
"she is wearing an apron, bustling around our apartment, always in motion, cooking, washing, ironing, sewing, after working all day downtown in the garment district as a seamstress,
sewing buttons and trim on clothing."[8] The whirling Arie was
also known for her extreme caution and incessant worrying,
especially about the family's finances and reputation in the
community.[9] Colin characterized his mother as "the perennial
worrier" possessing "a melting smile."[10] He recalled "a great
deal of status consciousness within West Indian families and Jamaican families; especially between those who have a little bit
of education and those who don't."[11] Arie's blend of tenderness
and willfulness contributed to him becoming "a bit of mama's
boy," a cautious and compliant son who avoided trouble so as
to remain in her good graces.[12] At a young age, he learned that
children must never embarrass their families and must always
"mind their adults."[13]

Standing atop the familial hierarchy was Luther Powell. A
mere five feet and three inches tall, he was the family "ring-
master," an unimposing optimist and a glad-hander.[14] Like Arie,
he was a dedicated worker who prized order and integrity; he

also loved to socialize. Dapper in appearance and carefree in attitude, he habitually chatted up the neighbors and became well known in Hunts Point for his generosity and gregariousness. Immensely proud of his American citizenship and personal achievements, he enjoyed reading newspapers and instigating debate on national and international affairs. At times when the more reserved Arie thought her husband was spouting off too self-confidently, she would mock him in her Jamaican dialect, "Him who never finished high school."[15]

Luther, ever ebullient, was the towering figure of Colin's childhood. Colin admired his father's confidence, cheeriness, and panache. Luther's unthreatening yet "take charge manner" was reassuring, and as a result, Colin yearned to please him.[16] One afternoon, Luther happened upon his son playing baseball with neighborhood kids. Colin wanted to impress his dad by batting well. It was not to be; he struck out repeatedly. Four decades later, Powell could still feel "the burning humiliation" of that day, as it was "always painful for me to disappoint my father."[17]

Throughout his childhood, Colin sought his parents' approval. They had taught him and his sister to obey authority and not shame the family.[18] Consequently, the Powell children were known to be agreeable, obedient, and morally upright. Schoolmate Marlene Charnizon remembered Colin as "an average, do-the-right-thing kind of guy."[19] Powell himself claimed that he, unlike other kids in the neighborhood, deliberately avoided experimentation with drugs because "my parents would have killed me."[20] Only on rare occasions did he get into mischief. When Powell was eight, neighbors caught him playing hooky from school, and several years later, his father found him dealing poker for some neighborhood men at the local shoe-repair shop. Such minor offenses never led to harsh consequences. In truth, Luther "rarely uttered a word of reproach" to his son.[21] The real punishment was the visceral pain of having displeased his parents. "The worst days of my life," Powell later said, "were . . . when I did something that disappointed my mother and my father."[22]

Young Powell's most severe transgression came while he attended a summer church camp in Peekskill, New York. The priest at the camp discovered several beers hidden inside the restroom. When Father Weeden asked who was responsible for the alcohol, Colin confessed to the crime and his coconspirators quickly followed suit. The sinners were sent home early. Powell's parents were livid; their boy had embarrassed the family, and at an Episcopalian function, no less. However, after learning that Colin had told the truth and taken responsibility, Luther and Arie allowed him to escape serious punishment. "Something from that boyhood experience, the rewards of honesty," Powell later recalled, "hit home and stayed."[23]

Despite occasional misadventures, Powell's disposition was, much like his father's, congenial and reliable. He was happy in the family home and even more so when playing outside with his clique of racially and ethnically diverse friends. Despite being black, young Powell never felt the sting of discrimination nor carried the burden of racism. "I grew up in neighborhood where everybody was a minority—blacks, Jews, Puerto Ricans," he later wrote. "And I never thought there was something wrong with me because I was black."[24] Although not a leader of his peers, Powell was popular. One friend recalled, "Colin had a great sense of humor. He always had a smile on his face. Kids wanted him around."[25] Beyond his amicability, another Powell attribute, according to childhood friend Gene Norman, was his unflinching fidelity: "He was fiercely loyal. . . . I could always count on his loyalty to take my side."[26] Like many other Hunts Point kids, Powell loved bicycling, playing stickball and sluggo, and attending weekend movie matinees. "I was a happy-go-lucky kid," he remembered; "My pleasures were hanging out with the guys."[27]

While happily disposed with many friends, Powell's academic record in the South Bronx public school system was mediocre at best, paling in comparison to his sister's well-known acumen. Although he worked hard at his studies, Colin admitted, "I was not one of the burning lights of this extended family."[28] At one point in elementary school, he was even classified as a slow learner and placed in a class with other subpar performers. Arie and Luther accepted that Colin was less academically talented than his sister, yet they expected "nothing less" than his best efforts.[29] Powell wanted to earn better grades for his parents' sake; his relatively weak marks in school were "the sort of secret to be whispered with shaking heads in our family circle."[30] His grades improved in junior high school, and in senior high school he demonstrated some affinity for history and geography. Still, Powell lacked intrinsic drive for intellectual endeavors and his overall academic performance failed to impress. He graduated high school with a 78.3 percent grade average and with "few screen credits" in the yearbook.[31] Years later, a classmate remembered Colin as "a friendly, always respectful gentleman," but added that she "never figured him as destined for national prominence."[32]

Standing six feet tall and approaching two hundred pounds, Powell might have demonstrated some athletic prowess in school, but it never materialized because he lacked motivation and commitment. He ran track for a season but eventually quit, unenthused. Likewise, he abandoned the church basketball team after faking a back injury, and he served only an abbreviated stint in the Boy Scouts. Powell also tried his hand at the piano and the flute, but ended up, much to Luther and Arie's chagrin, quitting both. "My inability to stick to anything," Powell acknowledged, "became a source of concern to my parents, unspoken, but I knew it was there."[33]

Two domains in which Powell's performance met his parents' expectations were church and work, and there he revealed a rich capacity for effective followership. Both environments provided formal structure and clear expectations, and neither required much critical or independent judgment. Following his father's lead as the parish board president and senior warden

of St. Margaret's Episcopal Church, Colin served as an aco-
lyte and was later promoted to subdeacon. The church, with its
"organization, tradition, hierarchy" and "pageantry, drama, and
poetry," captured Powell's imagination and inspired atypical
passion and commitment.[34] Later, as an adult, he reminisced af-
fectionately about his church activities, writing, "I loved it all."[35]
Similarly, Powell embodied the family work ethic as a part-time
employee at Sickser's children's furniture and toy store. Starting at fifty cents per hour, he diligently unloaded and assembled
merchandise and erected holiday displays. Powell's devotion
and friendliness impressed the store's owner, Jay Sickser, who
retained the teenager at the family business for five years. Recognizing Powell's underlying potential, Sickser eventually advised him, "Collie, I want you [to] get an education and do well.
You're too good to just be a schlepper."[36]

Despite his lackluster academic record, Powell applied for
college admission, not out of burning desire or intellectual in-
quisitiveness, but rather to meet his parents' expectations. Their
ultimate goal for him was to join the ranks of America's rapidly
expanding middle class, and university was the surest path to
that end. "I went to college for a single reason," Powell later
confessed to students at his alma mater. "My parents expected
it. I don't recall having any great urge to get a higher education.
I don't even remember consciously thinking the matter through.
I just recall that my parents expected it of me. And in those days
when your parents expected something, it was what you had to
do. In my family, especially, you did what your parents expected
of you."[37] Because of his middling grades and the family's limited financial means, Powell's choices for university were few. He
settled on City College of New York, which accepted most ap-
plicants with a high school diploma and the token ten-dollar
tuition.

Powell's lack of initiative and intrinsic drive for college extended to the selection of an academic major. This signal decision
was made not by Powell, but by his mother after consultation
with her sisters. Always conscious of status, Arie concluded that

an engineering degree would best serve her son because "that's where the money is, man."[38] Luther also thought it a wise choice, but Colin was nonplussed, given his mental "allergy" to science and mathematics.[39]

Powell's transition from the close-knit comforts of Hunts Point to the neo-Gothic campus of City College in Manhattan was unsettling. He was intimidated by the immense size and fast pace of the school, and by the mostly white, liberal students and faculty. He felt like an outsider, a discomfited interloper. In a 1954 college essay, Powell reflected on his experience: "I was awed by the great complexity of the school as well as all the people I met coming and going. . . . I felt alone."[40]

Not surprisingly, Powell also struggled academically. "I didn't quite know what I was doing in college," he later admitted, and in his second semester, the challenges of an entry-level mechanical drawing course proved overwhelming.[41] Powell dropped not only the course, but also the major, thus dashing his parents' dream of having an engineer in the family. Young Powell could hear the family whispers: "There goes Colin again, nice boy, but no direction."[42] Needing a new major, Powell made his first significant independent decision. After some investigation, he eventually settled on geology, primarily for its reputation as the least rigorous major on campus. Luther and Arie were confounded by the choice, but from Colin's perspective, he had found a realistic way to meet his parents' expectations.

At college, Powell came to recognize some of his own predominant attributes, including his congeniality, trustworthiness, and loyalty. These characteristics would contribute to his successful integration into college life and later to his stellar performance in the army. In a university paper, Powell wrote, "I consider myself a fairly decent person. I am easy to get along with and am able to make friends easily. . . . I am not two-faced and do not like anybody who is. . . . If I like a person I will stick by him all the way: even give him my last dollar."[43]

The major turning point in Powell's college experience—and an event crucial to his preprofessional development—transpired in fall 1954. He decided to enroll in City College's Army Reserve Officer Training Corps (ROTC), one of the largest contingents in the country. Powell's first six months at the university had been "kind of a bummer" because he had not made any friends, but circumstances changed when he met a group of cadets who "were guys a lot like me."[44] Powell believed that "all followers need to feel they belong to a team, a tribe, a band," and the teenager from Hunts Point had finally discovered his cohort.[45] Powell's parents, as befuddled as they were by his choice to join ROTC, grew to appreciate their son's new friends because, like him, "they were all good kids—nobody was a troublemaker."[46]

Powell had been attracted to ROTC by the sharp uniforms, but he soon realized that he had found much more: a genuine passion and a second home. With its well-established hierarchy and clearly articulated values and expectations, ROTC filled the void that he had felt since leaving his family and friends. "That happened to be the perfect niche for him," his sister later contended. "I think he liked the fact that it was structured. He came from a very structured family with rules and order."[47] Powell agreed: "The discipline, the structure, the camaraderie, the sense of belonging were what I craved. . . . I found a selflessness within our ranks that reminded me of the caring atmosphere within my family. . . . If this was what soldiering was all about, then maybe I wanted to be a soldier."[48] Whereas Powell's decision to change his major was born out of academic necessity and the need to achieve his parents' objectives, committing to ROTC was a significant independent choice arising from introspection and the pursuit of happiness.[49]

Within the ROTC program, Powell was befriended by Ronnie Brooks, one of the few other black cadets at City College. Brooks was the first in the extended line of military role models and mentors who helped to forge Powell into a skillful follower and leader. A year ahead of Colin in school, the tall and intelligent Brooks had a commanding presence and rose rapidly from cadet sergeant to battalion commander to drillmaster to cadet colonel. Powell, who described Brooks as an inspiring "driver" and "a hell of lot smarter than me," fully immersed himself in the military regimen.[50]

Powell followed his new idol up the chain of command and joined the Pershing Rifles, a precision drill team. Early on, he learned that competency and dedication were instrumental to receiving promotion in rank and public recognition, two extrinsic rewards he coveted. Moreover, Powell came to realize that the more he excelled as a responsible and agreeable follower, the faster he advanced and the more other cadets looked to him as their model and mentor. As his parents had done for him, Powell led his peers through the power of his example. And, while his academic coursework at City College still left much to be desired, his performance within ROTC was exceptional.

During his college years, Powell spent most summers either working at a soft-drink bottling plant or training at ROTC camps. In both environments he displayed an industrious work ethic and considerable ambition for advancement and praise. As he had done at St. Margaret's Church and Sickser's store, Powell dedicated himself to the work and demonstrated competence and reliability to superiors.

During one summer at the Pepsi bottling plant in Long Island City, Powell, along with other black porters, swung a wet mop for countless hours. "If that was what I had to do to earn $65 a week, I'd do it," he recalled. "I'd mop the place until it glowed in the dark. Whatever skill the job required, I soon mastered."[51] The following summer, again at the Pepsi plant, he was promoted to bottling and pallet-stacking jobs, working alongside white employees and even rising to deputy foreman. From this work experience, Powell deduced a lifelong followership maxim: "All work is honorable. Always do your best, because someone is watching."[52]

Powell similarly excelled during ROTC training. In the summer of 1957, he spent six weeks at Fort Bragg, North Carolina, with cadets from across the nation. Based on his superb military coursework, marksmanship, physical fitness, and leadership ability, Powell was named Best Cadet of Company D and was selected as the encampment's second-best cadet overall.[53]

Powell's academic performance outside of ROTC paled by comparison, but it did not prevent him from graduating. The dichotomy between his military and academic work stemmed largely from divergent motives, not ability. Powell had little passion for study unless it dealt with military affairs. In the end, he said, he graduated "by the skin of my teeth" with a dismal C– cumulative grade point average, which had been propped up by excellent marks in ROTC courses.[54] The latter allowed him to exit college as a Distinguished Military Graduate of the class of 1958. "After four-and-a-half no cost, undistinguished academic years," Powell later wrote, "the CCNY administration took pity on me and allowed my ROTC A grades to remain in my overall average. . . . To the great relief of the faculty, I was passed off to the U.S. Army."[55]

Much to Powell's delight, his extraordinary success in ROTC earned him a regular, not reserve officer commission in the army. After four years of college, he had secured respectable professional employment, a feat that had long been his parents' most prominent objective. Before his commissioning ceremony, Powell received candid career advice from another key mentor, Colonel Harold C. Brookhart, the ROTC commander at City College. Brookhart warned Powell about the harsh realities of racism in the army, despite its recent integration. If Powell wanted to be successful, he needed to conform, comply, and, above all, dodge controversy. "You may not like what you see, but you have to be prepared to compromise," Brookhart cautioned. "You have to try not to upstage or overturn . . . you need to go along."[56]

In brief, the well-intentioned white colonel had advised his top cadet to remain the kind of person Powell had been all of his young life. Significantly, Powell was not encouraged to become an independent critical thinker or a morally courageous military officer. If he intended to succeed in the predominantly white officer corps, he must not "rock the boat" and instead behave like a "good Negro."[57] The blunt advice did not offend Powell. Rather, he took the counsel to heart: "I do not remember being upset by what he said. He meant well. . . . He was a caring human being. I thanked him and left."[58] More crucial at that moment was that Powell had fulfilled Luther and Arie's parental dream. "What was most important," he later remembered, "was—and this was expected of me by my parents—that I had a job, even if it was in the military. In those days, you see, you went to school for the purpose of making yourself employable."[59]

On June 30, 1958, the once disengaged, directionless teenager from Hunts Point was officially sworn in as a second lieutenant in the U.S. Army. For much of his childhood, Powell's parents had worried about his aimlessness, his deficient motivation, and his "inability to stick with anything."[60] But Powell's experience at the university, especially in ROTC, had been transformative. More significant than achieving passing grades, he had discovered and cultivated a genuine calling: soldiering. His bachelor of science degree in geology was merely "an incidental dividend" to his newly declared military vocation.[61] True, at the age of twenty-one, Powell was still very much Luther and Arie's obedient, cautious, and amicable son, but at college and in ROTC he had also begun to demonstrate some central qualities of excellent followership, including commitment, competency, thoughtfulness, and independence. A childhood friend remarked on the transformation, stating that while Powell was still "very people-oriented," he had developed a new "bearing" and a "commanding presence." He could now be "very stern, very disciplined, very military-oriented."[62]

In subsequent decades, Powell's family and friends marveled at the unabating progression of his professional achievements. Remarkably, thirty years after graduating—narrowly—Powell, as an army general, would work directly for President Ronald Reagan as the first African American national security adviser and then under presidents George H. W. Bush and Bill Clinton as the first black chairman of the Joint Chiefs of Staff.

The intervening decades, however, were filled with trials and learning. Powell's first ten years of military duty, which included two tours in Vietnam, demonstrated not only impressive development as a subordinate and leader, but also the prominence of his ambition, his eagerness to please, and his submission to authority.

I was told, "If you do everything well and keep your nose clean for twenty years, we'll make you a lieutenant colonel."

—COLIN L. POWELL

CHAPTER TWO

Dutiful Soldier

(1958–1969)

The first decade of Colin Powell's military career witnessed significant development in his maturity and ability as a follower and leader. He had previously exhibited agreeableness, composure, and integrity as a deferential son in the South Bronx, and while at college, especially in ROTC, he had also displayed heightened levels of commitment and competency with a modicum of independence. As a junior infantry officer in the late 1950s and the 1960s, Powell focused on developing his professional capabilities and learning how to succeed in the army's hidebound, conformist culture. While stationed in West Germany and then at Fort Devens, Massachusetts, he quickly grasped the importance of learning from both personal experience and lessons taught by superiors, mentors, peers, and even subordinates. During two subsequent tours of duty in South Vietnam, Powell demonstrated not only physical courage in a war zone, but also his growing efficacy as a subordinate and leader. The Vietnam experience also revealed the limits of Powell's professional development: his unquestioning acceptance of orders, his unswerving allegiance to higher-ranking officers, his utilitarian ethics, and his overriding ambition to advance in rank.

Before deploying on his first overseas assignment, Second Lieutenant Powell was sent to Fort Benning, Georgia, for basic and advanced officer training. The often grueling and sometimes dangerous experience tested not only Powell's stamina and courage, but also his decision to make the military a career. He trained with enthusiasm and concluded that complete dedication and following orders strictly were the keys to achievement in the army. Powell's motivation was evident when he endured the infamous Slide for Life field exercise, which involved flying rapidly through the air on a cable suspended over a river. Soldiers are commanded not to let go of the cable—to drop safely into the water—until ordered to do so. In addition to testing one's performance under duress, Powell recalled, "the slide also tested our willingness to obey what seemed like suicidal orders."[1] The freshly minted lieutenant passed the harrowing slide test and many others. His die-hard commitment and ROTC training served him well.

Powell graduated from the eight-week Infantry Officer Basic Course in the top 5 percent of his class, which led to his selection for continuing education and training at Ranger School and the Airborne "Jump" School. In January 1959, Powell deployed to West Germany as an elite army airborne ranger. He was happy, confident, and determined to succeed. "Before this is through," he boasted, "I'm going to be the best lieutenant you ever saw."[2]

Powell began his on-the-job training as a professional army officer in Gelnhausen, West Germany. With a prized swagger stick in hand, he served first as a platoon leader and then assumed other duties in the Second Armored Rifle Battalion, Forty-Eighth Infantry Regiment, Third Armored Division. At twenty-one years of age, Powell was younger than some of the forty-five men placed under his command. His leadership style reflected both his friendly disposition and his competitive ROTC training. Not inclined to be loud or overbearing, Powell preferred to set clear goals, challenge his men, and model best behaviors. Drawing directly from his college success on the Pershing Rifles drill team, he sought to inspire quality performance by organizing competitions that allowed him to observe, evaluate, and reward soldiers. "I came to understand GIs during my tour at Gelnhausen," Powell remembered. "I learned what made them tick, lessons that stuck for thirty-five years. American soldiers love to win. They want to be part of a successful team. They respect a leader who holds them to a high standard and pushes them to the limit, as long as they see a worthwhile objective."[3]

With no experience leading noncommissioned officers and enlisted men, Powell at times found it challenging to boost the morale and motivation of his followers, a mixture of volunteers and draftees. Wisely, he observed the actions of a respected subordinate, a veteran platoon sergeant who led soldiers effectively through a combination of coercion and affection. Learning from this example, Powell, in addition to being attentive and compassionate, also employed pressure tactics. He even became known for losing his temper. On one occasion, his commander, Captain William Louisell Jr., overheard Powell berating another soldier. Louisell reprimanded his green lieutenant, instructing him, "Don't ever act that way in my presence or anyone's presence again."[4]

While in West Germany, Powell absorbed many lessons from senior ranking officers and mentors. They emphasized the value of focusing on details and extending consideration to errant subordinates. He was taught to know his troops, so he carried a pocket notebook and recorded military and personal information about each individual soldier. Powell and other inexperienced platoon leaders were held to high standards and regularly got their "asses kicked" for "not following through on various things."[5] On one occasion Powell lost his platoon's train tickets, and on another he misplaced his sidearm. An angry Captain

Tom Miller confronted the second lieutenant about the latter infraction to scare "the bejeezus out of him."[6] Mercifully, Miller did not write a reprimand. Instead, he warned Powell, "For God's sake, son, don't let that happen again."[7] The captain also taught his subordinates that leading soldiers required pragmatism and perseverance. Leadership, Miller insisted, was an endless process of problem solving. The best leaders do not have unrealistic expectations of sustained success or complain about the perpetual emergence of problems; they simply "suck it up and get started again."[8]

Powell also came to understand that successful followership in the army meant conforming. Consistent with the advice Powell had received at graduation, Captain Louisell advised him to avoid controversy by being a nonpolitical officer. As one of the few black officers in his Gelnhausen brigade, Powell worked diligently to fit in and earn the respect of subordinates, peers, and superiors. He wanted to be viewed not as an effective black lieutenant, but rather as an effective lieutenant who happened to be black.[9] In the military's post-segregation era, ambitious young African American officers sought to be indistinguishable from their white peers, and biographer Karen DeYoung concluded that "none was better at fitting in than Powell."[10]

The army's evaluations of Powell's performance in West Germany highlight his progress as a promising junior officer. A first assessment, in May 1959, rated Powell positively for his competency, dedication, and agreeableness. But thereafter his superiors also signaled some apprehensions. Captain Louisell wrote that Powell "has a quick temper, which he makes a mature effort to control."[11] Ironically, Powell was perceived by other superiors as being too calm and congenial. To them, he did not demonstrate sufficient gravitas. In an otherwise favorable evaluation, Lieutenant Colonel James T. Carter characterized Powell as "a refined, quiet, and easy going officer"; "from my observations of his leadership ability," he noted, "it appears he lacks forcefulness."[12] The negative comment stung Powell's ego but not his confidence or eagerness to please. He accepted such feedback as constructive criticism and dedicated himself to continuous improvement.

Overall, Powell's performance in West Germany was an excellent beginning to his army career. He was promoted to first lieutenant, and before completing his tour, he served short stints as a rifle company executive officer and as the commanding officer of a forty-man support detachment. Powell loved army life and demonstrated many characteristics of a superb soldier. In a December 1960 efficiency report, Lieutenant Colonel James B. Bartholomees extolled Powell's conduct as a follower and leader: "Lt Powell is one of the most outstanding young Lieutenants I have seen. . . . He is a driver and accepts responsibility willingly. He expresses his opinions quietly and convincingly. If his recommendation is not accepted, then he cheerfully and promptly executes the decision. He is calm and unexcitable. He is well liked by both superiors and subordinates. He has high standards and he demands and gets high standards."[13]

After Gelnhausen, Powell's professional development continued at Fort Devens, where he joined the First Battle Group, Fourth Infantry. Over a twenty-month period, he served as an operations and training liaison officer, as the executive officer for a rifle company, and even as a company commander before transferring to the Second Infantry battalion headquarters staff. During this time Powell also received first-rate schooling in followership and leadership. Major Richard D. Ellison taught him "how to push the smart proposals, derail the dumb ones, and strangle the most embarrassing in the cradle, all the while keeping our superiors happy."[14] Powell also absorbed ideas and information from other young officers, and he engaged his own soldiers in countless competitions as a means of boosting morale, confidence, and self-esteem. Some lessons he learned the hard way. Lieutenant Colonel William C. Abernathy taught Powell that a wise leader is attentive to the welfare of his troops and their families. On one occasion, Abernathy, to whom Powell had grown close, reluctantly admonished his subordinate for not properly executing a new family-support program. As with his parents, Powell hated to disappoint his superiors. "I would rather have had [Major] Red Barrett blister me with four-letter words," he confessed, "than hear Abernathy's pained reprimand."[15]

Despite occasional setbacks, Powell remained enthusiastic about his army career and proved a quick study and overachiever. He emerged from Fort Devens with a reputation as an excellent young staff officer who performed his duties with minimal supervision and an effective junior leader who improved the morale and productivity of an underperforming unit. Powell's superiors heaped praise on his demonstrated vigor and competency along with his "strong sense of duty and an unwavering loyalty."[16] In an October 1961 evaluation, Lieutenant Colonel Thomas Gendron described Powell as "a truly outstanding officer in every aspect and attribute of leadership. This officer is so unique in manner and performance that he could well be classified the 'Model Officer.' . . . He has in every case produced remarkably outstanding results. This young lieutenant has the professional knowledge equivalent to an officer of higher rank and greater experience."[17] Powell was promoted to captain in June 1962, six months before deploying to Vietnam.

By the time Powell arrived in Saigon on Christmas Day, 1962, he could draw upon four and a half years of active-duty experience. He was confident and gung ho, eager for the opportunity to demonstrate the skill and bravery of a well-trained infantry officer. According to Powell, he had been indoctrinated to "march into hell, if necessary, to accomplish the mission," and he believed that the "soul of the Army" was a courageous soldier's adherence to mission and authority.[18]

Captain Powell was assigned as a senior tactical adviser to the Second Battalion, Third Infantry Regiment, of the First Division of the South Vietnamese Army (ARVN). The unit executed counterinsurgency operations against Vietnamese communists in the highly contested A Shau Valley near the Laotian border. Powell was one of thousands of American military personnel sent to Southeast Asia by President John F. Kennedy to bolster South Vietnam's defenses against South and North Vietnamese communist forces. During this tour of duty, in which Powell demonstrated consummate skill and courage under fire, he advised three successive Vietnamese commanders. He adapted his behavior to fit their varying leadership styles and levels of competency and he shifted ably between roles as an adviser-follower and a battlefield leader.

Over time, Powell developed a close personal bond with Captain Vo Cong Hieu, a respected and capable commander of the Second Battalion. Hieu came to appreciate Powell's counsel on training, fortification techniques, and combat tactics. As an expert but foreign adviser, Powell worked carefully to be "useful without taking over."[19] When out on long jungle patrols in search of the enemy, the battalion came under frequent sniper attack and suffered gruesome casualties. Mindful that he was a role model for the South Vietnamese infantrymen, the American adviser consciously tamed his own anxieties. "Every morning," Powell later wrote, "I had to use my training and self-discipline to control my fear and move on. . . . [A]s a leader, I could show no fear."[20]

Soldiering alongside Captain Hieu, Powell relearned the necessity of earning the respect and trust of followers. Early in his assignment, when his ARVN battalion came under attack, Powell charged into the jungle in hot pursuit of the enemy, but before long he realized that not a single soldier had chosen to follow him. On another occasion, when his battalion was on patrol, a U.S. Marine helicopter gunner accidentally killed two soldiers in Powell's unit. "This bloody blunder had undermined their belief in me," he recalled. "I had trouble erasing the look of betrayal on the Vietnamese soldiers' faces."[21] But Powell's credibility rebounded when a U.S.-made protective vest saved a Vietnamese private who was on lead patrol. Powell had insisted that the vest be worn. Thereafter, soldiers hailed the American as "a leader of wisdom and foresight."[22]

Powell's second Vietnamese commander was the antithesis of a good leader. According to Powell, Captain Kheim was egotistical and rash, and unlike Captain Hieu, he was uninterested in the counsel of his American adviser. Powell and Kheim had opposing leadership styles. Powell delighted in developing bonds with rank-and-file soldiers. He was even known to lead them in song on a Saturday night. Decades after the war, a Vietnamese soldier wrote to Powell and reminisced about how the American had taught him to sing the song "The Fox" in a moonlit jungle outpost.[23] Captain Kheim's impersonal and ineffectual command came to an abrupt end when he was wounded during a mortar attack. "No great loss to the profession of arms," his American adviser thought.[24]

Powell's third Vietnamese battalion commander, "Captain Quang," was capable but lacked rapport and combat credibility with his four hundred soldiers. Powell, on the other hand, possessed both expertise and field experience, and he enjoyed the confidence of the troops. As a result, the battalion's sergeant major began looking to Powell for leadership. "I was supposed to be an advisor, not the leader," Powell later wrote. "Nevertheless, the two of us were in quiet collusion. Leadership, like nature, abhors a vacuum. And I had been drawn in to fill the void."[25]

During this time, Powell's battalion engaged in a rare and successful ambush against a Viet Cong patrol. He felt no remorse about killing the Viet Cong: "This was our fearsome unseen enemy. I felt nothing, certainly not sympathy. I had seen too much death and suffering on our side to care anything about what happened on theirs."[26] Powell's utter dedication to mission was also evident in his willingness to participate in the torching of South Vietnamese civilian villages, the slaughtering of livestock, and the destruction of farm fields. "This was counterinsurgency at the cutting edge," he later boasted.[27] He did, however, draw a moral red line at corpse mutilation, advising his fellow soldiers to discontinue the practice of cutting off enemy body parts.[28]

Powell's unofficial command of the Second Battalion ended abruptly in July 1963, when he stepped on a punji spike that pierced the instep of his right foot from bottom through top. "It was so quick," Powell recounted. "I didn't realize how injured I was. I just knew that I'd punctured my foot."[29] He managed to hike to a U.S. Special Forces encampment, where a helicopter eventually evacuated him from the battlefield. According to army records, "Captain Powell was wounded while moving to a vantage point where he could assist in the deployment of a rifle company. Despite this wound, Captain Powell continued to perform his advisory duties and remained with the unit until they arrived at the final destination."[30] After receiving medical treatment, he served the remainder of his tour as an assistant operations and training adviser at the First Division headquarters and as the airfield commander at the Hue Citadel airfield.[31]

From a career perspective, Powell's Vietnam experience had been a tremendous success. He demonstrated courage and competency, and he learned much about balancing the dual roles of following and leading, becoming better at both. His superior officers, American and South Vietnamese alike, wrote glowingly of his effectiveness. The Vietnamese commander of the First Infantry Division noted that despite the "arduous and hazardous" jungle environment, Powell had displayed "determination, physical stamina, and professional competence" that contributed to his unit's killing of "many Viet Cong" and the destruction of enemy "supply bases, crops and live-stock."[32] Powell's U.S. commanders also praised his performance, emphasizing his proficiency, work ethic, and affability. Lieutenant Colonel Joseph O'Connell wrote that Powell was "a tireless worker, cheerful and enthusiastic," someone who in the counterinsurgency effort exhibited "a professional touch not normally found in the work of an officer of his grade and time in service."[33] Major Thomas Ayers added that "Powell aided materially in the combat effectiveness of the battalion. His timely reports and analysis . . . enabled division to keep abreast of the situation. . . . By personal example he demonstrated the highest standards of professional competence and leadership."[34]

In recognition of Powell's combat performance, the army awarded him a Purple Heart and a Bronze Star. Despite the death and destruction that his battalion had wrought against Viet Cong soldiers and South Vietnamese civilians, Powell left Vietnam with no misgivings about the righteousness of his conduct and the broader American mission: "I was leaving the country still a true believer. . . . The ends were justified, even if the means were flawed."[35]

Powell would return to the war in Vietnam for a second tour in 1968, but for the better part of the four intervening years he worked as a student and a teacher. Both roles enriched his capacity to serve as an effective officer. Reassigned to Fort Benning, Powell furthered his formal education by participating in rigorous advanced airborne ranger training. Completion of the Pathfinder course marked an army officer as "an elite within an elite" group of paratroopers, and Powell, despite having a fear of jumping from aircraft, finished at the top of his class.[36]

Among the many leadership lessons etched into Powell's mind at Fort Benning were the importance of thoroughness and caution. On one blustery winter night, he and his classmates were aboard a helicopter preparing for a parachute jump. It was the jumpmaster's responsibility to check the static lines of all jumpers, but it was Powell who decided to examine each man's line. He, not the instructor, discovered that a sergeant's hook remained unattached to the floor cable, a potentially deadly oversight. The experience reminded Powell that even experts can blunder. He concluded, "Don't be afraid to challenge the pros. . . . Moments of stress, and confusion, and fatigue are exactly when mistakes happen. And when everyone else's mind is dulled or distracted the leader must be doubly vigilant."[37] By demonstrating the initiative of an exemplary student, Powell convinced at least one sergeant of his leadership ability.

After completing the Pathfinder course in early 1964, Powell remained at Fort Benning through the summer of 1967. He served as an army weapons and equipment tester, completed the Infantry Officers Advanced Course, and taught as a junior faculty member at the Infantry School. He excelled in all roles, whether student, instructor, or researcher. Powell's activities as a test officer, which included evaluations of a new field radio set, an all-terrain personnel carrier, and the tube-launched, optically tracked, wire-guided (TOW) antitank missile, were uneventful compared to the extremes of his experience in Vietnam. Still, his superiors and coworkers continued to extol his work ethic, composure, and friendliness. One colleague described him as "very impressive as a soldier. It was in his manner, his demeanor. There was no foolishness but he was very friendly. He was an intense, hard worker. People liked him."[38] In a March 1966 efficiency report, Colonel George Griswold wrote, "Captain Powell performed his duties in an exceptional manner. This officer is dedicated, intelligent, motivated, knowledgeable, and he tackles each task with the tenacity of a bulldog."[39]

At Fort Benning, Powell also proved an outstanding student in the highly competitive Infantry Officers Advanced Course, which he thought "inspired and intimidated in about equal doses."[40] Again, Powell impressed his instructors and classmates. He was perceived as "a team player," "a good listener," and a person with "a genuine concern" for others.[41] Colonel Tyron Tisdale, who believed Powell was destined for high command and general staff duty, described him as "a most outstanding young officer" with a "pleasing" personality.[42]

Despite such superlatives, Powell himself recognized a professional shortcoming. He was not an independent critical thinker, not someone who thought beyond the tasks the army put before him. At this stage in his career, he confessed to being "just another unquestioning captain, learning my trade."[43] Nevertheless, Powell graduated from the Advanced Course third in a class of four hundred captains and was rated the top officer from the infantry branch.

Powell's distinguished performance led to an early promotion to major and his appointment to the faculty of the Infantry School. In hindsight, this assignment, which included a teacher training course, proved critical to Powell's leadership development. He greatly improved his presentation skills, learning how to project his voice with authority and command center stage. "If I had to put my finger on *the* pivotal learning experience of my life," Powell later reflected, "it could well be the instructors course, where I graduated first in the class. Years later, when I appeared before millions of Americans on television . . . I was doing nothing more than using communicating techniques I had learned a quarter century before . . . at Infantry Hall."[44]

Powell's students, especially the greenest officer candidates, responded to his creative, informative, and charismatic teaching style, even when it focused on mundane topics such as unit readiness reports.[45] Whether leading soldiers in the field or the classroom, Powell believed that understanding and stimulating follower motivation was the "*sine qua non* of all learning"; therefore, he consistently incorporated firsthand "lessons learned in Vietnam" into his curriculum.[46] Students rated Powell's courses among the best at the school, and his immediate superior, Lieutenant Colonel Earl Adams, could not have been more satisfied. He characterized Powell as "not only the finest instructor that I know of in USAIS [Infantry School]," but also "a tremendous asset in preparing and developing new instructors as well. . . . His performance in duty, inherent abilities and extremely high potential are the finest I have observed in my service."[47] Steve Pawlik, a fellow faculty member, observed that Powell's friendly disposition and personal connection with students made him an ideal classroom instructor. "I used to kid him about being [a combat] adviser in Vietnam," Pawlik recalled. "He was misassigned as an infantry-man; he's not a killer by nature. He's a mediator."[48]

After nearly four years at Fort Benning, Powell was transferred to Fort Leavenworth, Kansas, assigned yet again to a student's chair, this time at the Command and General Staff College. A central purpose of the storied school was to broaden the command perspective of rising army officers from the platoon and company level to that of brigade and beyond. After completing the thirty-eight-week program, a graduate was expected to know "how to move a division of twelve to fifteen thousand men by train or road, how to feed it, supply it, and, above all fight it."[49] At Leavenworth, Powell also gained clearer insight into his own combat leadership decision making, which later evolved into the so-called Powell Doctrine. Wargaming at the school, Powell later wrote, "revealed a natural inclination to be prudent until I have enough information. Then I am ready to move boldly, even intuitively. . . . For me, it comes down simply to Stop, Look, Listen—then strike hard and fast with all the power you need."[50] Powell's dedication to his studies enabled him to graduate second in a class of more than one thousand officers, most of whom were senior in age, rank, and experience. As one of the top honors graduates, his picture appeared in the *Army Times* newspaper. Powell had come a long way from his subpar academic performance at City College of New York.

Powell graduated from the Command and General Staff College in the spring of 1968, and by mid-June he was assigned to the Third Battalion, First Infantry, Eleventh Infantry Brigade of the Twenty-Third Infantry Division—known as the American Division—in Duc Pho, Vietnam. The war had changed dramatically since his first tour; President Kennedy's successor, Lyndon B. Johnson, had ordered the deployment of hundreds of thousands of U.S. troops to defend South Vietnam from communist forces. Powell considered his return to Vietnam akin to attending "the graduate school of war, a school, a place, where people were shooting at you."[51]

By the time of Powell's arrival, the Duc Pho region had become a Viet Cong stronghold and American casualties were numerous. On this tour, Powell was not assigned to a battlefield advisory or pseudo-command position with South Vietnamese soldiers. Instead, he served as a U.S. Army staff administrator, first as the executive officer for the Third Battalion and then as a planning and operations officer at American Division headquarters. Powell, in fact, would not assume another command leadership position until 1973, when he was stationed in South Korea. Nevertheless, while in Vietnam he performed his follower duties exceptionally well, demonstrating impressive competency and masterful skill in the "performing art" of military briefings.[52]

As the Third Battalion's executive officer, Powell was tasked by his commander, Lieutenant Colonel Henry Lowder, with bolstering the unit's combat capabilities by mastering its troublesome bureaucracy. While Powell chafed at being in the rear of the fighting, he performed his responsibilities superbly and in the process demonstrated high degrees of initiative, reliability, and efficacy. One of his numerous managerial duties was to transport infantrymen, weaponry, and supplies to the battlefield. In the process, Powell untangled "endless reels of red tape" and prepared the battalion for the annual general inspection.[53] "He quickly took over," Lowder recalled, "absolutely did a fine job, and I had absolutely nothing to worry about. I knew we would always be supplied and our administration would be taken care of promptly."[54] Because of Powell's bureaucratic streamlining, the once poorly managed Third Battalion was rated the best unit by the division's inspector general.[55]

Powell's performance caught the attention of Lowder's superiors. The commander of the Eleventh Infantry Brigade, Colonel Oran Henderson, praised the young major for his exceptional trustworthiness, logistical acumen, and calm disposition. In an October 1968 evaluation report, Henderson wrote that Powell "performed duties . . . in a completely outstanding manner. He has demonstrated constantly his complete competence, levelheadedness, and dependability. . . . MAJ Powell is an outstanding officer in every respect."[56] The American Division's new commander, Major General Charles M. Gettys, also commended Powell's "spirit of cooperation" and "outstanding performance" as a battalion executive officer who, "in an amazing short time, revised and strengthened existing procedures, and required high performance standards on the part of all personnel in the Battalions Trains areas. . . . The level and quality of administrative and logistical support increased, thereby creating a higher state of morale among the troops in the field."[57]

Powell's many accomplishments as a battalion staff officer were especially remarkable given that he served in that position for only three months. After reading an old *Army Times* article, Major General Gettys discovered that the enterprising young major had just graduated second in his class at Fort Leavenworth. He immediately reassigned Powell, over Lowder's objections, to American headquarters in Chu Lai. Elated by the news, Powell began serving as Gettys's interim G-3, his top operations and planning officer. The sudden "stretch" opportunity validated the lessons that Powell had learned years earlier at the Pepsi bottling plant: "Always do your best, because someone is watching."[58] The G-3 job was a temporary posting but a monumental elevation in responsibility. "Overnight," Powell later wrote, "I went from looking after eight hundred men to planning warfare for nearly eighteen thousand troops, artillery units, aviation battalions, and a fleet of 450 helicopters."[59] Eventually, a more experienced senior officer replaced Powell, but he remained a valuable member of Gettys's staff as the deputy operations officer.

Although Powell did not lead soldiers in battle during his second tour in Vietnam, he visited infantry units in the field. On more than one occasion he returned to his post with dead and wounded soldiers aboard his helicopter. Powell himself demonstrated heroics in mid-November 1968, when he accompanied Major General Gettys on an inspection of a newly captured North Vietnamese base camp. Gettys's pilot attempted a difficult jungle landing, and the helicopter's rotor blade struck a tree trunk, which caused the helo to crash "like an elevator without a cable."[60] Powell fractured his ankle, but he still managed to pull Gettys from the smoking wreckage. With the help of others at the scene, he also rescued the general's aide, his chief of staff, and one of the pilots, all seriously injured. Powell's war notebook for that day simply reads, "Chopper crash. Tumelson, Carroll, Gettys, Treadwell, Hannon, Jacobs."[61] For his calm, decisive action, Powell earned the prestigious Soldier's Medal for heroism. The commendation states, "With complete disregard for his own safety and while injured himself, Major Powell returned several times to the smoldering aircraft which was in danger of bursting into flames. In one instance he had to break away part of the wreckage in order to get to a trapped individual. Through his efforts all personnel were saved."[62]

While working at American headquarters, Powell impressed higher-ranking officers with his tireless work ethic, extensive knowledge, positive attitude, confident demeanor, and unswerving loyalty. Armed with maps and charts, but never relying on notes, he demonstrated extraordinary presentation skills as he gave briefings on combat readiness, plans, and operations. Colonel John W. Donaldson, American's chief of staff, praised Powell as "the finest Major I have known and clearly one of the most outstanding all-round officers I have served with. . . . He knows his business through and through. . . . [P]ossessing great poise, he is a gifted speaker and talented writer. . . . [O]ne of those rare officers who should be marked for positions of the highest responsibility and promoted to General Officer rank ahead of his contemporaries."[63]

In May 1969, as Powell approached the end of his second tour in Vietnam, Gettys also proffered effusive praise for his subordinate's competence, courage, commitment, and temperament. He described Powell as both the most outstanding staff officer he had ever worked with and also the best "briefer I have ever known." Powell had earned a reputation, Gettys wrote, for

> working arduous extra-duty hours seven days a week, intense mental pressure, and frequent exposure to hostile fire while visiting troops. . . . He always maintained his calm and cheerful attitude, never reflecting the strain of his great responsibilities. . . . The briefings he conducted . . . were outstanding and earned him much respect. . . . He was instrumental in developing plans and implementing operations which were highly detailed and complex. . . . His ability, knowledge, and helpful, cooperative attitude were . . . widely known. . . . He earned the respect and admiration

of his superiors and subordinates alike. Major Powell's outstanding devotion to duty, diligent efforts, and high standards have contributed immeasurably to the success of the Americal Division in operations against hostile forces.[64]

After eleven years in the army, Powell was considered by his superiors to be an exemplary subordinate: enthusiastic, competent, courageous, collegial, loyal, and obedient. Still, Powell himself recognized that even as a highly decorated major, he had not yet developed a proclivity for independent thought or a willingness to question poor decisions made by superior officers. In the first decade of his career he had witnessed but not objected to pervasive "poor management practices" within the army, practices that egregiously promoted style over substance. This shoddy and potentially lethal mode of military operation was commonly referred to as "breaking starch"; he later wrote, "rather than blowing the whistle, . . . senior officers went along with the game, and junior officers concluded this was how it was played." Powell openly confessed that he "broke starch with the best of them."[65]

Regarding the Vietnam War, Powell also gave blind support to American foreign policy and the military's strategies and tactics. "I had no penetrating political insights into what was happening," Powell later acknowledged. "I thought like a soldier who knew his perimeter, and not much more."[66] Serving in South Vietnam, he never thought twice about the ethics of setting ablaze local villages, exterminating livestock, or ransacking food stores. After chronicling such activities in his 1995 memoir, he wrote, "However chilling this destruction of homes and crops reads in cold print today, as a young officer, I had been conditioned to believe in the wisdom of my superiors, and to obey. I had no qualms about what we were doing. . . . It all made sense in those days."[67] Powell's conformity and submissiveness also reflected his intense professional ambition. He readily acknowledged the dominance of his brain's "career lobe," and "for a long time," he wrote, "I allowed myself to think only on that side, an officer answering the call, doing his best, 'content to fill a soldier's grave.' . . . A corrosive careerism had infected the Army; and I was part of it."[68]

Powell's extreme conformity, career ambition, and desire to please superiors governed his small role in the army's cover-up of American atrocities against defenseless Vietnamese civilians. This includes the infamous March 16, 1968, My Lai massacre, in which five hundred Vietnamese civilians, mostly women, children, infants, and old men, were brutalized and murdered by American soldiers of the Eleventh Infantry Brigade, American Division.

Powell had joined that very brigade in June, just three months after the bloodbath. Although there was uncertainty about the exact number of casualties at My Lai, news of the killing spree spread throughout the Americal Division via formal and informal channels. American helicopter pilots, including Warrant Officer Hugh Thompson Jr., and their crews, had witnessed atrocities from the air and verbally reported what they had seen to multiple senior ranking U.S. officers, including a military chaplain. At one point during the massacre, Thompson and his men had heroically landed their aircraft to rescue civilians, all the while threatening to shoot American soldiers if they interfered with the effort. Within hours, word of the disturbing incidents at My Lai spread up the chain of command, reaching the Americal commander, Major General Samuel Koster, Gettys's predecessor.[69]

Koster's senior deputy recommended a formal investigation, but the Americal commander did not want to involve the army's Criminal Investigation Division. Instead, he directed Brigade Commander Colonel Henderson, Powell's soon-to-be superior, to conduct an "informal and quiet" investigation of Thompson's extraordinary allegations and the pilot's personal conduct.[70] Henderson suspected that his soldiers had killed a large number of civilians at My Lai, but not wanting to risk his own career, he conducted a superficial and biased investigation to satisfy his superior. In his March 20 oral report, Henderson exonerated his soldiers, who he asserted had killed 128 enemy combatants in a heroic firefight. He further informed Koster that twenty civilians had been accidentally killed by U.S. gunship fire and artillery, and dismissed Thompson as "an excitable young man" who mistook these unfortunate deaths for indiscriminate American killing. Henderson neglected to mention that other helicopter crew members had fully corroborated Thompson's claim of witnessing war crimes.[71]

The Eleventh Brigade's official after-action report on the My Lai mission and Henderson's April 24 written account of the operation excluded the firsthand accounts of the helicopter crews, instead brazenly praising Charlie Company for killing more than one hundred Viet Cong soldiers. The so-called "well planned, well executed, and successful" mission was also touted in America's divisional news sheets, in the *Stars and Stripes*, and in the *New York Times*.[72] Henderson, who participated in the cover-up for years, was eventually tried for willful dereliction of duty, and the Pentagon's formal investigation into the murderous affair concluded that his "deception . . . probably played a larger role in the suppression of the facts of [My Lai] than any other factor."[73]

Although the cover-up of the My Lai massacre had begun immediately, that did not preclude soldiers from discussing it. Some men of Charlie Company bragged about the operation, which had garnered high praise from the likes of Major General Koster and General William Westmoreland.[74] Soldiers also viewed photographs taken at the massacre site. Captain Ronald Tumelson, whom Powell would later rescue from Gettys's downed helicopter, admitted to seeing the gruesome pictures.[75] "Most of us in the brigade knew of the My Lai massacre," recalled Specialist Fourth Class Tom Glen of the Third Infantry of the Eleventh Brigade. "We knew they had killed civilians. We chuckled among ourselves at the all too common cynicism and vicious hypocrisy of the Army's body count system, and then forgot about the incident."[76]

Glen, however, did not forget what he had heard about the mass executions at My Lai nor his own firsthand observations of the army's brutal mistreatment of South Vietnamese civilians and prisoners of war. He, like Powell and other soldiers in Americal, knew of the intense animosity that existed between U.S. soldiers and much of the civilian populace, whose homes, food stores, and livestock had been destroyed.* In late November 1968, just before his tour of duty was completed, Glen penned a conscience-laden, eight-page letter to America's newly appointed top commander in Vietnam, General Creighton Abrams. In it, he assailed fellow soldiers for their inhumane and "overtly vicious" conduct against unarmed Vietnamese. Glen's heartfelt and scathing broadside, which did not specify names, dates, or places, read in part,

> Far beyond merely dismissing the Vietnamese as "slopes" or "gooks," in both deed and thought, too many American soldiers seem to discount their very humanity; and with this attitude inflict upon the Vietnamese citizenry humiliations, both psychological and physical . . . [And] fire indiscriminately into Vietnamese homes and without provocation or justification. . . . Does [a man's] presence in a combat zone and his possession of a rifle so absolve a soldier from moral responsibility? . . . What has been outlined here I have seen not only in my own unit, but also in others we have worked with, and I fear it is universal.[77]

---

*For example, the month after Powell arrived in Vietnam, Private First Class John C. Ebinger Jr. (also in Eleventh Brigade, Americal Division) wrote a letter to President Lyndon Johnson complaining about the torture and rape of Vietnamese civilians by U.S. soldiers. Ebinger concluded his letter by asking the president, "Can you or anyone higher up do anything about this kind of conduct in this war?" Ebinger to Johnson, July 30, 1968, My Lai Investigation Files, National Archives.

Glen's incendiary letter, which asserted gross violations of the Geneva Conventions, did not go unheeded. Several American officers, including Major Powell, were ordered to respond to the accusations brought against soldiers in their division. In his memorandum on the subject, Glen's former commanding officer, Lieutenant Colonel Albert L. Russell, dismissed the substance of the letter. And though he praised Glen's intelligence, ideals, and soldiering, he ultimately condemned him as a coward. Glen, he wrote, had demonstrated no "moral courage" by waiting to level such serious and yet general charges until after having rotated out of his unit.[78]

Russell did not attempt to contact Glen, and Powell chose to follow his lead.[79] Powell, too, criticized Glen for not following the chain of command and for not acting in a more timely manner. It was, according to Powell, "unfortunate that SP4 Glen did not bring these allegations to his immediate superiors or the IG [Inspector General] prior to the end of his tour."[80] Powell admitted that there might be "isolated cases of mistreatment" of civilians, but he reassured his superiors that all American soldiers were well trained on the proper treatment of civilians and even went so far as to boast that "in direct refutation of [Glen's] portrayal is *the fact* that relations between American soldiers and the Vietnamese people are *excellent*. The Vietnamese people are truly appreciative [of American's civic engagement]" (emphases added).[81]

In their detailed history of the My Lai massacre, journalists Michael Bilton and Kevin Sim conclude that Powell demonstrated "all the signs of a soldier who had triumphed in the battle of military paperwork" by writing "what his superiors clearly wanted to hear."[82] DeYoung, Powell's sympathetic biographer, concludes that "Gossip about that incident and other, less celebrated American assaults on civilians was so widespread that it was unlikely that Powell . . . was completely unaware of it."[83] In his comprehensive examination of My Lai, historian Howard Jones writes that Powell followed "a scripted procedure . . . ignore, deny, or call whatever happened a 'field expedient' and, if necessary, exonerate the army by finding a scapegoat."[84]

In 1994, when Powell drafted his autobiography, he chose not to mention Glen's letter and his whitewashed response to it. Both documents had been discovered in the National Archives several years earlier. Moreover, he chose not to make any reference to his close association with Colonel Henderson, who had extolled him as "an outstanding officer in every respect," performing his duties "better than any other officer I know."[85]

General Abrams's deputy, Brigadier General Howard H. Cooksey, signed the final, official rejoinder to Glen's letter. In it, the general freely admitted that some prejudice against the Vietnamese people existed within army ranks, but he rejected the notion that "overt acts" of aggression against civilians were common or tolerated. Furthermore, he castigated Glen for not speaking up sooner and for not providing details about alleged war crimes. Soldiers who commit such crimes are not absolved of moral responsibility, Cooksey wrote, "but neither is a person who keeps silent when he witnesses a war crime absolved of responsibility for that crime merely because he did not actively participate in it."[86]

Powell's 1968 memorandum responding to Glen's letter had grossly and intentionally exaggerated the state of friendly relations between U.S. soldiers and South Vietnamese civilians. He perpetuated the myth of cordial civilian-military relations for the benefit of his superiors and his own career. Even during Powell's first combat tour, when he unhesitatingly participated in burning villages and ransacking civilian food caches, he had recognized that innocent Vietnamese villagers were "caught in the middle" of the destruction wrought by American and South Vietnamese tactics. "I am sure these mountain people," he wrote, "wished they had never heard of the ARVN, the Viet Cong, or the Americans."[87] The level of suffering by South Vietnamese civilians was exponentially higher when Powell returned for his second tour.

Powell eventually admitted the truth: relations between Vietnamese civilians and American soldiers were severely strained. In August 1971 he volunteered an affidavit for the war crimes

trial of Brigadier General John Donaldson, who had commanded America's Eleventh Infantry Brigade and then became
divisional chief of staff during Powell's tour of duty. The army
was prosecuting Donaldson for having routinely "killed or ordered the killing of, unarmed and unresisting" Vietnamese civilians from his helicopter.[88] According to historian and journalist
Nick Turse, it had been an "open secret among the troops that
Donaldson and other commanders were killing civilians."[89]

Although Powell's autobiography excludes any mention of
Donaldson, the two had worked together at American headquarters, where the latter formally commended the junior officer as
"the finest major I have known."[90] In his 1971 sworn statement
supporting Donaldson's aggressive and lethal tactics in Vietnam,
Powell disclosed that "For the most part, the local population
was unsympathetic if not actually hostile to US/GVN efforts.
Willingly or unwillingly, they shielded enemy troops and thereby
made their detection and identification very difficult."[91]* This
was a complete reversal from Powell's description in his response to Tom Glen's damning letter.

Two decades after My Lai, when asked by an interviewer
about the massacre, Powell again described the Vietnamese civilian populace as hostile. "[It was] lousy Indian country," he said.
"I don't mean to be ethnically or politically unconscious, but it
was awful. There were *nothing* but VC in there. I'm not excus-
ing what happened, but when you went in there, you were fighting *everybody*" (emphases added).[92] Similarly, in his memoirs,
Powell vividly describes the region surrounding My Lai: "I knew

---

*In the original, hardback edition of *My American Journey*, 143, Powell
wrongly associates his sworn statement on behalf of Donaldson with the Peers
Commission, which investigated the My Lai massacre. There is no record of
Powell giving testimony to the Peers Commission. In the paperback edition
of *My American Journey*, 143, Powell deleted the reference to the Peers Commission but again failed to acknowledge his direct and faithful support of
Donaldson.

it had been a hellhole, a rough piece of territory inhabited by VC sympathizers. . . . Every time we sent units there, we could expect dozens of traumatic amputations at the evacuation hospital from mines and booby traps sown by enemy guerrillas and sympathetic peasants, including women, even children."[93] Consistent with his sworn statement in support of Donaldson, Powell's 1995 book defended the American practice of shooting male peasants from helicopters. If Vietnamese men, he wrote, wore "black pajamas," "looked remotely suspicious," and "moved" after a warning shot, then they were killed. "Brutal?" Powell asked. "Maybe so. . . . The kill-or-be-killed nature of combat tends to dull fine perceptions of right and wrong."[94]*

Glen's accusation that many soldiers from the U.S. Army's Eleventh Infantry routinely committed acts of violence against South Vietnamese civilians might have ended with General Cooksey's defiant retort, but in late March 1969, while Powell and Donaldson were still stationed at American headquarters, Ron Ridenhour, another veteran of the division, penned his own letter about atrocities committed by U.S. soldiers in Vietnam. He sent copies of his detailed statement not just to the army's upper echelon, but also to members of Congress, the secretary of state, and the president. Unlike Glen, Ridenhour provided a specific account of the My Lai massacre and pleaded for a public investigation.[95]

In May 1969, two months after Ridenhour's letter, Lieutenant Colonel William D. Sheehan, an army investigator from the Office of the Inspector General (OIG), arrived at Major Powell's Chu Lai office and conducted a ninety-minute interview. He asked twenty-two questions. According to Inspector General Robert Cook, Sheehan was there as part of "a sensitive

---

*In the paperback edition of *My American Journey*, 143, Powell felt compelled to add, "This part of Vietnam, jutting into the South China Sea, had had a long reputation for hard, bitter fighting even preceding our involvement in the war."

investigation . . . [into] an allegation that innocent civilians were killed during an operation on 16 March 1968."[96] Powell stated that being visited by an OIG officer is "about as welcome as learning that the IRS intends to audit you."[97]

While tape-recording the interview, Sheehan asked Powell if he knew of or had any records pertaining to Task Force Barker operations, especially for March 1968 in the vicinity of My Lai village. Powell emphasized that he was "not in country at this time," but had "hearsay" knowledge about Task Force Barker.[98] Powell eventually displayed and read aloud from America's doctored tactical operation journals for the first three weeks of March. He told Sheehan, "The most significant [contact with the enemy] occurred on 16 March 1968 . . . when C Company, 1st of the 20th, then under Task Force Barker, and the 11th Infantry Brigade conducted a combat assault into a hot LZ."[99] He proceeded to summarize the journal entries, which depicted "a hot combat assault . . . [that] continued hot and heavy with a variety of enemy kills, friendly wounded, and VC suspects detained."[100]

Sheehan next asked Powell whether there was any evidence that civilians had been advised to evacuate the area and whether he had any additional information about "the matters we have discussed."[101] Powell answered in the negative to both questions. According to Powell, at one point during the questioning his "guard [went] up."[102] Apparently not wanting to disclose anything that might displease his superiors, an anxious Powell brought the interview to a halt. He called America's chief of staff, who instructed him to continue answering questions.*

---

*Powell's account of the interview in his memoirs contains multiple factual errors, including the date of the interview, the questions asked, and the number of enemies he reported killed by U.S. soldiers. Regarding the latter, Powell's recollection mirrors a previous false report written by his then superior, Colonel Henderson, who wrote, "The results of this operation were 128 VC soldier KIA." See *My American Journey*, 142–43; Henderson to Commanding General, Americal Division, April 24, 1968, My Lai Investigation Files, National Archives.

The interview ended with Sheehan ordering Powell not to discuss any aspect of the inquiry with "anyone except as required by lawful authority."[103] As Sheehan was departing, he inquired whether Powell knew Captain Ernest Medina. Medina had led the attack on My Lai and would later be charged with premeditated murder. Powell indicated that "Medina was a member of my tactical operations center."[104] The investigator proceeded to interview Medina.

In the first edition of his autobiography, Powell claimed to be "mystified" by the OIG visit and stated that for the next two years he did not know that these interviews were connected to the My Lai massacre.[105]* This is implausible. Only six months after Powell's meeting with the investigator, the national media began extensive reporting on American and on Medina's direct involvement in the murderous operation.

Powell's small but unhesitating contribution to the army's cover-up of atrocities committed against Vietnamese civilians is hardly surprising. His superiors, including Henderson and Donaldson, had clearly set the tone and example. Little in Powell's personal development or professional training had prepared him—much less encouraged him—to critically assess and consciously challenge his leaders. Moreover, to have done so would have derailed his most promising career. DeYoung concludes that "the reluctance of midlevel and senior officers who knew better—himself included—to acknowledge the truth and speak it to those in power had indirectly given license to those below them to violate their own training and consciences."[106]

★　　★　　★　　★

---

*For the paperback edition of *My American Journey*, 143, Powell rewrote the text, stating that he had actually connected his OIG interview to the My Lai massacre only a few months afterward. Powell also deleted his prior statement that he had been called to testify before the Peers Commission, which investigated the massacre.

During his first decade in the army, Powell gained invaluable experience as a rising leader and a loyal, diligent subordinate. As before, he exhibited many qualities of superlative followership, including commitment, competency, agreeableness, and adjustment. Since the time of his posting in West Germany, Powell had effectively led soldiers at the platoon, company, and battalion levels and had demonstrated exceptional teaching skills at the U.S. Army Infantry School at Fort Benning. These successes were exceeded only by his consummate skill as a student at the Infantry School and the Command and General Staff College and as an administrator while working as a battalion executive officer and division planning and operations officer. By 1969 he had also demonstrated honor and valor on the battlefield.

Powell's potential to ascend the army's chain of command seemed unlimited, and he rightly began to look beyond his original objective of attaining the rank of lieutenant colonel. In late 1968, a prescient Major General Gettys forecast Powell's long-term future: "It is difficult to say at such a young point in his career that this young officer has general officer potential, but I am certain that he will be a general officer, that he possesses the necessary qualifications, and time and experience will develop his demonstrated potential to the point that he will be promoted to general officer rank."[107]

For eleven years, Powell had proven an adept player in the army's highly competitive career game. Again and again, he demonstrated professional competency and an uncompromised work ethic. His superiors consistently rated his loyalty and dependability among his best qualities. In excess, however, the latter traits can be counter to both exemplary followership and exemplary leadership. Powell's readiness—even eagerness—to conform to the army's faulty culture of "breaking starch," in which fidelity and appearances often mattered more than integrity and effectiveness, gave evidence of his burning ambition and underdeveloped capacities for independent critical judgment, ethical reasoning, and moral courage. In this context, Powell's willingness to embrace coercive and lethal tactics against un-armed civilians and to perpetuate the myth of cordial relations between U.S. troops and Vietnamese civilians was predictable.

Nevertheless, Powell entered the 1970s as one of the army's most talented and dutiful field-grade officers. He understood that to continue his rapid ascent, he would need to "keep his nose clean," performing in the same manner that had led to his early notable successes.

Colin was the best brigade commander we had. . . .
He was very reassuring to those above him also.
—MAJOR GENERAL JOHN A. WICKHAM JR.

CHAPTER THREE

Follower and Commander

(1970–1982)

In the dozen years following Powell's second tour of duty in Vietnam, he served in disparate leadership and followership roles, ranging from Pentagon staff officer and infantry field commander to White House Fellow and full-time graduate student. His ambition burned throughout, and in each assignment he continued to demonstrate characteristics of an exemplary follower: commitment, competence, adaptability, and amicability. Significantly, his wide-ranging experiences, including advanced military and civilian education, had broadened his perspective and cultivated his capacity and inclination for critical analysis and independent thought and action. During this period, when the army began its post-Vietnam reformation, Powell's well-regarded proficiency as a subordinate and burgeoning reputation as an effective leader attracted an array of powerful military and civilian mentors. These career "godfathers" and "rabbis," as he called them, intervened regularly to accelerate his already rapid ascent in the army officer corps.[1]

After Powell returned from Vietnam in the summer of 1969, he spent the next four years working in Washington, DC. From

Chu Lai, he had applied for the army's active-duty master's degree program and was accepted into George Washington University as a full-time student. Powell's motivation for graduate school, or "finishing school" as he derided it, was purely extrinsic; he wanted to advance his military career.[2] His decision to pursue a master's in business administration, with an emphasis in data processing, had more to do with meeting the military's preferences than any personal learning objective. "The army wanted me to get the M.B.A.," Powell recalled, because business management "was where they needed the expertise, and that's what they inclined me toward."[3]

Given his poor academic performance at City College, Powell, at thirty-two, entered George Washington with some apprehension and struggled initially with the coursework.[4] Nevertheless, he dedicated himself to the civilian master's program and soon excelled. One classmate, a navy veteran, remembered the army major's abilities and composure and lauded his "total control" and "unflappable competence."[5] Over a two-year period, Powell earned A grades in all classes but one, a "miserable course in computer programming."[6] His favorite and most influential field of study was management and leadership, which exposed him to the motivation research of prominent psychologists such as Abraham Maslow and Frederick Hertzberg.[7] Powell graduated in May 1971 after passing his comprehensive exam and completing his thesis, "The Impact of Separate Pricing on Computer Users and the Data Processing Industry."[8]

Having finished his MBA and earned promotion to lieutenant colonel, Powell was assigned to the army staff at the Pentagon. For the first time in his career, he appeared unenthusiastic as he anticipated a year of drudgery installing computer systems for the Management Information directorate. To his great relief, Powell was granted a transfer to the more prestigious Planning Programming Analysis directorate, which oversaw army organization, doctrine, and integration. Powell's ultimate superior, Lieutenant General William E. DePuy, the army's hard-driving assistant vice chief of staff, was a penetrating thinker and visionary reformer.[9] DePuy had a well-known disdain for officer incompetence and the "careerist games" that had come to predominate the service. In the wake of Vietnam, he was determined to make comprehensive reforms to the army's "doctrine, structure, . . . leadership . . . [and] ethical climate."[10]

DePuy assembled an impressive staff that included Powell and other exceptionally promising junior officers, and they became known as "DePuy's fair-haired boys."[11] Powell often worked closely with the lieutenant general, writing his speeches and traveling as his presentations assistant. Among the leadership principles DePuy inculcated in his subordinates was the importance of leading change, thinking imaginatively, and demonstrating moral courage.[12] DePuy, according to General William G. T. Tuttle Jr., "hated yes-men" and instead "wanted thinkers who had the guts to take a minority position because it was right. . . . His majors and lieutenant colonels were not mere recorders. They were expected to think above their pay grade, to be objective in analysis, and to be honest in clearly laying out their views, even when they ran counter to those of the boss."[13]

In one project, DePuy and his senior deputy, Major General H. J. McChrystal Jr., challenged Powell and several of his peers to think "the unthinkable," that the army must be shrunk from 1.6 million troops to 0.5 million.[14] Their task was to design the optimal organizational structure for a drastically smaller force. In the end, they outlined plans for an "absolute rock-bottom force called the 'Base Army,'" and while the project was never utilized, Powell appreciated an intellectual exercise that demanded his independent critical thinking.[15] "General DePuy taught me something invaluable," Powell recalled, "about holding on to one's core of individuality in a profession marked by uniformity and the subordination of self."[16]

Powell's performance on the army staff was superb, and his superiors foresaw "unlimited" potential.[17] Other observers were equally impressed. While working for DePuy, Powell was selected for the prestigious White House Fellows program, a one-year program designed to provide seventeen of the nation's most promising young leaders—mostly civilians but also a few military personnel—with a wide-ranging and applied education in public policy and administration. Special informational sessions enabled the fellows to converse with a cross section of influential leaders. Powell's group met with Justice Thurgood Marshall, Defense Secretary Elliot Richardson, Georgia Governor Jimmy Carter, psychologist B. F. Skinner, reporter Dan Rather, and feminist Gloria Steinem. The fellows also traveled internationally. Powell's cohort ventured behind the Iron Curtain with visits to Poland, Bulgaria, and the Soviet Union, and they also crossed the Pacific for a tour of communist China. With the benefit of hindsight, Powell described his fellowship experience as "a defining experience" of his career and "a seminal experience in my life."[18] His sister Marilyn agreed. "I think the fellowship was the real turning point of his career," she told a reporter. "[That's when] I first realized that this was a young man going someplace."[19]

Powell originally had no interest in the White House program. Having recently completed two years of civilian graduate school, he was happy to be among army ranks at the Pentagon and was looking forward to commanding troops in the field. But the army's chief of personnel, hoping to boost the service's prestige, urged Powell to apply for the program.[20] Powell thus did so not out of innate desire, but because of his superiors' preferences. "I was not looking for a detour," he wrote. "[But] the Infantry Branch was not asking me. It was ordering me."[21] Powell's application to the program benefited from an enthusiastic endorsement from his Vietnam commander, Major General Gettys.

One of the central components of the White House Fellows program was a service assignment inside a federal agency or department. Powell was assigned to work at the Office of Management and Budget (OMB). At first he was given a nondescript cubicle and conducted busywork research for the Directorate of Management office. There, Powell discovered how presidential directives filtered down through various cabinet departments, but he was uninspired: "They just shoved me off in a corner."[22] Through personal initiative, he secured a different position, one that allowed him to observe cutthroat bureaucratic politics and learn from civilian powerbrokers firsthand.

Powell's fellowship took this marked turn when Frederic V. Malek became the new deputy director of OMB. A West Point and Harvard graduate, Malek was earning a reputation as one of President Richard M. Nixon's "hatchet men," who labored to exert tighter White House control over the executive branch's sprawling bureaucracy. Having met Malek during the fellowship interview process, Powell felt comfortable sending the new deputy director a congratulatory note. In it, Powell hinted that he was being underutilized in the Directorate of Management, being left to languish "in the bowels of OMB."[23] Within days he was reassigned as Malek's executive assistant, complete with an adjacent office. Powell promptly became the deputy director's special projects manager, confidant, and gatekeeper: "If you wanted to see Malek, you had to see Powell first."[24] Powell watched with keen interest as Malek systematically fired career bureaucrats and replaced them with young, loyal Ivy League graduates. For a government official to hear that "Mr. Malek is on the line," Powell recalled, "was like hearing the Mafia tell you that the money was due by midnight and no excuses."[25]

As a self-described "fledging student of power" at OMB, Powell received a first-rate education on the "messy, disappointing, even shocking" processes of a functioning democratic government, in which "compromise can make the participants look manipulative, unprincipled, two-faced."[26] From his experience at OMB, Powell formulated a fundamental followership rule: "You don't know what you can get away with until you try."[27] Malek, like DePuy before him, proved an influential role model who demonstrated the rewards of risk-taking and assertiveness. Malek, in turn, recognized that Powell possessed certain traits of an ideal bureaucratic subordinate: "very smart . . . very good with people, and . . . very well organized."[28]

In 1973, much to Powell's satisfaction, he was ordered to South Korea to assume command of the Eighth Army's First Battalion, Thirty-Second Infantry Regiment, Second Infantry Division. Working under a legendary major general, Henry E. "The Gunfighter" Emerson, Powell further demonstrated his effective followership and proved his leadership capabilities. Powell readily embraced Emerson's vision and strategy for reforming the Eighth Army, which was suffering from poor discipline, racial tensions, alcohol and drug abuse, and abysmal morale and reenlistment rates. Just days after Powell's arrival, a "full-blown race riot" erupted that led to the arrest of more than two dozen of his soldiers.[29] He had inherited an "ill-disciplined, drug-infested mess."[30]

The Gunfighter's prescription for the Eighth Army's ills was a vigorous "Pro-Life Program" that emphasized strenuous physical training, intense group competition, live ammunition exercises, and basic academic education.[31] Incoming commanders such as Powell learned that their gung ho, results-oriented general was most focused on the morale and well-being of lower-ranking soldiers. This was evident in Emerson's aversion to pomp and circumstance and his policy of not awarding medals to any soldier above the rank of captain. Powell found inspiration in his commanding general's reforms and energetic manner. "Emerson had inherited a tough command," Powell later wrote, and "I found it heartening to hear a leader sound off with spirit and show a will to change."[32] Two years earlier, Powell had witnessed DePuy championing army reformation at the institutional level; working for the Gunfighter meant implementing meaningful reforms downrange.

Although he believed Emerson could be overzealous in his methods, Powell was determined to realize his boss's vision. Powell's approach to leading his undisciplined battalion began with setting the example. He ate breakfast early in the morning with his troops, and throughout the week he participated in the unit's grueling physical regimen. He set lofty performance standards and made a concerted effort to prepare his men to outperform other battalions. "I went flat out, following the same cycle as my men," Powell recalled, and "I was determined to have 1st Battalion of the 32nd Infantry win."[33] He also delegated authority to junior officers while holding them to high standards of performance and moral conduct. According to Ben Willis, his executive officer in South Korea, Powell "let his company commanders command their companies, and he set a great example. . . . [H]e cast a very jaundiced eye when any of his officers would stray downtown to visit the whorehouses. It's certainly something that he'd never do."[34]

To promote discipline and improve morale, Powell applied a judicious mixture of coercive, persuasive, and supportive tactics. On one occasion, he confronted a wildly drunk or drugged-out soldier who was swinging a pool cue and threatening to kill someone. Powell managed to calm him down without altercation. On another occasion, he discharged a corporal who was a notorious troublemaker. When the rebellious soldier protested, Powell barked, "You're out of my battalion. Out of this brigade. Out of this division. Out of this man's Army. And you are unemployed."[35] Word of the corporal's discharge spread throughout the battalion and earned Powell newfound respect and loyalty. Powell's brigade commander, Colonel Peter G. Grasser, was impressed, commending him as "a fantastic manager," "a fierce competitor," and a "hard charger" who had "won the complete respect and admiration of rank and file."[36]

Powell's leadership in South Korea produced the transformative results that his superiors wanted. He was known to be "completely responsive to Division and Brigade programs" and as a result, his battalion's racial tensions and AWOLs declined markedly while troop morale and reenlistment rates rebounded.[37] Powell also improved his unit's combat readiness, with an exceptionally large number of his soldiers qualifying for the Expert Infantryman Badge. Powell's tour of duty was not flawless, however. One night, he and his junior officers foolishly participated in a barroom brawl that erupted in the officers' club. Emerson's decision to ignore the fracas reminded Powell of a lesson in utilitarian ethics first learned in West Germany: leading strictly by the book was not always the wisest course of action. "In the end," Powell concluded, "results are what matter."[38]

Overall, Powell's stellar performance as a subordinate and as a leader made a lasting impression on his colorful boss. Emerson later proclaimed that while in South Korea, "Powell was out-fucking-standing."[39] The Gunfighter had intentionally assigned to Powell one of the worst-performing and most racially divided battalions in order to test his leadership mettle. For Powell, who had harbored some self-doubt about his ability to command, Korea had been a critical test of his leadership competency. According to Emerson, Powell passed the yearlong exam brilliantly: "I said, goddamn, this son of bitch can command soldiers. He was charismatic. He really raised the morale, especially the *esprit* of that unit. . . . He sure as shit showed me what he could do as a commander. . . . I put on his report this guy should be a brigadier general as quick as the law allows."[40] Powell was equally satisfied. He later described the assignment as "the happiest of my career" because he overcame "all self doubt."[41]

Toward the end of his stint in South Korea, Powell learned that he had been selected to attend the prestigious National War College in Washington, DC. Since his cohort would not begin classes for nearly a year, he was temporarily assigned to the Pentagon, where he worked as an operations research analyst for the Directorate for Manpower and Reserve Affairs. As of September 1974, Powell's primary duty was to help prepare the Defense Department's annual projection of military and civilian manpower needs for Congress. This daunting bureaucratic endeavor provided Powell with continuing education in working for senior ranking civilians and navigating the rocky channels of interservice rivalries. Powell recalled that he "worked like a dog" to balance and integrate the different priorities of the military branches and to complete the annual manpower report on schedule.[42] "It was a happy day for me," he recalled, "when we submitted the report to Congress—ahead of time."[43] From this experience Powell learned "an eternal paradox": competitive-ness among America's four military branches "produces both the friction that lowers performance and the distinctiveness that lifts performance."[44] The leadership challenge in the Defense Department, he concluded, was "to strike the right balance."[45] Powell's civilian bosses again rated his performance as outstand-ing, noting his "exceptional competence, initiative, and dedica-tion," for which he was awarded the Joint Service Commen-dation Medal.[46] Consistent with prior efficiency reports, his superiors recommended early promotion.

After the especially long work hours at the Pentagon, Powell was excited to begin classes at the National War College, an elite institution among the country's many military schools. The col-lege, which prepares students for elevated command and staff roles, draws top-performing officers from the U.S. Army, Navy, Marines, and Air Force. Powell's admission was due to the inter-vention of a future mentor, then Brigadier General Julius W. Becton Jr., himself a trailblazing African American soldier. Bec-ton chaired the selection board for the five senior service col-leges. The board first rated all of the candidates, and then assigned the best officers to the various schools. After reviewing Powell's record, Becton recognized his "great potential" to be-come a general and thus decided to "improve his chances by having him attend the best school." Over the objection of several junior ranking board members, who wanted Powell to attend the Army War College, Becton firmly announced that Powell "would be going to the National War College."[47]

The National War College's curriculum in politics, history, military theory, and diplomacy was intellectually stimulating for Powell and broadened his perspective on the place of military strategy within a political context. The course material and the renowned faculty, he wrote, "enabled me to connect my worm's-eye experiences to an overview of the interrelated history, cul-ture, and politics of warfare."[48] Dr. Harlan K. Ullman, a navy lieutenant commander and professor of military strategy who, decades later, became a principal author of the "Shock and Awe" warfighting doctrine, was instrumental in developing Powell's geopolitical-military outlook. The two became fast friends, and Powell credited Ullman for elevating his "vision several levels."[49]

Powell's reading of and reflections on Carl von Clausewitz, the Prussian military theorist, also had a pronounced and lasting effect on his thinking about the use of force. "Clausewitz was an awakening for me," he later wrote. "Like a beam of light from the past." In his memoirs, Powell quoted the Prussian and wrote reflectively about the relevance of Clausewitzian principles to the failure of American policy in Vietnam: "'No one starts a war, or rather no one in his senses should do so . . . without first being clear in his mind what he intends to achieve by that war and how he intends to achieve it.' Mistake number one in Vietnam. . . . Political leaders must set a war's objectives, while armies achieve them. In Vietnam, one seemed to be looking to the other for the answers that never came. Finally, the people must support a war. . . . That essential pillar had crumbled as the Vietnam War ground on."[50] Powell also agreed with "Clausewitz's greatest lesson" for successfully prosecuting a war: a country's leadership must fully comprehend the interdependence of the military, the civilian government, and public opinion. "Without all three legs engaged," he concluded, ". . . the enterprise cannot stand."[51] Within Powell's Clausewitzian analysis of the Vietnam War resided the basis for his future support of the Weinberger Doctrine on the proper application of U.S. military power.

Although Powell found the curriculum at the National War College rewarding, its rigor and the intellect of the faculty and fellow students presented unprecedented challenges. He was surprised—indeed, disappointed—that there were no multiple-choice exams, which he had long since mastered. "In fact," Powell later wrote, "we took no examinations. The courses . . . were designed for intellectual stimulation and growth rather than the mastery of technical material."[52] Powell's faculty advisor, Colonel James R. Stewart, himself a recent graduate of the war college, was not always impressed by his advisee's academic performance. Initially, he rated Powell favorably in every category, even describing him as "truly exceptional" and a probable distinguished graduate who routinely made "strong and valuable" contributions to class discussions.[53] By the end of the ten-month program, however, Stewart had tempered his evaluation. While he recognized Powell's leadership abilities and growth potential, he questioned his motivation for deep critical thinking, writing that Powell excelled only "if sufficiently challenged."[54] In the end, Stewart downgraded Powell in the categories of "Performance" and "Use of Time" from above average to merely average, and the faculty advisor did not recommend recognition as a distinguished graduate.[55] Graduating without the distinction would be perceived as a blemish on Powell's otherwise exceptional record.

Fortunately for Powell, his favorite professor and newest mentor intervened. Ullman made the case that Powell, who had just been promoted early to colonel, ought to be "singled out" as one of twenty-eight distinguished students.[56] In short, Ullman characterized Powell as a uniquely humble, "extremely smart," and truly outstanding officer. The war college's commandant, Major General James S. Murphy, concurred. In effusive praise, he wrote, "COL Powell most certainly has the executive ability, leadership techniques, and intellectual capacity to serve in the most senior positions within the defense establishment. He is without a doubt one of the finest officers I have encountered anywhere."[57] With these endorsements, Powell was selected as a distinguished graduate of the Class of 1976 even though he left the college six weeks prematurely to assume command of an air assault infantry brigade at Fort Campbell, Kentucky.[58]

In Kentucky, Powell was charged with leading the Second Brigade of the 101st Airborne "Screaming Eagles." There, he continued to demonstrate an extraordinary ability to succeed simultaneously as a subordinate and a leader. Powell came to admire the keen intelligence and quiet confidence of his division commander, Major General John A. Wickham Jr., who emerged as an influential mentor akin to Gunfighter Emerson (who was now Wickham's superior). Nevertheless, Powell still had to contend with his immediate superior, the brusque assistant division commander, Brigadier General Weldon C. "Tiger" Honeycutt, a Vietnam War hero who "may have been the most profane man in the Army."[59] Upon Powell's arrival at Fort Campbell, Honeycutt made clear that the Second Brigade was the worst-performing unit at the post. "We've got three infantry brigades," the general snapped. "Yours is dead-ass last. . . . So fix 'em. Now get your ass outta here."[60] The situation worsened for Powell when he discovered that his was the only brigade not invited to participate in annual war-game exercises in West Germany.

Powell's response to the challenging circumstances was that of an exemplary follower: he viewed the situation as an opportunity to exceed expectations. After all, he later wrote, "I was of the Gunfighter Emerson school. . . . If you get the dirty end of the stick, sharpen it and turn it into a useful tool."[61] Through concerted leadership, Powell set out to fulfill his boss's vision of an improved Second Brigade, and one of the keys to his success was setting high standards for soldiers, especially his junior officers. He decided, for example, that while the two other 101st brigades were in West Germany, all of his officers and many of his enlisted personnel should earn prestigious air assault badges, which required passing a demanding physical test. Leading by example, Powell, at thirty-nine years old, passed the test himself before informing his officers, including the chaplains, that they must become air assault qualified by winter. All of the officers met the challenge except one chaplain, who broke his leg and quickly transferred out.

When Wickham and Honeycutt returned from Europe, they were impressed by Powell's initiative and his unit's accomplishments. Honeycutt described Powell as a "first-class outstanding performer," a "totally reliable" subordinate who "requires no supervision" and who earns the respect of superiors and followers alike.[62] Wickham concurred, characterizing the "completely dependable" Powell as a follower-leader who was "candid in expressing his views. Works well under pressure. Solid in judgment. Has great rapport with subordinates. . . . Sets the example in everything he does." Both men recommended Powell for early promotion.[63]

Lieutenant General Emerson, who commanded the Eighteenth Airborne Corps, also viewed Powell as an exemplary follower-leader. The colonel, he contended, "was the best brigade level commander" in the entire Airborne Corps and thus deserved rapid promotion to brigadier general. In his evaluation of Powell, Emerson wrote, "He has everything it takes to reach four-star rank."[64]

Even years later, Wickham could recount Powell's extraordinary performance at Fort Campbell. "He was," the general remembered, "best in his tactical knowledge, in his feel for soldiers, and his ability to communicate. . . . He was very reassuring to those above him. He didn't seem to have an agenda, and he got results."[65] In short, by seizing the initiative in unfavorable circumstances and challenging his followers to perform beyond expectations, Powell had once again effectively led his soldiers and served his commanders.

By 1977, Powell's reputation as a consummate army officer was surging, and in February he was summoned to Washington, DC, for a meeting with Zbigniew Brzezinski, the national security adviser to President Jimmy Carter. Directed by the president to diversify the National Security Council (NSC) staff, Brzezinski offered the colonel a position as the manager of the NSC defense program. Powell, who had voted for Carter in the recent election, found the White House offer tempting. Confident that Powell would accept, Brzezinski underscored that the job held significant responsibility and would require untiring dedication. "It's a full-time commitment," Brzezinski told him. "So I'm glad you want to be with us. Isn't that right, Colonel?"[66] Powell politely declined the offer, stating that he preferred to complete his assignment as a brigade commander at Fort Campbell. He explained that leading soldiers in the field was his passion and that accumulating command experience was crucial to achieving his career goals.

Rather than being offended, Brzezinski was struck by the colonel's candor and self-determination. He informed Powell that he would call upon him again, after the colonel finished his posting with the Screaming Eagles. After nearly two decades in uniform, Powell's willingness to exert his independence was becoming increasingly apparent. As he later wrote, "Turning down the White House does not come easily to a soldier schooled in obedience."[67]

Three months after Powell returned to Fort Campbell, the nation's capital beckoned again. Not only did Brzezinski renew his offer with the NSC, but John G. Kester wanted Powell to interview for a job at the Pentagon. Kester, who was working as the White House liaison and the de facto chief of staff for Defense Secretary Harold Brown, needed an executive military assistant. Kester possessed a well-deserved reputation as a cagey bureaucratic infighter, and in their meeting Powell asked why he was being considered for the assistant position. Kester said, "I checked you out and I heard a lot of good things about you." Powell responded, "Well, as a matter of fact, I checked you out, too, and it wasn't all good." Kester was immediately taken with Powell, whom he judged "a very savvy fellow . . . very candid. You could tell he wasn't going to be a yes-man."[68] Kester extended an offer to Powell, who accepted after consulting with two mentors, Major General Wickham and Brigadier General Carl E. Vuono.

Although Powell did not know it at the time, he would be stationed at the Pentagon for the next four years, serving as the military assistant to three deputy defense secretaries, Democrats Charles Duncan and W. Graham Claytor Jr., and Reagan Republican Frank Carlucci. One of Powell's friends observed, "They didn't let you out of the Pentagon force-field very long, did they?"[69] Years earlier, as a White House Fellow in the Nixon administration, Powell had benefited from his introductory education in politics, policy making, and public administration. By comparison, this four-year tour at the Pentagon resembled graduate work in the realpolitik of institutional followership and leadership.

Kester, Powell's immediate superior, worked tirelessly to gain some control over the expansive Defense Department. As Kester's top subordinate, Powell was particularly observant of the friction between the Pentagon's senior civilian and military leaders. He watched Kester's power plays with keen interest, as they often came at the expense of the Joint Chiefs of Staff. Powell frequently found himself trapped in the middle of turf wars, but he remained loyal to his civilian superiors even though many of their decisions diminished the authority of the army's senior generals. Confident and trustful of Powell, Kester delegated to him considerable responsibility. "If the National War College had been my classroom in military politics," Powell later wrote, "I was now out doing field work."[70] He admired Kester's passion, confidence, and efficiency, but also concluded that his tactics could be unnecessarily harsh.

In a January 1979 performance review, Kester wrote that Powell was "a brilliant and trusted assistant" whose "advice, counsel, and sometimes needed cautions have had a positive impact" in the office of the defense secretary. He added further that Powell "should wear three or four stars some day." Defense Secretary Brown gave Powell a rave review, praising his candor, diplomacy, intellect, trustworthiness, and thoroughness.[71]

Powell's excellent performance as a staff officer led to another promotion and a new, if familiar, position as senior military assistant to Deputy Defense Secretary Duncan. In the spring of 1979, at the age of forty-two, Powell became the youngest general officer in the U.S. Army. While the early promotion boosted Powell's confidence and self-esteem, Army Chief of Staff George B. Rogers communicated to him and other newly promoted brigadiers that they were hardly indispensable. "All of you could board an airplane and disappear over the Atlantic tomorrow," Rogers told the group, "and the fifty-two colonels we'd replace you with would be just as good as you are. We would not be able to tell the difference. Furthermore, many of you have to accept that you have had your last promotion."[72] As a congratulatory gift, Powell received a framed quip by Abraham Lincoln: "I can make a brigadier general in five minutes. But it's not so easy to replace one hundred and ten horses." Powell displayed the quote in his office for the remainder of his career, calling it "the perfect cure" for sudden bouts of egotism.[73]

Working as Duncan's senior military assistant, Powell honed his administrative and politicking skills while participating in the Pentagon's interactions with the White House and Congress. He also began thinking more seriously about international affairs. In October 1978, Powell accompanied Duncan on a trip to the Middle East and Africa. At the time, Iran was governed by Shah Reza Pahlavi, a crucial U.S. ally. Duncan and Powell were entertained by Iranian generals and toured a modern-looking air force base equipped with American-made F-14 fighter planes. In spite of the impressive military display, Powell left Iran feeling unsettled. For one thing, a U.S. Air Force captain, who was training Iranian pilots, informed him that the quality of Iran's air force personnel was second-rate. Moreover, Powell had learned of the growing militancy of Iran's Islamic fundamentalist movement.[74]

Only three months after the trip, the shah was forced to flee his country when Ayatollah Ruhollah Khomeini and the Revolutionary Council seized control of the government. Reflecting on the course of events, Powell searched for lessons. Above all, perhaps, he was reminded that the best leaders and followers do not accept conditions at face value, but rather seek the unvarnished truth about their situation. "My suspicion of elites and show horse units deepened," he recalled. "Keep looking beneath surface appearances, I reminded myself, and don't shrink from doing so because you might not like what you find."[75]

During the summer of 1979, Duncan left the Pentagon to become President Carter's secretary of the Department of Energy. Powell accompanied him for three months to manage the transition and a reorganization of the department. After working directly and indirectly with Powell for two years, Duncan was most impressed with the young general's intelligence, work ethic, loyalty, and comity. "He's a person who has extremely good skills at working with other people," Duncan remarked, "and he's a very fast learner. . . . He is totally committed to what he's doing."[76] In his final evaluation of Powell's performance, the secretary characterized his military assistant as "my closest and most trusted advisor."[77]

After his brief stint at the Department of Energy, Powell returned to the Pentagon to serve as the senior military assistant to W. Graham Claytor Jr., Duncan's replacement as the deputy secretary of defense. While serving under Claytor, Powell learned valuable lessons about tactical planning and crisis management. In April 1980, President Carter approved Operation Eagle Claw, a joint military mission to rescue the fifty-two Americans taken hostage in Iran five months earlier. The mission, later known as Desert One, proved a debacle that led to the death of eight U.S. soldiers.[78]

Powell had no direct role in the botched rescue attempt, but he learned from the mistakes of his military and political superiors. He analyzed the operation with a Clausewitzian eye and from the perspective of an airborne commander, noting severe flaws in preparation, resources, communications, weather forecasting, and chain of command. "You have to plan thoroughly," he thought. "Train as a team, match the military punch to the political objective, go in with everything you need—and then some—and not count on wishful thinking."[79] In addition to the military operation, Powell also studied the Carter administration's approach to conveying its failure to the American people. He judged the president's management of the affair as a "public communications fiasco" since the administration refused to fully or quickly disclose the central facts of the tragedy and failed to admit that it had committed gross errors.[80]

Deputy Secretary Claytor admired Powell's critical thinking, confidence, and candor. Equally important was his subordinate's unquestionable loyalty. Claytor wrote that Powell "can be trusted absolutely . . . and he unfailingly represents his and others' views faithfully and objectively, while not hesitating to speak his mind when he thinks I might be pursuing an incorrect course of action. I have total faith in his ability to see that my decisions, once made, are carried out in the manner and spirit that I intended. He is unstinting in both time and effort in supporting me."[81] For his effective performance and unwavering devotion, Powell earned the Defense Distinguished Service Medal.

Seven months after the Desert One debacle, Ronald Reagan defeated Carter in the 1980 presidential election. Powell remained at the Pentagon for several months as the senior military assistant to Frank Carlucci, the new deputy defense secretary. By then, Powell had emerged as an elite senior staff officer, someone invaluable to Carlucci and his boss, Defense Secretary Caspar "Cap" Weinberger. Both Republicans had considerable government experience, but not in the Defense Department. As a consequence, they relied upon Powell's expertise and relationships. According to Carlucci, Powell "seemed to know everything. He was well liked, and he circulated widely around the building. He talked to people. He had good judgment, common sense and a wonderful personality."[82] Also significant to Carlucci was that Powell had been "unfailingly loyal to me."[83] For Powell and many others in the military, the arrival of the Reagan administration, with its promise to bolster defense spending, was most welcome.

Because of Powell's reputation as an excellent subordinate and talented administrator, Secretary Weinberger offered him the position of undersecretary of the army. If Powell accepted, he would have to retire from active duty. Fearing that he "was becoming more politician than soldier," Powell declined the offer.[84] Instead, Powell pressed Carlucci to get him out of the Pentagon and back into the field with infantry soldiers. Carlucci consented to the transfer and predicted that Powell "will become one of America's most valuable four stars."[85]

In June 1981, after four consecutive years of service in Washington, Powell was assigned to Fort Carson, Colorado, where he served as one of two assistant division commanders for operations and training with the Fourth Infantry Division (Mechanized). Powell understood that the new posting was a crucial "apprenticeship" before taking command of his own division.[86] Soon after arriving at his duty station, Powell wrote to Kester, "I continue to have a ball being back in a division and have absolutely no desire to return to the Pentagon anytime soon."[87]

As had been the case years earlier at Fort Campbell, Powell's new assignment presented a challenging leader-follower dynamic. His new commander, Major General John W. Hudachek, had a reputation as a hardnosed "difficult" boss with a "well known aversion" to fast-rising army officers, especially so-called political officers from Washington, DC.[88] Indeed, several generals had warned Powell about Hudachek. Major General Charles W. Dyke sent him a personal note underscoring that as Hudachek's assistant division commander, Powell would "find the younger officers and their families in particular looking to you for guidance, leadership, and example."[89] With such counsel, Powell took immediate action to allay any concerns that his new no-nonsense boss might have. Given his limited command record and inexperience leading tank soldiers, Powell set out to boost his standing, not only with Hudachek, but also with his own subordinates. He quickly qualified as an expert M60AI tank gunner, and his gung ho initiative seemed to please Hudachek, who informed Powell he was "doing a great job."[90]

The honeymoon did not last. After several months, Powell grew increasingly concerned that his commander's coercive leadership style was undermining the division's morale and performance. To make matters worse, Hudachek's high-profile wife behaved in a similar brusque fashion, which negatively affected many soldiers' spouses. As one of the two assistant division commanders, Powell served as "the buffer, lightning rod, and father confessor" between the post's disgruntled soldiers and spouses and their commanding general and his wife.[91] The fort's climate became so objectionable that he felt obliged to broach the subject with Hudachek. Even at the rank of brigadier general, Powell's greatest challenge stemmed from his position as a follower. Not surprisingly, neither Hudachek nor his wife appreciated his attempt to play the honest broker.

Powell's standing and influence with his commander continued to deteriorate.[92] There were miscommunications and disagreements over personnel decisions. On one occasion, Powell approached Hudachek with an unsolicited recommendation, this time regarding troop preparedness. Powell suggested that the division's performance could be improved by switching from the annual general inspection to a surprise inspection process whereby individual companies were inspected at different times of the year. Powell criticized the traditional process as "one gigantic exercise in breaking starch" and argued that a continual inspections would significantly enhance combat readiness. Hudachek "heard me out," Powell recalled, "but was not buying."[93]

When time came to write Powell's performance evaluation in May 1982, Hudachek rated his subordinate as "technically competent" and "an outstanding trainer" of soldiers.[94] Significantly, however, he did not laud his prospects for becoming a division commander, nor did he recommend that Powell be promoted ahead of his peers. Powell's senior rater, Lieutenant General Marion C. Ross, concurred with Hudachek's assessment. He, too, lauded Powell's skills as a training leader but did not recommend him for division command. Instead, he asserted that Powell should be given full "consideration to be a principal staff officer" because this is "more Colin's forte than command."[95] Powell read the evaluation in Hudachek's office and became visibly upset and, according to his boss, "highly defensive."[96] Reeling from the review, Powell attempted to plead his case, but Hudachek cut him off saying, "We're not going to argue about it."[97]

Powell feared that the evaluation would derail his fast-track career. "I had blown it," he thought. For the first time, he realized that his professional ascent might have peaked and began contemplating life after the military. He tried to take solace in having given his best effort. "I had done what I thought was right," he later wrote. "I was not going to whine or appeal, get mad at Hudachek, or go into a funk. I would live with the consequences."[98]

In the end, Powell overcame Hudachek's evaluation. By his own admission, his career had suffered "a gut wound" from which he learned to "watch his mouth and his step."[99] Powell's survival stemmed in part from the intervention of an influential mentor. During a visit to Fort Carson, Lieutenant General Julius W. Becton Jr. and his close friend General Dick Cavazos had learned of Powell's "problems" with his uncompromising commander. They instructed Powell, "Don't do anything dumb."[100] After leaving Fort Carson, Becton contacted General Edward C. "Shy" Meyer, the army chief of staff, who arranged for Powell's transfer to Fort Leavenworth, Kansas. Becton then sent Powell a letter of congratulations and scribbled in the margin, "No odds too great to overcome—even Hudachek notwithstanding."[101]

For a year at Fort Leavenworth, Powell served successfully as the deputy commanding general of the Combined Arms Combat Development Activity within the Training and Doctrine Command. He excelled. In Powell's performance review, his new boss concluded, "He could do my job today and do it better. He has 4-star potential and ought to command a division and then a corps."[102] With that evaluation, Powell's career was securely back on track, and he was promoted to major general. In a congratulatory if enigmatic note, General James V. Hartinger wrote that the promotion was an "indication that skill and cunning win out in the end."[103]

While Powell was stationed in Kansas, General Wickham intervened again to further bolster his career. In spring 1983, President Reagan and Secretary Weinberger selected Wickham to replace Meyer as the army chief of staff. One of Wickham's first actions was to organize a group of up-and-coming officers to draft a secret, close-held report. Their task was to articulate a new vision for the army, identifying the goals and priorities that should guide leadership for the next four years. Wickham asked Powell to lead "Project 14," a task force of thirteen colonels and lieutenant colonels. Powell relished the chance to influence Wickham's thinking and the army's future, and he applied lessons learned from the field and in Washington, DC.

In late May 1983, Powell briefed Wickham on the group's major conclusions. The report identified two major threats requiring better army preparation: (1) acts of terrorism and (2) the theft of or accidents pertaining to weapons of mass destruction. Against the backdrop of the Desert One rescue fiasco, Powell's task force also argued for more effective joint service operations and for improving the army's capacity to engage in small-scale conflicts. In the long shadow of Vietnam, the report evoked a Clausewitzian tone by underscoring the necessity of fighting wars with decisive military force and with stalwart public support. Regarding the latter, Powell and the officers of Project 14 advocated assertive and carefully managed relations with Congress: "We strongly recommend you mentally prepare yourself to aggressively work with the Congress throughout your tenure. . . . It won't always be pleasant—but the payoff will be astounding."[104] Wickham was pleased with Powell's "yeoman service" and "superb leadership," and the visibility that the assignment provided him among the army's top echelon.[105]

The army chief decided that Powell should return to Washington and recommended that he become Weinberger's senior military assistant. A week after the Project 14 briefing, Powell was at the Pentagon discussing the staff position with the defense secretary. Having already served three deputy secretaries and fearing "being branded permanently as a military dilettante," Powell resisted another political appointment.[106] To his chagrin, but to the betterment of his career, he was assigned as Weinberger's senior aide. Powell remained in that position for three years. It was another administrative—not command—assignment, but the experience positioned Powell for further advancement and for opportunities that exceeded even his own lofty aspirations. Wickham told his protégé that by working directly for Weinberger, "Your future will be assured."[107]

★   ★   ★   ★

Powell's second decade in the army had significantly developed his competencies as both leader and follower. Part of his development occurred as a student at George Washington University and at the National War College, and as a participant in the prestigious White House Fellows program. Powell matured in these educational experiences and also excelled in various staff positions at the Pentagon, where he honed bureaucratic skills and continued to demonstrate his renowned commitment, flexibility, and agreeableness. Moreover, he exhibited an expanded capacity for critical thinking and independent judgment. Given two challenging leadership assignments in South Korea and Kentucky, Powell also evidenced effective command ability at the battalion and brigade levels. His superiors, Emerson and Wickham, respectively, lauded his initiative and assertiveness, and his ability to motivate the rank and file by setting rigorous standards and serving as an inspirational role model.

Only once in this period, while at Fort Carson, did Powell stumble, and not with his soldiers but with a superior who rebuffed his attempts to lead from below. It was a defining experience for Powell. He had endangered his career by exercising the type of independent thought and moral courage that had been encouraged by leaders and mentors such as DePuy, Malek, Wickham, and Claytor. After surviving the Hudachek ordeal, he relearned "the overriding importance of pleasing the boss."[108] While Powell believed that the best subordinates offered their superiors independent thinking, he concluded that there was nothing more important than loyally executing the boss's decisions as if they were one's own.[109]

Despite the troublesome performance evaluation at Fort Carson, Powell's ascent in the army continued unabated, often thanks to the intervention of influential mentors such as Becton, Ullman, and Wickham who, unlike Hudachek, prized his effectiveness as a subordinate-leader. In the upcoming third decade of his military career, Powell's principal assignments, orchestrated by old and newfound "rabbis," were not with troops in the field. Instead, he would remain in Washington, DC, as a senior staff officer to powerful civilian leaders in the Reagan and George H. W. Bush administrations. Powell's Republican superiors expected and received his best effort—and his total loyalty.

CHAPTER FOUR

Loyalist

(1983–1988)

Powell spent little time commanding troops during the eight-year Reagan presidency. This, however, did not impede his ascension in the army nor within the Republican administration. In brief, his civilian superiors coveted his extraordinary skills as a subordinate and his unflinching loyalty. By the early 1980s Powell had earned a reputation among Republicans and Democrats as "one of Washington's best problem solvers. . . . a right hand man who delivered results. . . , [who] had strong views and would push for them but . . . knew when to follow orders and fall in line with the boss."[1]

At this time, the two most influential people in Powell's career were Caspar Weinberger and Frank Carlucci. For three years Powell served faithfully as Defense Secretary Weinberger's senior military assistant, and then in early 1987, after an abbreviated command assignment with the U.S. Army V Corps in West Germany, Powell returned to Washington, DC, to become the senior deputy to Carlucci, Reagan's fifth national security adviser. A year later, when Carlucci replaced Weinberger atop the Defense Department, Powell rose to the post of national security adviser to the president of the United States.

Throughout the Reagan years, Powell demonstrated impressive commitment and adaptability. He worked for superiors with vastly different leadership styles, ranging from Weinberger and Carlucci's focused and active management to Reagan's laissez-faire approach. The dangers and challenges of the latter became all too apparent during the Iran-Contra scandal and in its aftermath, when Carlucci and Powell rehabilitated the national security policy-making process. The Reagan administration's illegal arms-for-hostages operation and its illicit cover-up ensnared Weinberger and tested the boundaries of Powell's professional ethics, especially the extent of his loyalties. In addition, Powell's service to the Republican administration, including his tutelage under Weinberger, also afforded the army major general the opportunity to sharpen his thinking on the proper application of American military power.

Powell became Weinberger's senior military assistant during the summer of 1983. Despite being a two-star general, his responsibilities were those of a follower. As he later admitted, "I was working for someone else. I was not in charge of anything."[2] Among Powell's primary duties were satisfying the secretary's needs, no matter how small or large, and assuring the proper communication and effective execution of Weinberger's decisions. He also helped prepare the secretary's speeches and testimony before Congress. Powell described his position as "the Secretary's chief horse holder, dog robber, and gofer."[3] A significant part of the job was to act as Weinberger's gatekeeper, controlling people's access and helping the defense secretary manage his daily schedule. "I was a juggler," Powell wrote, "trying to keep the egos of three service secretaries, four service chiefs, the Chairman of the Joint Chiefs, and other Pentagon pashas all in the air at once."[4]

Powell discovered that he and his new boss held comparable views on the appropriate use of the military in foreign policy. Both were staunch cold warriors, but in the shadow of Vietnam, they were also reluctant to commit U.S. forces abroad absent a direct threat to national security and without clear, attainable military and political objectives.

Such thinking had led the defense secretary to oppose the deployment of U.S Marines as peacekeepers in Lebanon the year before Powell's arrival. Reagan's secretary of state, George P. Shultz, had supported the mission as a means to securing a broader Middle East peace. During one White House meeting, Shultz confronted Weinberger, asking him pointedly, "Why are you buying all this military equipment if you never want to use it?"[5] In this case, Reagan sided with Shultz and dispatched the marines as part of a multinational operation to oversee the safe evacuation of thousands of Palestine Liberation Organization forces out of Lebanon. Initially, the mission seemed successful. Even Weinberger acknowledged that the evacuation had "secured our objective" both "quickly and efficiently."[6]

However, in mid-September 1982, four days after the marines began their withdrawal from Lebanon, the newly elected Lebanese president was assassinated. The murder caused a surge of deadly violence against Palestinian refugees and led to the armed intervention of both Israel and Syria. Pressed by Shultz, Reagan ordered nearly two thousand lightly armed marines back into Lebanon to join a reconstituted multinational force charged with stabilizing the chaotic situation. Weinberger and the Joint Chiefs of Staff objected to the redeployment, perceiving the mission as ill-defined and perilous.[7] With Israel and Syria occupying much of Lebanon, a period of relative peace ensued until spring 1983, when a car bomb exploded outside the American embassy in Beirut. The explosion killed more than a dozen Americans, including eight CIA officers.

In spite of the embassy bombing, Shultz appeared to be making diplomatic progress in the region. In August 1983, one month after Powell joined Weinberger's staff, Reagan renewed his commitment to the American peacekeeping mission in Lebanon. Weinberger and his senior military advisers, including Powell, opposed the continuing deployment. "What I saw from my perch in the Pentagon," the major general recalled, "was America sticking its hand into a thousand-year-old hornet's nest with the expectation that our mere presence might pacify the hornets."[8] On August 29, the U.S. Marine contingent came under mortar fire from a Syrian-backed Lebanese militia; two marines were killed. Two more died in early September and another two on October 16. Supported by Powell and the Joint Chiefs, Weinberger counseled Reagan to reposition the marines onto nearby warships. The president demurred.

On the morning of October 23, Powell received news that a massive truck bomb had detonated outside of the marines' barracks at the Beirut airport. Distressed, he telephoned the news to Weinberger. The explosion killed 241 U.S. servicemen, marking the deadliest day for the nation's military since the Vietnam War. The tragedy scarred Powell and Weinberger and solidified their cautious approach to overseas military operations. The redeployment of the marines into Beirut, they thought, had been unnecessary and wrongheaded. For Weinberger it was "a sad and grievous error."[9] Powell agreed with a U.S. Marine Corps officer who concluded, "Lebanon was a goat fuck."[10] For the remainder of their public careers, Weinberger and Powell viewed Lebanon as a horrifically painful lesson on the improper use of military force, and it colored their thinking on all future troop deployments. The next year, Reagan withdrew the marines from Lebanon. He would later describe the barracks bombing as "the lowest of low" in his presidency.[11]

At the time of the Beirut bombing, the Reagan administration was also addressing a foreign policy crisis in the Caribbean. On October 13, 1983, Bernard Coard, the deputy prime minister of the island nation of Grenada, orchestrated a violent coup against Prime Minister Maurice Bishop and Governor-General Sir Paul Scoon. The rebels imprisoned Scoon and later executed Bishop. Grenada's volatility provided Reagan with an opportunity, even if a minor one, to roll back communist influence in the region. Long supported by Cuban financial and technical assistance, the Grenadian government had begun constructing an unusually large airfield, one that Washington feared would expedite the transfer of arms and equipment from the Soviet Union to allied states in Latin America.[12] Seven months earlier, in March 1983, Reagan had publicly expressed his opposition to "the Soviet-Cuban militarization of Grenada," which could "only be seen a power projection into the region."[13] Furthermore, in the aftermath of the Iranian hostage crisis of the Carter era, administration officials also feared for the safety of hundreds of American medical students attending St. George's University on the island.[14]

Reagan, supported by Weinberger, Shultz, and National Security Adviser Robert McFarlane, believed conditions in Grenada presented a danger to American security. Shultz later wrote, "the situation on the ground was deteriorating into total anarchy. Conditions were ripe . . . for hostage taking."[15] On October 22, the Organisation of Eastern Caribbean States, along with Jamaica and Barbados, formally requested American assistance in pacifying the tumult in Grenada. Reagan decided to invade the island with the goals of rescuing the students, ousting the Cuban soldiers, and replacing the Coard regime with a democratically elected government. Powell, like Weinberger, wished for more time to conduct "massive pre-landing reconnaissance," but he too supported the operation given the threat to American citizens, the mission's well-defined objectives, and the president's willingness to commit a decisive military force.[16] Recognizing that the sudden invasion would garner immense press coverage, Powell persuaded Weinberger to alert the Pentagon's communications office in advance of the surprise attack.[17]

Operation Urgent Fury, which dispatched a dozen warships and seven thousand ground troops, began on October 25. After several days of intense combat, the outnumbered and underequipped Grenadian and Cuban forces surrendered. The U.S. military suffered 135 casualties, including 19 fatalities. Enemy causalities were four times as high. Reagan terminated the operation on December 15. Four days later, citizens on the island held new elections. The rescue of the Americans, the overthrow of the rebel regime, and the establishment of a new government received widespread public support in the United States and in Grenada.[18]

Although many foreign governments, including key U.S. allies, criticized the precipitous invasion, Powell and Weinberger considered it a marked contrast to Lebanon and an example of the proper application of American military might. This belief was reinforced a year later when Powell accompanied Weinberger and Reagan to Grenada to celebrate the first anniversary of the invasion. Powell marveled at the ebullient reception, writing, "I have never witnessed an outburst of mass emotion to match the President's welcome in Grenada. . . . Ronald Reagan was introduced as the liberator, the Messiah, the savior, and the crowd went wild."[19]

As Weinberger's senior military aide, Powell played only a minor advisory role in the Granada invasion, but as someone who worked daily alongside the defense secretary, he was well positioned to analyze the operation. He had supported the secretary's use of substantial land, air, and sea power against the weak military opponent. Because the operation represented America's first major offensive since Vietnam, Weinberger and Powell aimed for a swift and certain victory. While Weinberger and his advisers had been somewhat reluctant to launch the invasion without extensive intelligence, the defense secretary, like Reagan and Shultz, considered the mission justified and its outcome a military and political success.

On the other hand, Powell was disturbed by various aspects of the campaign. Although not in the chain of command, he had carefully monitored the operation. Yes, American forces had been victorious and achieved their objectives, but Powell deemed the military's execution problematic. Most troubling was the shoddy collaboration between the army, navy, and marine corps. "Relations between the services," he contended, "were marred by poor communications, fractured command and control, inter-service parochialism, and micromanagement from Washington." Furthermore, he thought that "the operation demonstrated how far cooperation among the services still had to go. The invasion of Granada succeeded, but it was a sloppy success. I was only a fly on the wall at the time, but I filed away the lessons learned."[20]

While Powell pondered the tactical mistakes of Operation Urgent Fury, his boss grew increasingly apprehensive about American interventionism. Tragedies as large as Vietnam and as small as Lebanon were at the forefront of his thinking. Within the administration, Weinberger jousted frequently with Secretary Shultz over the appropriate application of U.S. military power, with the former arguing for increased restraint and the latter urging its actual or threatened use in achieving foreign policy objectives. To influence the debate, Weinberger planned to make a public declaration to specify preconditions for the use of military force. Powell largely agreed with Weinberger's principles, but he knew that such a speech would be controversial within the administration and might disclose too much information about U.S. military decision making. In the end, Powell and officials at the White House persuaded the secretary to postpone any pronouncements until after the pending presidential election. "We talked him out of it all through the '84 campaign," Powell recalled, "so that we wouldn't have another Shultz-Weinberger fight."[21]

Three weeks after Reagan's landslide reelection, Powell accompanied his superior to the National Press Club, where the defense secretary outlined his prerequisites for the use of American military power. Weinberger argued that force should be applied only as a last resort to ensure the protection of vital national interests and those of U.S. allies. Before any deployments were made, all military and political goals had to be clearly identified and have the support of Congress and the American people. Finally, the size of the force should be flexible and always commensurate with achieving the stated objectives to demonstrate "the clear intention of winning."[22] The secretary's war philosophy was soon dubbed the Weinberger Doctrine, and over time and with some modification it would also become known as the Powell Doctrine. "Clausewitz would have applauded," Powell wrote. "And in the future, when it became my responsibility to advise Presidents on committing our forces to combat, Weinberger's rules turned out to be a practical guide."[23]

By the time of the National Press Club speech, Powell and Weinberger had become inseparable. They trusted each other completely. The secretary characterized his senior military aide as "my closest advisor and confidant," while Powell viewed his boss as a father figure and "a strong manager" with a "will of steel."[24] Powell conferred with Weinberger "a dozen times a day," sat with him at most meetings, and traveled with him domestically and internationally.[25] Their relationship, personal and professional, was based on mutual respect and a shared military philosophy. "Colin could and did speak for the secretary in some areas," Brigadier General Peter Dawkins recalled. "I would meet him in his office and I would feel I had just been to the schoolmaster. He displayed the kind of virtuoso mastery of the political complexities of the Pentagon that is rare."[26] Weinberger also admired Powell's proficiency, intelligence, and dedication. "I assess Major General Powell's professional competence as categorically superlative, in the uninflated, unadulterated sense of the word," the secretary wrote in a performance evaluation. "This very gifted and supremely dedicated officer stands head and shoulders above his peers."[27]

For both men, loyalty was a deep-seated core value. On occasion, Powell had to rely on Weinberger's protection and support. As the defense secretary's personal representative and gatekeeper, Powell often had "to play the heavy" with senior ranking Pentagon officials who wished to exert more influence on Weinberger.[28] Secretary of the Navy John F. Lehman Jr., for example, thought Powell overzealous in controlling access to Weinberger. The increasingly frustrated Lehman, described as "a Pentagon powerhouse" and "the ablest infighter in the building," attempted to have Powell reassigned. Weinberger would hear nothing of it, leading Powell to conclude, "Power corrupts; but absolute power is really neat."[29]

As the defense secretary's principal assistant and trusted confidant, Powell had significant knowledge of the Reagan administration's 1985–1986 attempts to rescue American hostages in Lebanon by selling weapons to Iran through Israel—part of the infamous Iran-Contra affair. In early 1986, Powell would orchestrate the transfer of four thousand TOW missiles from the Defense Department to the CIA, which, through various intermediaries, sold the arms to Iran. Powell was not involved with the government's parallel program that provided illicit military aid to anticommunist Contra rebels in Nicaragua.

The Iran-Contra scandal, which included an illegal diversion of proceeds from the Iranian arms sales to the Nicaraguan Contras, threatened to bring down the Reagan presidency. And while Weinberger and Powell largely opposed Reagan's policy of trading weapons for hostages, their unswerving loyalty to the president rendered them complicit in the unlawful dealings with Iran. Despite his direct participation in the controversial arms-for-hostages program, Powell would also come to play a leading role in the administration's rehabilitation and in its overhaul of the national security policy-making process, all of which served to advance his career.

Powell's involvement in the Iran-Contra saga began midyear 1985. On June 17, National Security Adviser McFarlane provided Weinberger, Shultz, and CIA Director William J. Casey with an eight-page, top-secret memorandum. It was a bold Cold War policy proposal recommending that the United States develop closer political relations with Iran—a declared terrorist state—in order to promote American interests in the region. In the draft national security decision directive, McFarlane reasoned that if Washington did not seize the initiative with Tehran, Moscow would. He promised that the sale of U.S. military equipment and arms would draw the Iranian government into the American camp, and he wanted support from Weinberger, Shultz, and Casey before he presented the radical policy to the president.[30]

Powell, who read all of Weinberger's mail, including the most highly classified, thought the idea of aiding Iran was disturbing, "a stunner," so he rushed the memorandum to the defense secretary.[31] Like Powell, Weinberger considered the proposal unfathomable, writing across McFarlane's document, "This is almost too absurd to comment on."[32] In mid-July, Weinberger sent his formal and unambiguous response: "Under no circumstances . . . should we now ease our restrictions on arms sales to Iran."[33] In a rare moment of policy solidarity, Shultz concurred with the defense secretary. Casey, on the other hand, was "enthusiastic" about the initiative.[34]

McFarlane was undeterred by Weinberger and Shultz's objections. After communicating with a senior ranking Israeli official, he came to believe that moderate Iranians, if properly motivated, would use their influence to secure the release of American hostages held by Lebanese terrorists. In early July, he informed Weinberger and Powell by telephone and later Shultz by secret cable that the Israeli government, which was already selling weapons to Iran, had offered to play an intermediary role between Washington and Tehran.[35] The defense secretary, who considered Iran a "barbaric, 13th century empire," dismissed the proposal in conversations with Powell. He opposed any negotiations with Iranian officials because "the only moderates in Iran are in the cemetery."[36] Shultz, on the other hand, had warmed to "the prospect of gaining the release of . . . seven hostages" and the establishment of ties with political moderates in Iran, especially with Israel's support.[37] Despite Weinberger's objection, McFarlane's commitment to a new Iranian policy persisted. On July 13 he informed the president about the Cold War initiative, which he said was aimed, in part, to rescue the hostages in Lebanon. The latter resonated with Reagan.[38]

McFarlane's proposal, including Israel's offer of support, was debated on August 6 at a White House meeting of the president's senior national security team. According to McFarlane, the discussion included "the legal ramifications, the political risks, [and] the matter of Congressional oversight."[39] Shultz and even Weinberger expressed a willingness to open back-channel communications with Tehran but objected to "the very bad idea" of Israel shipping batches of its U.S.-made missiles to Iran in return for hostages.[40] Weinberger believed "that any shipment of arms was probably illegal" and that even a third-party transfer must be reported to Congress.[41] The meeting ended without resolution. A rueful Powell later admitted that "this scheme looked, at the time, as if it would die of its own foolishness anyway. But we underestimated the President's support for the plan or the determination of the NSC staff to pull it off."[42]

Despite Weinberger and Shultz's objections, Reagan approved McFarlane's plan to negotiate with Tehran. In his memoirs, the president wrote, "The truth is, once we had information from Israel that we could trust the people in Iran, I didn't have to think thirty seconds about saying yes to their proposal. . . . I said there was one thing we wanted: The moderate Iranians had to use their influence with Hizballah [*sic*] and try to get our hostages freed."[43] According to McFarlane, he informed Shultz, Weinberger, and others of the president's decision.[44] Meanwhile, the Israeli government had launched the operation.[45]

On August 22 Israeli officials notified McFarlane that they had successfully delivered ninety-six TOW antitank missiles to Iran. The Reagan administration, which had a policy of never making "deals" with terrorists or state sponsors of terrorism such as Iran, had now sanctioned an illegal shipment of U.S.-made weapons to Tehran.[46] The 1976 Arms Export Control Act prohibited the delivery of arms to any nation that supported terrorism, and it further required the president to notify Congress if there was suspicion that the law had been violated.[47] Reagan accepted the CIA's recommendation to keep congressional leaders in the dark and never provided the required authorization, known as a presidential finding, for the operation, in part because it, too, would require congressional notification.[48]

McFarlane understood the political and legal significance of the arms shipment, and after hearing from the Israelis, he arranged an impromptu, nighttime meeting at the Pentagon to debrief Weinberger, Powell, and the acting chairman of the Joint Chiefs of Staff. There, McFarlane recounted the recent course of events, including Reagan's sanctioning of the arms transaction.[49] Afterward, Weinberger appeared more willing to negotiate with Iran for the hostages. He wrote in his diary, "I argued that we tell them we wanted *all* hostages back."[50]

On the following day, McFarlane telephoned Reagan and Weinberger. The defense secretary subsequently noted, "Iranian proposal to let us have our Kidnappees—agreed we should deal directly with Iranians & not thru Israelis & that we should get guarantees that we'll get them all & take them off w helos fm [with helicopters from] Tripoli Beach."[51] Anticipating the release of hostages, Reagan wrote in his diary, "They will be delivered to a point on the beach north of Tripoli & we'll take them off to our 6th fleet. . . . Now we wait."[52]

On August 29 McFarland communicated to Weinberger that the "Iranians will offer to give us back our hostages. Want meeting in Vienna Tuesday/Wednesday. Asked for Defense representative."[53] The secretary agreed to send an emissary. Shortly thereafter, a "senior military officer" traveled to Austria under a false passport along with a member of McFarlane's staff, Marine Corps Lieutenant Colonel Oliver North.[54] Their mission, according to Weinberger's diary, was to "see if Iranians will release our hostages."[55] Two years later, when Powell was shown a number of the defense secretary's diary entries, he admitted to knowing "by this time that there was a serious deal going on with the Iranians."[56] In his memoirs, Powell wrote how during the summer and fall of 1985, it was becoming all too evident that the president "wanted the hostages freed, and was willing to take political risks to do it."[57]

The arms shipment of August 22 did not lead to the release of American hostages. Iran demanded an additional four hundred TOW missiles in return for freeing a single captive. Israel indicated a willingness to continue its intermediary role. Reagan, without legal authorization or congressional notification, approved a second shipment of American-made arms from Israeli stockpiles.[58]

It is evident from Weinberger's diary that he and Powell were again anticipating a release of hostages, including William Buckley, the captured CIA station chief. On September 11, the defense secretary wrote, "Bud McFarlane—says Iranians told Israelis our 7 hostages would be released in 3 groups . . . [and] we will extract them by helicopter."[59] The second batch of missiles was delivered to Iran on September 15, and Weinberger wrote, "A delivery I have for our prisoners."[60] To the president's absolute delight, this shipment led to the immediate release of Reverend Benjamin Weir. His release, according to journalist Bob Woodward, was "treated almost as high mass at the White House."[61] The next day, however, a disappointed Weinberger noted, "Saw Colin Powell—no news of release of Buckley—he was not delivered to Cyprus on time."[62]

Weinberger also learned from Powell that his office had not been receiving all of the National Security Agency intelligence intercepts pertaining to the Iran initiative. The defense secretary demanded, through Powell, that he be kept fully informed. "We straightened that matter out in a hurry," Powell recalled.[63]

In the weeks following Israel's September 15 shipment of missiles to Tehran, the Iranians requested still more weaponry for the release of additional American hostages. Reagan, delighted by the release of Reverend Weir, sanctioned further negotiations to be coordinated by McFarlane and the NSC staff. For its part, the Israeli government agreed to ship more missiles to Tehran, but it wanted the United States to replenish its diminished stockpiles. McFarlane assured the Israelis of replenishment and informed Weinberger and Shultz about the continuing operation.[64]

By this time, North, as a member of McFarlane's NSC staff, began playing an even larger role in the arms-for-hostages operation. The marine lieutenant colonel later testified, "If I recall properly what happened in '85—my original point of contact was General Colin Powell, who was going directly to his immediate superior, Secretary Weinberger. . . . The Israelis expected . . . to have gratis given to them, 508 TOWs in replenishment for what they had shipped in August and September."[65]

In November 1985, McFarlane contacted Weinberger and Shultz to provide updates on the Iran initiative, including the possibility of shipping U.S. Hawk antiaircraft and Phoenix air-to-air missiles to Iran. Both secretaries questioned the prudence of the arms-for-hostages program. On November 9 McFarlane telephoned an increasingly wary Weinberger on a secure line. After the conversation, the defense secretary wrote in his diary, "Bud McFarlane . . . wants to start 'negot' exploration with Iranians (& Israelis) to give Iranians weapons for our hostages. I objected."[66] The following day, after talking to McFarlane again, Weinberger expressed some flexibility: "We'll demand the release of all hostages. Then we might give them through Israelis Hawks but not Phoenix [missiles]."[67] For his part, Shultz concluded that a shipment of U.S. Hawk and Phoenix missiles to Iran would be "highly illegal" and doubted that Weinberger would condone it.[68]

Nevertheless, on the morning of November 19, McFarlane received Reagan's approval to sell U.S.-stocked missiles to Iran through Israel.[69] The national security adviser first informed Shultz, who registered his objection to the mission but declined to take his opposition directly to the president. McFarlane then telephoned Weinberger. The defense secretary wrote in his diary, "[McFarlane] wants us [the Defense Department] to try to get 500 Hawks for sale to Israel to pass on to Iran for release of 5 hostages Thurs."[70] Weinberger seized the opportunity to express his disapproval. He immediately tasked Powell with drafting a memorandum, one that painted the proposed shipment of Hawk missiles "as negatively as possible."[71]

Powell's "Point Paper" emphasized that such a transaction required Congress to be notified immediately.[72] Weinberger wrote in his diary, "Colin Powell in office re data on Hawks—can't be given to Israel or Iran w/o Cong. notification."[73] According to

Powell, the defense secretary then telephoned McFarlane to say the proposed arms transaction "is illegal, it's a bad idea."[74] Undeterred, McFarlane trumped Weinberger the following day. He told the secretary that Reagan decided to bypass the Defense Department and "do it thru Israelis."[75] Like Shultz, Weinberger did not take his protest to the president. Robert M. Gates, then the deputy director of the CIA, later wrote of the Iran initiative, *"No one* was willing to put his job on the line to stop it. . . . The arms deal could have been stopped at any time if Shultz or Weinberger had thought it important enough."[76] Instead, Weinberger and Powell renewed their vigil, hoping for the release of hostages. On November 23 the defense secretary wrote, "Colin Powell— . . . no hostage release last night."[77] In fact, due to logistical complications, the Israeli arms had not yet reached their destination.

Eventually, eighteen Hawk missiles from Israel's arsenal arrived in Iran. This third shipment of arms had been illegally facilitated by the CIA.[78] Weinberger and Powell received confirmation of the delivery the next day. Under the subject line "Lebanese Kidnappings," the intelligence report read, "Delivery Made on 24 November 1985."[79] But the Hawk shipment did not lead to the release of a single hostage.

Two weeks later, on December 7, Reagan convened his senior foreign policy team at the White House. He wanted to discuss "continuing and possibly even expanding the covert operation begun the previous summer."[80] In his diary, the president referred to the Iran initiative as "a complex undertaking with only a few of us in on it."[81] Just before the meeting, Weinberger huddled with Powell and Richard Armitage, the assistant secretary of defense of international security affairs, for an update on a new "NSC Plan to let Israelis give Iranians 50 Hawks & 3300 TOWs in return for 5 hostages."[82] Earlier, Armitage had presciently concluded that there "is no good way to keep this project from ultimately being made public."[83]

At the White House, McFarlane recounted the history of the Iran initiative, including all previous arms shipments.[84] An intense debate ensued, with Weinberger and Shultz renewing their opposition to the program on both policy and legal grounds.[85] The defense secretary reiterated the need to notify Congress given the embargo on weapons sales to Iran and asserted that "washing" arms shipments through Israel did not make such transactions legal.[86] Reagan, however, remained adamant about rescuing the hostages.[87]

Undeterred by Weinberger and Shultz's warnings, the president expressed his willingness to break the law and risk impeachment to secure the freedom of the hostages. "They can impeach me if they want," Reagan told his advisers. He even joked that "visiting days are Wednesday" at the Leavenworth federal penitentiary. Weinberger snapped, "You will not be alone."[88] The secretary summarized the meeting in his diary entry of December 7: "I argued strongly that we have an embargo that makes arms sales to Iran illegal & the President couldn't violate it—& that 'washing' transaction thru Israel wouldn't make it legal. Shultz, [and Chief of Staff] Don Regan agreed. President sd. [said] he could answer charges of illegality but he couldn't answer charge that 'big strong President Reagan passed up a chance to free hostages.'"[89]

Separate from the president's plans for another arms shipment to Iran was the lingering issue of replenishing Israel's depleted stockpiles. On December 10 McFarlane again briefed Reagan, Weinberger, and others in the Oval Office.[90] After the meeting, Weinberger met with Powell and wrote on his daily notepad, "We still must replace 500 TOWs to Israel."[91]

A January 15, 1986, NSC memorandum signaled Weinberger's ongoing, if futile, opposition to additional arms deals with Iran. In the document, North complained about the defense secretary's obstructionism to John Poindexter, who had recently replaced McFarlane as the president's national security adviser. North wrote, "Casey believes Cap [Weinberger] will continue to create roadblocks until he is told by you that the President wants to move NOW and that Cap will have to make it work. Casey points out that we have now gone through three different methodologies in an effort to satisfy Cap's concerns and that no matter what we do there is always a new objection. . . . [Casey] is concerned that Cap will find some new objection unless he is told to proceed."[92]

On January 17 Weinberger met with Powell to discuss U.S. laws "prohibiting" arms sales to Iran.[93] Later that same day, the defense secretary reminded Shultz, Casey, and Poindexter of the "Statutes forbidding sales to Iran."[94] Nevertheless, Weinberger relented to White House and CIA pressure, accepting Reagan's utter determination to secure the return of more hostages. Casey was informed that Weinberger's staff, led by Powell, "had signed off" on the new plan. It called for the Defense Department to transfer missiles to the CIA, which, working with NSC staff and through intermediaries, would sell and deliver the arms to Iran.[95] When one of Weinberger's deputy assistant secretaries asked half-jokingly, "Do we have a legal problem with this, is somebody going to jail?" The defense secretary responded, "Yes, we could go to jail, or someone could."[96]

Weinberger had acquiesced to the sale of U.S. arms because Reagan had signed a top-secret presidential finding of necessity that authorized the direct sale of U.S. missiles to Iran. Acting on the president's order, the defense secretary told Powell to personally facilitate the transfer of four thousand TOW missiles to the CIA. A perturbed Weinberger informed his senior military assistant, "I want nothing to do with the Iranians. I want the task carried out with the department removed as much as possible."[97] Apparently, Weinberger even kept the shipment secret from his chairman of the Joint Chiefs of Staff, Admiral William J. Crowe Jr.[98]

With these instructions, Powell contacted an old friend, acting army chief of staff General Maxwell "Mad Max" Thurman, and had the weapons transferred from the Defense Department to the CIA. Powell did not tell Thurman or anyone else in the military where the missiles were going. He and Weinberger "treated the TOW transfer like garbage to be gotten out of the house quickly" and "with as few fingerprints as possible on it."[99] The defense secretary had instructed Powell to ship the weapons "in a way that does not contaminate us any more than we are."[100] Powell worked assiduously to minimize intradepartmental knowledge of the arms-for-hostages operation and, utilizing the power of Reagan's executive order, adeptly orchestrated the arms transfer without informing his senior ranking military colleagues of the weapons' ultimate destination, a designated terrorist state.[101] Powell later told federal investigators that his army superiors "had no need to know" about Iran and thus they had no reason or responsibility to notify Congress.[102]

By February 13, 1986, the Defense Department had received a wire transfer of $3.7 million from Iran through various intermediaries, including the CIA. Four days later, the first five hundred U.S. TOW missiles *under the new arrangement* were delivered to Iran via Israel. A second batch of five hundred was transferred on February 20.[103] It seems that neither Powell nor Weinberger was aware that the Iranians had been charged $10 million for the weapons and that part of the profits from the sale would be illegally diverted to Nicaragua to support the anticommunist Contra resistance movement.[104] Later that year, when FBI agents asked Powell if he knew of the diversion, he replied, "No, No, No."[105] Many years later, when Powell admitted that laws had been broken during the Iran-Contra affair, he considered the diversion of funds the most flagrant violation. In his memoirs, he wrote, "I knew that Weinberger, as well as the rest of us at Defense, had no knowledge of *the most illegal aspect* of the affair, the diversion of Iranian arms sales profits to the contras" (emphasis added).[106]

The hyper-secretive nature of the Defense Department–CIA transaction and Powell's bypassing of normal arms-transfer protocols raised serious concerns at the highest levels of the army. At one point, the director of the army staff called Powell with a warning: "If arms in that amount are going to a foreign country, Congress has to be notified."[107] Powell was among only five people, including Weinberger and Armitage, in the entire Defense Department who knew that the U.S. weapons were bound for Iran. A crucial question was whether the administration, including Defense, would provide Congress with timely notification of the arms sales as required by law. Powell, understanding that "this kind of a transfer requires a notification," attempted to reassure the army leadership that everything about the arms shipment was above board and congressional notification would be made.[108] Following Weinberger's order to minimize the involvement of the Defense Department, Powell told army leaders that it was the CIA's duty to inform Congress "and that the Army did not have responsibility to do that." He asked the army's assistant deputy chief of staff, Lieutenant General Vincent Russo, who was himself "very uncomfortable" with the secret operation, to assure Army Secretary John O. Marsh Jr. that "[congressional] notification was being handled . . . that it had been addressed and it was taken care of."[109]

Marsh was not reassured by Powell's expressed confidence. He and Army Chief of Staff General Wickham, one of Powell's mentors, insisted that a memorandum be drafted for Powell to underscore the need for congressional notification. Wickham would later testify, "I felt very uneasy about this process. And I also felt uneasy about the notification dimension to the Congress."[110] The memo was delivered on March 7. Powell showed it to "an unhappy Weinberger," who foresaw trouble for the administration.[111] On March 12, just days before Powell completed his three-year assignment as Weinberger's senior assistant, he handed the army's communique regarding "statutory requirements" to National Security Adviser Poindexter. Powell told him, "Handle it . . . however you plan to do it."[112] Poindexter proceeded to hide the memorandum in a safe.[113] Neither he nor anybody else in the administration ever complied with the law and notified Congress about the weapons shipments to Iran.

For Powell, the arms-for-hostages operation was unseemly business, and he was happy to leave it and the Pentagon behind. Nevertheless, he viewed Weinberger as "one of the true heroes of the Iran-Contra matter" because he "spoke up forcefully inside the government in an effort to prevent it from occurring."[114]

In other words, he thought the defense secretary had demonstrated intellectual honesty and moral courage by frequently opposing McFarlane's "absurd" and "illegal" program.

There is much to respect in Weinberger and Powell's conduct during the Iran initiative. They were highly dedicated and independent-minded senior subordinates who not only recognized and communicated the dangers of implementing the unlawful foreign policy but also expressed their opposition to it. Their ultimate deference to the president's decision making, however, made them complicit in the illegal 1985 arms transfers and in the administration's ongoing failure to notify Congress. As evidenced by the defense secretary's diary, Weinberger and Powell were well aware of the missile shipments to Iran and the need to replenish Israel's arsenal. Throughout 1986, neither of them insisted on congressional notification, even after they themselves had arranged for the transfer of U.S.-based missiles to Iran through the CIA. As Powell later admitted, "Timely congressional notification might have blown this scheme out of the water."[115]

For his years of effective and loyal service to the administration, Powell received a promotion to lieutenant general and was given a plum assignment as commander of V Corps in West Germany. Weinberger's final evaluation of Powell's performance was effusive: "He was directly involved in every issue I faced as Secretary of Defense. Moreover, he played a pivotal role in the functioning of the entire Department of Defense. In every way, MG Powell's performance was unfailingly superlative. . . . Soldier, scholar, statesman—he does it all. . . . Colin Powell is an emerging national leader with unlimited potential, capable of, indeed deserving of, leadership at the highest levels of the American military."[116]

Powell left the Pentagon with enormous respect and admiration for the defense secretary.[117] He considered Weinberger "extremely astute" and "a great fighter, a brilliant advocate," someone who "projected strength, unflappability, and supreme self-confidence."[118] Most important, Powell believed his boss was a sage leader of the Defense Department, appropriately cautious in the application of military power. Under Weinberger, Powell had further developed his own thinking on the subject, which had been maturing since Vietnam and his study of Clausewitz at the National War College. The invasion of Grenada, he concluded, had been justified because of the direct threat to U.S. security and because Reagan had articulated clear objectives and deployed ample force to achieve them. In contrast, the president's decision to send peacekeeping marines into the heart of the volatile Middle East was inconsonant with Powell and Weinberger's martial philosophy, which valued reasoned restraint as much as calculated aggression.

With his new assignment in West Germany, Powell had finally secured a premier field command position. He was responsible for leading 75,000 soldiers. It was a superb opportunity to demonstrate to doubters such as Major General Hudachek that he was, in fact, a highly capable commanding general and not a just a Pentagon politico. Powell began his tour in July 1986 with a belief that his army career was approaching its zenith. He had come full circle since serving as a platoon leader at Gelnhausen. At V Corps, Powell enjoyed working with soldiers of all ranks, and while the task of preparing his troops for a potential conflict with Soviet forces was a significant one, the pressures of the command paled in comparison to the stressful years under Weinberger. He later wrote, "I had jumped from the frying pan into the easy chair. . . . It was pleasant to have others performing for me my old roles as gofer and horse holder."[119] But the joys of field command came to a sudden and dramatic end when the Iran-Contra programs became public.

News of the Reagan administration's secret dealings with Iran first surfaced in early November 1986. After initially denying the story, the president eventually admitted that arms had indeed been sold to Iran in hopes of securing the freedom of American hostages in Lebanon.

When the administration also acknowledged that some proceeds from the Iranian missile sales had been diverted to the anticommunist Contra rebels in Nicaragua, "the crisis," according to the CIA's Robert Gates, "went nuclear and . . . threatened to destroy Ronald Reagan's Presidency."[120] As a result of the scandal, Poindexter resigned as national security adviser and Lieutenant Colonel North, who along with his boss had destroyed many relevant government documents, was fired from the NSC staff. Revelations about Iran-Contra led to three separate major investigations: a special presidential review board known as the Tower Commission, a joint congressional committee, and an independent counsel team led by Lawrence E. Walsh, a former federal judge, the deputy attorney general in the Eisenhower administration, and a onetime president of the American Bar Association.

On December 2, 1986, as the investigations got underway, Reagan selected Carlucci as his new national security adviser. Carlucci intended to direct a major overhaul of the NSC structure and processes, and he needed a capable, loyal, and motivated deputy to help him. He immediately called Powell in Frankfurt with a job offer. Carlucci knew Powell to be an excellent subordinate: self-assured, intelligent, trustworthy, and collaborative. It was Carlucci's opinion that Powell had developed into "the world's best staff officer" with an "upbeat and inclusive style and sense of humor," that, "combined with his military bearing and crisp efficiency, radiated competence and confidence."[121] Above all, Carlucci needed Powell's political "savvy" and superior administrative skills to help "impose order and procedure" on the NSC, which was left "rudderless, drifting, [and] demoralized" in the wake of the scandal.[122]

The last thing Powell wanted was to surrender his comfortable command and return to the heat of the Washington pressure cooker. He resisted Carlucci's impassioned pleas: "Frank, I'm finally back in the real Army," he explained, continuing that he did not want to leave until he had proved himself "an able corps commander."[123] More significant and problematic, Powell reminded Carlucci that he had played a major part in orchestrating weapons shipments to Iran, saying, "You know I had a role in this business" and was "up to my ears."[124] Carlucci, believing the presidency to be in peril, was undeterred in his efforts to enlist Powell's help. He arranged for the FBI to interview the lieutenant general about his role in the Iran-Contra affair. Acting out of a "sense of caution and self-preservation," an anxious Powell took the extraordinary step of tape-recording that interview and others that followed.[125]

The FBI reported to the White House that the army general was not a suspect in their criminal investigation of the Iran-Contra affair. Carlucci also had Weinberger call Peter J. Wallison, the White House counsel, to further assure Reagan that "Colin had no connection with Iran arms sales—except to carry out President's orders."[126] Weinberger himself prodded Powell to "do what's right in this hour of the President's need."[127] In the end, Powell agreed to join the NSC staff as Carlucci's sole deputy on the condition that the president himself order the reassignment. That was the only way, Powell told Carlucci, "I can make this departure honorable, the only way I'll be able to face my fellow officers. . . . That's the one thing my world will understand."[128] Reagan telephoned Powell on December 12, and within days the White House had announced his appointment as the new deputy assistant to the president for national security affairs.

In the throes of the Iran-Contra investigations, Powell and Carlucci proved a formidable team in reforming and revitalizing the NSC. "Our situation was similar to taking over a demoralized battalion," Powell later wrote, "where the commanding officer had just been relieved, or inheriting a team after the coach had been fired, or acquiring a company recently looted by its officers."[129] Powell recognized that many people, including the president, were to blame for the security council's damaged condition. McFarlane, Poindexter, and North had run amok, to be sure, but Reagan's delegatory management style and inattention to detail had created the unbridled environment that promoted rogue behavior without accountability. To Powell and Carlucci's amazement, Reagan's leadership passivity continued after the scandal broke, and this, according to Powell, "placed a tremendous burden on us. Until we got used to it, we felt uneasy implementing recommendations without a clear decision."[130] At one point, Carlucci complained to Powell, "My God, we didn't sign on to run this country!"[131]

Still, in a matter of months and without engaged leadership from the president, Carlucci and Powell revamped the NSC and together assumed the role of the "honest broker" in making national security policy.[132] They shuttered its secret communications room and the political-military affairs branch, which North had led, and reduced the overall staff by some 50 percent. They had, according to Powell, "cut out the infection" and stemmed "the bleeding."[133] Carlucci and Powell also hired new NSC legal counsel and conducted a detailed review of every active covert operation. In the end, they canceled many programs, including all of those operated by NSC staff.

While the national security adviser invested his time working directly with the president and the secretaries of state and defense, he gave Powell "a lot of latitude" to manage the NSC staff and lead the newly created Policy Review Group (PRG), where, Carlucci later said, "the actual business was done."[134] The PRG was a forum for subcabinet-level officials to openly communicate, debate, and coordinate the policy positions of various government departments and agencies, such as State, Defense, and the CIA. "After years of obfuscation and intrigue" by the NSC staff, Armitage remarked, the transparency of the PRG "was like the clouds opening up and the sun coming out."[135] In the end, Powell said of his work under Carlucci, "We had a plan, we executed that plan, and we were rather successful in putting that process back on a firm footing."[136]

By fall 1987, Powell was receiving public accolades for his competency as Carlucci's deputy. In "National Security Council; Case of the Reluctant General," *New York Times* reporter Richard Halloran depicted Powell as an effective reformer and a well-regarded manager of people and processes who, while preferring to be in the command of soldiers, had obediently returned to Washington, where his exceptional organizational skills were needed in a time of presidential crisis. "By all accounts," Halloran wrote, "General Powell . . . has won the respect of top bureaucratic operatives who often wield sharp knives" and "become a key player in the rebuilding of the staff of the National Security Council and in reviving the interagency process through which recommendations on policy are submitted to the security council and the President."[137]

Powell's effectiveness and loyalty led to another promotion, not in military rank but in title and authority. In November 1987, after Weinberger announced his resignation, Reagan selected Carlucci as his next secretary of defense. The president then accepted Shultz's recommendation to elevate Powell as his national security adviser. According to the secretary of state, "Powell had proved to be extraordinarily knowledgeable and gifted intellectually. He had a great touch with Congress."[138] A profile in the *Los Angeles Times* concluded that the lieutenant general's rapid ascent had been grounded in "political savvy, efficiency, and loyalty."[139] Powell was elated with his new status and very happy to shed the title of deputy assistant. "I was no longer someone's aide or number two," he thought. "I would be working directly with the President, the Vice President, and the secretaries of State and Defense. . . . And I would not only be organizing the views of others to present to the President; I was now expected to give him my own national security judgments. I had become a 'principal,' with cabinet-level status, if not the rank."[140]

Powell was also cognizant of the bizarre reality that the Iran-Contra debacle had actually benefited his career. "If it hadn't been for Iran-Contra," he later wrote, "I'd still be an obscure general somewhere. Retired, never heard of."[141] Robert Gates was not as lucky. In 1986 he was forced to withdraw his nomination to become Reagan's CIA director because of congressional concerns that he had contemporaneous knowledge of the Iranian and Nicaraguan initiatives and because he had been "less than candid" during the subsequent investigations.[142]

Although Powell had assumed the leadership of the NSC staff, his primary roles remained that of a follower and manager. He emerged as a masterful honest broker, coordinating and presenting the views of the secretaries of state and defense and helping them to execute the president's policies.[143] On most mornings at 7:00 a.m., Shultz and Carlucci convened in Powell's West Wing office to briefly discuss and debate issues on his "neutral ground."[144] According to Carlucci, "Those meetings were the key to the effective functioning of foreign policy in the last year and half of the administration."[145] Unlike previous national security advisers, Powell rarely originated or significantly influenced policy, deferring instead to the more experienced Carlucci and Shultz. In his memoir, Powell admits his role was "largely as an administrator, the guy who made the NSC trains run. I was not Henry Kissinger or Zbigniew Brzezinski, with their Ph.D.s and international relations backgrounds."[146]

Powell found particularly rewarding his role in organizing diplomatic summits for Reagan and Soviet Premier Mikhail Gorbachev. Those meetings, held in Washington and Moscow, resulted in the historic intermediate-range nuclear forces treaty, an agreement to mutually destroy hundreds of intermediate-range missiles. Powell was exceedingly impressed with Gorbachev's intelligence and determination to bring the reforms of perestroika and glasnost to the Soviet system. In spring 1988, while meeting with Gorbachev and Shultz in Moscow, Powell became convinced that the Soviet leader was intent on ending the Cold War. "That night, back in my hotel room," Powell recalled, "I thought over this extraordinary day, and I felt a conviction deep in my bones. This changed Soviet line was no ruse to disarm us. This man meant what he said. . . . Now, I had to think about a world without a Cold War."[147] With the Reagan administration coming to an end in late 1988, a new president, George H. W. Bush, would have to grapple with the drastically changing geopolitical landscape.

Powell's one-year tenure as Reagan's national security adviser was judged widely as a success. The president characterized him as a "brilliant" subordinate who, along with Carlucci, "revitalize[d] and restore[d] honor to the NSC."[148] Like Carlucci, Powell had served the president well by maintaining order, discipline, and transparency at the NSC and by effectively coordinating policy between the White House and the Departments of State and Defense. While neither "a global strategist nor a covert activist," he had, according to the *Los Angeles Times*, been "the grand facilitator of foreign policy, not so much an initiator as a compromiser."[149] Once again, Powell had proven a highly capable and greatly admired follower, and he was amply rewarded for it.

On December 1, 1988, less than a month after Bush won the presidential election, the White House announced that Powell would be nominated for a fourth star and for appointment as the commanding general of Forces Command (FORSCOM), a position responsible for the readiness of all U.S.-based army reservists, guardsmen, and active-duty soldiers—nearly one million troops. In the history of the army there had been other black four-star generals, but Powell would be the first to have responsibility for a massive command. Bush had given Powell two other options within the new administration, including director of the CIA and deputy secretary of state under James Baker. But Powell was not inclined to either position, especially the latter, which he considered a demotion. Instead, he trained his eye on becoming the army's chief of staff, and the FORSCOM job best positioned him to realize that goal.[150]

During the Reagan presidency, Powell had again demonstrated many key characteristics of an exemplary subordinate. His work for Weinberger, Carlucci, and Reagan reflected remarkable managerial competency, professional knowledge, commitment, and adaptability. "One of his principal assets," Weinberger noted, "was that he clearly knew more about the subject matter than did any of the other participants. He also knew exactly what had to be accomplished at each meeting, and as a result he was able to participate in the most effective way possible."[151] Powell's superiors also valued his intellect and initiative, characterizing his judgment as "impeccable," "critical," and "insightful" and his leadership as "readily evident in every undertaking."[152] Powell's competence and reliability garnered extraordinary trust and confidence from his superiors, and Weinberger, who considered the general his "closest advisor and confidant," concluded that he "could not have chosen a more loyal, capable, or dependable officer" as his senior military assistant.[153]

Fidelity to one's superior was always a paramount virtue for Powell, and it had served him well throughout his career.[154] He himself characterized the ideal subordinate as someone who not only expressed honest and independent opinions, but also embraced and loyally executed the boss's final decisions.[155] In short, Powell believed that "loyalty is disagreeing strongly, and loyalty is executing faithfully."[156]

But during the Iran-Contra affair, Powell and Weinberger's loyalties were misaligned. Their complicity in the 1985 and 1986 illegal arms shipments to Iran and their failure to notify Congress speaks to both men's ethical shortcomings as senior ranking government officials. Their ultimate loyalty should have been to the Constitution and the American people, not the president. Worse, after the scandal erupted, Powell and Weinberger compounded their misdeeds by knowingly participating in a cover-up of the Iran-Contra operation in order to protect each other and the president.

Starting in December 1986 and continuing through November 1992, government investigators questioned Powell nearly a dozen times about his and Weinberger's roles in Iran-Contra. The interviews were variously conducted by the FBI, the White House, Congress, the Army Inspector General, the General Accounting Office, and the Office of Independent Counsel.

In a clear obstruction of justice, Weinberger and Powell concealed from federal investigators their knowledge of the defense secretary's voluminous diary, which contained incriminating information related to Iran-Contra. In June 1987, when the defense secretary was asked if he had any personal notes pertaining to national security meetings, he was purposefully misleading: "[I] occasionally take a few notes, but not really very often."[157] That same month, when investigators asked Powell if Weinberger kept a diary, he said, "The Secretary, to my knowledge, did not keep a diary."[158] Powell also misled investigators about his own note-taking habits.* Five years later, in April 1992, after the independent counsel discovered Weinberger's large collection of notes—some seven thousand pages—Powell reversed himself.[159] In a sworn affidavit and in his memoirs, he confirmed that the "small mountain" of notepads did indeed constitute the defense secretary's "personal diary which reflected a record of his life."[160]

Weinberger's diary contained incontrovertible evidence that he and Powell had lied under oath about their contemporaneous knowledge of the illegal 1985 arms shipments to Iran and the need to resupply Israel. In November 1986, Weinberger told Congress he did not learn of Israel's 1985 shipments and the need to replenish Israeli stockpiles until 1986. "No," he said. "I heard about that only much later after these things started to come out, and as I say I heard—only heard that statements were being made, not that that [arms shipments] had actually hap-

*In 1987, when investigators asked Powell if he had taken notes in meetings with Weinberger, he replied, "I would occasionally take notes, sometimes not." Powell, in fact, had a reputation as a habitual note taker. His closest friend at the Pentagon, Richard Armitage, testified that Powell "took extensive notes in spiral notebooks while he was Caspar Weinberger's military assistant," going through as many as five books a week. Powell informed investigators that he purposely destroyed all of his meeting notes. "Deposition of General Colin L. Powell," June 19, 1987, "Colin Powell's Notes," February 3, 1992, and "The Testimony of Colin Powell, April 22, 1992, Records of the Independent Counsel Lawrence Walsh, National Archives.

pened."[161] In July 1987, Weinberger was asked again whether he knew, in 1985, of the need to resupply Israel. He answered, "No, I have no memory of that."[162] When asked more specifically if he had had contemporaneous knowledge of the November 1985 Hawks shipment to Iran, Weinberger lied again: "No, I did not."[163]

In the years before Weinberger's notes were discovered, Powell repeatedly denied that he and Weinberger knew, in 1985, of Israel's arms shipments. In April 1987, congressional investigators asked Powell about the Iran operation and Israel's 1985 shipments. Powell told them that he was "aware of the Iran Initiative, but that the transfer of Israeli arms to Iran was *new* to him" and that "he is *now* aware that Israeli shortages existed in certain areas at that time" (emphases added).[164] In June 1987, Powell was asked again when he learned of the multiple 1985 Israeli shipments. He said, "It would be in calendar year 1986." When asked specifically about the November 1985 Hawk shipment, Powell said, "It was '86 not '85." He later stated that his recollections of the Iran initiative before mid-January 1986 "*all* have to do with discussions about a *possible* initiative [with Iran]" (emphases added).[165] In July 1987, Powell again told federal investigators that he had no contemporaneous knowledge of "Israel's involvement in the shipping of HAWK missiles to Iran in 1985."[166]

In 1992, after the independent counsel discovered Weinberger's daily notes, Powell admitted that he and the defense secretary had some contemporaneous knowledge of the 1985 arms shipments and of the need to resupply Israel. Powell also confessed that he had regular and concurrent conversations with Weinberger about the Iran initiative as represented in the secretary's notes. He said, "I would have discussed the events [the Iran initiative] referred to in the notes with Secretary Weinberger when they were happening."[167] The independent counsel later reported that the defense secretary and Powell "were consistently informed of proposed and actual arms shipments to Iran during 1985 and 1986."[168]

In April 1992, Powell was shown Weinberger's November 22, 1985, diary entry: "Israelis will sell 120 Hawks, older models to Iranians—Friday [hostage] release. Called Colin Powell—re above." In response, Powell said, "I assume this is an accurate statement by Mr. Weinberger." Powell was also shown Weinberger's December 10, 1985, diary entry: "We still must replenish 500 TOWs to Israel." Powell said, "This implies obviously that 500 TOWs have gone somewhere that must be replaced and I assume we were aware of it by this time." Powell was asked if Weinberger debriefed him after the December 10, 1985, White House meeting about Iran and Israel. Powell told the investigator that "he would be surprised if he was not briefed on the Israeli missile replenishment issue."[169] Seven months later, when a federal attorney asked Powell if the Israelis expected their missile stockpiles to be replenished by the Defense Department, the general barked, "You can't buy them at Kmart."[170]

Weinberger also made new admissions after his diary was uncovered. In May 1992 he told Lawrence Walsh, the independent counsel investigating Iran-Contra, that his diary notes were accurate, that he had contemporaneous knowledge of the November 1985 arms shipment to Iran, and that he always believed the weapons transfers to Iran through Israel had been illegal. Weinberger offered to testify to those facts, but he refused to plead guilty to any crime, not even a misdemeanor.[171] The latter was unacceptable to Walsh. A month later, a grand jury indicted Weinberger on five felony charges for lying to Congress about the 1985 arms sales and for obstructing federal investigations. He was arraigned on June 19, 1992.[172]

Powell was fortunate to escape indictment. Walsh had determined that general's misleading testimony regarding Weinberger's diary alone "seemed corrupt enough to meet the . . . test of obstruction."[173] In his final 1993 report to Congress, Walsh concluded that "Weinberger lied to investigators to conceal his knowledge of the Iran arms sales" and that "General Powell was one of the handful of senior DoD officials who were privy to detailed information regarding arms shipments to Iran during

1985 and 1986. . . . [I]nvestigators quickly learned that Powell was a knowledgeable party." The report further stated that some of Powell's statements to investigators "were questionable and seem generally designed to protect Weinberger."[174] And while Powell was characterized as a frequently "cooperative witness," the report condemned his sworn testimony as being "at least misleading" and "hardly constituted full disclosure."[175] In the end, Walsh decided not to indict the four-star general, concluding that "while Powell's prior inconsistent statements could have been used to impeach his credibility, they did not warrant prosecution."[176] While Powell has admitted that his frequent testimony in the Iran-Contra saga was often oriented toward protecting Weinberger, he has long presented himself as a victim of an unethical independent counsel who recklessly impugned his character and sullied his reputation by characterizing him as "a liar."[177]

Weinberger's trial was scheduled for January 5, 1993, and Powell was to be an important witness. James Brosnahan, Walsh's lead prosecutor in the case, knew that the general and others would face "the hard choice of either telling the truth or risking their own prosecution for perjury or obstruction of justice."[178] Powell was saved from testifying when just a week before the trial, Bush, who had supported Reagan's Iran initiative, pardoned Weinberger. Powell and many others had encouraged the president to do so. The last-minute reprieve outraged Brosnahan and Walsh. The latter immediately issued a statement of condemnation: "President Bush's pardon . . . undermines the principle that no man is above the law. It demonstrates that powerful people with powerful allies can commit serious crimes in high office—deliberately abusing the public trust without consequence."[179] Arthur Liman, the chief counsel for the Senate committee investigating Iran-Contra, later wrote that Bush's pardon set "a terrible precedent, since it said that a cabinet officer could lie to a prosecutor and the Congress with impunity."[180]

Powell and Weinberger's unethical conduct during the Iran initiative—acquiescing to the illegal 1985 arms shipments and failing to comply with statutory requirements to notify Congress—and in the subsequent cover-up reveal the potentially disastrous consequences of excessive loyalty to one's superiors. It was insufficient for the defense secretary and his trusted military assistant to express internal opposition to an unlawful policy. As senior government officials, they had an obligation to report the president's illicit program to Congress and the Justice Department. As a major general in the U.S. Army, Powell should have recognized that in such extreme circumstances loyalty is not "disagreeing strongly, and executing faithfully," but disagreeing strongly and refusing complicity in illegal activities.

In his autobiography, Powell praised Weinberger for not resigning in protest, writing that "Senior officials cannot fall on their swords every time they disagree with a President."[181] But the debate over the Iran initiative was not a rudimentary policy disagreement; it was about the president's willful violation of the law. Writing in 1990, Pulitzer Prize–winning journalist Thomas Oliphant appropriately singled out Powell and Weinberger as two actors in the Iran-Contra drama "whom history is going to judge harshly for not having stopped the scandal cold."[182]

Despite the vagaries and criminalities of the Iran-Contra affair, Powell's career continued to prosper. During the Reagan years, he had refined his thinking about the use of military force, a philosophy that had been maturing since Vietnam, Lebanon, and his studies at the National War College. Reagan's invasion of Grenada, he thought, had been appropriate because there was a clear and present danger to American security; moreover, the president had articulated well-defined objectives and deployed abundant resources to achieve them. Powell's own war doctrine, which prized thoughtful restraint as much as decisive action, would become famous during the George H. W. Bush presidency. During the general's tenure as the chairman of Joint Chiefs of Staff, he would demonstrate all the hallmarks of an exemplary senior subordinate.

If there's anybody that has the integrity and the honor to
tell a president what he feels, it's Colin Powell.

—GEORGE H. W. BUSH

CHAPTER FIVE

Chairman

(1989–1993)

Colin Powell became the commander in chief of FORSCOM in April 1989, but this assignment was truncated. During the summer, Secretary of Defense Dick Cheney recommended to George H. W. Bush that Powell become the next chairman of the Joint Chiefs of Staff. Cheney had been impressed with the general's "cleaning up" of the NSC "apparatus" after Iran-Contra.[1] The president also admired and respected Powell—"I love the guy," Bush wrote in his diary—but he worried about Powell's lack of "command experience" outside of Washington, DC.[2] Nonetheless, given the defense secretary's "insistence," the president embraced the recommendation.[3] Years later, Cheney concluded that recommending Powell "was a stroke of genius . . . one of my best decisions. . . . It's not possible to conceive of my tour [as defense secretary] without Colin Powell as an integral part of it."[4]

In August the president announced that Powell was his nominee for chairman of the Joint Chiefs of Staff. At fifty-three years old, Powell would be the youngest officer to ever hold the position and the first African American, the first ROTC graduate, and the first former national security adviser. His selection was lauded in the press, as he represented "the very model of a modern Army general for a time when diplomatic finesse and foreign policy expertise may be as important as combat experience."[5] After a unanimous Senate confirmation, Powell assumed the post on October 1. Two days earlier, Bush had confided to his diary, "The Powell decision has gone down well."[6]

During his four years as chairman, first under Bush and then under Bill Clinton, the United States waged victorious wars in Central America and the Middle East. Powell also witnessed the end of the Cold War, the disintegration of the Soviet Union, and the development of horrific humanitarian crises in Somalia and Bosnia. Amid the international tumult, Powell emerged as America's most admired and trusted leader. Speaking in the aftermath of the Persian Gulf War, Republican senator John McCain declared Powell "the greatest military leader this country has produced since World War II."[7] Likewise, Democrat Madeleine Albright perceived the chairman as "a larger-than-life hero" and "the hero of the Western world."[8]

Paradoxically, Powell had risen to this pinnacle leadership position because of his record as an exceedingly effective and loyal *subordinate* to powerful military and civilian leaders. For most of his career he had exhibited remarkable competency, commitment, composure, fidelity, and amicability. In serving as chairman, Powell would exercise heightened levels of independence, critical thinking, and moral courage. After three decades in government service, the new chairman evolved into the quintessential follower.

Powell had a clear understanding of his role and responsibilities as chairman. In addition to leading the Joint Staff and supporting all branches of the military, his primary obligation was to act as the principal military adviser to the president and defense secretary. He knew well that his influence with his superiors rested on his ability to persuade, not command. As chairman, he was determined to ask his civilian leaders probing questions about national security objectives and provide them with unambiguous military options and judicious recommendations. Powell would draw on his thirty years of experience and use lessons learned from Vietnam, Lebanon, and Grenada as guides for the proper use of America's armed forces. Regarding the latter, the chairman became renowned for his promotion of caution and diplomacy before exercising lethal force; if military force was deemed necessary, he insisted on well-defined mission objectives and the application of decisive combat power. This philosophy of war became known as the Powell Doctrine.

Volatile political developments in Panama, including a coup attempt against the country's dictator, Manuel Antonio Noriega, immediately challenged Powell as both leader and follower. On October 1, 1989, less than two weeks after his Senate confirmation, the chairman received word of the planned coup. For years, the Panamanian dictator had cooperated with the CIA and the U.S. Drug Enforcement Administration, but by fall 1988 Noriega had become persona non grata. He was suspected of election fraud and complicity in the murder of a political rival and had been indicted by two Florida grand juries for international narcotics smuggling.

Powell had met Noriega six years prior while touring Latin America with Defense Secretary Weinberger. The Panamanian strongman made a bad first impression. "I immediately had the crawling sense," Powell recalled, "that I was in the presence of evil."[9] As Reagan's national security adviser, he had supported a policy of escalating economic sanctions against Panama, and while he told reporters that Reagan was contemplating "additional pressure" against Noriega, Powell opposed Secretary of State Shultz's recommendation to send two additional army brigades to the Panama Canal Zone.[10]

In May 1989 a new crisis emerged when Noriega, supported by the Panamanian Defense Forces (PDF), stole the country's presidential election from an opposition candidate, Guillermo Endara. Noriega then launched a violent campaign against his political opponents. In October, Chairman Powell faced the question of whether to recommend U.S. military support for the rumored coup against the dictator.

The role and authority of the chairman of the Joint Chiefs of Staff had changed two years earlier with passage of the Goldwater-Nichols Department of Defense Reorganization Act.[11] Under the new law, which sought to diminish interservice rivalry and promote better communication and coordination among the service branches, the chairman alone, not the collective Joint Chiefs, acted as *the* principal military adviser to the president and defense secretary. Powell relished the enhanced powers of the position, not wanting to be "limited to presenting the chiefs' watered-down consensus recommendations and then whispering his personal views."[12] He was also elated that Defense Secretary Cheney wanted all civilian orders to combatant commanders to be channeled through Powell. The looming crisis in Panama represented the first significant test of the Goldwater-Nichols Act and the empowered chairman.

After consultation with the commander of U.S. forces in the Panama Canal Zone, Powell advised Bush and Cheney not to intervene. Secretary of State James Baker viewed the chairman as being "wary" of involvement in "a poorly organized effort."[13] Powell, like other senior administration officials, wanted Noriega deposed, but, suspicious of the limited intelligence, he concluded that a "half-baked" coup led by a "half-baked" Panamanian major would not transform Panama's troubled situation.[14] In other words, removing Noriega but leaving his army intact would not promote Panamanian stability or U.S. security. "I thought that we would have to . . . eventually . . . take it all down," Powell later said. "We would really have to take the PDF down or else you couldn't solve the problem."[15] The chairman's superiors, while eager to oust Noriega, accepted his counsel and withheld military support for the coup.[16]

Proceeding without U.S. military intervention, the coup failed. Members of Congress and political pundits flailed the Bush administration for not seizing the opportunity to oust Noriega. In hindsight, the president and many of his advisers regretted their inaction.[17] Cheney later recalled this "first test" of the new national security team and concluded, "We did not perform as well as we might have."[18] Bush, however, did not blame Powell for his cautiousness. In fact, the president told reporters, nobody was going to be fired, and "certainly not General Powell."[19]

Anticipating further destabilization in the small but strategically important country, Powell ordered updated war plans to remove Noriega and defeat his armed forces. He instructed his staff to be ready "on very short notice." Cheney assured the president that "General Powell and his commanders were refining a plan for vigorous military intervention in Panama."[20] In October and November, amid the new planning efforts, Powell solicited and received approval to increase troop and equipment levels at American defense installations in and around Panama.[21]

In mid-December the situation took a dramatic turn. Standing before Panama's National Assembly, a machete-wielding Noriega proclaimed himself "Maximum Leader of National Liberation" and declared Panama in a "state of war" against the United States.[22] Shortly thereafter, the PDF killed a young U.S. Marine Corps officer and detained, interrogated, and abused a U.S. Navy lieutenant and his wife, who had witnessed the shooting. Powell discussed these developments and potential responses with the defense secretary and the Joint Chiefs.[23] Cheney recounted that "General Powell was particularly eloquent on the consequences of Noriega's PDF killing an American soldier in cold blood. This was not the kind of thing we could let go unanswered."[24]

At an emergency White House meeting, Powell, with the full support of Cheney and the Chiefs, advised Bush that there had been "sufficient provocation" for military action to protect U.S. citizens and secure the Panama Canal.[25] The defense secretary later characterized the killing of the marine officer as "the action-forcing event."[26] Powell presented multiple options, ranging from a small commando raid to a full-scale invasion. He advocated the latter, which prompted Bush to ask, "Does it have to be that big?"[27] The chairman answered affirmatively. Only overwhelming force would ensure the overthrow of Noriega, the dismantlement of the PDF, and the protection of U.S. civilians and national security. Powell also cautioned that a successful invasion would make the United States responsible for ruling Panama until the government and police force were reconstituted. When Bush asked for casualty estimates, Powell said, "There will be a few dozen casualties if we go." He added, "If we don't go, there will be a few dozen casualties over the next few weeks and we'll still have Noriega."[28] After further discussion with his national security team, the president rose from his chair and said, "Okay, let's do it. The hell with it."[29]

Before launching Operation Just Cause, the Bush administration secured the support and cooperation of Endara, Noriega's political rival, and with that the president was convinced that an invasion was fully justified. Powell, however, was suddenly overcome with "self-doubt" and "foreboding."[30] In his first significant act as chairman, he had urged the president to launch a war that would certainly lead to the death of American personnel. When the invasion commenced, Powell's self-confidence rebounded, and from the confines of the National Military Command Center in Washington, DC, he labored to support the generals in the field.

The American force, which included hundreds of aircraft and twenty-four thousand ground troops, routed the PDF.[31] Twenty-three Americans died in the fighting along with some six hundred Panamanians, mostly soldiers and militia.[32] It was the largest U.S. military operation since the Vietnam War. Endara was quickly sworn in as Panama's new president. Noriega was eventually captured and sentenced to prison in Florida. Although the Organization of American States and many other countries condemned the action, it received widespread support within Panama and the United States.[33]

Utilizing his powers under the Goldwater-Nichols Act, Powell had demonstrated superb followership during the Panamanian crises. In October he had been tempted to support the rumored coup against Noriega, but after exercising critical judgment, he concluded that the risks of intervening without sufficient provocation and under ambiguous circumstances were too great. His reasoning persuaded his anxious superiors. Furthermore, Powell and his staff took the initiative to develop contingency plans, should the president decide to engage, and when circumstances deteriorated in Panama, Powell was prepared to present military options and his own recommendation to intervene with decisive force. In the end, Powell convinced his civilian leaders that a major invasion was necessary to achieve the administration's objectives: ejecting Noriega, debilitating his army, establishing temporary martial law, installing a new popular government, and protecting American citizens and the Panama Canal. In short, Powell had effectively led his superiors.

Operation Just Cause also afforded Powell the opportunity to assess his bosses and solidify his own role within the chain of command. He noted the president's attentiveness, composure, and tolerance for "free-swinging" debates among his senior subordinates.[34] "Bush very much enjoyed listening to us all bat away. And it was never personal," the chairman recounted. "I would say something and [Brent] Scowcroft would say, 'You know you got your head up your butt.' In front of the president of the United States!"[35] As for Cheney, Powell perceived him as "a cerebral Wyoming cowboy," someone who asked smart questions, made distinct judgments, and encouraged his senior subordinate to express contrary opinions to the president.[36]

Likewise, the defense secretary praised Powell for his initiative and decisiveness. "You're off to a good start as chairman," Cheney told him. "You're forceful and you're taking charge. . . . That's the way I want it."[37] Thus, Powell was pleased overall with his integration into the administration and his conduct as its senior military adviser. He had concerns about White House officials trying to micromanage the invasion "from the sidelines," but ultimately, the chairman expressed appreciation for the "clean and clear" command structure in which he was the conduit and facilitator between the president and defense secretary on the one hand, and the commanders in the field on the other. [38] "I was empowered . . . by Dick Cheney to be his partner in helping him run the Pentagon," Powell recounted, and had "pretty clear rein to speak my mind."[39]

While satisfied with Powell's early performance, Cheney was not hesitant to remind him of his subordinate status. The secretary balked, for example, at the chairman's attempt to control all information being sent to the secretary's office. Cheney insisted that he was to receive input from multiple sources. "Information is power. . . . And I had tended to control it," Powell later wrote. "I was being shown my place." He recognized that the defense secretary and the president, and not the chairman, were accountable for national security policy. Ultimately, they, not he, "would have to bear the responsibility."[40]

Powell's subordinate role did not prevent his emergence as a uniformed public celebrity. In televised press briefings during the Panama War, he conveyed authority, competence, and candor. Shortly after the invasion and the installation of Endara, Powell assured the American people that "the operation is a success already because we cut off the head of that government" and restored democracy to Panama.[41] The chairman personified "calm and confidence," and journalists began to laud the country's newest "Four Star Warrior."[42] He was depicted as "politically attuned" and having significant influence with the president.[43]

Although the war in Panama had achieved its military and political objectives, Powell acknowledged that leadership mistakes had been made, and he intended not to repeat them. At the operational level, an insufficient number of American forces had been deployed to secure the Punta Paitilla airport, resulting in the death of four Navy SEALs. Four army airborne rangers had also died, and many more were injured after they parachuted from dangerously low altitudes with extra-heavy packs. Moreover, there had been inadequate planning to maintain civil order and prevent looting following the collapse of the PDF. In addition, Powell criticized National Security Adviser Brent Scowcroft for trying to manage the battlefield from Washington and admitted that the Pentagon had failed to adequately accommodate the press corps' coverage of the fighting.[44]

Perhaps the most significant lesson Powell extracted was Panama's validation of the emerging Powell Doctrine as an antidote for avoiding quagmires such as Lebanon and Vietnam. As with Reagan and Grenada six years prior, Bush had identified an imminent threat to American interests and articulated unambiguous military and political objectives. Equally important, the president had authorized the use of decisive military force, which led to a conclusive victory and a timely drawdown. "Panama confirmed all my convictions . . . since the days of doubt over Vietnam," Powell wrote in his memoirs. "Have a clear political objective and stick to it. Use all the force necessary, and do not apologize for going in big if that is what it takes. . . . Whatever threats we face in the future, I intended to make these rules the bedrock of my military counsel."[45] Weinberger, Powell's old boss and mentor, applauded his protégé's conduct toward Panama, telling a reporter that the chairman's approach to war means "you go in with overwhelming force, you go in very quickly, and once it's over you get out. That is a refreshing change from the Vietnam era."[46]

Over the course of Powell's military career, he had come to believe that exemplary subordinates learn from experience, assess their circumstances, anticipate potentialities, and develop and execute plans to help their superiors define and achieve objectives. Before and during the Panama crisis he had routinely demonstrated these followership qualities, and they remained evident throughout his years as chairman. "More than intelligence and discipline," journalist David Halberstam wrote of Powell, "he had an exceptionally refined sense of anticipation, so important in a bureaucracy . . . the ability to sense what was going to happen next, and thereby to help his superior stay ahead of the play."[47]

Powell further demonstrated independent and anticipatory thinking when he decided that his main mission as chairman was to convince the president and defense secretary, as well as his military colleagues and Congress, of the need to downsize and restructure the U.S. military in a new post–Cold War world. "My thoughts were guided simply," he wrote, "by what I had observed at world summits, by my experience at the NSC, by what I like to think of as informed intuition. I was going to project what I expected to happen over the next five years and try to design an Army, Navy, Air Force, and Marine Corps to match these expectations."[48] While serving in the Reagan administration, Powell was among the few who had grown certain that the Cold War was coming to an end. It was evident to him that "Gorbachev was a new man in a new age offering new opportunities for peace."[49]

In May 1989, when still the FORSCOM commander, Powell began to share his crystallizing view of a radical future. In the speech "The Future Just Ain't What It Used to Be," later printed in *Army* magazine, Powell declared the Soviet Union a "bankrupt" and "benign" enemy and intimated that communist Poland, Hungary, and Czechoslovakia would one day seek admission to NATO.[50] Amid such fast-changing geopolitical realities, Powell argued that America's armed forces should undertake momentous changes in both strategy and structure.

Powell's maverick views were controversial. He was, for example, the leading proponent of ditching the army's stockpile of artillery-fired, tactical nuclear weapons. Cheney informed the chairman that none of his "civilian advisors," including Under Secretary for Policy Paul Wolfowitz, supported him. Powell responded half-jokingly, "That's because they're all right-wing nuts like you."[51] But the chairman eventually convinced his Pentagon superior, who later said, "I'd have to give General Powell some credit in this area. I mean he certainly influenced my thinking on it. . . . He had been arguing successfully, and I think correctly, that this was a mission we could get rid of."[52] Powell believed that as the Soviet Union's decline became more apparent, Congress would swiftly slash the defense budget, thus forcing a restructuring upon the Pentagon. Anticipating the latter, he recognized the need to seize the initiative: "We had to get in front of them if we were to control our own destiny" and not have military reorganization "schemes shoved down our throat."[53]

Since Powell's Senate confirmation hearing in September 1989, he had stated regularly and bluntly that his "principal challenge" as chairman was to reformulate defense policies to better contend with a fast-changing world and budgetary realities.[54] Thus, for several years, Powell oversaw the development and promotion of a "Base Force" plan that balanced "our superpower base force requirements and what the American people are willing to pay for."[55] In brief, the plan was designed to reduce the military force structure by approximately 25 percent while maintaining its capability to serve multiple vital missions: (1) to act as a nuclear deterrent, (2) to wage two simultaneous wars across the Pacific and the Atlantic, and (3) to fight and control regional "hot spots" such as Grenada and Panama.[56] Powell's belief in a declining Soviet threat and the appropriateness of a substantially reduced defense budget provoked skepticism and outright opposition among administration officials, the Joint Staff, and members of Congress. Undaunted, he pursued his "missionary work" inside the White House, at the Pentagon, and on Capitol Hill.[57]

By August 1990, nine months after the fall of the Berlin Wall, Powell's visionary Base Force strategy had won the support of Cheney and Bush. As for the Joint Chiefs, the chairman later recounted, "I told them we either cut or Congress will cut idiotically. I got buy in before the Salami slicing began."[58] The president credited Powell for being "at the forefront of planning for this critical restructuring."[59] It had not been an easy road to acceptance. "At times," Powell recalled, "I had been discouraged by setbacks and had almost given up hope. . . . The changes envisioned were enormous, from a total active duty strength of 2.1 million down to 1.6 million. . . . The plan . . . would effectively mark the end of a forty-year-old strategy of communist containment."[60] In originating and championing the controversial plan,

Powell had personified the independence, foresight, intelligence, resolve, and moral courage of an exemplary follower-leader.

Powell continued to demonstrate such superlative characteristics in the prelude to the Persian Gulf War. On August 1, 1990, the Iraqi Republican Guard invaded the State of Kuwait. The Bush administration quickly determined that it was in the United States' vital interests to mount a massive military defense of neighboring Saudi Arabia. Within a matter of days, American forces would mobilize to protect the Saudi kingdom. Much less clear and far more complex was the issue of whether the United States should wage a war to liberate Kuwait.

Cheney wanted the president to have military options, and Powell informed the secretary that his staff was working on viable alternatives. The chairman's instinct was to oppose a rushed retaliation using air strikes. "[That] would be like pissing into the wind," Powell told Cheney, and worse, it could provoke Iraq into invading Saudi Arabia.[61] Reluctant to commit U.S. forces to war, the chairman advised drawing "a firm line" at the Saudi border. "We must start with policy and diplomatic overtures," he advised. "We can't make a case for losing [American] lives for Kuwait, but Saudi Arabia is different. I am opposed to dramatic action without the President having popular support."[62] Powell told U.S. Central Command (CENTCOM) commander General Norman Schwarzkopf that he doubted that Bush would go to war over Kuwait.[63]

During an NSC meeting on Friday, August 3, when support for Saudi Arabia was reconfirmed, Scowcroft pushed for a policy of intervening in Kuwait. Powell pushed back, questioning whether it was "prudent" for the United States to forcibly rescue the small country. Not seeing Kuwait as a vital interest and still haunted by the ghosts of Vietnam and Lebanon, he feared the risks of a full military engagement with Iraq.[64] The chairman cautioned the president and his national security team: liberating Kuwait "would be the NFL, not a scrimmage. It would mean a major confrontation."[65] In other words, a war in the Persian Gulf would not be a replay of the invasion of Panama.

Powell's warning was met with a stony silence. He "detected a chill in the room" and realized that as an adviser he might have exceeded his military portfolio by asserting a foreign policy position.[66] Regardless, he was determined to put all alternatives on the table so that he could formulate the best military options for the president and defense secretary. The NSC meeting concluded with Bush agreeing that the "defense of Saudi Arabia has to be our focus" but not answering the Kuwait question.[67]

Shortly thereafter, Cheney chastised Powell for broaching the political issue of Kuwait. "You're not Secretary of State," he blasted. "You're not the National Security Advisor anymore. And you're not Secretary of Defense. So stick to military matters."[68] Powell knew that he had "overstepped," but he did not regret pressing his superiors to clarify their policy objectives. "There had been cases in our past," Powell later said, "particularly in the Vietnam period, when senior leaders, military leaders, did not force civilians to make those kind of clear choices, and if it caused me to be the skunk at the picnic . . . [they could] take a deep smell."[69] In his memoirs, Powell further explained his motivation for speaking out: "I had been appalled at the docility of the Joint Chiefs of Staff, fighting the war in Vietnam without ever pressing political leaders to lay out clear objectives for them. Before we start talking about how many divisions, carriers, and fighter wings we need, I said, we have to ask, to achieve what end?"[70] From the Vietnam experience and even the Iran-Contra scandal, Powell had learned that the best subordinates must demonstrate moral courage and insist that their superiors clarify policy objectives.

Five days after Iraq invaded Kuwait, Bush approved Operation Desert Shield, which included the deployment of 250,000 U.S. troops to defend Saudi Arabia. But the question of whether to dislodge Iraq's army from Kuwait remained open throughout September, even though the president had publicly stated that Saddam Hussein's aggression "will not stand."[71] Powell still wondered whether saving Kuwait was worthwhile, and he worried that Bush, being encouraged by Scowcroft, was moving too swiftly to a war footing without considering viable alternatives.[72] Cheney recalled that Powell "repeatedly pressed the case for long-term sanctions, for waiting and hoping that economic pressure would drive Saddam out of Kuwait."[73] Consistent with the qualities of an exemplary follower, he sought to provide his superiors with policy options.

Scowcroft was impressed with Powell's ability to tactfully render independent judgments even when they were contrary to the thinking of his bosses. "Colin was very good that way," he later wrote. "I never heard him contradict Dick Cheney directly, but by the end of the meeting, you always knew where Colin stood. He was very deft at things like that. Colin kept thinking—longer than I did or Dick Cheney did, and probably longer than the president."[74]

On September 24, 1990, Powell met with Bush, Cheney, Scowcroft, and White House Chief of Staff John Sununu at the White House. The general laid out options for removing Iraqi forces from Kuwait, including military intervention, defensive containment, and economic sanctions. Convinced that the administration was leaning toward an aggressive military policy, Powell cautioned against an offensive engagement with the battle-hardened, one-million-man Iraqi army, and he promoted the benefits of a "strangulation" containment policy with international economic sanctions and defensive forces in Saudi Arabia. The objective was "to bring the Iraqis to their senses and reverse the invasion without having to go to war."[75] Powell feared a premature or unnecessary conflict with Iraq. "I do not believe in spending the lives of Americans lightly," he later wrote. "My responsibility . . . was to lay out all options for the nation's civilian leadership."[76] After Powell completed his briefing, Bush responded, "Thanks, Colin, that's useful. That's very interesting. It's good to consider all the angles. But I really don't think we have time for sanctions to work."[77] Powell was disappointed. He confided to his predecessor, retired Admiral William J. Crowe Jr., "I've been for a containment strategy but it hasn't been selling around here [the Pentagon] or over there [the White House]."[78]

With Bush and Scowcroft seemingly bent on an offensive campaign, Powell shifted his focus to advising the president and defense secretary on the best strategy for defeating the Iraqi military and liberating Kuwait. He ordered his staff to reorient their planning. "In our democracy," he thought, "it is the President, not generals, who make decisions about going to war. I had done my duty. The sanctions clock was ticking down. If the President was right, if he decided that it must be war, then my job was to make sure we were ready to go in and win."[79]

Powell grew alarmed when he learned that Bush hoped to prosecute the war by airpower alone. Earlier in August, the chairman had warned Cheney against surgical air strikes, as they might provoke an Iraqi invasion of Saudi Arabia. Instead, to restore Kuwaiti sovereignty, Powell advocated a comprehensive, multinational air, land, and sea campaign. He later told a reporter, "I don't believe in doing [limited] war. . . . I'm more of the mindset of a New York street bully, here's my bat, here's my gun, here's my knife, I'm wearing armor, I'll just take your ass."[80] Given Bush's penchant for a military offensive, the challenges for Powell were to construct a formidable war plan and to amass commensurate forces in the region. To solve these problems, Powell relied extensively on General Schwarzkopf, then charged as CENTCOM commander with defending Saudi Arabia.

In working under Bush and Cheney and over Schwarzkopf during the Persian Gulf crisis, Powell again found himself in the simultaneous roles of follower and leader. Schwarzkopf's volatility and coercive style only complicated Powell's position between the civilian leadership and the senior field commander. On several occasions, a skeptical Cheney asked Powell if the hot-tempered Schwarzkopf was the best person to execute the president's military strategy. Powell said yes. He recognized Schwarzkopf's shortcomings but considered him an extremely capable commanding general. As a result, Powell consistently supported Schwarzkopf in discussions with Cheney and the president. "For all of his pyrotechnics and histrionics," Powell wrote, "Norm was a brilliant officer, a born leader, and a skilled diplomat in the region. He was the right man in the right place and I was happy to reassure Cheney from time to time."[81]

By early October 1990, with Schwarzkopf overseeing the buildup of the Saudi defense force, Powell was under continuous pressure from his superiors to produce an offensive war plan for ejecting Iraqi forces from Kuwait. The chairman telephoned Riyadh, seeking a preliminary strategy from his field general. "I got no goddam offensive plan," Schwarzkopf hollered, "because I haven't got the ground forces."[82] Moreover, he had not completed his defensive positioning. Regardless, Powell asserted himself and demanded an attack plan for the president. Schwarzkopf's preliminary strategy, which focused largely on a strategic air campaign, was presented to Bush and his national security team on October 11. Senior officials were enthused about the cutting-edge air campaign but deemed the overall proposal "a loser" because of its limited and uninspired ground offensive.[83]

Although sympathetic to Schwarzkopf's plight, Powell agreed that the first-cut plans were problematic and instructed the general to revise them. In the process, he intentionally relayed an insult made by Scowcroft, Deputy National Security Adviser Robert M. Gates, and others on the NSC. After hearing of the inadequate ground plan, they had derided Schwarzkopf as the second coming of General George B. McClellan, the Civil War commander who all but refused to lead his sizable army into battle. Schwarzkopf reacted predictably, shouting at Powell, "You tell me what son of a bitch said that. I'll show him the difference between Schwarzkopf and McClellan!" Powell had deliberately and effectively "shoved the bayonet between his ribs to goad him into thinking harder about our ground offensive plan."[84]

Two months after Iraq's invasion of Kuwait, Powell still hoped that Saddam Hussein would realize the precariousness of his situation and withdraw from Kuwait. To avoid a land war in Southwest Asia, the chairman sought to intensify international pressure on Iraq. He requested a private Saturday meeting with Secretary of State Baker. As two veterans of the Reagan administration, they enjoyed, according to Baker, "a simpatico relationship": "We often found ourselves on the same side of the barricades." At their October 19 meeting, the two reached "a consensus" that the best course of action was a more aggressive "coercive diplomacy" that included the buildup of enormous multinational military force and the authorization to use it from both the United Nations and the U.S. Congress. The next day, Baker broached the plan with the president, who seemed "generally sympathetic."[85] Some of the president's other senior advisers, including Secretary Cheney, later opposed the idea of seeking endorsements from the United Nations and Congress.

On October 21, after convening a select group of Joint Staff war planners, Powell flew to Saudi Arabia to assist Schwarzkopf in devising a new, bold attack plan. He also sought to reassure Schwarzkopf. Powell sympathized with his field commander; neither of them wanted to enter into battle without adequate forces. Indeed, both intended to wage war with decisive power. "Don't worry," Powell informed his general, "you won't be jumping off until you're ready. We're not going off half-cocked."[86] For Schwarzkopf this was welcome news. He later wrote of Powell, "I felt as though he'd lifted a great load from my shoulders."[87]

By early fall, Bush had all but decided to liberate Kuwait by force, but he relied on his senior military subordinates to determine the best means of achieving it. "Colin Powell, ever the professional," the president later wrote, "wisely wanted to be sure if we had to fight, we would do it right and not take half measures. He sought to ensure that there were sufficient troops for whatever option I wanted, and then the freedom of action to do the job once the political decision had been made. I was determined that our military would have both. I did not want to repeat the problems of the Vietnam War."[88] Once again leading his superior, Powell convinced the president to hold off the attack until adequate forces had been marshaled in the theater.

In his memoirs, Powell elaborated on the constant challenge of his dual leader-follower role during the Gulf crisis. "Between his [Bush's] impatience and Norm Schwarzkopf's anxieties," he wrote, "I had my own juggling act. Norm displayed the natural apprehensions of a field commander on the edge of war, magnified by his excitable personality. I had to reassure him constantly that he would not be rushed into combat. At the same time, the President was leaning on me: 'When are we going to be ready? When can we go?' Dealing with Norm was like holding a hand grenade with pin pulled. Dealing with the President was like playing Scheherazade, trying to keep the king calm for a thousand and one nights."[89]

On October 30, 1990, Powell returned to Washington, DC, to update the Bush war council on the defensive positions in Saudi Arabia and on a new offensive strategy for liberating Kuwait. The next day, the chairman announced that the defense of Saudi Arabia had been completed ahead of schedule. If the president also wanted to conduct an offensive operation, he needed to deploy an additional 250,000 U.S. troops. "Mr. President," Powell said, "this is one of the biggest military offensives ever put together. And it is one of the most complicated. If you decide to liberate Kuwait by force, it is going to take half a million troops, a couple thousand aircraft, thousands of tanks, and handful of carrier groups, a couple of hundred ships, and billions of dollars of ordinance."[90]

Powell's assessment astonished many in the room, and he recalled hearing audible gasps and gulping sounds. Scowcroft thought the chairman's recommendation was excessive, but Cheney supported the Powell-Schwarzkopf estimate, which had the backing of the Joint Chiefs. Still, the defense secretary considered Powell's force request as one "hell of a shopping list."[91] Bush asked, "Now Colin, you and Norm are really sure that airpower alone can't do it?"[92] Powell responded that a restricted battle campaign would not be worth the risks. He had already persuaded Cheney of the necessity of a ground war.[93] After some deliberation, the president reached his decision. If sanctions failed to move Iraq out of Kuwait by the end of the year, he would order Powell's massive assault. Bush biographer Jon Meacham concluded that the president "had thoroughly absorbed the post-Vietnam Powell Doctrine of American warfare."[94]

Powell's commitment to organizing a comprehensive war campaign and his willingness to challenge his superiors was aired publicly on December 3, when he and Cheney appeared before Congress to discuss the Persian Gulf crisis. In his opening statement, Powell chastised the "many experts, amateurs and others in this town" who believed airpower alone could oust Iraqi forces from Kuwait. "Such strategies," he declared, "are designed to hope to win, they are not designed to win."[95] A senator asked if the chairman had the will and moral courage to challenge the president if he disagreed with him. Powell replied, "I am not reluctant or afraid to give either the Secretary of Defense, the President or any other members of the National Security Council my best, most honest, most candid advice, whether they like it or not. And on—some occasions, they do not like it." Powell, smiling, then turned to Cheney and asked, "Isn't that right?" The defense secretary replied, "I will confirm that." Powell followed up, "Which part, sir?" Cheney said, "All of it, Colin."[96]

By New Year's Day 1991, war against Iraq was imminent. Powell and Baker's strategy of coercive diplomacy had not compelled Saddam Hussein to withdraw from Kuwait. An enormous multinational force had been assembled and the U.N. Security Council had authorized its use if Iraq did not draw down by January 15. On January 12, Bush received a joint resolution from Congress authorizing him to remove Iraqi forces from Kuwait. Bush, Cheney, and Powell would initiate the attack if Iraq failed to meet the U.N. deadline; fail it did.

The first phase of Operation Desert Storm featured relentless aerial bombing of Iraqi armed forces and installations. After one month, coalition forces had flown tens of thousands of missions and destroyed four thousand Iraqi tanks and thousands of artillery pieces and armored vehicles.[97] As with the U.S. invasion of Panama, Powell emerged as the public face of war. His televised press conferences detailed the campaign's objectives and operations. On January 23 he gave a curt and memorable articulation of the war plan: "Our strategy in going after this army is very, very simple. First, we're going to cut it off, and then we're going to kill it."[98] Two weeks later, while in Khamis Mushait, Saudi Arabia, Powell told a crowd of cheering airmen and airwomen, "We told [the Iraqis] to move it or lose it. They would not move it and now they are going to lose it."[99] Writing for *Newsweek*, Howard Fineman characterized Powell as "a leader-soldier who was a combination of Harry Truman and Dirty Harry."[100]

To dispatch the Iraqi army, Schwarzkopf needed to launch a major ground offensive. When Cheney and Powell visited him in early February, the CENTCOM commander projected that the ground phase of the war would commence on February 21. The timing was conveyed to an increasingly anxious Bush, who sought a rapid victory. On February 18, the president wrote in his diary, "The meter is ticking. Gosh darn it, I wish Powell and Cheney were ready to go right now."[101]

After Powell and the defense secretary returned to Washington, Schwarzkopf shifted the timetable, delaying the invasion until February 24. Powell thought the move was excessively cautious. By telephone, he reminded Schwarzkopf, "The President wants to get on with this."[102] Nevertheless, the chairman supported his general and recommended the delay to his disappointed superiors.

On February 20, Schwarzkopf, citing a bad weather forecast, advocated further postponement of the ground war until February 26. Under immense pressure to prosecute the war as quickly as possible, Powell communicated Bush and Cheney's desire to launch the attack. He also sought to reaffirm his respect for Schwarzkopf's decision making. When Powell reached the general on the telephone, Schwarzkopf threw a tantrum. "You're pressuring me to put aside my military judgment out of political expediency," he shouted. "I've felt this way for a long time!"[103] Powell yelled back, "My President wants to get on with this thing. My [defense] secretary wants to get on with it. *We need to get on with this.*"[104]

After regaining his composure, Powell reassured Schwarz-kopf, "We've just got a problem we have to work out. You have the full confidence of us back here. At the end of the day, you know I'm going to carry your message, and we'll do it your way."[105] Only minutes after this heated exchange, Schwarz-kopf telephoned Powell to say that the poor weather was clearing and that he would commit ground forces on February 24 as previously planned. Again, Powell had effectively prodded Schwarz-kopf to act.

After only three days of ground operations, the war was essentially won. American-led forces killed some twenty thousand Iraqi soldiers, captured some sixty thousand more, and destroyed the vast majority the enemy's tanks, all while suffering minimal casualties. Coalition warplanes continued to decimate the Iraqi army as it fled from Kuwait, and U.S. pilots and journalists dubbed the freeway out of Kuwait City to Basra as the "Highway of Death."[106] With this success, Powell's thinking turned to the "nearing endgame," and his actions demonstrate how the morality and responsibility of exemplary followers can influence the decisions of their leaders.[107]

Having achieved the principal objective of liberating Kuwait, Powell worried about the ethics of "killing literally *thousands* of people" after an enemy was obviously defeated.[108] He believed that the administration "held the high moral ground" in prosecuting the war but could "lose it by fighting past the [point of] 'rational calculation.'"[109] He first shared his concern with Schwarzkopf, who was sympathetic, and then he advised Bush and Cheney to conclude the war sooner rather than later.[110] At the White House on February 27, Powell informed the president, "It's going much better than we expected. The Iraqi army is broken. All they're trying to do now is get out. . . . We don't want to be seen as killing for the sake of killing, Mr. President."[111] Bush agreed and suspended the offensive campaign the next day. In the years that followed that decision many would criticize Bush and Powell for ending the war prematurely, "but stopping the war was no mistake," writes military historian Rick Atkinson. "Rather, it was a rare triumph for the better angels of our nature."[112]

Victorious in a second war, Bush's popularity soared. Powell lauded the president's approach to war. Bush had identified a threat to vital national interests, articulated unambiguous political and military objectives, and rallied congressional and public support. Also important to Powell was the president's willingness to order a massive deployment, one large enough to "guarantee" the achievement of his objectives.[113] Thus, out of the Persian Gulf War, the Weinberger Doctrine had evolved fully into the Powell Doctrine, with its predominant principle of "using all the force necessary to achieve the kind of decisive and successful result" previously realized in Panama.[114]

The successful war against Iraq also boosted Powell's popularity with the American people. But the publication of a new book by journalist Bob Woodward in May 1991 threatened the chairman's good standing. In *The Commanders*, Woodward underscored Powell's misgivings about rescuing Kuwait by force and his preference for a defensive policy of containment and sanctions. Powell was depicted as appropriately cautious in the application of military force, while Bush was portrayed as too gung ho. On May 2, the day before the book was officially released, the *Washington Post* published an excerpt under the headline, "Book Says Powell Favored Containment; Image of Harmony on Gulf Policy Dispelled."[115] Powell's heart sank as he read the article. The chairman had been one of Woodward's sources for the book, and now he worried about the administration's reaction.[116]

Fortunately for Powell, he had a deep and abiding relationship with the president. After seeing the *Post* article, Bush called Powell with a message of reassurance. "Colin, I don't pay attention to all that crap," he said. "Don't worry about it. Don't let them get under your skin."[117] Later that day, the president publicly proclaimed his support for Powell, praising the chairman's followership and leadership, and especially his candor and moral courage: "If there's anybody that has the integrity and the honor to tell a president what he feels, it's Colin Powell, and if there's anybody that is disciplined enough and enough of a leader to instill confidence in his troops, it's Colin Powell. Nobody's going to drive a wedge between him and me."[118]

Three weeks later, now branded in the press as America's "Reluctant Warrior," Powell joined the president in the White House Rose Garden.[119] There, Bush announced his decision to reappoint Powell for a second two-year term as chairman of the Joint Chiefs of Staff. The president offered effusive praise and conveyed his respect and admiration for the general. Bush said that Powell's performance had been "fantastic" and that his military counsel had been "absolutely remarkable." When a reporter asked the chairman about his "serious misgivings" before the Iraq War, Powell dodged, saying only, "It's a pleasure working within a team that you can give advice on all options." Bush then interjected with an energetic defense of his subordinate's conduct during Desert Storm:

> We had a lot of meetings. And General Powell leveled with me. . . . And to the degree they [military leaders] were not rushing to commit our young men and women to battle, that's exactly the way they should have been. . . . And he [Powell] gave me sound advice. He gave me straightforward advice. I never had any concern about where he stood. I expect the Secretary of Defense feels exactly the same way. And I just want to be on the record as saying that he spoke his mind; he did it openly. And then when we had to get together in meetings and figure the next steps, he was a constructive force all the way along the line.
>
> And it was Colin Powell, more than anyone else, who I think deserves the credit for the time we had to—after all options, in my view, were exhausted—draw the line in the sand. It was he that suggested to me, sitting right up here in

that office. And so, I feel that he did what any general officer should do. He told me the risks; he told me what was at stake in human life. He told me what his view is to how it would go, which was always very positive, if we had to commit forces.[120]

Powell's cautionary prewar counsel to the president was of particular interest to senators who had opposed the war with Iraq. Some, including presidential aspirant Democrat Sam Nunn of Georgia, were furious with Powell for not sharing his apprehensions more broadly and for having confidential conversations with Woodward. Despite the controversy, the Senate ultimately gave unanimous consent to Powell's reappointment as chairman.[121]

In the coming years, criticism of Powell's conduct during Desert Storm focused less on his initial reluctance to rescue Kuwait and more on the Bush administration's decision not to topple the Iraqi regime. On the first anniversary of the Persian Gulf War, critics, both civilians and retired military officers, carped publicly that the American offensive had been halted prematurely—in large measure because of Powell—and that this had resulted in "something less than a complete victory" and "a case of unfinished business."[122] As a result, the critics contended, Saddam Hussein violently repressed Kurdish and Shiite rebellions, reconsolidated his political power, and reconstituted his military.

In January 1992, Powell agreed to discuss the war on all three major television networks and CNN. He defended the decision to launch the offensive, pointing to Iraq's refusal to withdraw its forces from Kuwait despite political, economic, and diplomatic pressure. Powell further emphasized that the president had received use-of-force authorizations from Congress and the United Nations. When asked why he urged Bush to call a cease-fire, the chairman said the principal factor was that the military and political objectives had been achieved: Allied forces had ousted Iraqi troops from Kuwait and restored the country's legitimate government. Moreover, Powell asserted, there was an ethical issue at stake: "To continue the killing at that point would in my judgment have been irresponsible."[123] He reminded his television audiences that "it was not our intention to totally decimate the entire Iraqi army, it was not our intention to go to Baghdad. And had we done that, we would have gotten ourselves into the biggest quagmire you can imagine, trying to sort out 2,000 years of Mesopotamian history."[124]*

Powell was also asked whether Saddam Hussein remained a threat to national security and whether the United States might have to fight him in another war. The chairman, who described Hussein as "a very, very skilled gangster," said the dictator represented a diminished threat because Iraq's offensive military capabilities had been "thoroughly trashed" and his nuclear weapons capacity seriously damaged.[125] "What we have to do now," Powell said, "is keep the pressure on, keep the pressure on with U.N. inspections, keep the pressure on with U.N. sanctions."[126] As to whether the United States would find itself fighting Saddam Hussein again, Powell said, "I do not expect that we will be fighting him down the road. I have contingency plans for everything, but I don't expect that."[127]

Although Powell served as chairman of the Joint Staff for two years after Operation Desert Storm, his superb followership and leadership during the war marked the zenith of his army career. In the war's aftermath, he received countless accolades and prestigious honors. Bush awarded him the Presidential Medal of Freedom for "especially meritorious contribution" to the security of the United States.[128] Congress bestowed a Congressional Gold Medal for extraordinary excellence in his roles as the

---

*Later that year, Powell wrote that seizing Baghdad would have come "at unpardonable expense in terms of money, lives lost and ruined regional relationships" and with "major occupation forces in Iraq for years to come and a very expensive and complex American proconsulship"; see Powell, "U.S. Forces: Challenges Ahead."

president's principal military adviser and the de facto leader of U.S. armed forces.[129] Queen Elizabeth appointed Powell an Honorary Knight Commander in the Military Division of the Most Honourable Order of the Bath for his role in the Gulf War and his promotion of U.S.-British relations.[130]

After three decades of professional experience, Powell, as chairman of the Joint Chiefs of Staff, had demonstrated the hallmarks of a consummate leader-follower. Cheney characterized Chairman Powell's performance as "superb."[131] During the Iraqi crisis he had evidenced not only commitment, competence, and a propensity for independent critical thought, but also the moral courage to disagree with his superiors and proffer well-considered alternative courses of action. In this respect, Powell's relationship with Bush and Cheney epitomized political scientist Eliot Cohen's ideal of civil-military relations wherein political leaders "must demand and expect from their military subordinates a candor as bruising as it is necessary; that both groups must expect a running conversation in which, although civilian opinion will not usually dictate, it must dominate; and that that conversation will cover not only ends and policies, but ways and means."[132]* Schwarzkopf marveled at Powell's close relationship with the president and his tremendous effectiveness as chairman. "And there is no doubt in my mind," Schwarzkopf wrote, "that General Powell was the best man for the job during this crisis. Not since General George Marshall during World War II had a military officer enjoyed such direct access to White House inner circles—not to mention the confidence of the President. Powell could get decisions in hours that would have taken another man days or weeks."[133] The chairman was, according to Schwarzkopf, "a political genius."[134]

---

*Unlike the author, Cohen is highly critical of the Bush administration's civilian wartime leadership, asserting that it granted too much authority to the military, Cohen, *Supreme Command*, 188–207.

While victory in the Gulf War boosted Powell's and Bush's popularity, the special effect was fleeting for the president. In the face of a faltering domestic economy, Bush lost his 1992 bid for reelection to Bill Clinton. Powell, on the other hand, continued to enjoy tremendous bipartisan popularity. According to Senator McCain, the general had been "treated with deference and respect on Capitol Hill" before the Iraq War, and afterward "it bordered on adulation."[135] Similarly, a *Los Angeles Times* profile declared that the chairman's wartime press conferences had "seared Colin Powell in the national consciousness" and had the effect of turning him into "a folk hero . . . being immortalized on posters and bubble-gum cards, hounded by autograph seekers and, more significantly, being promoted as a potential candidate for national office."[136]

Powell repeatedly denied any personal interest in partisan politics. In fact, just two days before the 1992 presidential election, he rebuffed an overture from the Clinton campaign to become secretary of either state or defense.[137] Instead, Powell chose to serve his final year in uniform as the principal military adviser to Clinton and his defense secretary, Leslie "Les" Aspin Jr. Powell came to like both men personally, but he frequently found working for them and with other administration officials exasperating.

The first major issue Powell confronted in the Clinton administration was the prohibition of homosexuals serving in the U.S. military. During his presidential campaign, Clinton had promised to terminate the ban, which still had broad support within the armed forces and in Congress. Powell described the proposed policy shift as "the hottest social potato tossed to the Pentagon in a generation."[138]

On November 19, 1992, during his first one-on-one meeting with President-elect Clinton, the chairman broached the controversial subject.[139] Powell sought to provide the incoming president with sound political counsel and evidence of his professional integrity. He first warned that a proposal to terminate the ban would prove an extraordinarily difficult issue for the new administration because of the staunch political and military opposition. Any policy change toward open integration, he said, "ain't going to be easy."[140] To avoid getting bogged down in a protracted conflict, Powell recommended that the new defense secretary review the policy for six months. This way, the chairman reasoned, Clinton would gain "some breathing space" on Capitol Hill and prevent the divisive issue from becoming "the first horse out of the gate with the armed forces."[141]

Powell also offered to resign if Clinton possessed any reservations about working with a general so closely identified with Republican national security policies. Powell pledged his "total loyalty" if kept on and added, "Sir, anytime I find that I cannot, in good conscience, fully support your administration's policies because of my past positions, I will let you know. And I'll retire quietly, without making a fuss."[142] Clinton was impressed. Immediately after their session, the president-elect told reporters that he enjoyed the meeting. He liked Powell "very much" because the general had "laid it on the line and did not fudge one of our disagreements." Moreover, Powell had stated unequivocally, "You're the boss."[143] Reflecting on this initial encounter with Powell a year later, Clinton said, "I knew that one thing I would never have to worry about was having a strong and wise, a forthright and honest Chairman of the Joint Chiefs of Staff."[144]

The chairman and his fellow Joint Chiefs favored the ban on homosexuals, but they would implement a new policy if the president ordered one. Powell had already made his position clear while testifying before a congressional committee in February 1992. There, he praised homosexuals as "proud, brave, loyal, good Americans," but proceeded to spar with Barney Frank, an openly gay congressman from Massachusetts.[145] Powell asserted that ending the ban would damage morale and stir conflict and disorder among the rank and file, thus diminishing the military's ability to perform at maximum capacity. Powell told Frank, "It would be prejudicial to good order and discipline to try to integrate that in the current military structure."[146] The chairman also rejected any comparison of the ban on homosexuals to the military's historic discrimination against African Americans. When Congresswoman Pat Schroeder equated the two in a letter to Powell, the chairman drafted a biting response that concluded, "I can assure you I need no reminders concerning the history of African-Americans in the defense of their nations and the tribulations they faced. I am part of that history. Skin color is a benign, non-behavioral characteristic. Sexual orientation is perhaps the most profound of human behavioral characteristics. Comparison of the two is a convenient but invalid argument."[147]

Regardless, Powell also stated that he would dutifully follow Clinton's directive on the issue and manage the fallout. In November 1992, the chairman told reporters that while the Joint Chiefs "strongly" supported the ban, they also understand that the ultimate decision would be made by the nation's "political leaders" and "the armed forces of the United States will do what we are told to do."[148] On December 5, Powell reiterated the point on CNN: "The armed forces are subordinate to the president and to the instructions from the Congress. So if a judgment is made to move in this direction, we will move in that direction."[149] Again on January 12, 1993, just before the presidential inauguration, Powell told a U.S. Naval Academy audience that while he favored the ban on homosexuals serving openly, "we're all Americans," and he would fall in line if Clinton commanded its reversal. He further instructed the midshipmen that if any military officer thought such an order violated his or her "personal moral beliefs" and thus refused to execute it, then that officer had an obligation to resign from duty.[150]

The matter came to a head on January 25, 1993, when Powell and the Joint Chiefs of Staff met with Clinton, Defense Secretary Aspin, and other administration officials in the Roosevelt Room at the White House. The president presented his case for wanting to end the military's discriminatory ban. Then each of the service chiefs expressed their opposition to a change in policy, citing "practical problems that gay integration presented on crowded ships, in cramped barracks, and in other intimate situations."[151] Nevertheless, the flag officers also assured the president that they would obey his final orders.[152] In the end, Powell endorsed a compromise called "Stop asking and stop pursuing."[153] The chairman recommended to the president and defense secretary that the military simply cease inquiring about the sexual orientation of new recruits and stop actively pursuing active-duty homosexuals "as long as they kept their lifestyle to themselves."[154] Powell and the Joint Chiefs thought they had provided a face-saving solution for their new commander in chief, one that would be supported by Congress. Senior presidential adviser George Stephanopoulos characterized the military's proposal less charitably: "Permit us to allow you an honorable surrender."[155]

Powell was pleased with the "very excellent discussion" with Clinton, who he thought had proved a courteous if not sympathetic listener.[156] The president was disappointed by the military's opposition but was also impressed by the chairman. In a private conversation with Stephanopoulos, he expressed regret for not pressing Powell harder to join his cabinet as secretary of state. "I think he would have taken it," Clinton confided. "But the moment's passed."[157]

Six months later, Clinton announced "Don't Ask, Don't Tell" as his official policy on the service of homosexuals in the U.S. military. The president considered it "an honorable compromise," and Congress ratified it in November.[158] Stephanopoulos later wrote what everyone knew to be true at the time: the policy was "essentially identical to Powell's initial proposal."[159]

Powell could not savor the policy victory. For the first time in his storied career, he was widely excoriated in press. Some attacked him for being disobedient to the president, others painted him as homophobic and bigoted, and still others lamented that one of the nation's most prominent African Americans stood as an impediment to civil rights progress. The *New York Times* editorial board charged Powell with defying his president "almost to the point of insubordination."[160] Likewise, *Time* characterized the chairman as "The Rebellious Soldier."[161] Veteran journalists Jack Germond and Jules Witcover demanded to know "Who's in Charge?"[162] Cynthia Tucker of the *Atlanta Constitution* wrote damningly that "Colin Powell, of all people, is enforcing bigotry."[163] Three years later, still scarred by the attacks on his character, Powell wrote, "My life would have been easier if he [Clinton] had simply lifted the ban by executive order. The military leadership would have said, 'Yes, sir.'"[164]

Powell had approached the controversial issue of homosexuals in the military with confidence and integrity, and, despite the press's criticism, his approval rating with the public was an astounding 71 percent.[165] He had offered Clinton thoughtful and candid advice, knowing full well he was at odds with the president. The chairman's stance on the ban reflected his conscience and what he believed best served the military and national security.[166] As a consummate subordinate, Powell both pledged his loyalty to Clinton and proposed a viable compromise policy. Clinton appreciated the general's frank and pragmatic counsel. "Despite our differences," the president later wrote, "General Powell made it clear that he would serve as best as he could, including giving me his honest advice, which is exactly what I wanted."[167]

Clinton also relied on Powell's counsel during evolving crises in the Balkans and in Somalia. Again, the chairman's advice proved influential and controversial. During the second half of the Bush administration, the Socialist Federal Republic of Yugoslavia had begun to fragment into smaller, independent nation-states. In 1991, when war broke out between Croatian and Serbian-led Yugoslav forces, the United States supported a U.N. arms embargo in the Balkans, hoping to curtail the fighting. In April 1992, the Bosnian parliament declared its independence from Yugoslavia. The declaration sparked a bloody civil war between supporters of the nascent government and the Bosnian Serb population, which received substantial military and political support from Serbian President Slobodan Milosevic. The

Bush administration protested Milosevic's intervention and immediately applied diplomatic and economic pressure. The president recalled the U.S. ambassador from Belgrade, closed U.S. consulates in Serbia, and honored the U.N. arms embargo. In June 1992 the United States, through the U.N. Security Council, also supported the deployment of a small U.N. protection force but not the inclusion of U.S. troops.[168]

Powell and Cheney supported Bush's policies, including the decision not to intervene militarily with U.S. troops. They did not believe that the Bosnian civil war and Serbia's sponsorship posed a danger to American security. The chairman recited Bismarck's famous line that "all the Balkans were not worth the life of one Pomeranian grenadier" and then added, "The man knew what he was talking about."[169] The conflict in the Balkans, Powell thought, represented a post–Cold War European problem in need of a European solution. He reminded a reporter that "there are many air forces in the world who have the capability of flying air power besides the United States Air Force" and that Bosnia "is also more of a European issue . . . than it is a U.S. issue."[170]

By summer 1992, the Bush administration had come under increasing pressure to intervene. The international media had exposed Serbian atrocities in Bosnia, including a network of concentration camps that were starkly reminiscent of the Holocaust. On the presidential campaign trail, Clinton contended that the United States should intervene forcefully to stop the ethnic cleansing. He declared that the military should launch air strikes against Serbia because "we cannot afford to ignore what appears to be a deliberate, systematic extermination of human beings based on their ethnic origin."[171] Polling data in August showed that 53 percent of Americans supported U.S. military intervention, up from 35 percent the prior month.[172]

As a result of these developments, Secretary Baker convinced Bush to fly humanitarian relief supplies into Sarajevo. As a precaution, the president also ordered the deployment of a marine amphibious ready group to the Adriatic Sea.[173] The Bush administration also championed a new U.N. resolution authorizing the small U.N. military contingent in Bosnia to use force if needed to protect aid convoys. Administration critics considered this policy shift weak-kneed and compared it to Neville Chamberlain's appeasement of Hitler in 1938. In early August, Bush held a press conference to express his concerns about the humanitarian crisis. He associated the ghastly Bosnian concentration camps with the Holocaust but avoided the term *genocide*. Nor was there mention of American military intervention. Instead, Bush underscored the need for the "international community" to gain "access to any and all detention camps."[174]

Consistent with the Weinberger-Powell Doctrine, Powell had advised Bush against armed intervention. He viewed the Bosnian War as rooted in "ancient ethnic hatreds" that did not threaten vital U.S. interests. Moreover, nobody in the administration was articulating clear-cut military and political objectives in Bosnia, much less a viable exit strategy.[175] Bush said as much in an interview with *USA Today*: "Before I'd commit forces to a battle, I want to know what's the beginning, what's the objective, how's the objective going to be achieved and what's the end."[176]

Nonetheless, public and political pressure mounted in the fall of 1992. In late September Powell aimed to influence the debate by agreeing to an interview with Michael R. Gordon, a military reporter for the *New York Times*. This decision, occurring just weeks before the presidential election, would spark another controversy for the chairman.

With the Reagan-era Lebanon catastrophe etched in his mind, Powell sought to support Bush's cautious Bosnian policy and explain his own opposition to limited military engagements that lacked clear and achievable objectives. "As soon as they tell me it [military intervention] is limited," he told Gordon, "it means they do not care whether you achieve a result or not. As soon as they tell me 'surgical' [warfare], I head for the bunker."[177] Gordon's account of the interview, which appeared in the newspaper the following day, portrayed the typically "calm and collected" Powell as angry and rigid. According to Gordon, Powell still suffered from Vietnam syndrome and thus had impulsively declared a "Resounding No" to any proposals for armed intervention in Bosnia.[178]

A week later, the *New York Times* editorial board published a retort to Powell's comments. The editors opined that what was transpiring in Bosnia was not a war or even a "fair fight," but rather a massacre of Bosnian Muslims and Catholics by Serbians. At a minimum, the editorial argued, the president should override Powell's recommendation and intervene to "slow the slaughter." The *Times* further advised Bush to tell his chairman what Lincoln told General McClellan during the Civil War, "If you don't want to use the Army, I should like to borrow it for a while."[179] Now it was Powell, not Schwarzkopf, who was being prodded.

Powell read the editorial and "exploded" in anger.[180] He penned a lengthy rebuttal, with Bush and Cheney's approval, and the *Times* printed it under the banner "Why Generals Get Nervous." The chairman drew from American history and adhered to Clausewitzian logic and the Weinberger-Powell Doctrine. He explained his opposition to endangering military personnel in a war with "deep ethnic and religious roots that go back a thousand years." There are, he contended, "unclear purposes" for the United States in Bosnia. "Military force is not always the right answer," Powell insisted. Moreover, he praised Bush for his prudent matching of "the use of military force" to "political objectives" and thus preventing debacles like the Bay of Pigs, Lebanon, and Vietnam. "So you bet I get nervous," Powell concluded, "when so-called experts suggest all we need is a little surgical bombing or a limited attack. . . . History has not been kind to this approach."[181]

A month after Powell's article, Bush lost his bid for reelection. As a lame-duck politician, the president supported a new U.N. resolution that, for the first time, recognized Serbian ethnic cleansing as "a form of genocide."[182] By then, approximately one hundred thousand people had been killed in the Bosnian War. The Bush administration's belated recognition of the genocide elicited more disdain from its critics. One State Department official said it was equivalent to telling President-elect Clinton, "Oh, by the way, this is genocide. We haven't been doing anything about it. Oops. It's all yours!"[183]

Soon after the election, Clinton arranged a meeting with Powell. He asked about Bosnia and the utility of using air power to improve the situation on the ground. During the campaign, Clinton had said, "The United States . . . must take action. If the horrors of the Holocaust taught us anything, it is the high cost of remaining silent and paralyzed in face of genocide."[184] In the meeting, Powell suppressed his visceral reaction to the idea of limited air strikes and told the president-elect that airpower was "not likely" to be effective. Still, he agreed to have the Joint Staff investigate it further.[185] During the next nine months as Clinton's principal military adviser, Powell never wavered in his opposition to limited intervention in Bosnia. His influence on the president proved significant.

Once in office, Clinton grew less enthusiastic about intervening militarily in Bosnia even though Holocaust survivor Elie Wiesel exhorted him to do so. As president, Clinton took pains to differentiate the Holocaust from the Bosnian situation. The Holocaust, he told Wiesel, was "on a whole different level." America, Clinton said, must "stand up against" ethnic cleansing, but "that does not mean that the United States or the United Nations can enter a war."[186]

In meeting after meeting, Powell argued that despite much "belligerent rhetoric" the administration had failed to identify the national security interests or associated political objectives in the Balkans.[187] The chairman received some support from Defense Secretary Aspin, National Security Adviser Anthony Lake, and Secretary of State Warren Christopher. According to Christopher, "the Balkans had the look and feel of a Vietnam-like quagmire," and that prospect forestalled military intervention.[188]

After much internal debate, the president came to agree with Powell, who had given him a copy of Robert D. Kaplan's book *Balkan Ghosts* to underscore the region's long history of ethnic conflict.[189] The risks of military intervention in the Balkans seemed too great. In his memoirs, Clinton wrote, "I . . . didn't want to divide the NATO alliance by unilaterally bombing Serb military positions. . . . And I didn't want to send American troops there, putting them in harm's way under a UN mandate I thought was bound to fail."[190] Powell had offered the president options, including limited or heavy aerial bombings in an attempt to "change Serb behavior," but the chairman always concluded his presentations with his firm belief that significant ground forces were necessary to check Serbian offensives and guarantee peace and stability in Bosnia.[191] He was teaching lessons learned from Grenada, Panama, and Iraq: "When we go to war, we go to war to win. We don't fiddle around or see if we can kind of push somebody a certain way."[192]

Not everybody in the Clinton administration sided with Powell. U.N. Ambassador Madeleine Albright, who advocated air strikes in Bosnia, grew increasingly frustrated with the chairman. She recalled, "Time and again he led us up the hill of possibilities and dropped us off on the other side with the practical equivalent of 'No can do.'"[193] Albright thought Powell's reluctance to intervene, even on a limited basis, was excessively cautious. In an echo of George Shultz's haranguing of Caspar Weinberger, she challenged Powell: "What's the point of having this superb military that you're always talking about if we can't use it?"[194] Powell found the question deeply disturbing, and other senior advisers supported his position. At one point, National Security Adviser Lake reminded Albright, "You know Madeleine, the kinds of questions Colin is asking about goals are exactly the ones the military never asked during Vietnam."[195]

Many desk officers in the State Department shared Albright's frustrations with Powell and the administration's inaction. In August 1993, a month before the chairman retired, three officers resigned in protest. They could not in good conscience abide by a Balkans policy that legitimated belligerence and genocide.[196] Powell, however, continued to advocate his unpopular position, being "the skunk at the picnic." He argued repeatedly that only the deployment of U.S. ground troops "was guaranteed to change Serb behavior" and insisted on well-established goals before intervening.[197] "My constant, unwelcome message at all the meetings on Bosnia," Powell later wrote, "was simply that we should not commit military forces until we had a clear political objective."[198] In the end, Clinton did not intervene in Bosnia with substantial military force until the summer of 1995, more than a year after the chairman had retired.[199]

The Bosnian War demonstrated both the nature and influence of Powell's followership under two presidents. As chairman, he thoughtfully analyzed geopolitical developments and humanitarian crises and proffered his best independent advice to his superiors. For him, turmoil in the Balkans, unlike that in Panama and the Persian Gulf, did not justify the application of American military power. An ethnic war in Bosnia, Powell concluded, posed no threat to U.S security. Moreover, he opposed intervention because his superiors failed to articulate achievable political and military objectives. While Powell sympathized with the innocent victims of the Balkans conflict, he doubted that surgical interventions by the United States would curtail the suffering. The chairman feared that a policy of limited engagement would inadvertently lead to a costly and bloody escalation. For Powell, if the American goal was to bring meaningful peace and stability to the Balkans, the only strategy was a comprehensive war campaign. During his tenure as chairman, neither he, Bush, Cheney, Clinton, nor Aspin thought limited or large-scale armed intervention were worth the risks.

Despite the Bosnian example, Powell was not entirely opposed to limited military engagements. His priority was always to match mission objectives with appropriate levels of armed force. The Clinton administration's approach to Saddam Hussein provides a case in point. On the night of June 23, 1993, Powell and the rest of Clinton's national security team were reaching agreement on how to respond to an audacious Iraqi provocation. Investigations by the FBI and CIA concluded that Saddam Hussein had attempted to assassinate former President Bush two months earlier when he had been in Kuwait to commemorate the second anniversary of the Persian Gulf War.

In a secret meeting at the president's residence, Powell advised a proportionate response. "Don't oversell and don't undersell," he counseled.[200] "You need a response, but not another war. If Saddam had killed Bush or wounded him, you would have to take Saddam out."[201] The chairman, who had previously characterized Saddam as "'toothache' that we could live with," recommended a retributive air attack on Iraq's intelligence headquarters.[202] Nobody wanted a hollow gesture. The president favored "hitting Iraq harder," but Powell persuaded him that a limited strike would sufficiently deter further Iraqi terrorism and also minimize casualties.[203]

In the end, the NSC agreed and supported a cruise missile strike on downtown Baghdad. On June 25, twenty-three Tomahawk missiles exploded Iraq's intelligence headquarters. That evening, after Powell confirmed the strikes, he and Clinton assessed the administration's handling of the operation. From Powell's perspective, the decision-making process for the president's first use of force had been sound: "All of the options were properly explored."[204] Clinton was equally satisfied, even elated to have won the chairman's "seal of approval."[205] Moreover, according to the president's Middle East adviser on the NSC, "Powell proved correct in his assessment that the strike would deter more such schemes by Saddam. For the next seven years, we saw no evidence that his intelligence services were involved in any terrorist or assassination activities against American or Western targets."[206]

Powell demonstrated his willingness to advocate limited and even risky military engagements elsewhere. In the summer of 1992, a bloody clan-based war erupted in Somalia after the overthrow of dictator Siad Barre. To make matters worse, a severe drought wreaked starvation and havoc upon the populace.[207] With Powell's eventual support, the Bush administration intervened despite a dire warning from the U.S. ambassador to Kenya, Smith Hempstone, who cabled, "If you liked Beirut, you'll love Mogadishu."[208]

In August, amid his reelection campaign and public criticism for not intervening in Bosnia, Bush announced Operation Provide Relief.[209] The deployment consisted of ten military cargo planes and $77 million worth of food to be sent to a Kenyan airfield to supplement U.N.-Somalian relief activities, which included 550 Pakistani peacekeepers in Mogadishu.[210] Even with the delivery of thousands of tons of food and other relief supplies, the combined international efforts failed to halt the fast-expanding catastrophe. In October, Powell and his chief deputy toured Somalia, only to be "shocked" by the gruesome conditions on the ground, where several hundred thousand people had perished.[211] Marine General Anthony Zinni described the scene as a "wasteland 'future' exactly like a postapocalypse movie. It was a shock. . . . Anarchy and chaos were total."[212]

While highly reluctant to intervene in an East African civil war, by early winter 1992 Bush was moved by Powell's ultimate determination that the United States was "the only nation that could end the suffering."[213] On November 25, the chairman presented to the NSC plans for Operation Restore Hope, which entailed a U.N.-sanctioned deployment of twenty-eight thousand U.S. military personnel, primarily the army's Tenth Mountain Division and the First Marine Division. The objective was to "take charge of the place and to make sure the food got to starving Somalis."[214] A week later, the U.N. Security Council adopted a resolution authorizing U.S.-led coalition forces to use "all necessary means" to establish a secure environment for humanitarian relief operations.[215]

Bush approved the mission but expressed his desire for a short-term commitment. His goal was for the United Nations to assume long-term control of the occupation. "We'll do it," the president told his senior advisers, but "try to be out by

January 19" so as not to encumber Clinton.[216] Many people, including Powell, knew that a rapid buildup and swift withdrawal were unrealistic, but nobody argued against the mission of mercy.

On December 4, Powell and Cheney held a joint press conference to provide details on the African operation. They emphasized the clarity of president's military objective: restore enough stability to Somalia to ensure that U.N. relief supplies could again be delivered to the population. The U.S. mission, they insisted, was not nation building; that was a task "best handled through the United Nations." Once adequate stability was achieved by the U.S. military, then a sizable U.N. peacekeeping force would take over responsibility. "So that's how we get out," Powell said. "It's sort of like the cavalry coming to the rescue, straightening things out for a while, and then letting the marshals come back in to keep things under control."[217]

When a reporter asked why the Bush administration was willing to intervene in Somalia but not Bosnia, Cheney provided a rehearsed answer meant to draw a stark contrast between the two situations. In Bosnia, unlike Somalia, he said, the United States did not have a well-defined and achievable mission, nor a viable exit strategy. Moreover, he said, the ethnic conflicts in the Balkans were "decades, century old," and the "executability" of a military operation would be further troubled by difficult terrain and the opponent's formidable armaments.[218]

U.S. forces landed in Somalia on December 9, and their effectiveness was visible from the outset. Stephen Rosenfeld, the deputy editor of the *Washington Post* editorial page, praised the "uncommonly political soldier" Powell for leading "this first use of force for humanitarian purpose in a region of no strategic significance to the United States"[219] The *New York Times* editorial board, however, issued a warning: "Mr. Bush has executed a dramatic takeoff," but "Bill Clinton, who backs the mission . . . may well be stuck with a messy crash landing."[220] The latter proved all too prophetic.

By the spring of 1993, Powell believed that Operation Restore Hope had accomplished its limited objectives of "ending the civil disorder" and improving the distribution of food.[221] More than twenty-three thousand tons of relief supplies had been delivered to famine victims.[222] In March, however, the U.N. Security Council, supported fully by the Clinton administration, expanded the scope of the mission in Somalia from humanitarianism and peacekeeping to nation building, including the disarmament of the population. This led to the establishment of a new U.N. military operation commanded by retired U.S. Admiral Jonathan Howe.[223]

Powell flew to Mogadishu in early April, just before the transfer of mission leadership from the United States to the United Nations. He held an upbeat press conference at the American embassy. The chairman stated that the United States had accomplished its objective of restoring hope in Somalia and that the United Nations was now poised to build a viable political structure. The United Nations, Powell said, "will be more into nation-building then we were."[224] Except for a battalion-sized quick reaction force (QRF), the majority of U.S. forces were withdrawn by the end of May.[225]

In early June, twenty-four U.N Pakistani soldiers were murdered and dozens wounded by Mohammed Farah Aidid's militia. As a result, the U.N. Security Council immediately expanded the mission to include the apprehension and prosecution of Aidid and his paramilitaries. Powell later told congressional investigators that this variation of mission creep—the Clinton administration's full-fledged support of the March and June U.N. resolutions—had been decided without consulting him. "I was not involved in any way," he said.[226]

Fearing the consequences of escalation in Somalia, the chairman resisted calls for the redeployment of U.S. troops. According to the military's official history of the Somalia intervention, "General Powell . . . saw many dangers and little hope of success."[227] "It was exactly what Powell hated," David Halberstam later wrote, "mission expansion, slipping toward an open-ended commitment."[228] After the killing of the Pakistani soldiers, Admiral Howe "pushed hard" on the Clinton administration to send U.S. special operations forces to find and apprehend Aidid. Powell and CENTCOM commander General Joseph P. Hoar successfully resisted the plea for two months. Hoar considered the hunt for Aidid "a dumb thing to do" and the deployment of U.S. Special Forces "a bad thing." The chairman, Hoar later testified, "felt even more strongly than I did."[229]

Nevertheless, Powell eventually acquiesced and recommended to Aspin and Clinton that the Special Forces be deployed. There had been many points of pressure. On August 8, four American military policemen stationed in Somalia were killed by a remote-controlled land mine. Ten days later, the chairman also received a dire briefing by Ambassador David H. Shinn, who was coordinating the administration's Somali policy with the United Nations. Powell's own senior strategic planner, Lieutenant General Barry McCaffrey, also recommended the deployment, as did Major General Thomas Montgomery, the commander of U.S. forces in Somalia. Moreover, Powell told the president, "We couldn't behave as if we didn't care that Aidid had murdered UN forces who were serving with us."[230] Aspin and Clinton approved the chairman's recommendation. "We sent Task Force Ranger with the greatest reluctance," Powell recounted.[231] "It was a recommendation I would later regret."[232]

In September, with Aidid still evading capture, Admiral Howe and Major General Montgomery requested Abrams tanks and Bradley armored vehicles, not to support the Special Forces operations, but as a precautionary measure to back up the QRF. CENTCOM Commander Hoar reluctantly supported the recommendation and forwarded the request to Powell. While the chairman did not want "M1A1 tanks to blast buildings in Mogadishu," he recommended the deployment to Aspin after consulting with the Joint Chiefs of Staff.[233] "This was . . . quicksand," he thought. But with "our commander on the ground pleading for help to protect American soldiers, I had to back him, as I had with the Rangers and Delta Force."[234] Aspin, who was searching for ways to extricate U.S. forces from Somalia, denied the request.

In public, Powell continued to claim that the U.S. mission in Somalia was "incredibly successful" and spoke optimistically about the United Nations' ability to increase its force structure and solve the "murky" problem of Aidid in Mogadishu. The American QRF would remain in place, he said, stationed as "a posse over the ridge."[235] But within the Pentagon and the White House, Powell had begun to plead for a full policy review. "In my last few weeks as Chairman," he later told congressional investigators, "I pushed for it. I aggressively pushed Secretary Aspin for such a review and on . . . September 25th when we had a meeting at the White House on Bosnia, I said at the end of the meeting that we need to do something about Somalia— either reinforce our forces or change our policy."[236]

On September 30, 1993, the day of Powell's retirement, he met privately with Clinton. The outgoing chairman warned the president, as he had Aspin, about the vexing situation in Somalia: "We could not substitute our version of democracy for hundreds of years of tribalism. We can't make a country out of that place. We've got to find a way to get out, and soon."[237] A few days later, Somali guerrillas shot down two Black Hawk helicopters, and eighteen U.S. soldiers from Task Force Ranger were killed in a bloody and frantic firefight in Mogadishu. The carnage appalled the American people, and the outcry led the president to halt all offensive operations and order a full policy review. Clinton considered the tragedy among "the darkest days of his presidency."[238] In December he accepted Aspin's resignation and eventually withdrew all U.S. armed forces. "Thus ended," U.N. Secretary-General Kofi Annan later wrote, "the greatest experiment ever attempted to use peace enforcement in a mission motivated purely by humanitarian goals."[239]

For Powell, as the principal military adviser to the president and defense secretary, Somalia had presented an especially vexing problem. The heartbreaking humanitarian crisis was not a threat to American national security, but the intervention of U.S. forces could establish a secure environment, improve food and aid distribution, and save lives. When Bush originally announced the deployment, he told the American people that "only the United States has the global reach to place a large security force on the ground in such a distant place quickly and efficiently."[240] Powell agreed and backed the mission. He saw the president's policy objectives as being clear, just, and viable.

Unlike Bosnia, Powell had deemed Somalia a manageable crisis with a feasible exit strategy. The country could be stabilized by a large contingent of U.S. ground forces and effectively turned over to the United Nations. After the deployment's initial success, however, the situation changed. Ground conditions worsened, and mission's objectives were expanded. While uneasy with this shift, Powell's propensity to support commanders in the field led him to endorse the very kind of escalation that he had come to dread. In 2012 Powell wrote that unlike the Bush administration, the Clinton team "was determined to achieve a far more ambitious goal. They took on the task of creating a democracy where democracy never existed and where there was never much appetite for it." He contended that the disaster, which was the basis for the 1999 book and 2001 film named *Black Hawk Down*, "illustrated the futility of that effort."[241] But Powell bears some responsibility for the tragedy. As Clinton's principal military adviser, he had supported an American escalation to capture Aidid. Moreover, Powell was too slow in calling for a full policy review, especially given the U.N. Security Council's expanded missions of March and June 1993.

While the Somalian operation marked an anticlimactic, even tragic end to Powell's four years as chairman, his tenure included many successes that bore witness to his excellence as a subordinate and a leader. Nowhere was his remarkable deftness in both roles on better display than during the Persian Gulf crisis. As an exemplary follower of Bush and Cheney, the chairman demonstrated ethical integrity, untiring commitment, supreme competence, emotional stability, and a proclivity for independent critical judgment. Moreover, Powell expressed moral courage through his willingness to disagree with his superiors, all the while designing alternative strategies and tactics to meet their objectives. Cheney later recounted that his own policy perspectives and warfighting decisions were directly "influenced by General Powell" and that he "absorbed without even thinking about it a lot of his attitudes and views."[242] In addition to his influence from below, the chairman also provided exceptional leadership during the Gulf crisis by effectively leading the Joint Staff and a volatile, combative field commander while inspiring the troops, Congress, and the American public.

Ongoing criticisms of Powell's role and influence during the Persian Gulf War, especially regarding his advocacy of a so-called premature cease-fire, are mostly overblown. To be sure, mistakes were made, but they were not, as Andrew Bacevich and others have asserted, "monumental blunders" that "led ultimately to 9/11 and yet another major war [against Iraq in 2003]."[243] It is correct that had the war continued for another week, more of the Iraqi Army, including a portion of the Republican Guard, could have been destroyed. Even Powell has conceded that "That's a legitimate criticism. . . . More of them got out than perhaps should have been the case."[244] But the mission given to Powell by the president was not the destruction of the Iraqi Army nor the toppling of Saddam Hussein's regime; it was the liberation of Kuwait. With that prime objective clearly accomplished, Powell is to be commended for reminding his superiors and colleagues about moral judgments in warfare and of the sanctity of human life: "We're talking about young kids getting killed on both sides. . . . These are the children of people."[245] Moreover, it was the president's decision, not Powell's, to declare the cease-fire, a decision firmly supported by Cheney, Schwarzkopf, Scowcroft, Baker, and the Joint Chiefs. Had Bush ordered Powell to continue the fight, he would have saluted.

Likewise, Powell and Schwarzkopf have been sharply criticized for the "magnanimous" terms of the cease-fire given to Iraq.[246] There is, however, scant evidence that Powell "exerted his considerable influence to minimize civilian involvement in efforts to arrange the ceasefire."[247] In fact, the White House, Defense Department, and State Department all reviewed and approved the military conditions presented by Schwarzkopf, who, in negotiating with the Iraqis, ultimately did err in assenting to their request to fly armed helicopters.[248] It is true that just weeks after the cease-fire, Saddam Hussein used the gunships to help suppress indigenous Kurdish and Shia uprisings. But it is equally true that the dictator did not need the helicopters to defeat the insurgents because much of his army, which had never been committed to the Kuwait theater, was still intact. "People say the helicopters did it all," Powell later commented. "Well, if there were no helicopters, then I assure you, he had other ways of killing all those Shias."[249] Similarly, Schwarzkopf wrote, "grounding the Iraqi helicopter gunships would have had little impact. The tanks and artillery of the twenty-four Iraqi divisions that never entered the Kuwaiti war zone were having a far more devastating effect on the insurgents."[250]

In the end, Dick Cheney's recollection of the decision making at the Persian Gulf War's end is closest to the mark. In his 2011 memoirs he wrote, "No one on President George H. W. Bush's national security team was arguing in 1991 that we should continue on to Baghdad to oust Saddam. And though there were arguably some misjudgments at the end of the war, I think you would be hard-pressed to argue that they fundamentally altered the strategic landscape."[251]

The trajectory of Powell's thirty-five-year career, from ROTC cadet to chairman of the Joint Chiefs, had been nothing short of astonishing. His staunch loyalty, dedicated work ethic, and bureaucratic skill account for a great deal of his professional success. In 1999, when an interviewer asked about his selection as chairman of the Joint Chiefs of Staff, Powell said, "I worked very hard. I was very loyal to people who appointed me, people who were under me, and my associates. I developed a reputation as somebody you could trust. I would give you my very, very best. I would always try to do what I thought was right and I let the chips fall where they might."[252] Such qualities were at the heart of his effective followership.

Also central to Powell's development and success were his constant reflection on his experience and his study of and engagement with role models, mentors, and superiors. Powell was always seeking to learn from others' examples, whether good or bad, to enhance his own capabilities as a follower and leader. Early on, his parents had inspired hard work and personal accountability, and fellow ROTC cadet Ronnie Brooks had encouraged him to aim for excellence in the military profession. In West Germany, Captains Miller and Louisell taught their green lieutenant about human fallibility and the need for "humane leadership."[253] From general officers such as DePuy and Emerson, Powell came to value independent judgment and imaginative thinking. At the Pentagon and in the White House, Powell learned to master bureaucracies from many civilian mentors, including Malek, Kester, Weinberger, and Carlucci.

In retirement, Powell reflected on the many nuances of the leadership process. He came to believe that "leadership is all about followership" and that success in one role is tightly intertwined with success in the other.[254] Moreover, it was evident that many of the central factors of exemplary followership underpin the best leadership as well. Powell's military career illustrates not only the commonalities of effective followership and leadership, but also the reality that most organizational leaders, even those holding prominent positions, also serve in concurrent roles as followers of others.

Despite the controversies over Bosnia, Somalia, and "Don't Ask, Don't Tell," Powell entered retirement immensely popular with the American people. Opinion polls reflected and pundits acknowledged that the general had become the nation's most trusted and admired leader, ranking well ahead of all contenders, including President Clinton. There was much speculation, even hopefulness, that Powell would channel this widespread popularity into a political career. "Not since Douglas MacArthur and Dwight D. Eisenhower," wrote Eric Schmitt in the *New York Times*, "has a soldier's retirement prompted such political speculation."[255]

Before the 1992 presidential campaign, there was a "Washington fantasy" that Bush would "ditch" Vice President Dan Quayle in favor of the popular general.[256] After the election, Clinton reached out to Powell, offering a cabinet position. The general declined the latter entreaty, confirming his commitment to military service and his loyalty to Bush.[257] Not long after Clinton's electoral victory, an earnest movement emerged to draft Powell for a presidential bid of his own. Perhaps the time had come to shed his role as the consummate follower and assume the country's preeminent leadership position.

PART II

The Civilian Years

And in Powell's case, he is . . .
[the] most trusted man in America.
—NEWT GINGRICH

Presidential Icon

(1993–2000)

Retired from government service at just fifty-six years old, Colin Powell contemplated his options for transitioning into the private sector. A well-trodden path for general officers is negotiating an executive position at a large corporation, often a defense contractor. A select few are paid to write their memoirs and travel the lecture circuit. Given Powell's prominence as chairman of the Joint Chiefs of Staff and his public celebrity after the invasion of Panama and the Persian Gulf War, he had vastly better opportunities than most. By the time of Powell's retirement in 1993, he had emerged as the country's most beloved leader. According to a national opinion poll, 71 percent of Americans expressed "a very warm feeling" for the general, compared to 55 percent for President Bill Clinton.[1] In a lengthy profile in the *Atlantic*, Steven Stark reported that the general possessed "an almost unheard of" favorable-versus-unfavorable rating of 64 to 6 percent.[2]

Powell's exalted status, a by-product of his extraordinary military career, is central to understanding the contours of his life in the decade following his retirement. His broad popularity and masterful communication skills led to the publication of a best-selling autobiography and a lucrative second career as a motivational speaker. Both endeavors fortified his standing with the American people and provided him with complete independence. For the first time in his professional life, Powell was his own boss, not obligated to follow anybody.

Powell's stature and commitment to public service ensured some involvement in political affairs. In 1994 Clinton appointed him as a provisional envoy to Haiti in a U.N. effort to restore that country's democratically elected president. Subsequently, the president again asked Powell to join his administration.[3] By fall 1995, with the publication of his memoirs and "Powell-mania" surging across the country, the retired general publicly declared himself a Republican and privately plotted a presidential campaign for the 1996 election. During his military career, he had worked as a chief subordinate to three presidents, and now the time seemed ripe for him to ascend to the presidency, the definitive leadership position. The prospect of Powell's election, however, generated sharp and unprecedented criticism from both the political left and right. In the end, Powell made a tortured decision not to enter the Republican primaries. With the exception of his keynote address at the 1996 Republican National Convention, he removed himself from politics and retreated into the comfortable life of self-employment.

By 2000, Powell, still remarkably popular with the American people, had grown restless and desired a return to government service. In April, after George W. Bush emerged as the presumptive Republican presidential nominee, Powell agreed to support the Texas governor's candidacy. In December, just three days after Democrat Al Gore conceded the presidential election, Bush named Powell as his choice for secretary of state. After a seven-year hiatus, Powell found himself in that familiar dual role of following a superior while also leading subordinates.

After retiring in September 1993, Powell launched his new career as motivational speaker, earning up to $60,000 per speech.[4]

He relished the adulation and independence. Years earlier, Treasury Secretary Don Regan had given Powell some candid advice: "If you really want to be somebody in this town, you've got to go out and make a buck on your own. The 'fuck you' money. Until then, you're never really free."[5] Best-selling novelist Tom Clancy had written to Powell in 1992, encouraging him to publish his memoirs and predicting that the general "could count on a seven-figure advance."[6] In August 1993, just weeks before Powell's army retirement ceremony and after a frenzied bidding war among major publishing houses, he inked a $6.5 million book deal with Random House.[7] In collaboration with veteran nonfiction writer Joseph E. Persico, Powell dedicated himself to the project, which came to fruition in the fall of 1995.

A year into retirement, Powell was enlisted as an emergency emissary to help forestall a U.S.-led and U.N.-approved military invasion of Haiti. The troubled Caribbean nation had been in crisis for three years since army officers instigated a bloody coup and ousted Jean-Bertrand Aristide, the country's first democratically elected president. Backed by a U.N. Security Council resolution, Clinton planned a massive U.S. operation to "end a reign of terror" and restore Aristide to power. In desperation, Haiti's senior ranking army general, Raoul Cédras, reached out to former president Jimmy Carter, who had observed the nation's democratic elections in 1990. On September 13, after telephoning Cédras, Carter proposed to the White House that he, Powell, and Senator Sam Nunn would travel to Haiti to negotiate a peaceful resolution and reinstate Aristide.[8]

Two days later, in a nationally televised address, Clinton threatened Haiti's generals, demanding that they abdicate. That same day, the president reluctantly approved the Carter-Powell-Nunn mission, giving them a deadline of noon, September 18. Unbeknownst to the delegation, Clinton had ordered that the invasion of Haiti begin one minute after midnight September 19. Powell had initially resisted the call to duty but relented after the president personally asked him to serve. Clinton's instructions were clear: the three envoys were to negotiate "how," not "if"

U.S. forces will "go ashore."[9] Powell later described his Caribbean adventure as a "fascinating, exciting, two-day period of my life, unlike any other I have ever had."[10]

After landing in Port-au-Prince aboard an air force jet on Saturday, September 17, 1994, the American delegation was rushed to Haitian military headquarters. The trio had thirty-six hours to persuade the generals to stand down. The first day included two long sessions with Cédras and his staff. Possessing the gravitas of a famous four-star general, Powell played an instrumental role in the negotiations. With a Haitian soldier's M-16 assault rifle leaning against the meeting room wall, Powell accentuated the importance of "soldierly honor" as a guiding leadership principle, and he spoke with great concern for the welfare of the Haitian people. "Let me tell you what true honor is," he told Cédras. "It means having the courage to give up power rather than cause pointless death."[11] Cédras proved defiant. He even recounted Haiti's historic battle against Napoleon's imperial army. The night ended with Cédras contemplating a settlement proposed by the U.S. delegation.

On the morning of the second day, in light of Clinton's noon deadline, the U.S. emissaries met with Cédras's wife, Yannick, who had considerable political influence with the general. Robert A. Pastor, a Carter aide, described her as "serious as shit."[12] He also noted that Powell was "the key figure" in the room.[13] Because Yannick Cédras came from a prominent military family, she had tremendous respect for the American general. Powell advised her as he had her husband: "There is no honor in throwing away lives when the outcome is already determined. You and your husband should accept the inevitable and spare Haiti further suffering. Let's talk about life and not death."[14] She seemed somewhat persuaded that the "honorable path" for a soldier like her husband was to reach a peaceful agreement.[15]

The delegation then met with Haiti's eighty-one-year-old provisional president, Émile Jonassaint, who appeared most amenable to a deal. At one point, Jonassaint even told Powell that he wished the general would return to Haiti to help rebuild its military, "just as MacArthur had done in Japan!"[16]

After meeting with the president, the envoys shuttled back to Haitian military headquarters to resume direct negotiations with Cédras. The invasion was still set for midnight, and Clinton wanted the U.S. delegation to evacuate, but progress was afoot. Cédras, having digested the Americans' last proposal, made a counterproposal that would allow for a U.S./U.N. occupation force, but under strict conditions. Knowing that Clinton would reject any restrictions, a determined Powell leaned over the table and threatened, "Let me make sure you understand what you're facing . . . two aircraft carriers, two and a half infantry divisions, twenty thousand troops, helicopter gunships, tanks, [and] artillery."[17]

By noon, Cédras had agreed to allow U.S. forces into the country, but he had not agreed to a timetable for Aristide's return nor his own departure. By then Powell had been informed that American war planes would soon be in the air.[18] Needing more time, the delegation faxed a draft settlement to Washington for review. An hour later, the White House faxed back a significantly revised document.[19] Carter and Powell were in regular phone contact with an impatient Clinton, who was bent on military action.[20] Powell assured the president that the talks were progressing favorably, and he emphasized that war with Haiti was not worth the life of a single American soldier. "It would be terrible," he cautioned the president, "if we were to fail at this point, to pull out and to have American troops killed when they can come in peacefully."[21]

At 4:00 p.m., with talks still deadlocked, Philippe Biamby, Cédras's chief of staff, burst into the meeting room; he had just received intelligence that the Eighty-Second Airborne was mobilizing. Biamby declared the negotiations over and that he would take Cédras to a secure location. In this "very intense moment," Powell tried to calm Biamby, assuring him that "We are in direct touch with the President. We are in control of events . . . we told you they were coming, so let's stop wasting time and get this deal concluded."[22] Carter wisely recommended that they bring President Jonassaint into the negotiations, and Cédras accepted.[23] Powell drove with Cédras and an armed escort to the presidential palace with pinned hand grenades rolling on the car floor. Once there, Powell called Clinton to inform him of the progress. Against the advice of several Haitian cabinet members, Jonassaint agreed to sign the delegation's settlement agreement, which sanctioned the immediate and uncontested entry of U.S. peacekeeping forces and the restoration of Aristide by October 15. Cédras assented. When American helicopters and three thousand soldiers landed in Port-au-Prince the next day, they met no resistance.[24]

On the morning of September 19, Clinton greeted Carter, Nunn, and Powell at the White House, and they held a joint press conference to comment on the Haitian mission. Clinton praised the delegation for orchestrating a peaceful transfer of power. Powell spoke with confidence and satisfaction. "I am very pleased this morning," he said, that "the transition of power has begun." He added that Haiti's top general did "the right and honorable thing."[25] Standing assuredly alongside two American presidents, Powell himself appeared presidential. Richard Armitage, his close friend, thought him the commanding figure at the press conference, so much so that he worried that the Clinton team would be jealous. "You know," Armitage advised, "you've got to stop that, man, because you just dominate it."[26] The success of the Haitian mission fortified Powell's popularity and boosted his credentials as a statesman. "He's a hero and a nonpolitical figure in the eyes of most Americans," pollster Andrew Kohut declared. "Clearly, our research shows he's the most popular man in America."[27]

Powell's celebrity rocketed further with the publication of his memoir, *My American Journey*. In September 1995 he embarked on a barnstorming book tour and media blitz that included a slew of nationally televised interviews, ranging from ABC's *20/20* with Barbara Walters to NBC's *The Tonight Show with Jay Leno*.[28] Adoring crowds mobbed Powell in each city, and the 613-page book became an instant best seller, quickly moving more than a million copies in the United States. It was the fastest-selling book in Random House's history.[29] The general was amazed by the fervor and warmth of the public's reception, often commenting to his aide, "Do you believe this?"[30]

Before and during the whirlwind book tour, there was tremendous curiosity about Powell's political views and future. He had never declared as a Republican or a Democrat, but the book provided some insights. The general had previously voted for both Democratic and Republican presidents and described himself as a determined centrist, "a fiscal conservative with a social conscience."[31] He advocated for free-market capitalism, lower taxes, and national debt reduction. At the same time, he championed a "vigorous and active" government that provided for public transportation, safety, and education, as well as worker protections, collective bargaining, Social Security, and Medicare.[32] Because he felt out of place among extremists in both the Republican and Democratic parties, Powell suggested that the time had arrived for a major third party, one that represented the "sensible center of the American political spectrum."[33] As to his own political future, Powell equivocated. While not ruling out a campaign for public office, he wrote that he did not yet hear that essential inner "calling" of "a successful politician."[34]

Powell's widespread appeal among Democrats and Republicans could hardly go unnoticed, and with the 1996 elections on the horizon, leaders in both parties hoped to capitalize on his popularity. Clinton had been attracted to Powell's star power for several years, and on three separate occasions between May 1992 and December 1993 he had offered him a position in his cabinet.[35] In 1994, after the Democrats suffered a devastating defeat in the midterm elections, Clinton renewed his interest in bringing the general into his administration. Secretary of State Warren Christopher's desire to step down created a golden opportunity. A week before Christmas, just two months after Powell's Haitian diplomatic mission, the president invited Powell to the White House for "a chat." For a second time, Clinton offered him the position of secretary of state. Powell again declined.[36]

The Republicans, including some stalwart conservatives, also wanted Powell on board in any way they could entice him: as a governor, a senator, as vice president, or even president. But Powell resisted. During his first two years of retirement, he chose to remain America's "mystery man," or, as one commentator put it, "a riddle wrapped in a mystery inside a uniform."[37]

After the six-week book tour, Powell felt empowered like never before. His prominence was at an all-time high, and he had become independently wealthy. The general had also reached two political decisions. First, he was more a Republican than a Democrat, even if barely so. Second, he had decided to enter national politics by launching a campaign for the presidency. He possessed absolutely no interest in settling for the vice presidency. After spending most of his professional career developing and exercising prodigious skills as a subordinate, Powell would not be the next president's second-in-command. He was ready to serve as the leader of the free world. In late October, Powell drafted his announcement speech. He planned to deliver it at his alma mater, City College of New York, on November 22, the day before Thanksgiving and the anniversary of John F. Kennedy's assassination.[38]

Some of Powell's closest friends thought him ill-suited for the rough and tumble of American politics. Harlan Ullman, his Naval War College professor, mentor, and friend, detailed the mismatch between Powell's personality and experience and the attributes and behaviors needed for effective executive politics. "You are superb role model . . . an honest broker and a facilitator of the first order. . . . [But] you have always worked 'for someone,' providing you a degree of political cover; that may not work so well when there is no such cover." Harlan continued, "You are honest, direct and nicely irreverent—traits I admire, but ones that may get you into political trouble."[39] Armitage, Powell's closest adviser and best friend, was more succinct in his opinion about a presidential bid: "Don't do it! Don't do it!"[40]

Although Powell decided to enter the political arena as a Republican, he kept the decision close for as long as possible.

In the meantime, speculation on his political future ran rampant in Washington, DC, and the national media. Since his retirement, countless journalists had imagined him as a presidential candidate, one who would be supported by both Republican and Democratic voters. In September 1993, *U.S. News & World Report* had published the cover story "Colin Powell Superstar: From the Pentagon to the White House?"[41] A year later, Joe Klein of *Newsweek* penned the lengthy profile, "Can Colin Powell Save America?" In it, Klein declared Powell "the most respected figure in American public life," someone whose personal approval rating is "somewhere close to Mother Teresa."[42] Likewise, in December 1994, Jon Meacham described Powell as "everybody's dream candidate." He, like many others, compared Powell's bipartisan popularity to that of General Dwight D. Eisenhower.[43]

By September 1995, amid Powellmania and the *My American Journey* book tour, the *Evans-Novak Political Report* proclaimed Powell as the unofficial candidate of the Washington establishment.[44] Democratic operatives considered Powell's potential candidacy "mind-boggling," while Republicans gazed at the "dazzling prospect" of his appeal to black Democrats.[45] At the White House, Clinton grew jealous of Powell's press coverage and became more and more concerned about facing him in the 1996 election. The president was "apoplectic on the subject of Colin Powell, terrified of Colin Powell," said Clinton's political adviser Dick Morris.[46] "That fall," George Stephanopoulos wrote, "one man was increasingly the source of Clinton's foul moods. His book was a best seller, his poll numbers were soaring, and his potential presidential run had pundits swooning. General Powell was pissing the president off."[47]

The viability and likelihood of a Powell candidacy inspired a bevy of critics, and the sniping came from both the right and left. From the left, civil rights leader Jesse Jackson assailed Powell's support for Republican national security policies and questioned the veracity of the retired general's support for organized labor, the working class, and civil rights activism. "We do know that very right-wing white people can trust him," Jackson stated. "They can trust him to drop bombs. We know that Reagan could trust him. . . . But have we ever seen him on a picket line? Is he for unions? Or for civil rights? Or for *anything*?"[48] Writing in an April 1995 edition of the *New Republic*, Charles Lane raised earnest questions about Powell's obsequious nature, which, he said, had contributed to the army's cover-up of the My Lai massacre and the Iran-Contra scandal. During his long career, Lane wrote, "Powell often disagreed with the Army or the government, or with the direction of the country. But he rarely spoke out. Rather, he made a point of keeping his head down and doing his job."[49]

Such criticism continued into summer 1995. Retired Marine Corps Lieutenant General Bernard E. Trainor and Michael R. Gordon, Pentagon correspondent for the *New York Times*, penned an exposé in *New York Times Magazine* that characterized Powell, the "Beltway Warrior," less as a heroic military leader to be worshipped and more as an astute political animal of which to be wary. Gordon and Trainor lashed Powell for being deficient in moral courage and abundant in subservience to authority. Their article's subtitle was "Colin Powell has fought most skillfully behind closed doors, where winning is less important than escaping blame."[50] The duo, who had recently published a book critical of the Bush administration's decision making before, during, and after the Persian Gulf War, rebuked Powell for being overly cautious, both in his initial approach to the war and in bringing about its conclusion.[51] Powell was no "modern MacArthur," the authors contended, but rather "a master bureaucrat, skillful in dealing with the press and adept at escaping blame for questionable decisions, risk-averse to the point of timidity."[52]

While some conservative Republicans, including William Kristol, Jack Kemp, and William Bennett, were amenable to a Powell presidency, right-wing criticism of the general was often unsparing.[53] Republican stalwart Pat Buchanan mocked Powell as a Democrat in Republican clothing, a "Bill Clintonite."[54]

Likewise, Laura Ingraham and Stephen Vaughn argued that Powell was "a New Democrat" with positions on domestic policy that sounded "more like Bob Dylan than Bob Dole."[55] Meanwhile, retired Marine Lieutenant Colonel Oliver North not only disparaged Powell as a faux Republican, but also posited that something nefarious lay buried in the general's military past. On his national radio show, North insisted that the public had a right to know about Powell's "real role in the so-called Iran-*contra* affair, his real role in the cover-up of the My Lai massacre in Vietnam, his role in what was done to prevent Desert Storm."[56]

Similarly, in Irving Kristol's conservative magazine *The National Interest*, University of North Carolina professor Richard Kohn, a former senior air force historian and past president of the Society for Military History, excoriated Powell for having frequently exceeded his authority as chairman of the Joint Chiefs of Staff. Powell's "troubling" and "astounding" leadership during the Bush and Clinton administrations, Kohn contended, had contravened tradition and "eroded" civilian control over the military. He criticized Powell for pushing his personal "vision" of a post–Cold War national security strategy and a major restructuring of the armed forces. He chastised the general for his reluctance to wage war against Iraq and his "extraordinary efforts to control his civilian superiors' inclinations to formulate a strategy and move rapidly into combat." Powell's "very worst breach of civilian control," Kohn asserted, was his public opposition to openly integrating homosexuals into the military. He also harangued the general for wielding inordinate influence on policy in places such as Bosnia and Somalia. "General Powell took it upon himself," Kohn wrote, "to be the arbiter of American military intervention overseas, an unprecedented policy role for a senior military officer, the most explicit intrusion into policy since MacArthur's conflict with Truman."[57]

A more coordinated assault on Powell's suitability for the White House came on November 2, 1995, when a group of emboldened conservatives, including Gary Bauer and Grover

Norquist, convened a press conference to warn fellow Republicans that a Powell candidacy would doom the conservative movement and the party. The charges against the general were familiar: he was not a Republican but rather a closeted big-government Democrat who supported abortion rights and affirmative action; and he was dangerously cautious in national security decision making. Powell was disparaged as a reluctant supporter of Reagan's Star Wars missile defense initiative and an opponent of Bush's decision to eject Iraqi forces from Kuwait. At the gathering, former Pentagon official Frank Gaffney derided Powell as "a risk averse and politically hypersensitive military officer."[58] Reporting for the *Washington Post*, Dan Balz and Paul Taylor characterized the conservatives' onslaught as "unusually vituperative."[59]

Despite the criticism, Powell remained the frontrunner in preliminary presidential election polls. In early November, according to a *Wall Street Journal*/NBC poll, he was fifteen points ahead of Bill Clinton.[60] On November 8, two weeks before his planned announcement, Powell convened a press conference. There, he officially declared himself a Republican. He also announced that he would not seek the presidency or any other elective office. At that very moment, wrote Steven Holmes, "the sound of air leaking out of the body politic could be heard in Washington and throughout the country," and for many Americans "a moment had been lost, a moment of importance for the country, for history, for the Republican Party, for race relations, for voter enthusiasm, and even for media interest in the campaign."[61]

Somber in tone, Powell confessed that he lacked the innate drive and enthusiasm required to lead a successful presidential campaign. "Ultimately . . . I had to look deep into my own soul, standing aside from the expectations and enthusiasms of others," he said. Presidential politics, he continued, is "a calling I do not yet hear. And for me to pretend otherwise would not be honest to myself, it would not be honest to the American people."[62] As for the right wing's orchestrated strike against him, Powell said,

"When you move away from just disagreeing with someone's views and you move into ad hominem attacks to destroy character, you're adding to the incivility that exists in our political life right now, which we ought to do something about."[63]

Many people were heartbroken by the news of Powell's announcement. No one seemed more forlorn than columnist Maureen Dowd, whose pining on the subject bordered on the absurd: "The graceful hard male animal who did nothing overtly to dominate us yet dominated us completely, in the exact way we wanted that to happen at this moment, like a fine leopard on the veld, was gone. . . . 'Don't leave, Colin Powell' I could hear myself crying from somewhere inside."[64] Late-night television host David Letterman tallied a Top Ten List of the "Real Reasons Colin Powell Isn't Running" against Bill Clinton:

10. Have you ever moved into a house after hillbillies have lived there?
9. Afraid his secret draft-dodging past would be revealed
8. Was under the impression he'd have to marry Hillary
7. Duties as President would take time away from duties as secretary/treasurer of Leonard Nimoy fan club
6. Taking relaxing 2-month vacation on O. J.'s "Search for the Real Killers"
5. Thought it might be fun to sit back, watch Clinton screw up another 4 years
4. Afraid he'd be embarrassed by his deadbeat brother, Roger Powell
3. Would rather get a job Americans still respect
2. Same reason I'm not hosting next year's Academy Awards—the people want Whoopi
1. Five words: "White House Correspondent Sam Donaldson"[65]

There were, in fact, multiple reasons for Powell's withdrawal. He detested the idea of waging a grueling campaign with its requisite fundraising, deal-making, and mudslinging.[66] As an *undeclared* candidate, he had already suffered from unprecedented attacks on his character and professional record. Moreover, being pragmatic and risk averse, and having like-minded political advisers such as Armitage, Powell also came to the dreadful realization that he might not even win the Republican Party's nomination.[67] "It was about as miserable a period I've ever had in my life," he later said. "I can usually handle problems and I can usually handle stress, but I was losing weight. It was a bad time."[68]

In a prescient article, written a year before Powell's press conference, journalist Jon Meacham predicted that the general would bow out of a presidential horse race. "It seems probable that Powell, a proud man who has a military man's love of precision, won't put up with what it takes to run," Meacham wrote, adding, "A presidential campaign, with its Alice-in-Wonderland quality and slap-dash reporting, is not designed for a man of Powell's temperament. He may decide, with his lucrative lecture fees and his already-mythic reputation, to lead a comfortable, quiet life as an undisputed hero."[69]

After the press conference, Powell removed himself as much as possible from the political scene. This disappointed many Republican politicians, who had hoped that the immensely popular Powell would campaign for them. When such requests came, as one did from G.O.P. Speaker of the House Newt Gingrich, the general responded that he was otherwise occupied and that "While I am a proud Republican, my plans and schedule for the foreseeable future will not permit me to participate in fundraising or campaign activities."[70] Senate Majority Leader Bob Dole came courting as well. By spring 1996, Dole had emerged as the presumptive Republican presidential nominee, and he wanted Powell as his running mate. The prospect of a Dole-Powell ticket was, according to Dole's campaign manager, simply "orgasmic."[71] Powell dutifully met with Dole in June but promptly scotched the idea of being his number two.[72]

Powell did agree to give a couple campaign speeches and a keynote address at the Republican National Convention. Securing the recalcitrant general was boon for party organizers who envisioned him as "our Walter Cronkite (the most trusted man in America)."[73] Powell refused to be managed by party officials and insisted on writing his own speech, which was not subject to their approval. The address, given on the evening of August 12, mostly skirted foreign and defense policy and instead focused on his parents' immigrant experiences, the American Dream, economic growth, free enterprise, lower taxes, and family values. Powell also sought to stave off the growing influence of right-wing conservatives. He declared that he had joined the Republican Party to "help fill the big tent," wherein members are both compassionate and free to disagree with one another. To the disappointment of conservatives, Powell expressed his unabashed support for affirmative action and women's right to choose an abortion. "I was invited here by my party to share my views with you," Powell said, "because we are a big enough party—and big enough people—to disagree on individual issues and still work together for our common goal: restoring the American dream."[74] The general received a raucous standing ovation.[75] Powell's speech, which barely mentioned Dole, was a significant political declaration. He would not make another for four years.

Thereafter, Powell returned to the profitable lecture circuit and dedicated himself to numerous charitable causes. He joined the boards of the United Negro College Fund, the Boys and Girls Clubs, the Children's Health Fund, and Howard University. In 1997, at the invitation of President Clinton and the living former presidents, he also helped to create the nonprofit foundation America's Promise—The Alliance for Youth, which coordinated with businesses, other nonprofits, church groups, and government agencies to provide improved education, health care, and work opportunities for disadvantaged urban youth.[76] Powell told *Life* magazine, "I want every American to say, What can I do? Not what can I do for the neighbor who looks just like me, but what can I do for a kid who is hurting and needs me to come across town and put myself out."[77] All the while, Powell's popularity soared with the American people. Poll after poll indicated that the general was not just the nation's most admired Republican, but the country's "most trusted person."[78]

Looking toward the 2000 presidential election, many people hoped Powell would finally mount a campaign. In fall 1997, as the chairman of America's Promise, he was traveling the country to boost volunteerism. At a rally in San Antonio, he was joined by Governor George W. Bush, who announced, "General Powell, Texas is reporting for duty." At a joint press conference, Bush commented that the retired general "would make a great president," and Powell responded in kind: "As would this guy."[79] Unlike Bush, Powell had no desire to make a run for the White House, and while he continued to squash all suggestions to the contrary, he had warmed to the idea of becoming secretary of state.[80]

Powell did not see Bush again until April 2000, when the governor emerged as the presumptive presidential nominee for the Republican Party. At their next meeting, in a Washington, DC, hotel room, Bush asked for and received the general's support for the coming contest against Democrat Al Gore.

Powell's visible return to national politics occurred on May 23, when Bush gave a foreign policy address.[81] Weeks before, Powell had reviewed a policy paper and draft speech written by Bush's national security advisory team, headed by Condoleezza Rice. The documents outlined Bush's support for reductions in offensive nuclear stockpiles, for the termination of the Anti-Ballistic Missile Treaty, and for the development of a defensive shield to fend off "that horrifying day when North Korea or Iraq launches—or threatens to launch—a nuclear attack."[82] Standing behind Bush at the National Press Club were Powell and four Republican elder statesmen: George Shultz, Brent Scowcroft, Henry Kissinger, and Donald Rumsfeld. Two days later, when Powell was again in Texas promoting his foundation's charitable work, a reporter inquired about his interest in becoming Bush's vice-presidential nominee. Powell replied emphatically, "I'm not seeking it, and the governor knows that."[83] Two months later, Bush selected Dick Cheney as his running mate.

Powell made several personal appearances for Bush in the fall campaign, but, as in 1996, his principal contribution was a keynote address at the opening of the Republican National Convention. His message was similar to his previous convention speech: he wanted to inspire and challenge the party. He again underscored the importance of family values and "all that is good and right in America," and he argued for a more inclusive Republican Party, one that promoted the American Dream and equal opportunities for all citizens. Powell reiterated his support for affirmative action and decried the decline of urban communities, including their failing schools. Unlike 1996, Powell singled out the Republican presidential nominee as a bold and caring leader, someone with a genuine understanding of the nation's ills and a proven record of reform that had benefited "all Texans—white, black, Latino, Asian, Native American." Courting favor from the nominee, Powell contended that Bush was the party's best hope because he "has been successful in bringing more and more minorities into the tent by responding to their deepest needs." To rousing applause, the general issued a proclamation: "In Governor George Bush we have the leader."[84]

Republicans and pundits widely praised Powell's address, which had been interrupted by applause more than forty times. Rumsfeld immediately conveyed his appreciation for the inspiring address.[85] Speaking on CNN after the speech, news anchor Judy Woodruff gushed, "When you look at Colin Powell, you really do see the embodiment of not only one of America's most popular politicians—maybe the most popular politician in the country. . . . Someone who could have run for president . . . could have had the vice presidential nomination, you know, just by the asking."[86] Political analyst William Schneider agreed, declaring, "Colin Powell is hands down the most popular public figure in America. . . . And we can prove it. Let's look at where the voters are. He has an 81 percent favorable rating, higher than George W. Bush, John McCain, Dick Cheney, even Bill Clinton. Eight-one percent favorable. You know, an elected official would kill or at least pay a consultant a whole lot of money to get that kind of rating."[87]

Powell's public support for the Bush-Cheney ticket proved invaluable, especially his ability to attract politically moderate voters. The number of self-identifying moderates voting for the Republican nominee increased 36 percent from 1996 to 2000.[88] Powell's extraordinary popularity and national security credentials bolstered Bush's credibility. "If you're George Bush, and the biggest weakness you have is foreign policy, and you can have Cheney on one flank and Powell on the other, it virtually eliminated the competence issue," Gingrich reflected. "And in Powell's case, he is an African American, chairman of the Joint Chiefs, best-selling writer, most trusted man in America."[89]

Al Gore conceded the hotly contested election on December 13, 2000. Three days later, Bush arranged a press event in Crawford, Texas, to introduce Powell as his nominee for secretary of state. Since Powell's May appearance with Bush at the National Press Club, it had been presumed that the retired general would be Bush's top choice to lead the State Department. In actuality, Bush had never promised the position to Powell. "It just sort of happened," Powell recalled, "as it was assumed to happen."[90] Recounting his initial happiness with Bush's selection of Powell, Cheney wrote, "I was proud of the Powell pick and glad he had agreed to join us. We had worked together well during my time in the Pentagon, and I was looking forward to the chance to work with him again."[91]

Before bringing Powell to the podium, the president-elect, with Cheney standing nearby, outlined the parameters of his planned foreign policy, which he characterized as bipartisan, purposeful, formidable, and humble. Bush's policy precepts included close cooperation with "friends and allies," the promotion of democracy and free trade, support for a secure Israel and the Middle East peace process, and a determination to stop the proliferation of WMD. "I know of no better person to be the face and voice of American diplomacy," Bush said, "than Colin Powell." He commended Powell's storied service to the nation and his record of "providing good counsel, strong leadership, and an example of integrity for everyone with whom he served." Visibly moved, Bush characterized Powell as "an American hero" who possessed a "soldier's sense of duty and honor" and who, like Secretary of State General George Marshall, was "a tower of strength and common sense."[92]

Powell took the podium to boisterous cheers from the assembled crowd. He told local and televised audiences that he was happy to return to public service. Echoing Bush, he emphasized the importance of international engagement, especially collaboration and coordination with allies, which, he said, would be the "the center of our foreign policy activities." Powell deftly articulated a foreign policy vision that was "uniquely American internationalism," not isolationist but activist and open, and "rational" in its approach to major powers like China and Russia. He also identified antiterrorism as a priority: "We will stand strong with our friends and allies against those nations that pursue weapons of mass destruction, that practice terrorism. We will not be afraid of them. We will not be frightened by them. We will meet them, we will match them, we will contend with them. We will defend our interests from a position of strength." Powell also sent an unambiguous message to employees at the State Department by pledging "as a priority of my stewardship as secretary of state" to apply considerable pressure on Congress to increase resources for the department.[93]

In the question-and-answer period with reporters, Powell, not Bush, offered responses. In the process, he reiterated the president-elect's commitment to the Middle East peace process, to a national missile defense system, and to a review of U.S.-Bosnian policy. He also promised "reenergized sanctions" against Iraq, which had not yet accounted for its WMD.[94]

Powell was pleased with the coming-out party. His performance, conducted without notes, had been a tour de force. He exuded competence and confidence. Some, including Cheney, thought Powell had badly upstaged Bush.[95] Armitage urged him to be more careful in his public appearances with the president.[96] *New York Times* columnist Thomas L. Friedman fretted that Powell's enormous stature might give him unchecked influence over Bush.[97] Robert Kaplan concurred, writing in the *New Republic*, "Last week's press conference during which

Powell lectured about his foreign policy priorities while Bush stood mutely beside him, offered an early glimpse of what lies ahead."[98] To most people, however, Powell's return to government service reinvigorated their respect and admiration for him. At CNN, Schneider posited that Powell's nomination as secretary of state was "especially important at this moment, because it's a moment when the nation wants healing, consensus, unity. And no figure symbolizes that [so well as], the most respected figure . . . in American public life, Colin Powell."[99]

During the seven years between his retirement and his selection as Bush's secretary of state, Powell had lived an independent life, serving no masters. Moreover, he had sustained remarkable bipartisan popularity while taking positions on controversial domestic issues and despite the criticisms engendered by his possible presidential bid. With the success of his autobiography and his continuous lecturing, he had also earned millions of dollars, "the fuck you money" that Regan had once prescribed. The retired general had been his own boss, pursuing his own agenda on his own terms.

Powell's return to government service meant the loss of autonomy and a return to that familiar dual follower-leader role, which he had perfected as chairman of the Joint Chiefs of Staff. As the principal military adviser to the Bush and Clinton administrations, Powell had demonstrated his brilliance as a subordinate and his effectiveness as the de facto leader of America's armed forces. He had displayed the exemplary characteristics of competence, dedication, integrity, adaptability, agreeableness, thoughtfulness, and independence. As secretary of state, Powell would face the biggest challenges of his career, both as a senior subordinate to an inexperienced president during a time of crisis and as the leader of an ailing State Department.

I am not coming in just to be the foreign policy adviser to the President. . . .
I'm coming in as the leader and manager of this department.

—COLIN POWELL

CHAPTER SEVEN

Leader, Follower, Odd Man Out

(2001–2004)

As America's sixty-fifth secretary of state, Colin Powell assumed two broad responsibilities: advising and following the president on foreign policy and leading the State Department. In these capacities, Powell drew upon three and half decades of government experience, especially his time as national security adviser and two terms as chairman of the Joint Chiefs of Staff. As a senior counselor, Powell aimed to provide the president with a range of policy alternatives, including his own assessments of their suitability and likely outcomes. If measured by the degree of his influence on George W. Bush's decision making, Powell achieved some notable successes, including the administration's management of a crisis in the South China Sea, its promotion of global programs to combat the spread of HIV/AIDS, and its decision, immediately after September 11, 2001, to focus on the security threat in Afghanistan, not Iraq. Powell also enjoyed monumental success as the leader of the State Department, where he boosted morale and confidence and significantly increased the organization's effectiveness by upgrading facilities, security, technology, and personnel.

On January 21, 2001, the U.S. Senate confirmed Powell's nomination as secretary of state by a unanimous vote. Four days earlier, at his confirmation hearing, he had expressed his great joy in returning to public service after "my seven-year sabbatical."[1] In his prepared statement and during the question-and-answer session, Powell articulated his pragmatic views on America's proper role in the world. He was committed to a thoughtful policy of international engagement, a "distinctly American internationalism" that precluded protectionism and isolationism and promoted cooperation and multilateralism. In that context, he pledged to fortify and expand U.S. alliances and to work constructively with major-power adversaries, such as Russia and China, to meet the security challenges of the new century. Powell further promised to continue the Clinton administration's policies of reducing tensions on the Korean Peninsula and promoting stability in the Middle East. As he had vowed at his December coming-out party in Crawford, Texas, Powell also made a case for increased funding for the State Department. In the process, he decried the department's personnel shortages, dilapidated facilities, and ramshackle infrastructure. "We need to do better," Powell said, adding, "I know that we do not have enough to accomplish the mission; we do not have enough. And we need not just a little increase, we need a step increase."[2]

In his confirmation hearing, Powell also expressed concerns about the development and proliferation of WMD. He gave particular attention to Iraq. "I understand that a nuclear, biological or chemical weapon of Saddam Hussein," Powell said, "threatens not only the children of Iraq, but the entire region." He characterized that country as a "weakened" and "failed state" that still "utters threats and pursues horrible weapons to terrorize its neighbors." As a result, Powell promised to reshape and "reenergize" economic sanctions against Saddam's regime and to support the reinsertion of U.N. weapons inspectors, back anti-Saddam opposition movements, and respond to any provocations. The "ultimate goal" of tightening sanctions, he stated, was to prevent Iraq "from having such terrible weapons in their arsenal."[3]

Powell faced numerous and significant challenges as the State Department's new chief executive officer. He inherited an underfunded, sprawling global enterprise with forty thousand employees operating in run-down buildings with inadequate security and antiquated information and communication technology. Before Powell arrived, more than a thousand department employees had signed a letter of protest that characterized the State Department as "a rusted-out diplomatic hulk that is no longer seaworthy."[4] During the Clinton years, congressional funding for State had declined precipitously. Moreover, morale in the understaffed organization was palpably low. "All in all," historian J. Robert Moskin writes, "it was a period of deplorable neglect for the State Department and its Foreign Service."[5] As demonstrated throughout his army career, Powell viewed such organizational problems as leadership opportunities. Furthermore, if the challenges were dealt with effectively, he would significantly enhance the department's ability to execute the nation's foreign policies.

From the onset, the secretary set a fresh, energetic tone, one that emphasized his intention to lead constructive—indeed, transformational—changes and champion the needs of State Department personnel. He made an immediate and positive impression during several televised addresses to employees around the world.[6] His inspiring talks were frequently interrupted by applause, and as *Newsweek* reported, "staffers line up to shake his hand. Some wept."[7] In full recognition of his dual responsibilities as their leader and as Bush's subordinate, Powell informed his people, "I am not coming in just to be the foreign policy adviser to the President, although that is what the principal title is. . . . I'm coming in as the leader and manager of this department."[8] The secretary told his followers that he respected their expertise and experience and wanted to encourage their independence in thought and action. Moreover, he stated his preference for direct, unadulterated information flow throughout the department, and he emphasized his high standards and expectations. "If you perform well, we are going to get along just fine. If you don't," he joked, "you are going to give me push-ups."[9]

Powell's upbeat, candid, and collaborative message had a resounding effect on morale.[10] One retired Foreign Service officer told the secretary, "We do recognize that you have a tremendous job ahead of you. We are very, very enthusiastic about your appointment."[11] Another senior officer exclaimed, "Here was a guy who understood institutions, who was going to rely on the institution and support it. It was just what we'd been waiting a decade to hear. We were like the Army at Valley Forge when George Washington showed up."[12]

Crucial to Powell's transformational initiatives at the State Department was his influence on Capitol Hill. Improving the department's relations with Congress was a major priority, and Powell personally testified before most budget and appropriations committees. "Now is the time," he told the lawmakers, "to provide to the practitioners of foreign policy the resources they need to conduct it."[13] In November 2001, at Powell's urging, Congress agreed to significantly increase the State Department's multibillion-dollar budget, and it continued to do so in subsequent years. According to Ambassador Charles Hill, "Powell worked budget issues in the Congress with briefing skills that he honed through decades of military and public service," and he used the additional resources to update hardware, software, and infrastructure and to improve embassy security and increase staffing and training.[14]

The nonpartisan Foreign Affairs Council (FAC) published an independent assessment of Powell's stewardship after his first two years. The glowing report praised the secretary on multiple fronts. His hand-picked senior staff, including Deputy Secretary Richard Armitage, was considered "one of the strongest management teams in the history of the State Department," and Powell's "remarkable success" with Congress was providing desperately needed resources to revolutionize "woefully inadequate" information technology and restore the department's "decrepit facilities" abroad.[15] Regarding the technology challenges, Powell himself later wrote, "I entered a Department that had an out of date, not functioning information system. Still using Wang computers 8 years after the company died. I had just left the AOL board and needed to bring the Dept. into the 21st Century."[16] Moreover, the secretary's Diplomatic Readiness Initiative, which aimed to hire more than a thousand civil service personnel, Foreign Service officers, and other specialists within three years, had made "impressive" strides in rebuilding the department's "hollowed out" human resource base. The FAC concluded that in two short years, Powell's achievements were "substantial, even historic."[17]

Powell's effective leadership brought wholesale positive changes to the State Department, and this inspired tremendous appreciation and loyalty among his civilian troops.* "During his four years at State," Ambassador Hill wrote, "Secretary Powell had endeared himself to the Foreign Service as few before him. He knew how to earn loyalty and respect."[18] In December 2004, Richard Lugar, chairman of the Senate Committee on Foreign Relations, sang Powell's praises from the Senate floor. Among his "greatest achievements," Lugar said, was his reformation of "the leadership culture" of the State Department. The secretary's emphasis on "management, training, and empowerment" had elevated morale and intradepartmental cohesion, which together enhanced the State Department's execution of foreign policy. Lugar also noted that Powell had brought major improvements

---

*While many State Department employees strongly disagreed with Bush administration policies, a large majority seemed to respect Powell's institutional leadership. See *From Colin to Condi: The Handoff at State*, the February 2005 issue of the *Foreign Service Journal* (February 2005), esp. 13–59.

to information technology and had "overcome a crisis" in embassy security and construction.[19] A November 2004 report from the FAC was equally laudatory, stating plainly that Powell and his "gifted" senior team had fixed "a broken institution," making it "infinitely stronger." Under the secretary's leadership, the report continued, advances in staffing, morale, technology, facilities, and security were extraordinary. "The Powell team," the FAC concluded, "has 'talked the talk' and 'walked the walk.' The Secretary has been an exemplary CEO of the State Department."[20]

The first major foreign policy crisis of the Bush administration occurred on the night of March 31, 2001, when a U.S. Navy EP-3 reconnaissance plane collided midair with a Chinese F-8 fighter jet approximately seventy miles off of the Chinese coast.[21] The Chinese interceptor crashed into the South China Sea, killing the pilot. Meanwhile, the pilots of the badly damaged U.S. plane had little choice but to violate Chinese airspace and make an emergency landing on the island of Hainan. Chinese authorities detained the twenty-four-person American crew and demanded that Washington issue an apology and promise to cease such surveillance missions. Bush, in turn, publicly demanded that China release the naval crew safely and promptly.[22] Wanting to avoid a hostage crisis and the dangerous major-power escalation, the president turned to Powell and the State Department to secure a diplomatic solution. Management of the incident validated Bush's selection of Powell as his chief diplomat. It also demonstrated the president's willingness to accept Powell's counsel over the opposition of Vice President Cheney and Defense Secretary Rumsfeld.

Powell established a benevolent tone for the negotiating with the Chinese by sending a personal communique to Vice Premier Qian Qichen. The secretary expressed his regret for the downed Chinese pilot and communicated that the president's "thoughts and prayers are with the pilot's family and loved ones, as are mine and all Americans'."[23]

During the course of the next week, the State Department crafted two official letters for the Chinese government, one in English and the other in Chinese. The carefully constructed, even cagey documents, which were to be signed by the American ambassador in China, expressed regret for the loss of the Chinese pilot and aircraft and for the U.S. plane's forced landing on Chinese soil. The letters did not accept blame for causing the collision, nor did they promise to stop flying reconnaissance missions over international waters. The English-language version offered an expression of sorrow but purposefully avoided the word *apology*. The Chinese version, however, could easily be interpreted as a formal apology.[24] Rumsfeld and Cheney disliked Powell's nuanced approach, preferring to penalize China for the incident.[25] The defense secretary jabbed at the secretary, saying he might as well ask "pretty please" of the Chinese.[26]

On April 8, Powell appeared on the CBS Sunday morning television show *Face the Nation* to clarify the administration's position: "We're sorry" about the death of the pilot, "no matter what the fault was," and for violating Chinese airspace during the emergency landing, but, the secretary said, the United States was not offering "an apology accepting responsibility" for the deadly collision.[27] The two letters were delivered to the Chinese on April 11; the unharmed American crew was released immediately and their dismantled aircraft was eventually returned to the United States.[28]

The peaceful resolution of the South China Sea crisis and safe return of naval personnel was largely seen as a success for Bush and his secretary of state. The president complimented Powell on his performance and later noted that the secretary's "role in resolving the EP-3 incident . . . showed . . . calm judgment and steady resolve."[29] Still, Rumsfeld, Cheney, and other hardline conservatives thought Powell's diplomacy made the United States appear "a weak supplicant."[30] The *Weekly Standard* blasted Bush and Powell for their deferential diplomacy, which had supposedly brought upon the United States a "profound national humiliation."[31] Nevertheless, the president was content. He had avoided a major escalation and thus "passed the commander-in-chief test."[32] Powell, too, was pleased, and he publicly dismissed the conservatives' carping as "very unfortunate, and it is also absurd."[33] According to Armitage, Powell's senior deputy, the president's support of Powell during the crisis and the safe return of the U.S. service personnel left the State Department "feeling pretty lusty and bold."[34]

Early in the Bush administration, Powell also found the president open to and ultimately passionate about a major initiative on international health care. In March 2001, Bush met with Kofi Annan, the Secretary-General of the United Nations. Annan proposed a new U.N. fund to combat HIV/AIDS, malaria, and tuberculosis. Wary of foreign development programs and especially distrustful of the United Nations, Bush did not commit himself. Powell, however, recognized a prime opportunity for American leadership. He telephoned Tommy Thompson, Bush's secretary of Health and Human Services, and explained that the HIV/AIDS pandemic was "not just a health matter," but had implications for global stability and was thus "a national security matter."[35] With that perspective, he enlisted Thompson's help in convincing the president that the United States should be the first contributor to Annan's U.N. fund. It worked.

Bush later admitted that he was reluctant to support the U.N. project because he viewed the world organization as "cumbersome, bureaucratic, and inefficient."[36] But Powell and Thompson proved a formidable team. "They felt it would send a good signal for America to be the first contributor," Bush wrote. "Their persistence overcame my skepticism."[37] Powell and Thompson proceeded to cochair a task force on how best to organize and manage the relief fund. In May 2001, at the White House Rose Garden with Powell, Thompson, Annan, and others nearby, Bush announced a $200 million "founding" commitment to the U.N. Global Fund, and he promised "more to follow as we learn where our support can be most effective."[38] Annan later wrote favorably of Bush's "resolute" commitment to "the most important international financing facility for aid established in the last twenty years."[39]

To Powell's delight, Bush delivered on his promise, and then some. In 2002 he not only increased America's commitment to the U.N. Global Fund to $500 million, but also launched a separate U.S. AIDS initiative. Returning to the Rose Garden in June 2002, the president announced "another important and new initiative in the fight against HIV/AIDS," the International Mother and Child HIV Prevention Initiative, a $500 million program to prevent mother-to-child transmissions. Bush again commended Powell and Thompson for their "hard work" in combating a pandemic that "staggers the imagination and shocks the conscience."[40]

The Bush administration's leadership continued on the tragic international health crisis. In his January 28, 2003, State of the Union speech, the president announced a massive $15 billion, five-year program to "turn the tide against AIDS in the most afflicted nations of Africa and the Caribbean." Annan considered this program the single most important foreign policy achievement of the Bush administration.[41] Five months later, in the Dean Acheson Auditorium at the State Department, Bush signed the United States Leadership against HIV/AIDS, Tuberculosis, and Malaria Act of 2003. He characterized the enormous health program as "a great mission of rescue" in the tradition of the Marshall Plan, the Berlin Airlift, and the Peace Corps. Bush credited Powell and Thompson for "their leadership on this crucial issue," stating that there were "no better people to trust in seeing that the great heart and compassion of America is recognized in our world through accomplishment."[42] Later that year, the U.S. Senate confirmed the State Department's first U.S. Global AIDS Coordinator, a position with ambassadorial rank. For Powell, Bush's enthusiastic commitment to fighting the spread of HIV/AIDS was the height of "bold" presidential leadership.[43]

Bush had been open to Powell's influence during the China crisis and on the global health initiative, but on other occasions the president gave diplomacy short shrift. In mid-March 2001, Powell received an unexpected phone call from National Security Adviser Condoleezza Rice concerning U.S. energy policy. She informed him that the White House was sending a letter to Capitol Hill regarding the Kyoto Protocol on climate change and she wanted him to review it. The letter had been drafted by Cheney's office for the president's signature. Earlier, several Republican senators had asked Bush to clarify his policy on global warming and domestic greenhouse gas emissions. Cheney's document declared, in essence, that the administration prioritized domestic energy production and opposed mandated reductions in emissions, something Bush had supported during the presidential campaign.[44]

Powell assessed the letter from a diplomatic perspective and promptly sent Rice new language to make it clear that the United States was also committed "to work with our friends and allies" on the issue. The secretary advised further that the administration inform its major allies before the letter was issued. After receiving his recommendations, Rice telephoned again to say the White House was not going to incorporate Powell's changes. Fearing a diplomatic blunder was in the works, the secretary instructed Rice to "slow this thing down" until he could get to the Oval Office. By the time Powell arrived, it was too late. Cheney was already delivering the signed document to senators on Capitol Hill.[45]

Powell and Rice were troubled by the episode. They thought the president and vice president had acted impetuously, not contemplating the diplomatic fallout.[46] Powell thought, "They all got together . . . and said to hell with everybody else and they just signed it with no reference to our allies, no reference to 'Let's work with them and find a way forward on carbon emissions.'"[47] When Bush explained to Powell that he simply wanted to give the senators a timely response, the secretary warned, "Well, you're going to see the consequences of it."[48] Powell would later admit to the *New York Times* that the issue "was not handled as well as it should have been."[49] The White House did not appreciate this frank assessment, but Powell felt no remorse. "They were all mad at me that day, too," Powell recalled. "What are they going to do? Send me to Vietnam?"[50]

The Bush administration's policy toward the Israeli-Palestinian conflict further tested Powell's influence on the new president, especially since it was another topic where the secretary's views differed from those of other senior advisers. The Middle East conflict had been escalating since President Clinton's last-ditch effort to negotiate a peace agreement at Camp David in 2000. With poor prospects for peace, Bush was reluctant to intervene. He possessed deep sympathy for Israel but believed that U.S. intervention would not contribute to a lasting solution or even curb the rising violence. Moreover, Bush was loath to adopt any policy that resembled his predecessor's. Like Bush, Powell was skeptical that the administration could orchestrate a permanent peace settlement. In fact, Clinton had called him soon after Bush's election to warn the incoming secretary of state of Palestinian leader Yasser Arafat's unreliability: "Don't you ever trust that son of a bitch. He lied to me and he'll lie to you."[51] Nevertheless, Powell feared that further escalation in the Israeli-Palestinian struggle would threaten national security as it pertained to U.S. allies Jordan, Egypt, and Saudi Arabia. As a consequence, Powell advocated engagement.[52]

Rising violence in the Middle East was a primary topic of the Bush administration's first NSC meeting on January 30, 2001. Powell provided an overview of the burgeoning crisis and called for a policy of active diplomacy. He was opposed by Rumsfeld and Cheney who, in addition to supporting Israeli policy, believed that the president should not inject the administration into an unsolvable and divisive international problem. Doing nothing, Powell thought, was irresponsible, as disengagement would lead to "dire" consequences, most especially for the Palestinian people.[53] The world's only superpower, he believed, could not take the position of "No, it's too hard. I don't want to waste energy on it."[54] In the end, Bush said he wanted U.S. policy to "tilt back" toward Israel and away from Arafat. "Sometimes a show of strength by one side can really clarify things," the president said, but he still authorized Powell to visit the region and assess the situation.[55] Years later, the president commended his secretary of state for being "a key architect" of the administration's "Broader Middle East initiative."[56]

Powell traveled to the Middle East in February and June 2001. He held meetings with newly elected Prime Minister Ariel Sharon in Israel and with Arafat in Palestine. Although Powell disliked shuttle diplomacy, which he likened to a "root canal," he persisted.[57] Once back in Washington, he recommended that the president deliver a major speech on the conflict and clearly express America's desire to play a constructive role in alleviating the violence. Bush agreed to give an address and even entertained the idea of meeting with Arafat. Powell was pleased; Cheney and Rumsfeld opposed his policy of engagement, but Bush remained open to it.[58]

September 11, 2001, changed everything. The al Qaeda terrorist attacks jaded Bush's outlook on the Israeli-Palestinian conflict. Even more than before, the president viewed Palestinian leaders, especially Arafat, as terrorists bent on wreaking havoc upon Israel. Nevertheless, Powell remained steadfast in his belief that the United States needed to engage in constructive diplomacy, and sometimes he compelled the president to act. In early October Bush, for the first time, announced publicly that he supported the creation of an independent Palestinian state.[59] By November Powell had convinced the president to renew his support for the Middle East peace process in his upcoming speech before the U.N. General Assembly.

Two months after 9/11, Bush proclaimed at the United Nations that the United States "stands by its commitment to a just peace in the Middle East. We are working toward the day when two states—Israel and Palestine—live peacefully together within secure and recognized borders as called for by the Security Council resolutions."[60] Bush pledged to do "all in our power to bring both parties back into negotiations."[61]

Seeking to build on this momentum, Powell delivered his own policy speech nine days later. Cheney had opposed the address, especially anything that hinted of criticism of Israel, but Powell secured Bush's preapproval. Speaking at the University of Louisville, the secretary emphasized the need for both Israelis and Palestinians to compromise if they were to achieve the grand objective of "peace, security and dignity."[62] The Palestinians, he said, must cease all terrorist acts, and Israel must end its military and civilian occupation of Palestinian territory. Powell underscored the Bush administration's commitment to the peace process, declaring that "The Middle East has always needed active American engagement for there to be progress, and we will provide it."[63] Much to Powell's satisfaction, Bush commended him for a well-balanced address.[64]

The secretary then persuaded the president to move beyond rhetoric. He had obtained Bush's approval to appoint retired Marine Corps General Anthony Zinni as the administration's new special representative for Middle East peace negotiations. Zinni, the former CENTCOM commander, had been inspired by Powell's Louisville speech and was "excited" to learn that the administration's commitment to the peace process "had moved way up."[65] The retired general accepted the mission in large part because of Powell's commitment to the enterprise. "If he was ready to put his ass on the line for this," Zinni later wrote, "then I was glad to be part of it."[66] Before Zinni departed in late November, he met with Powell for his "marching orders," which were "to achieve an immediate cease-fire" and implement security and political plans previously formulated by CIA Director George Tenet and former U.S. senator George Mitchell.[67] Afterward, Zinni and the secretary went to the White House to meet with Bush, Cheney, and Rice. There, the president told Powell, "Well, Colin, this is your baby . . . you convinced me, now it's your show."[68]

Despite good intentions and genuine effort, the Zinni mission failed. Lethal violence between Israel and Palestine escalated to new heights. Zinni returned to Washington after only a few weeks; in that short period of time forty-four people had been killed. In public and private, Powell heaped blame on both

Israel and Palestine and also told Zinni to prepare for another trip. That mission transpired in January 2002, but as the special envoy later wrote, "the spiral of violence grew more horrific."[69] The instability worried U.S. allies in the region, including Jordan and Saudi Arabia, which pressured Bush to do more. On March 7, 2002, the president agreed to Powell's recommendation to send Zinni on a third mission; several days later the administration supported a new resolution by the U.N. Security Council that called for an end to the violence and the establishment of a two-state solution. This resolution floundered as well after a Palestinian suicide bomber murdered thirty Israeli civilians and injured more than a hundred others in Netanya. Israel responded forcefully, sending troops into the Gaza Strip, the West Bank, and Bethlehem. Diplomats and world leaders feared the arrival of all-out war.[70]

Bush understood that he could not be idle. On April 1 he consulted with his national security team. Cheney and Rumsfeld opposed any substantial initiative. Powell, on the other hand, pressed the president to take a direct and personal stand, and he did. On April 2, Bush gave a speech from the Rose Garden that condemned Palestinian terrorism and urged Israel to withdraw its troops.[71]

Thereafter, Bush assigned Powell the herculean task of traveling to the Middle East to calm Palestinian and Israeli leaders, quell the violence, and resurrect peace negotiations. The president knew full well that Powell possessed more international credibility than anybody in his cabinet, and the secretary's direct engagement was to signal the administration's commitment to ending the conflagration. "This is going to be tough," Bush told his secretary of state. "You're going to have part of your butt burned off. But you have more butt than any of the rest of us, so you can afford it."[72] It was not the last time that Bush capitalized on Powell's global stature.

Powell was not optimistic about his chances for success, but at least the president had "stuck with it" over the opposition of other senior advisers.[73] On April 4 Bush and Powell met with reporters outside the White House to announce the diplomatic mission.[74] The trip was a modest validation of the secretary's influence on the president's decision making.

Powell's peace mission proved every bit as challenging as Zinni's. On his way to the Middle East, he laid over in Spain to meet with diplomatic representatives of the United Nations, the European Union, and the Russian Federation. The so-called Madrid quartet endorsed a comprehensive strategy for curtailing Israeli-Palestinian violence and restarting negotiations for a permanent settlement. "To my relief and satisfaction," U.N. Secretary-General Kofi Annan wrote, "the international community was now at least pulling together, and there was the prospect of a serious political discussion on the way forward."[75]

However, after Powell arrived in the Middle East, he realized what limited support he had from Washington. There was new resistance to the idea of him meeting face-to-face with Arafat, who was branded a terrorist. Powell was incredulous. How could he help arrange a cease-fire without meeting directly with Arafat? Undeterred, the secretary arranged two conferences with the Palestinian leader. This prompted a volley of backbench criticisms from the vice president's office and from senior ranking civilians at the Pentagon. "People are really putting your shit in the street," Armitage informed his boss by phone.[76] Cheney later wrote that Powell's controversial trip represented "a watershed moment" in the deteriorating relationship between the State Department and the White House: "a tie had been cut."[77]

Powell's diplomacy made little tangible progress. Before returning to Washington after "ten of the most miserable days imaginable," the secretary was determined to make a public statement to inspire a modicum of hope.[78] Powell "cooked up" a possible international conference to include the two belligerents and the Madrid quartet.[79] The idea of the multilateral peace conference was opposed by the hardline, pro-Israeli conservatives in Washington. When Cheney learned of Powell's draft speech, he telephoned Rice and pressed her to rein him in.[80] She called the secretary and advised him to say nothing except that he was returning to Washington to consult with the president. Powell snapped back, "I'm the secretary of state. I'm representing the president. He sent me over here. I can't just say, 'It's been nice,' sign the guest book and leave."[81]

At a press conference on April 17, 2002, Powell read from a lengthy statement crafted the night before. He recounted the planning progress of the Madrid quartet and underscored Bush's commitment to the peace process, including the president's "clear vision" of "a Palestinian state . . . that will respect its neighbor." Powell pointed to his own shuttle diplomacy as evidence of the president's "leadership role." He also announced that he would discuss the idea of an international conference with Bush, and that he would return to the region to keep working toward a just and peaceful settlement.[82] But privately Powell was not optimistic, and he came to believe that Arafat's unwillingness to curb the violence was an insurmountable obstacle to peace. "Believe me," he later said, "I worked hard for a year and half on Arafat before I had to give up, he was hopeless."[83]

Powell did not return to the Middle East for more than a year. During that time, Bush made sporadic pronouncements promising diplomatic leadership. "I and my country will actually lead" the way to peace, he said in June 2002.[84] Arab and Israeli leaders traveled to Washington for consultations, but little was accomplished. The Middle East battle raged on, leaving hundreds of Palestinians and Israelis dead.[85] For Powell, a rare high point in Middle East diplomacy came in spring 2003, when Bush, against the counsel of Cheney and Rumsfeld, publicly endorsed a "Road Map" for peace aimed at the cessation of violence and the creation of a Palestinian state.[86] The plan, championed by Powell, was backed by the European Union, the United Nations, Great Britain, and Russia.[87] In her memoirs, Rice praised Powell's critical efforts, "work for which," she wrote, "he has never gotten enough credit."[88]

In June 2003 Bush and Powell toured Europe and the Middle East. The president again stated that he would "expend the energy and effort necessary to move the [peace] process forward."[89]

Powell and others were impressed that the president was applying pressure to both Palestinian and Israeli leaders. In July, leaders from Israel and Palestine met with Bush at the White House. "That period was a high for Powell," one Arab diplomat concluded, because "he felt that his views prevailed, he felt vindicated."[90] Indeed, Powell had helped to convince the president that the United States could not isolate itself from tumult and instability in Middle East. Nevertheless, the limits of American diplomacy and Powell's influence were all too apparent in August 2003 with a resurgence of Palestinian suicide bombers and forceful Israeli retaliations.

Consistent with his promotion of U.S. engagement in the Israeli-Palestinian conflict, Powell and the State Department believed that Bush should engage North Korea, as Clinton had done, to minimize a threat to regional and national security. Powell had articulated that position during his confirmation hearing. Cheney and Rumsfeld characteristically advocated a hardline approach to Pyongyang, and Bush was sympathetic to their perspective.[91] As a result, the president was unhappy to read Powell's comments in the *Washington Post* saying that the administration planned "to engage with North Korea to pick up where President Clinton and his administration left off. Some promising elements were left on the table."[92]

Furious, Bush telephoned Rice at home.[93] She thought the "touchy" president was overreacting, but she called Powell to tell him, "We have got a problem." The secretary's statement supporting a policy of engagement with North Korea was one issue, but the bigger mistake was aligning with the much-despised Clinton.[94] The secretary of state dutifully backtracked with reporters, clarifying that the administration will "determine at what pace and when we will engage with the North Koreans" and that there were no "imminent" plans for negotiations.[95]

Chastened, Powell thought the White House had overreacted. "He's not easily stunned," one of his aides remarked, "but he was stunned by that."[96] Powell admitted to State Department staffers that he had erred by getting ahead of the White House with the press, but he assured them he could convince the president that engagement with Pyongyang was prudent national security policy. "Don't worry about this," he told them. "This will come our way in the end because we're right about it, and we're going . . . to talk to the [North] Koreans about their nuclear program."[97]

Notwithstanding his "Axis of Evil" speech in January 2002, Bush again demonstrated a willingness to overrule his more hawkish advisers and granted Powell some latitude on North Korea. The president felt some attraction to Powell's flexible and pragmatic approach to managing the nuclear threat. During his first year as secretary of state, Powell quietly and effectively embarked on a campaign "to bring the boss along slowly."[98] While on a tour of Asian countries in the summer of 2002, Powell arranged for an informal sit-down with his North Korean counterpart, Foreign Minister Paek Nam Sun. Hardliners in Washington accused Powell of overstepping again, but Bush had approved the secretary's seemingly impromptu get-together.[99] The meeting was largely symbolic, but it signaled a turning point in Bush's policy and provided a measure of the secretary's persistence and influence.

In early 2003, while in Beijing, Powell encouraged Chinese officials to participate in multilateral negotiations aimed at freezing and eventually dismantling North Korea's nuclear weapons capabilities. If compliant, North Korea would receive security guarantees, international economic aid, and full diplomatic recognition. The so-called three-way talks began in April. When progress stalled, Powell convinced Bush to support U.S. participation in six-way talks that included Russian, Japan, and South Korea. Those negotiations commenced in the August and continued into 2004.[100]

Throughout, the hawks in the Bush administration, led by Cheney, frustrated Powell by attempting to delimit the instructions given to American diplomats, whom they did not want negotiating directly with the North Koreans.[101] Rice recalled Powell's anger over "this infringement on his turf" and admitted "that this was no way to treat the secretary of state."[102] Nevertheless, Powell guided his emissaries, actively encouraging them to engage in "dialogue" with North Korean diplomats while at the same time avoiding the appearance of "direct negotiations."[103] The secretary was also quick to defend his subordinates when they were criticized for being "too soft" with the North Koreans.[104]

In late February 2004, Cheney, circumventing Powell, convinced the president that American negotiators should demand the "irreversible dismantlement" of North Korea's nuclear program. These instructions were never executed because the security talks adjourned, but when Powell found out he warned Bush that an uncompromising approach "would have blown up the whole six-party framework."[105] Armitage characterized the White House's hardline diplomacy as "Alright, you fuckers, do what we say."[106]

Powell never approached Cheney about the incident, and his aversion to direct confrontation disappointed some subordinates in the State Department. To have more influence on policy, they expected their leader "to take more risks and make more demands of the president."[107] Lawrence Wilkerson, the secretary's chief of staff, even wanted Powell to threaten to resign as a way of influencing major policy decisions, but he knew that his ever-loyal and practical boss "wasn't prepared to do that."[108]

Despite Cheney's and Rumsfeld's frequent opposition, Powell had, on important occasions, demonstrated his ability to influence the president's decision making. During the U.S.-China aircraft incident, Bush had sided with the secretary of state, agreeing that diplomatic compromise and not retributive action was the best way to safeguard American service personnel and prevent the major-power crisis from escalating. The president had also embraced the U.N. Global Fund to combat the HIV/AIDS pandemic, and he showed a willingness, if halting and ultimately inconsequential, to side with Powell on the subject of U.S. engagement in the Middle East and with North Korea. The supreme test of Powell's influence on presidential decision making, however, was in determining how best to respond to the 9/11 terrorist attacks.

When two airplanes struck the World Trade Center on the morning of September 11, Powell was at breakfast with the Peruvian president and his cabinet in Lima. The secretary had arrived the night before to attend a Special Assembly of the Organization of American States, which was scheduled to adopt the Inter-American Democratic Charter. During breakfast, Powell's executive assistant alerted him to the attacks on New York City. Peru's prime minister inquired, "Who's behind it?" The U.S. secretary of state did not hesitate in answering, "Osama bin Laden."[109]

Powell and the other principals of the NSC were familiar with bin Laden and al Qaeda. In January 2001 Richard A. Clarke, the NSC's lead expert on counterterrorism, had briefed Cheney, Rice, and Powell on the severity of the threat and proposed an offensive campaign against the terrorist network. Clarke was especially impressed with Powell because the secretary "took the unusual step" of asking for a special meeting with the Counterterrorism Security Group, which included senior counterterrorism specialists from the NSC, FBI, CIA, and Defense and State Departments.[110] In that meeting, the terrorism experts delivered a unified and unambiguous message to the incoming secretary of state: al Qaeda presented a serious danger to American interests, and it was enjoying "a safe haven" in Afghanistan.[111] According to Clarke, Powell was engrossed, asking many questions and taking copious notes.

In late March 2001, Powell assigned Armitage to oversee this portion of the State Department's portfolio. During the spring and summer, Armitage and deputies from other departments and agencies crafted a strategy "for eliminating the threat provided by al Qaeda."[112] Meanwhile, the State Department began to pressure Pakistan to "cut its losses" with the Taliban in Afghanistan.[113]

On September 11, as Powell's plane was being prepped for an expedited return to Washington, the secretary was chauffeured to the Organization of American States convention. On the way he telephoned Armitage, who informed him of a third plane attack, this one against the Pentagon. Powell remained at the convention long enough to cast America's vote in support of the new democratic charter and to express a few words to the thirty-four ministers in attendance.[114] His message was a call for international unity against terrorists. "A terrible, terrible tragedy has befallen my nation, but it has befallen . . . all those who believe in democracy," Powell said. "Terrorism . . . is everyone's problem. . . . It is something we must all unite [against]."[115]

During the eight-hour flight home, Powell had technical difficulties in communicating with Washington. For most of the flight he contemplated the consequences of the attacks. If he was right about bin Laden, then that probably meant war in Afghanistan. And, if there was to be war, the State Department would be responsible for assembling a reliable allied coalition reminiscent of Desert Storm. When Powell's plane finally reached the nation's capital, the 9/11 sun was setting as smoke rose from the Pentagon. The secretary raced to the State Department for an expedited briefing and then sped to the White House, where the president was about to address the nation.

Six decades after the Japanese surprise attack on Pearl Harbor and Franklin Roosevelt's Infamy Speech, Bush delivered a comparably brief and potent address to a shocked and grieving country. Although the television broadcast lasted less than ten minutes, it contained a central element of a bold new national security policy, later dubbed the Bush Doctrine, which aimed to punish not only the terrorists responsible for the day's deadly attacks, but also all nations that had lent them support. "We will make no distinction," the president declared, "between the terrorists who committed these acts and those who harbored them."[116] That precise language, seeking maximum global "impact," had been cleared by Powell, Cheney, Rumsfeld, and Rice.[117]

Later that night, in the bunker beneath the White House, the president convened his senior advisers, including CIA Director George Tenet, to discuss how to respond to the attacks. Bush reiterated his determination to punish the 9/11 "perpetrators" and all those who harbor terrorists.[118] The latter suggested the targeting of any nation that supported any terrorists, a policy even broader than the one he had broadcast on television. The CIA believed that Osama bin Laden was responsible. When Tenet informed Bush that al Qaeda operated in sixty nations around the world, the president snapped, "Let's pick them off one at a time."[119] Cheney worried that Afghanistan, a remote and underdeveloped country, did not offer many easy or meaningful targets for punitive bombing. Rumsfeld cautioned that the Pentagon was not yet prepared for a major military retaliation and added that there were many countries besides Afghanistan that embraced terrorists.[120] "We must think broadly," the defense secretary said. But Powell disagreed.[121]

The secretary of state argued for a focus on al Qaeda in Afghanistan, and he emphasized America's unique opportunity to build a global coalition for combating international terrorism.[122] Powell told the president that pressure must be applied to the Taliban government in Afghanistan and its chief supporter, Pakistan. "It was clear that we could start pulling a coalition together," the secretary said, "[and] as you looked at where this [the 9/11 attack] probably came from—al Qaeda, Osama bin Laden and Afghanistan—it immediately meant that Pakistan was going to play a key role, as well as Afghanistan."[123] Powell declared, "This is showtime" for Kabul and Islamabad.[124]

Bush reconvened his principal advisers the next morning. By then, the CIA and the FBI were convinced that bin Laden and al Qaeda, not Iraq or Iran, were behind the 9/11 attacks.[125] Powell assured the president that the State Department would deliver a list of hard-hitting demands to the Taliban and Pakistan to motivate their cooperation. Rumsfeld and Cheney, as they had done the night before, questioned the practicality and benefits of an American reprisal that concentrated solely on terrorists based in Afghanistan. "Do we focus on bin Laden and al Qaeda," Rumsfeld asked, "or terrorism more broadly?"[126] For Cheney, an expansive definition of U.S. policy objectives, one targeting various governments that aided terrorism, was preferable because "then we get at states. And it's easier to find them than it is to find bin Laden."[127] But Powell thought that the group directly responsible for the hijackings and suicide attacks should be the president's priority. He was advising adherence to the Weinberger-Powell Doctrine: political and military objectives should be unambiguous. "The goal is terrorism in its broadest sense," Powell admitted, but what made the most sense regarding immediate military action was "focusing first on the organization that acted yesterday."[128]

The president, who suspected that Saddam Hussein was somehow involved in 9/11 and had tasked the NSC's Clarke to investigate the connection, agreed with Powell.[129] Clarke was relieved. He did not believe there was a nexus between Iraq and 9/11, and he told Powell, "Having been attacked by al Qaeda, for us now to go bombing Iraq in response would be like our invading Mexico after the Japanese attacked us at Pearl Harbor."[130] The secretary concurred, but he warned Clarke that attempts by the administration's hawks to implicate Saddam Hussein were "not over yet."[131] Bush instructed his senior advisers, "Start with bin Laden, which Americans expect. And then if we succeed, we've struck a huge blow and can move forward. . . . We don't want to define [it] too broadly for the average man to understand."[132] When Bush met with reporters and congressional leaders that same morning, he characterized the assault on the United States as an act of war and pledged to "rally the world" in the "monumental struggle between good and evil."[133]

Because Pakistan was a major benefactor of the Taliban, the president instructed Powell, "Do what you have to do" to bring Islamabad into the fold.[134] Coincidentally, Pakistan's director of intelligence, Mahmood Ahmed, was visiting CIA headquarters. Armitage arranged a confidential meeting with Mahmood and Pakistani Ambassador Maleeha Lodhi. According to Tenet, Armitage "dropped the hammer on them," declaring that America's new "You're with us or against us" foreign policy should cause "deep introspection for Pakistan."[135] Armitage arranged a second meeting for the next day at which he would share more details on the president's fast-developing response and its implications for Pakistan. "We're talking about the future," the deputy secretary emphasized, "and for you and for us history starts today."[136]

At a gathering of the NSC, the president and his advisers agreed that the international coalition against terrorism must be dynamic, one of "variable geometry."[137] Rumsfeld called it a coalition of coalitions, with different countries playing different roles at different points in time. The defense secretary and Cheney argued yet again for a broadening the military mission beyond al Qaeda, to target other nation-states that sponsored terrorism.[138] Rumsfeld asked directly, "Why shouldn't we go against Iraq, not just al Qaeda?"[139] Powell objected, as he had done earlier that morning. So did General Hugh Shelton, the chairman of the Joint Chiefs of Staff, who was soon to retire.[140] "What the hell, what are these guys thinking about?" Powell later asked Shelton. "Can't you get these guys back in the box?"[141]

At the NSC meeting, Powell emphasized another tenet of the Weinberger-Powell Doctrine, the importance of domestic approval for a war against al Qaeda. "Any action needs public support," he told the president. "It's not just what the international coalition supports; it's what the American people want to support. The American people want us to do something about al Qaeda."[142] The president, who believed the pending war against terrorism would be "fought with many steps," sided with Powell again, saying that al Qaeda was the top priority and "the American people want a big bang."[143]

In the late morning of September 13, Armitage held his second meeting with Mahmood. The deputy secretary and Powell had drafted a list of demands to be communicated to General Pervez Musharraf, Pakistan's president. The demands included sealing the border with Afghanistan, granting the United States access to Pakistani military bases, eliminating domestic support of terrorists, and assisting in the destruction of al Qaeda, should the Taliban government continue to harbor it. Armitage delivered these nonnegotiable demands to Mahmood and informed him that Powell would telephone Musharraf within two hours. When Powell made the call, he addressed the Pakistani president "as one general to another" and stated that America needed "someone on our flank fighting with us." Moreover, he warned that "the American people would not understand if Pakistan was not in this fight with the United States."[144] Musharraf assented to the demands. Pakistan, in short order, had been turned from a Taliban supporter to an indispensable, if not completely effective or reliable, ally in the war on terrorism. Tenet believed that Musharraf's reversal was "the most important post-9/11 strategic development after the takedown of the Afghan sanctuary itself."[145]

Powell announced his diplomatic feat that afternoon at an NSC meeting. The president was delighted, telling Powell, "You got it all."[146] Bush then informed the group that he favored a CIA plan to expand covert paramilitary operations in Afghanistan and increase collaboration with indigenous rebels organized as the Northern Alliance. Earlier that morning, during the CIA's briefing, Tenet's chief counterterrorism officer, Cofer Black, predicted a quick and decisive victory in Afghanistan, telling Bush, "By the time we're through with these guys, they're going to have flies walking across their eyeballs."[147] The president said he wanted his advisers to meet at Camp David over the weekend to develop a comprehensive war strategy, one that should include a distinct role for Great Britain. "I want a plan—costs, time," he ordered. "I need options on the table. I want Afghan options by Camp David. I want decisions quick."[148]

On Friday morning, September 14, at a full meeting of the president's cabinet, Powell reemphasized that the brazen terrorist attacks against the homeland provided a special opportunity for the administration to build an effective and lasting international coalition. Both a global war against terrorism and the singular war against al Qaeda in Afghanistan would be less effective if attempted unilaterally. "This is not just an attack against America," Powell declared, "this is an attack against civilization and an attack against democracy."[149] The secretary provided an update on the State Department's extensive outreach during the week and promised that "we are engaging with the world. We want to make this a long standing coalition."[150] He joked, "I've been so multilateral the last few days, I've been seasick."[151] Still, while the president wanted America's reprisal to be buttressed by Powell's international coalition, he was willing "to go it alone" if need be.[152]

Later that day, as Bush's senior advisers prepared for the weekend strategy session at Camp David, the president toured Ground Zero in New York City. Climbing onto some rubble, he assured surrounding relief workers that "the people who knocked these buildings down will hear all of us soon!"[153]

The Camp David meeting featured formal presentations and free-flowing discussions, including renewed debate over the probity of focusing exclusively on Afghanistan. The day before, Congress had passed a joint resolution granting Bush broad military power to punish the terrorists associated with 9/11 and all nations, organizations, and individuals who "aided" or "harbored" them.[154] Powell began the meeting with an update on his efforts to build a coalition, which centered on NATO members and featured Pakistan's support and Russia's influence with former Soviet republics in Central Asia. Bush thought Powell's diplomacy had been "impressive," especially the turning of Pakistan.[155] Tenet gave an in-depth presentation on how the CIA could effectively lead the war against al Qaeda's network and destroy the Taliban government. His integrated plan meshed CIA operations with military air and sea power, commando teams, and indigenous anti–al Qaeda and anti-Taliban groups in northern and southern Afghanistan. Bush considered the CIA presentation a model of strategic and operational thinking.[156]

After Tenet's briefing, Rumsfeld turned to his deputy, Paul Wolfowitz, who renewed the case for targeting Iraq, even if there was only a "10 percent" chance that Saddam Hussein was involved in 9/11.[157] "Dealing with Iraq," Rumsfeld said, "would show a major commitment to antiterrorism."[158] Knowing Bush's priority, Cheney remained largely silent, although in recent days he had clearly supported a broadening of military targets. Unsurprisingly, Powell objected to the Rumsfeld-Wolfowitz line. He argued that expanding military action beyond Afghanistan would jeopardize international goodwill and the coalition that the administration was building. Powell warned Bush, "You're going to hear from your coalition partners. They're all with you, everyone, but they will go away if you hit Iraq."[159] Powell explained that he did not see any justification for bombing Iraq as there was no evidence of its role in the terrorist attacks against the United States. "There was an obvious choice to be made," the secretary said. "We could go after the known perpetrators" or go after Saddam Hussein.[160] Powell concluded that if new evidence emerged later, he would support military action against the Iraqis. "If you get something pinning September 11 on Iraq, great," he told the president. "Let's put it out and kick them at the right time. But let's get Afghanistan now. If we do that, we will have increased our ability to go after Iraq—if we can prove Iraq had a role."[161]

During a break, Bush engaged General Shelton in a private conversation about Iraq. Supportive of Powell's position, the chairman advised the president to concentrate on al Qaeda because there was no evidence linking Iraq to 9/11 and because U.S. aggression against Iraq "will destroy us in the eyes of the Arab world."[162] Shelton would later write, "Both Colin and I had reiterated that there was *not one shred of evidence that Iraq was involved in the 9/11 attacks.*"[163] Bush viewed Afghanistan as the priority; however, he also informed Shelton, "We're going to get that guy [Saddam Hussein], but we're going to get him at a time and place of our own choosing."[164] The president later instructed Rumsfeld to quietly update plans for a possible war against Iraq.[165]

When the war council regrouped, Bush asked Shelton for the military's plans for attacking al Qaeda and the Taliban in Afghanistan. The general laid out preliminary options, ranging from cruise missile and aircraft strikes to the deployment of ground forces. Wolfowitz interrupted Shelton's presentation. "But we really need to think broader than that right now; that's not big enough," he said. "We've got to make sure we go ahead and get Saddam out at the same time—it's a perfect opportunity."[166] Powell and Shelton exchanged disgusted glances. According to Shelton, Bush became "irate" and scolded Wolfowitz: "How many times do I have to tell you we are *not* going after Iraq right this minute, we're going after the people we know did this to us. Do you understand me?"[167]

After an extended lunch break, the Bush war council reconvened. The president asked for personal recommendations. Powell led off. He argued for immediate military action against al Qaeda. He wanted the administration to present evidence to the public that connected Osama bin Laden to the September 11 attacks. The secretary advised Bush to give the Taliban an ultimatum: surrender al Qaeda within forty-eight hours or subject itself to direct attack by the American-led coalition. He also recommended that the administration manage news coverage of the fighting to moderate swings in public opinion and suggested that Saudi Arabia could play an important role in negotiating a settlement with the Taliban once al Qaeda had been defeated. Powell reiterated his position that if evidence later linked Iraq or any other nation, such as Iran or Syria, to the 9/11 attacks, that the administration should retaliate at that time. "If we weren't going after Iraq before September 11," he asked matter-of-factly, "why would we be going after them now when the current outrage is not directed at Iraq. . . . Keep the Iraq options open if you get the linkages," he advised, but added, "[I] doubt you'll get the linkages."[168]

Bush's other senior advisers responded in turn. Rumsfeld avoided any specific recommendations, though he reemphasized the need for improved target selections in Afghanistan. In response to Powell's concern about the fragility of the nascent international coalition, the defense secretary spoke dismissively. If Powell's coalition was not willing to go after Saddam Hussein, then perhaps "it is not a coalition worth having."[169] Wolfowitz, having been chided by the president, remained silent. Tenet largely agreed with Powell's focus on Afghanistan. "Meet at least the al Qaeda target. Take out the majority of Taliban military structure," he said.[170] Rice concurred, though she did not say so until after the meeting. The president's chief of staff, Andrew Card, argued for a massive buildup of American forces in the Persian Gulf and for multiple small commando raids "around the world," but he did not believe that an effective case had been made against Iraq.[171] Cheney supported the CIA war plan for Afghanistan. He agreed with Powell that the September 11 attacks had created a unique opportunity for the United States to rally a new coalition of allies in the Middle East. Launching a precipitous war against Iraq, he said, would squander the opportunity and jeopardize "our rightful place as good guy."[172]

The president concluded the Camp David meeting by restating his views on al Qaeda and Iraq. "Everybody will understand us going after the perpetrators," he said. "Iraq will be there."[173] On that parting note, Bush informed everybody that he would take some time to consider his options in Afghanistan. Powell was impressed with the president's deliberative process, recounting how "he very wisely went off, reflected on it, thought about it."[174]

The next day, the vice president appeared on *Meet the Press*. He told Tim Russert that "at this stage," the president's "focus" was on al Qaeda because there was no evidence connecting Iraq to 9/11. "Saddam Hussein's bottled up, at this point," he said.[175] Powell had won the day. The crisis of 9/11, the *Guardian* soon reported, "has seen Powell, in his deceptively quiet way, gain ascendancy over his many rivals" within the administration.[176]

By Monday morning, September 17, Bush had shifted from deliberation to determination and launched a war against al Qaeda in Afghanistan. According to Powell, "he came down, called us into the Cabinet Room in the White House, gave us his decision and started barking instructions."[177] Much to the secretary's relief, Iraq was relegated to the back burner. The president presumed Saddam Hussein's involvement in 9/11 and had ordered the CIA to continue searching for links, but he was still reluctant to act against Baghdad. "I believe Iraq was involved," he told the NSC, "but I'm not going to strike them now. I don't have the evidence at this point."[178] Instead, the CIA's covert war plan for Afghanistan was operationalized, and the Pentagon finalized a battle campaign that featured "missiles, bombers, and boots on the ground." Bush wanted to "rain holy hell" on the terrorists.[179]

The president instructed Powell to issue an ultimatum to the Taliban later that day. If the Afghan government did not turn over bin Laden and the al Qaeda terrorists, then the Taliban would also be targeted. Bush told his secretary of state to have the Taliban "quaking in their boots."[180] Powell requested and received extra time to draft the demand letter. He wanted to consider the timing for the ultimatum and its likely effects on U.S. allies, including Pakistan. A quasi declaration of war, he thought, should not be rushed.

In the end, the president delivered the message to the Taliban. On September 20, in a televised address to a joint session of Congress, Bush said, "The Taliban must act, and act immediately. They will hand over the terrorists or they will share their fate."[181] Four days later, in the White House Rose Garden, the president, Powell, and Treasury Secretary Paul O'Neill announced an executive order freezing the financial assets of twenty-seven suspected terrorist groups. With that action, Powell declared, "the campaign has begun. We're going after Al Qaeda, we're going after terrorism. And this is an indication of how we're going to use all the elements of our national and international power to do it."[182]

During the next three weeks, the State Department constructed an international alliance for war against al Qaeda in Afghanistan. Bush was willing to fight the war without allies, but he admitted to his war council that a truly successful global campaign against terrorists and their sponsors "requires a coalition, it can't be done without one."[183] Two of the more important contributor nations were Russia and Uzbekistan. Powell worked with his Russian counterpart by phone and dispatched Armitage to Moscow as part of a Washington delegation to ask for general assistance and to assure the Kremlin there was no intention of establishing permanent U.S. military bases in Central Asia. "We wanted to impress upon the Russians that we were deadly serious about the prosecution of the war against al Qaeda," Armitage recalled. "We wanted their help, and we wanted the benefits of their experience of their activities in Afghanistan."[184] On September 22 Bush spoke directly with President Vladimir Putin, who pledged not only to use his influence with former Soviet republics, but also to allow U.S. military aircraft to enter Russian airspace.[185]

Garnering the cooperation of Uzbekistan, which borders Afghanistan, proved vexing. The U.S. military needed temporary bases in Uzbekistan to effectively launch its operations, which included sending arms to the Northern Alliance and humanitarian aid to Afghan civilians. The diplomatic negotiations were protracted but ultimately successful. "After a period of discussion, they said yes to our first set of requests," Powell remembered. "Then there was a second and a third and a fourth set of requests. Each one required reassurance once again, and there was a little bit more of a commitment and a little bit more support to their efforts. But they came along."[186] In the end, more than sixty nations contributed either troops or aid to the U.S.-led campaign in Afghanistan.[187]

In this same period, Powell debated two policy positions with senior presidential advisers. Consistent with his own war doctrine, he sought mission clarity and public support. The first question was whether the administration should share with its allies and the public detailed evidence tying al Qaeda to 9/11. The second was whether the primary U.S. objective in Afghanistan was regime change—ousting the Taliban government—or only destroying al Qaeda. From the beginning, Powell had argued for a white paper detailing bin Laden and al Qaeda's role in the 9/11 attacks. He thought it critical to sustaining public and congressional support for war and for securing coalition partners. "There's a lot of evidence," Powell contended. "We've been asked by some of our closest allies for some of this information. . . . The allies expect it, it enhances our case and it's going to be to our benefit."[188]

Rumsfeld opposed the white paper, arguing that the U.S. government was not obligated to share classified evidence and that it was mistake to do so. "I think the precedent is bad," the defense secretary asserted, "of having to go out and make your case publicly, because we may not have enough information to make our case next time, and it may impair our ability to pre-empt against the threat that may be coming at us."[189] This issue became pointless on October 4, when British Prime Minister Tony Blair took up Powell's reasoning and released to the public a sixteen-page report linking al Qaeda to 9/11. Blair then went before Parliament to make the case for war.[190]

Regarding regime change in Afghanistan, Powell had asserted frequently that destroying al Qaeda, but not necessarily the Taliban government, should be the prime object of U.S. policy. The overthrow of the Taliban could spark a protracted civil war, he thought, which could in turn destabilize Pakistan, a nuclear power. If, however, the Taliban obstructed the American mission in Afghanistan, then Powell supported all-out attacks against its military. "It is not the goal at the outset to change the regime," the secretary contended, "but to get the regime to do the right thing."[191] From the beginning, however, Tenet favored a simultaneous war against the 9/11 terrorists and their Afghan hosts. "We need to go after the Taliban leadership," he argued, "and then go after the Taliban more generally."[192]

Rumsfeld agreed with the CIA and argued that unlike al Qaeda, the Taliban's military offered easy targets for the United States. "We have to have something to hit," he proffered. "There is not a lot of al Qaeda to hit."[193] On September 24 Powell advised the president, "We want Afghanistan to be terrorist-free. If the Taliban can do that, fine. If not, we will work with someone else as long as they make it terrorist-free. Our rhetoric should avoid suggesting we are trying to determine who runs Afghanistan at the end of the day."[194] Cheney sympathized with Powell's approach, hoping that the Taliban would break from al Qaeda, but by early October he shifted toward Tenet and Rumsfeld's position. "In the short term it would be useful," the vice president concluded, "to obscure on the future of the Taliban to exploit fissures in the Taliban. But the long term—we need the Taliban to be gone."[195]

On September 27 the CIA successfully deployed the first of seven teams of covert operatives into Afghanistan.[196] The Taliban was not cooperating. According to Armitage, "It was looking more and more as each day went on that the Taliban would not be throwing out al Qaeda, and hence evading prosecution. . . . It became very clear that we were talking about a Taliban-less Afghanistan. That was understood and accepted."[197] That realization led to last-minute planning for Afghanistan's postwar reconstruction. Bush assigned that responsibility to Powell and the State Department. The president had only recently decided that "helping a democratic government emerge" in Afghanistan was an important policy objective.[198] One of the reasons Powell had been against the hasty destruction of the Taliban was his recognition that someone had to assume responsibility for the postwar environment. Without the Taliban, the United States and its allies would be forced into a major reconstruction role.

On October 7 Bush announced to the world that the U.S. Navy and Air Force had begun bombing al Qaeda and Taliban targets in Afghanistan. The Taliban, he said, "will pay a price" for not surrendering the 9/11 terrorists. The president assured American military personnel that the "mission is defined; your objectives are clear; your goal is just . . . and you will have every tool you need to carry out your duty."[199]

During the first week of the war, there was considerable discussion within the NSC about the responsibility for governing post-conflict Afghanistan, and the question often pivoted on the Taliban-controlled capital city, Kabul. Powell asked, "Do we want to take it? Do we want to hold it? If we want to hold it, what are we going to do with it?" When the president suggested that the United Nations should take over Kabul, Powell seconded the idea immediately. "Yeah, the U.N. is the best way to handle it," he said with some relief. "Have a U.N. mandate plus third country forces ruling Kabul."[200] The idea of having the United Nations govern Kabul had widespread support with senior members of the administration; nobody wanted a protracted U.S. military presence in Central Asia. On October 12, the president told his advisers, "I oppose using the military for nation building. Once the job is done, our forces are not peacekeepers. We ought to put in place a U.N. protection and leave."[201] Powell began pressuring Annan.[202] He also told reporters, "Clearly the United Nations, it seems to me, will be playing a leading role . . . with respect to the new political regime" in Afghanistan.[203] Bush then instructed his cabinet to focus less attention on the postwar aspects of the conflict and more on winning the war itself.

During October, despite relentless U.S. bombardment, allied Afghan opposition forces were hesitant to attack urban enclaves, thus leaving al Qaeda and the Taliban in control of most of the country. Moreover, there were delays in inserting U.S. ground forces. On October 10 Rumsfeld chided his own commanders for not being more "thoughtful, creative, or actionable."[204] He reminded the chairman of the Joint Chiefs of Staff that Powell's State Department had effectively organized a large multinational coalition, while the Defense Department "has come up with a goose egg."[205]

The lack of progress on the ground also led to a sharp debate between the CIA and the Pentagon over which organization owned the war's leadership. In a NSC meeting on October 16, Rumsfeld, already frustrated because of delays in getting Special Forces on the ground to coordinate with Afghan allies, blamed the CIA for not communicating better targeting information. The defense secretary told Bush, "This is the CIA's strategy. They developed the strategy. We're just executing the strategy."[206] The CIA's deputy director, John McLaughlin, countered by saying that the CIA was merely supporting General Tommy Franks, commander of CENTCOM, which was overseeing military operations in Afghanistan. "No," Rumsfeld said, "you guys are in charge."[207]

For Powell's senior deputy, the lack of leadership and accountability was ridiculous. "I'm hearing FUBAR [fucked up beyond all recognition]," Armitage blurted out. When asked by the president to explain, the deputy secretary said, "I don't know who's in charge. . . . I want to know who's in charge out there. It's about who's taking responsibility on the ground over there."[208] A noticeably piqued Bush ordered Rice to establish a clear chain of command. Rumsfeld was eventually put in control.

Without visible territorial gains, politicians and pundits in Washington began criticizing the Bush war plan, even suggesting that the United States was embarking on a Vietnam-like quagmire.[209] Powell himself was concerned that the military strategy lacked crystalline objectives. The continuous aerial bombardment began to feel like bombing for the sake of bombing. Although his official portfolio was diplomacy, not defense, Powell began calling for concentration on the strategic northern city of Mazar-e Sharif, which was close to the Uzbekistan border. "We ought to try and consolidate the north and east before winter," he argued. "Seize Mazar-e Sharif, control the border and the valleys."[210] Like the president, Powell wanted to avoid a large deployment of American ground forces, declaring that "I'd ruled out the United States going after the Afghans, who have been there 5,000 years."[211] Instead, he advocated for extensive military support and training of the Northern Alliance rebels during the fast-approaching winter season. On November 2, at a meeting of the NSC, Powell asked pointedly, "What's the capability of the [allied] opposition forces? Do we need to train them?"[212] He was dismayed by General Franks's response: "I don't place any confidence in the opposition."[213] During the next week, as the stalemate on the ground persisted and al Qaeda and the

Taliban retained power, there was little optimism in Washington. "Yes, there was a great deal of nail-biting," Powell later admitted.[214]

On the morning of November 9, the CIA expressed some faith that Afghan rebels with U.S. support might overtake Mazar-e Sharif, but there were few believers on the NSC.[215] Nevertheless, on the next day, the Northern Alliance, backed by the CIA, U.S. airpower, and Special Forces, seized Mazar-e Sharif. It proved the tipping point. By November 14, thousands of al Qaeda and Taliban forces had abandoned the capital city of Kabul. In less than a week, the Northern Alliance had taken control of nearly half of Afghanistan.[216] On December 7 Kandahar, the last major Taliban stronghold, fell to the Northern Alliance and its Pashtun allies. From there, the U.S. forces, which had never exceed four thousand "boots on the ground," and Afghan allies pursued fleeing Taliban and al Qaeda militants into the mountains at Tora Bora, near the Khyber Pass leading to Pakistan. By December 17 the Taliban and the terrorists had been overrun, with more than eight thousand killed in battle. Even though bin Laden had escaped into Pakistan, talk of a Vietnam-like quagmire in Afghanistan vanished.[217]

With the major combat offensive ending, Powell and his team scrambled with the United Nations to lay a foundation for a new Afghan government. He appointed James F. Dobbins, a veteran diplomat and an expert on postwar stabilization and reconstruction, to lead the U.S. mission. Beginning in November 2002, Germany hosted an U.N.-sponsored conference of Afghans, including leaders of the Northern Alliance, to chart a path for the creation of a new sovereign government. Those meetings concluded in December with the so-called Bonn Agreement, which established Hamid Karzai, a Pashtun tribal and military leader, as chairman of the Afghan Interim Authority, and chartered a process for the creation of an entirely new government.[218] "For all its imperfections . . . ," Kofi Annan wrote, "the agreement was a remarkable achievement in such a short span of time."[219] The next month, representatives of dozens of nations gathered in Japan and pledged a combined $4.5 billion toward Afghan reconstruction. Thereafter, NATO agreed to assume command of an U.N.-authorized international security force.

The Bush administration had made substantial progress toward its military and political objectives: debilitating al Qaeda, ousting the Taliban, and promoting a new democratic and antiterrorist Afghan government.[220] But the war in Afghanistan had created a nettlesome problem: what to do with captured al Qaeda and Taliban fighters?

In November 2001, unbeknownst to Powell, Rice, and the chairman of the Joint Chiefs of Staff, Cheney had circumvented an interagency group working on the issue.[221] He secretly collaborated with the Justice Department to draft a new presidential directive that authorized Bush to confine, indefinitely, "unlawful enemy combatants," who, if formally charged with crimes, would be tried by a U.S. military commission.[222] On November 13 Bush signed the order and appointed the secretary of defense as the "detention authority."[223] Cheney's top lawyer, David Addington, who had drafted the directive, thought much like his boss: "Fuck the interagency process."[224]

Powell and Rice were blindsided by the decision. The secretary learned about the order while watching CNN and was left asking, "What the hell just happened?"[225] Rice threatened to resign if "cut out of the process" again. Bush apologized.[226] In his memoirs Rumsfeld admitted, "There are things the administration could have done differently and better with respect to wartime detention. As the administration grappled with these difficult decisions, there were remarkably few interagency meetings devoted to detainee policy."[227] Years later, the Supreme Court ruled aspects of the presidential order unlawful for disregarding constitutional due process.[228]

During the military campaign in Afghanistan, thousands of captured enemy fighters had been placed in battlefield prison camps. By early January 2002, the administration had decided to transfer hundreds of prisoners to the U.S. Navy base at

Guantanamo Bay, Cuba. Avoiding American soil held the promise of evading constitutional protections for the detainees. The question remained whether the prisoners would be afforded international legal protections under the Geneva Conventions.

Powell was traveling in Asia when he learned from William H. Taft IV, his chief legal adviser at the State Department, that the president had decided that neither the al Qaeda terrorists nor the Taliban fighters were entitled to prisoner-of-war status under the Geneva Conventions. Rumsfeld had already relayed that judgment to U.S. armed forces, and on January 12 he told reporters that these "unlawful combatants do not have any rights under the Geneva Convention."[229] Distressed, Powell telephoned Rice at the White House. He warned her to "hold on" because "we're making some mistakes here."[230] According to Rice, Powell was "particularly worried" about not granting Taliban fighters legal rights because Afghanistan had been a signatory to the Geneva Conventions.[231]

The president's decision, encouraged by Cheney, rested on a forty-two-page opinion drafted by John Yoo, a deputy assistant attorney general at the Justice Department. Yoo contended that because Afghanistan was a "failed state" and al Qaeda was a stateless organization, none of the detainees warranted Geneva protections. They were not prisoners of war, Yoo argued, but rather unlawful combatants.[232] Taft, who thought it highly suspicious that these decisions were being made while Powell was traveling abroad, quickly drafted a detailed and biting rebuttal to Yoo. "Both the most important factual assumptions on which your draft is based and its legal analysis are," Taft wrote, "seriously flawed."[233] As a consequence, Taft wrote he could not advise the secretary of state nor the president to circumvent America's obligations under the Geneva Conventions.[234] Years later, in 2006, the Supreme Court voted 5 to 3 to repudiate the presidential order establishing military commissions. The court ruled that Common Article 3 of the Geneva Conventions, which requires humane treatment and judicial guarantees for captured combatants, applied to a terrorist group such as al Qaeda.[235]

When Powell returned to Washington, he asked to see the president. They met in the Oval Office on January 21. Powell made an impassioned plea for giving all detainees, al Qaeda and Taliban, some coverage under Geneva. Accordingly, all prisoners should receive due process: a review of their status to determine whether they qualified as prisoners of war. Not to do so, the secretary argued, put American service personnel in jeopardy. Powell reminded Bush that giving the detainees Geneva consideration did not automatically grant them POW status, nor did it preclude them from being jailed, interrogated, and tried. Bush disagreed, but he promised to discuss the matter at the next meeting of the NSC.[236]

Before the NSC met, somebody in the administration leaked a related draft memorandum to the *Washington Times*. The memo to Bush was technically from White House Counsel Alberto Gonzales, although it had been written by his deputy and Cheney's senior attorney. The newspaper article and the memo not only depicted Powell as kowtowing to liberals regarding Geneva, it also misrepresented his and the State Department's position. As a result, the *Times* headline read, "Powell Wants Detainees to Be Declared POWs."[237] This was inaccurate. Powell actually wanted the president to state that Geneva applied to the war in Afghanistan *and* that under the conventions al Qaeda and Taliban detainees probably did *not* warrant POW status. In other words, it was unnecessary to completely disregard the Geneva Conventions. Powell was furious with the blatant misrepresentation.[238] His view was soon clarified in the *New York Times*, which reported, "The position of the State Department is that the Geneva Conventions do apply . . . but that these people [al Qaeda and Taliban detainees] don't qualify under the Geneva Conventions to be prisoners of war."[239] The original leak to the *Washington Times*, the secretary later said, was a preemptive strike meant "to screw me" and "blow me out of the water" before the meeting.[240]

In preparation for the NSC meeting, Powell drafted a stark memorandum responding to the leaked document. He listed the major pros and cons of applying and not applying the Geneva Conventions. He also included an attachment that corrected "the most important factual errors" in the original Justice Department opinion, which he characterized as "inaccurate or incomplete." Powell wanted the president to have the clearest understanding of his options and their consequences. In restating his case for granting the detainees due process, Powell moved beyond the argument of safeguarding U.S. service personnel overseas and appealed for the preservation of "U.S. credibility and moral authority by taking the high ground," which "puts us in a better position to demand and receive international support."[241] In the memo, Powell made clear that he personally believed that al Qaeda terrorists "are not entitled to POW status" and that the Taliban fighters "could be determined not to be POWs." [242]

On February 2, Taft sent another memo to Gonzales. In it, he further argued that the application of Geneva, without automatically granting POW status to all fighters in Afghanistan, was "consistent with the plain language" of the conventions and the "unvaried practices" of the United States since 1949.[243] He also made clear that while lawyers at the State Department did not consider Afghanistan a failed state, they did agree with the Department of Justice that al Qaeda and the Taliban fighters "are presumptively not POWs."[244]

The NSC debated the issue on February 4, 2002. The new chairman of the Joint Chiefs of Staff, General Richard B. Myers, supported Powell. Together they argued that at a minimum the detainees should have hearings to determine whether they qualified for Geneva protections. They rejected the "failed state" argument concerning Afghanistan.[245] Myers contended that the issue at hand was not a legal matter, but a military and moral one. "Mr. President," the air force general stated, "you'll notice everybody's here with a lawyer. I don't have a lawyer with me; I don't think this is a legal issue."[246] Powell added, "We have an image to uphold around the world. If we don't do this, it will make it much more difficult for us to try and encourage other countries to treat people humanely."[247] In their opposition, Cheney and Attorney General John Ashcroft adhered to Yoo's opinion, arguing that the detainees were not lawful combatants because al Qaeda was stateless and Afghanistan was a failed state. Cheney warned the president, "we don't want to tie our hands. We need to preserve our flexibility."[248] The meeting ended without Bush stating his position.

Several days later, the president sided with Powell and Myers by rejecting the "failed state" argument regarding the Taliban. But, more consequentially, he aligned with Cheney and Ashcroft and refused to grant due process or POW status to any of the Afghan War captives, whether Taliban or al Qaeda. Instead, the president directed the U.S. military to treat detainees humanely and in the spirt of Geneva. But he also allowed the humane treatment to be suspended if found not "appropriate and consistent with military necessity."[249] Moreover, Bush's directive made no attempt to circumscribe the CIA's treatment of detainees.

In his account of the wars in Iraq and Afghanistan, Army Lieutenant General Daniel P. Bolger recounted that Bush's ambiguous order "left a lingering perception up and down the chain of command that maybe the normal rules for treatment of prisoners of war didn't apply. . . . Leaving the detention situation so loosely defined would come back to bite them [the Bush administration] in ways nobody foresaw in late 2001."[250] Indeed, a scathing bipartisan Senate Armed Services Committee investigation into detainee treatment later concluded, "Following the President's [February 7, 2002,] determination, techniques such as waterboarding, nudity, and stress positions used in SERE [Survival, Evasion, Resistance, and Escape] training to simulate tactics used by enemies that refuse to follow the Geneva Conventions, were authorized for use in interrogations of detainees in U.S. custody."[251]

★ ★ ★ ★

Although Powell did not agree with the president's decision on due process under the Geneva Conventions, he accepted it. The disagreement with Bush and Cheney had been but one more in a series of intense policy debates that marked Powell's tenure as secretary of state. Some debates he lost; others he won. "There were many instances when my colleagues lost the argument," the secretary later wrote, including Bush's support for diplomacy during the South China Sea crisis and the Powell-Zinni missions to the Middle East. In the "Geneva Convention debate," he recalled, "I recommended a different course than that which he [Bush] had decided upon. After a spirited debate, he compromised on our different points of view. His decision had the backing of his Attorney General, his intelligence and law enforcement officials and, I might add, the Congress and the American people." It was, according to Powell, just another "a policy dispute," and certainly not something worth resigning over. "If we all quit over policy disagreements," he wrote, "no one would be around."[252]

Powell's role in the Geneva episode reflected the nature of his followership under Bush. As secretary of state, he frequently took the initiative, engaged in serious critical thinking, and provided the president with thoughtful assessments, policy alternatives, and candid counsel—even when it ran contrary to Bush's own views. Powell also readily accepted that not all of his recommendations would be adopted. He believed, in short, that the best subordinates develop good independent ideas and demonstrate a willingness to "disagree strongly" with their superiors, but ultimately they fall in line with the boss's final decisions.[253]

The Bush administration's approach to the Geneva Conventions issue (and to Kyoto, North Korea, and the Middle East) also reflected the limited nature of Powell's relationship with the president and cabinet colleagues. It is telling—indeed, shocking—that the president, vice president, attorney general, and defense secretary all wittingly excluded the secretary of state, a former chairman of the Joint Chiefs of Staff no less, from the initial decision making on the prisoner-of-war status of the Afghan War captives.

By comparison, it is impossible to imagine George H. W. Bush bypassing Secretary of State James Baker during the first Bush administration. And Baker knew well that when "the Secretary of State and the President are not really close, it doesn't work for the Secretary of State, because everybody wants a piece of that foreign policy turf, everybody, and you need a President who is going to protect you and support you and defends you even when you are wrong, which is what Bush did for me."[254] Secretary Powell did not enjoy such a partnership George W. Bush. "In 43's administration," he later said, "we were not philosophically as close enough to each other. The differences were too severe." In contrast, Powell continued, "[George H. W.] Bush had unerring loyalty to all of us, and when I would get in trouble. . . . It would be Bush who would say, . . . Don't worry about that. That's nothing. . . . It meant a lot to me. It meant a lot to me to know that even if I had screwed up . . . I always had him in my corner."[255]

Nevertheless, one of Powell's most significant victories as secretary of state was his staunch opposition to an ill-considered attack on Iraq in the immediate aftermath of 9/11. Rumsfeld and Cheney had begun lobbying for the bombing of Iraq on the night of September 11, but Powell, supported by Chairman Shelton, persuaded the president otherwise. For the secretary, the focused war against al Qaeda and the Taliban, a war supported domestically and internationally, represented a proper retaliatory projection of American military power. The terrorist organization and its benefactor had presented a clear and present danger to national security. By comparison, the Iraqi threat was distant and complicated. The Bush administration's ongoing attempts to grapple with the problem of Iraq would plague Powell's last two years as secretary of state.

If we had known there were no WMDs, there would have been no war. . . .
I am mad mostly at myself for not having smelled the problem.

—COLIN POWELL

Adviser

(2002–2003)

Colin Powell proved himself a remarkably effective leader of the State Department and also a loyal, skillful, and independent-minded follower of the president. Beyond his transformational leadership at State, the secretary had served Bush exceptionally well on multiple occasions, especially after 9/11 when he successfully blocked Rumsfeld, Cheney, and Wolfowitz's campaign for a precipitous attack on Iraq. A year later, however, after the allied coalition's rout of al Qaeda and the Taliban in Afghanistan, the Bush administration's civilian war hawks renewed their drive to overthrow the Iraqi regime. For Powell, confronting this second offensive and the president's own inclination to oust Saddam Hussein presented the ultimate test of his capabilities as a senior subordinate.

In the ramp-up to war with Iraq, Powell won some hard-fought policy battles, including his determination to secure a new U.N. resolution against Iraq and reinsert weapons inspectors, and to get congressional authorization for the use of military force if necessary. By the time of the U.S. invasion, shortly after Powell's historic February 2003 presentation at the United Nations, the secretary of state was at the apex of his power within the Bush administration. Not long thereafter, in the absence of Iraqi WMD, it became increasingly evident that Powell, and other senior advisers, had gravely failed the president and country by not detecting perhaps the most disastrous intelligence failure in American history. "It was," Powell later confided in personal emails, "a collective disaster" and "a total, catastrophic intel failure."[1] Bush, of course, bears the ultimate responsibility for taking the nation to war and for its calamitous consequences.

In late 2001, with al Qaeda and the Taliban depleted and retreating toward Pakistan, Bush directed increased attention to Saddam Hussein and the threat of WMD proliferation. Iraq had long been on the administration's agenda. Before taking office, President-elect Bush and Vice President-elect Cheney had received a classified intelligence briefing titled "Iraq: Steadily Pursuing WMD Capabilities."[2] Ten months later, immediately after 9/11, the president ordered Richard Clarke, his chief counterterrorism adviser on the NSC, to investigate whether Iraq had sponsored the September attacks.[3] On September 26, 2001, the president ordered Rumsfeld to begin a secret review of war plans for an invasion of Iraq.[4] In late December, CENTCOM commander General Tommy Franks briefed Bush and his principal advisers on updated plans to force Saddam Hussein to relinquish his WMD. At that meeting the president said, "We should remain optimistic that diplomacy and international pressure will succeed in disarming the regime," but contingent war planning was absolutely necessary.[5]

In his January 2002 State of the Union, Bush identified Iraq, along with North Korea and Iran, as an "evil" nation with an active WMD program, and thus a threat to the United States. The president declared that he would "not stand by, as peril draws closer and closer."[6] "To be sure," CIA Director Tenet later wrote, "a number of people were fixated on Iraq, and a number of decisions and actions during the late fall of 2001 and into 2002 created a momentum all their own."[7]

Powell did not oppose contingent war planning for Iraq or even the final stark language in the president's "Axis of Evil" speech.[8] Like Bush, he believed that Saddam Hussein had stockpiled biological and chemical weapons and represented a serious international threat. In December 2001, Richard Armitage, not wanting the State Department to appear dovish on the issue, told the *New York Times*, "I don't think there is any question that an Iraq with weapons of mass destruction is a threat . . . and so we will do what we need to do to obviate that threat."[9] Armitage later admitted that he wanted to convey an overt message of "[Let's] get these fuckers."[10] Powell firmly supported the objective of disarming Iraq and the tactic of applying steady political and economic pressure to that end. Before 9/11, he had persuaded the president to reject "the crazy-ass idea" of a bold "enclave strategy," advocated by Cheney and the Pentagon's civilian leadership, in which the United States would recognize and support an opposition government in areas of Iraq not controlled by Baghdad.[11] That plan included seizing control of Iraq's southern oil fields. Instead, the secretary convinced Bush that continued containment through no-fly zones and the application of new U.N. "smart sanctions" against Saddam Hussein was the most appropriate policy.[12] The president assured Powell, "I'm in no hurry to go look for trouble."[13]

In other words, in early 2002, Powell and Bush did not yet view the Iraqi threat as imminent. The danger was clear, yes, but not fully present. From the secretary's perspective, the president was pursuing a pragmatic strategy of "coercive diplomacy," one that aimed to simultaneously rally international support against Saddam Hussein and pressure him to disarm.[14]

After 9/11, Powell encouraged Bush to consider multiple policy alternatives for solving the ongoing problem of Saddam Hussein. In early February 2002, the secretary reminded members of Congress that "regime change" had been the policy of the United States since 1998, and as a result, "The President is examining a full range of options of how to deal with Iraq." Ultimately, Powell said, the United States might have to act unilaterally, but that "doesn't mean an invasion is imminent."[15] Two weeks later, Powell assured reporters from the *Financial Times* that the administration's policy was to tighten sanctions on Iraq and support opposition groups, but, he also added, "if there is ever a point where we believe it's necessary to do something else, we'll do it."[16]

In June 2002, speaking at the U.S. Military Academy at West Point, Bush articulated a new national security policy of preventive warfare. The strategy went far beyond deterrence or containment. The president contended that in an era of global terrorism, the proliferation of WMD presented extraordinary risks that justified preventive action because "if we wait for threats to fully materialize we will have waited too long."[17] Bush told the cadets, "The gravest danger to freedom lies at the perilous crossroads of radicalism and technology. When the spread of chemical and biological and nuclear weapons, along with ballistic missile technology, when that occurs even weak states and small groups could attain a catastrophic power to strike great nations."[18] The Pentagon termed the strategy "anticipatory self-defense," which was codified as official U.S. policy in September.[19]

Soon after the West Point address, the CIA presented Bush with an opportunity to implement his threat-prevention policy. The agency had gathered intelligence that a Sunni extremist group, Ansar al-Islam, had established an encampment in the Kurdish-controlled mountains of northeastern Iraq. The camp was thought to harbor known terrorists, including Jordanian Abu Musab al-Zarqawi, and possibly a chemical weapons laboratory for the production of cyanide and ricin. The principals on Bush's national security team disagreed on whether to attack the suspected facility.[20]

Cheney, Rumsfeld, and Joint Chiefs chairman General Richard Myers all advised Bush to bomb the camp and then deploy Special Forces to search for evidence of a weapons lab. The military assessed the operation as "doable, but challenging."[21] Always hesitant to launch "surgical" air strikes, Powell counseled restraint and questioned the veracity of the intelligence. Moreover, he feared that a unilateral attack would undermine Bush's ongoing efforts to build international support against Iraq. Worse still, there was the possibility that an offensive attack could ignite a full-scale war. "This would be viewed as a unilateral start to the war in Iraq," the secretary advised.[22] Bush and Rice agreed with Powell; the risks were too high to take military action at this time. "There was a sense of urgency to do something about Iraq," Rice recounted, "but we wanted to get it right."[23]

Powell had again restrained the president, but by the end of July 2002, the secretary was growing increasingly worried that the administration was moving hastily toward a war footing. He and Armitage, a former Navy SEAL, were wary of hawkish political leaders who had never experienced combat. "You know the problem with some of the guys in this administration?" Armitage asked and then answered, "They ain't never smelt fucking cordite."[24] Earlier in the month, one of Powell's policy deputies, Richard Haass, had informed him about a troubling conversation with the national security adviser. Haass had expressed to Rice his apprehension that a war with Iraq would be inordinately problematic and would predominate U.S. policy. Rice's response was curt. She "brushed away" his concerns, snapping that "the president had made up his mind."[25]

By July 19, General Franks announced that he had successfully deployed two U.S. Army brigades into Kuwait. That same month, the British government detected "a perceptible shift in attitude" in Washington, DC.[26] Powell's counterpart, Foreign Secretary Jack Straw, told Prime Minister Tony Blair that it appeared Bush had decided on war with Iraq and there was minimal American support for working through the United Nations. Moreover, the British concluded that "intelligence and facts were being fixed" to support a war policy and that little thought was being given to a war's aftermath.[27]

Like the British, Powell feared the rush to war. In mid-July he confided to Ambassador Christopher Hill his "strong misgivings about a war" with Iraq as well as his "disgust at the war fever" in the administration.[28] Powell requested a private meeting with the president to discuss Iraq. "I have to do it alone," he told Rice, "without all the warlords in the room."[29]

On the evening of August 5, after Franks presented to the NSC an update of his "shock and awe" invasion plan of Iraq, Bush, Powell, and Rice convened for "a relaxing dinner" at the White House.[30] At that meeting, the secretary urged Bush to reconsider and clarify his objectives in Iraq. Powell shared with the president that he "was not comfortable with the political and diplomatic considerations relevant to a potential conflict with Iraq."[31] Did the president want to forcibly oust Hussein from power or just eradicate the dictator's WMD stockpiles? Powell asked point blank, "Is his elimination worth a war?"[32]

Powell also wanted Bush to comprehend the consequences of an invasion. If the president opted for war, he said, there was little doubt of a swift military victory. But the outcomes of the war would include the economic and political destabilization of Iraq and perhaps the broader Middle East. "It isn't getting to Baghdad," Powell cautioned. "It is what happens after you get to Baghdad. And it ain't going to be easy."[33] Causing instability in the region, Powell said, would undermine the administration's global war on terror and U.S. foreign policy more generally. The secretary warned Bush that a war "would probably suction all the air out of his presidency and that he needed to understand that when you take out a government, you become the government. If you break it [Iraq], you own it."[34] Powell continued, "When you hit this thing [Iraq], it's like crystal glass . . . it's going to shatter. There will be no government. There will be civil disorder. . . . You'll have twenty-five million Iraqis standing around looking at each other."[35] In later years, Powell would point to this August meeting as his personal attempt "to avoid . . . war."[36]

Among all his senior advisers, Bush knew that Powell was the most apprehensive about a war with Iraq. Still, the president was struck by the level of the secretary's distress that evening.[37] "Colin," the president later wrote, "was more passionate than I had seen him at any NSC meeting."[38] After Powell finished his presentation, Bush asked for recommendations: "What should I do? What else can I do?"[39] Powell was unequivocal in his response. The president, along with Great Britain, should take the case against Iraq to the United Nations. Doing so had numerous advantages. A multilateral diplomatic strategy was best, Powell reasoned, because Iraq was already in violation of multiple U.N. resolutions. When faced with renewed and united international pressure, Hussein would most likely capitulate and allow weapons inspectors back into the country. If the dictator gave up his WMD, there would be no war, but he would stay in power. "If not, and war becomes necessary," Powell advised, "you will be in a better position to solicit the help of other nations to form a coalition," which, he argued, was needed to prosecute a full-scale war and rebuild the country.[40]

The secretary was persuasive. Rice thought he had made "a terrific" two-hour case for both "making an aggressive approach" to Iraq via the United Nations and the costs of not doing so.[41] Bush judged Powell's recommendation as a smart "tactical" move in support of the administration's larger "strategic" vision for transforming Iraq and the Middle East.[42]

Powell's meeting with the president in August was an example of exemplary followership. Drawing upon his considerable national security experience, the secretary of state determined that Bush was rushing to war without adequately contemplating his policy objectives, the strategic options for achieving them, and their risky ramifications. "My goal in this period," Powell later said, "was to make sure that the president was taking into account all the consequences of military action."[43] As a mark of his integrity, Powell took the initiative to share his concerns with Bush and to provide a viable policy alternative that might achieve the president's goals without launching a costly and unpredictable war in the volatile Middle East.

At this same time, several prominent Republicans expressed their fears that the administration was imprudently marching toward war; indeed, one of Powell's senior deputies believed that Bush, Cheney, Rumsfeld, and Rice had already "crossed the political and psychological Rubicon."[44] The day prior to Powell's dinner with the president and Rice, Nebraska senator Chuck Hagel and former National Security Adviser Brent Scowcroft appeared on CBS's *Face the Nation*. Their questions and commentary on Iraq complemented the secretary's own thinking. Hagel launched into a series of thoughtful questions: "What's the urgency of the threat?" "Would we do this in a unilateral way with no allies?" "What comes after Saddam Hussein?" and "What would we hope to gain?" A Vietnam veteran with two Purple Hearts, Hagel stated, "We didn't ask any of these questions before we got into Vietnam. That's why this process is so important now."[45]

Scowcroft piled on, saying war with Iraq was not justified because there was no link between Saddam Hussein and al Qaeda. He recommended that the United Nations insist on new weapons inspections, and if Iraq refused, then at least "that gives you the *casus belli* that we don't really have right now." Scowcroft also warned that toppling Hussein's regime would cause "an explosion in the Middle East" and "could turn the whole region into a cauldron and thus destroy the war on terrorism."[46] Scowcroft's critique was highlighted in newspapers and on television news shows. Powell appreciated the external support.[47] The vice president did not. Cheney derided Scowcroft's cautious thinking as reflecting an antiquated "pre-9/11 mind-set."[48]

Soon thereafter, Scowcroft reiterated his views in the *Wall Street Journal*, and Hagel did the same on MSNBC. The senator told *Hardball* host Chris Matthews, "It's interesting to me that many of those who want to rush the country into war and think it would be so quick and easy don't know anything about war. They come at it from an intellectual perspective versus having sat in jungle or foxholes and watched their friends get their heads blown off. I try to speak for those ghosts of the past a little bit."[49] Hagel's and Scowcroft's pronouncements were followed by a *New York Times* opinion piece by former secretary of state James Baker.[50] For Baker, going to the United Nations for a new resolution and demanding the renewal of weapons inspections was simply the best policy. True, the United States could take unilateral action against Iraq, but he advised the president to "try our best not to have to go it alone" and to "reject the advice of those who counsel doing so."[51]

Powell took comfort in the chorus of his like-minded old friends. He telephoned Scowcroft to thank him for providing "me some running room."[52] The secretary later said that he had appreciated Scowcroft's "principled concern" and "always listened to him."[53] Cheney, on the other hand, rebelled against the external interference and Powell's plan to engage the United Nations.[54] Speaking before television cameras at a convention of the Veterans of Foreign Wars, the vice president dismissed the efficacy of the United Nations and painted an ominous picture of Iraq as a clear and present danger to all of civilization.[55] In a speech not vetted by the CIA, Cheney made unequivocal statements about Iraq's WMD stockpiles and Saddam Hussein's menacing intentions. "Simply stated, there is no doubt," he said, that Iraq already possessed WMD. "There is no doubt" that Hussein was "amassing them to use against our friends, against our allies and against us" and "many of us are convinced" that he would soon possess nuclear weapons. He then denigrated the value of U.N. weapons inspectors, saying it was "right to question any suggestion that we should just get inspectors back into Iraq and then our worries will be over. . . . A return of inspectors would provide no assurance whatsoever of his compliance with U.N. resolutions. On the contrary, there is a great danger that it would provide false comfort."[56]

Powell was furious with Cheney's public dismissal of the diplomatic strategy against Iraq. He immediately called Rice, complaining that the vice president was "undercutting the president before the president has tossed the pitch."[57] The speech also offended Tenet and White House Communications Director Karen Hughes. Tenet knew that Cheney's pronouncements on Iraq's WMD programs had not been verified. While the director later admitted that the CIA had provided Bush and Cheney with "overly assertive" briefs on Iraq's WMD, the vice president's speech had gone "well beyond what our analysis could support."[58] Hughes, a close friend of Bush's, worried that the president was "being steered down a path toward a dangerous confrontation."[59]

Bush and Rice had been angry about Scowcroft's public cautioning against a war, but now they were perturbed with Cheney for making war sound inevitable.[60] The president directed Rice to rein in Cheney; she failed. The vice president gave a comparable address two days later.[61]

Powell attempted damage control, especially with the British, and received Bush's personal assurance that he still supported a diplomatic initiative and weapons inspections.[62] In an interview with British journalist David Frost, Powell said that a strength of Bush's national security team was its willingness to engage in "full, open debate without pulling punches." He then underscored the need for weapons inspectors in Iraq because the inventory levels of chemical or biological weapons were "not known." Powell said that the president was exploring all options for Iraq and assured Frost that Bush would honor his pledge to "consult closely" with friends, allies, and the United Nations.[63]

The president was scheduled to deliver an address to the United Nations on September 12. Powell urged him to call for a new Security Council resolution against Iraq. During the week prior, there was contentious debate over the issue. Cheney and the civilian leadership at the Pentagon argued against a new resolution, positing, in part, that Bush already possessed the authority to attack Iraq because of its ongoing failure to comply with existing U.N. resolutions. "It's time to act," Cheney implored. "We can't delay for another year. . . . An inspection regime does not solve our problem."[64] Powell counterpunched, saying that none of the prior resolutions had authorized military force and that no country currently serving on the Security Council was advocating the use of force. Therefore, the secretary called for a new resolution that both demanded the reinstatement of weapons inspectors and stated the consequences if

Iraq refused. Such a policy, he argued, would enable to president to construct a larger allied coalition if war came.[65] According to Tenet, the president "pretty much let Powell and Cheney duke it out."[66]

Powell's recommendation was strengthened on September 7 when Prime Minister Blair met with Bush and Cheney for dinner at Camp David. The British government "prized" Powell for being a voice of restraint and multilateralism.[67] Foreign Minister Straw and the secretary had become friends and confidants, so much so that Powell could freely express his frustrations with "the Cheney-Rumsfeld-Wolfowitz group," whom he derided as those "fucking crazies."[68] Blair, who had publicly and unequivocally stated that Iraq possessed WMD, endorsed the secretary of state's position on Iraq, saying that a Security Council resolution was crucial to legitimizing a war and building a broad international coalition.[69] Bush agreed and reiterated his intention to call for a new resolution. He joked with Blair, "I suppose you can tell the story of how Tony flew in and pulled the crazed unilateralist back from the brink."[70]

Six days later, while addressing the U.N. General Assembly, Bush reviewed Iraq's history of thwarting the will of the world body and characterized Saddam Hussein's regime as "a grave and gathering danger." Consistent with his strategy of coercive diplomacy, he pledged to work with the Security Council in devising the necessary resolutions "to meet our common challenge." If Iraq did not comply, he stated, then "the world must move deliberately, decisively to hold Iraq to account."[71] Although the speech failed to elicit any applause from U.N delegates, Powell was satisfied. The president had followed his counsel and thus impeded Cheney and the Pentagon's civilian hawks.

During the next month, the secretary of state labored to craft a U.N. Security Council resolution against Iraq. To the dismay of other senior advisers, Powell also persuaded Bush to seek support from Congress. On the morning of September 4, the president met with congressional leaders to discuss the "serious threat" of Saddam Hussein. Bush stated that Iraq had to be disarmed and he hoped that Congress agreed. He also informed the lawmakers that he would try to rally the United Nations, but he was willing to act unilaterally if necessary. The House majority leader, Republican Dick Armey, expressed the most skepticism about a war, and his predictions echoed Powell's. "If you invade Iraq, you're going to win the war in two or three weeks and then," he warned, "you're going to own the place and you'll never get out of it. It'll be such a burden on your presidency."[72] Bush countered that the severity of the Iraqi threat was too grave to ignore. After the meeting, the president told reporters that "at the appropriate time" he would seek from Congress authorization to use all force "necessary to deal with the threat."[73] Subsequently, he flew Congressman Armey to Camp David and arranged for a secret intelligence briefing by Tenet.[74]

Bush enlisted Cheney, Rice, Rumsfeld, and Tenet to help win over Congress. Powell played only a limited role, as the president knew he possessed "the deepest reservations" about a war with Iraq.[75] Rice and Cheney appeared on the Sunday morning television shows to issue dire warnings of Iraq's attempts to acquire nuclear arms. "We don't want the smoking gun," Rice said, "to be a mushroom cloud."[76] On the one-year anniversary of 9/11, Tenet, Rumsfeld, and Cheney briefed nearly three dozen senators on Iraq's weapons programs. Afterward, Senator Max Cleland, a decorated Vietnam War veteran, noted, "It was pretty clear that Rumsfeld and Cheney are ready to go to war. They have already made the decision to go to war and to them that is the only option."[77]

In a pivotal meeting on September 24, 2002, Cheney held a one-on-one session with Majority Leader Armey to win his support for a congressional resolution against Iraq. The vice president reviewed Iraq's history of making and using chemical weapons and presented photographs and satellite imagery supposedly showing weapons laboratories and materials that could be used for making nuclear bombs. Cheney linked Iraq with al Qaeda and made the unsubstantiated claim that Hussein was close to developing a suitcase-size nuclear weapon. "Dick," he said, "how would you feel if you voted no on this [authorization to use force] and the Iraqis brought in a bomb and blew up half the people of San Francisco?"[78] The stark meeting converted the majority leader. Years later, an embittered Armey snapped, "I deserved better than to have been bullshitted by Dick Cheney."[79]

On September 26, Bush told a group of lawmakers that Iraq had definite connections to al Qaeda and possessed stockpiles of WMD. Moreover, he claimed, Saddam Hussein could launch a chemical or biological attack in "as little as 45 minutes" after his order and was building a nuclear bomb that could be deployable in twelve months.[80] The next day, Secretary Rumsfeld assured reporters that the administration had "bulletproof" evidence linking Iraq and al Qaeda.[81] Four days later, the CIA delivered to the Senate Select Committee on Intelligence a newly prepared National Intelligence Estimate: "Iraq's Continuing Programs for Weapons of Mass Destruction." The ninety-three-page report, especially its summary of "Key Judgments," corroborated, if erroneously, much of what the Bush administration was arguing.[82]

On October 10, the House, with Armey's backing, voted overwhelmingly, 296 to 133, to authorize the use of force to eliminate the Iraqi threat.[83] The Democratic-controlled Senate provided an even larger margin of support, with 77 in favor and only 23 against. Powell considered it "a handy majority."[84] By comparison, congressional authorization for the 1991 Persian Gulf War had passed with far less support.

With congressional approval secured, focus shifted to Powell and the drafting of a new U.N. Security Council resolution. The NSC principals disagreed on whether the resolution must detail the consequences should Iraq fail to comply with new demands. Cheney and Rumsfeld wanted a stark all-in-one resolution that authorized "all necessary means" to disarm Iraq if it did not abide by the terms.[85] For Powell, the most important objective was getting a new resolution passed.[86] Knowing that the Cheney-Rumsfeld approach would be "totally unsellable" to the Security Council, Powell agreed to submit a version of their explicit "all necessary means" draft. It was quickly and widely rejected.[87]

Powell then, in close cooperation with the British, French, Chinese, and Russian foreign ministers, engaged in weeks of intense negotiations to revise the draft to make it amenable to the entire Security Council.[88] The new document, which declared Iraq already in material breach of prior resolutions, did not explicitly authorize the use of military force against Iraq. Instead, it offered Hussein a "final opportunity to comply with disarmament obligations" or "face serious consequences."[89] Regardless of the exact language, the British foreign minister later wrote, "Everyone who had been involved in the negotiation knew what 'serious consequences' meant: military force. . . . That's why those words were in there."[90]

As the negotiations progressed, Powell embarked on a media blitz to sway council members and public opinion in favor of the resolution. He channeled the ominous language frequently utilized by Bush, Cheney, Rumsfeld, and Rice. On CNN, he told Larry King, "We do know that he has stocks of biological weapons, chemical weapons. We don't believe he has a nuclear weapon, but there's no doubt he has been working toward that end."[91] On the *Oprah Winfrey Show*, Powell said categorically, "They have chemical weapons; they have biological weapons; they're trying to acquire nuclear weapons," and thus the United States must threaten war and be prepared to wage war.[92] On October 30, while being interviewed on a national radio program, the secretary warned, "If the United Nations won't deal with it [the Iraqi threat], then the United States, with other likeminded nations, may have to deal with it. We would prefer not to go that route, but the danger is so great, with respect to Saddam Hussein having weapons of mass destruction, and perhaps even terrorists getting hold of such weapons, that it is time for the international community to act, and if it doesn't act, the President is prepared to act with like-minded nations."[93]

On November 8 the Security Council, including France, China, Russia, and Syria, unanimously passed the American and British–led resolution. "There was a genuine sense of achievement in the Council that day," wrote U.N. Secretary-General

Kofi Annan, "a belief that through tough negotiations, the member states had found a formula that would preserve the prerogative of the Council while making clear to the Iraqis that time was running out on their games and obfuscations."[94] Powell was immensely pleased with this diplomatic achievement. "It took me six weeks of intense negotiations," he later wrote, to design a solution "that gave Hussein a 'get out of jail card.'"[95] He telephoned Bush and said, "Hey, Boss. We got it done."[96] Rice considered the U.N. vote "a triumph for U.S. diplomacy . . . and for Colin Powell."[97] Bush recounted that he had worried about Powell's "negotiating strategy," but "in the end, we got a great resolution, and to Colin's credit."[98]

The passage of U.N. Security Council Resolution 1441 and Congress's authorization of force against Iraq signaled not only Powell's war doctrine, which prized political and public support for military engagements, but also his ability to influence the president's decisions despite opposition from other senior subordinates.

Bush and his secretary of state were pleased with the progress of their coercive diplomacy. Soon after the U.N. vote, the two met with reporters in the White House Rose Garden. The president lavished rare praise on the United Nations for taking a momentous and courageous stand. "If we are to avert war," the president said, all nations must further pressure Iraq into compliance. Coming on the heels of Congress's authorization of force, Bush declared that "The world has now come together to say that the outlaw regime in Iraq will not be permitted to build or possess chemical, biological or nuclear weapons." Credit for this remarkable accomplishment, the president proclaimed, belonged to Powell and the State Department. "I want to thank the Secretary of State Colin Powell," Bush said, "for his leadership, his good work and his determination over the past two months. He's worked tirelessly and successfully for a resolution that recognizes important concerns of our Security Council partners and makes Iraq's responsibilities clear. . . . Secretary of State Powell's team has done a fine job."[99] For Powell, wrote Karen

DeYoung in the *Washington Post*, the unanimous U.N. resolution had been "a long road to victory" and marked "his vindication as the leader of President Bush's foreign policy team."[100]

After the passage of Resolution 1441, Iraq proclaimed that it no longer possessed any WMD. Saddam Hussein allowed the reintroduction of weapons inspectors, and his government submitted to the United Nations some twelve thousand pages of documents for review. Iraq's denial of WMD disappointed Annan, who saw it as further evidence of Hussein's "intransigent modus operandi."[101] Upon hearing Iraq's seemingly preposterous claim about not possessing WMD, Cheney advised Bush to immediately and formally declare Iraq in material breach of 1441.[102] Powell, too, disbelieved Iraq's seemingly brazen claim, but he argued for more time.[103] To the secretary's relief, the president rejected Cheney's counsel. Bush had promised Hans Blix and Mohamed ElBaradei, the chief weapons inspectors, that he would support their efforts to secure hard evidence against Saddam Hussein. Moreover, the president knew that American armed forces would not be prepared for war for another two months.[104]

After six weeks of U.N. inspections, Powell observed his boss losing patience.[105] On January 9, 2003, Blix reported to the Security Council that Iraq was continuing to cooperate, but weapons inspectors had not discovered any "smoking guns."[106] The following day, Bush and Cheney met with several Iraqi dissidents, who told them that the Iraqi people would greet U.S. soldiers "with sweets and flowers."[107] Growing ever more doubtful that the inspectors would uncover Saddam's supposedly well-hidden WMD, Bush concluded that war was inevitable. He did not convene his NSC for deliberation. Powell privately contemplated a nightmare scenario. One day, he walked into the office of his chief of staff, gazed out the window and said, "I wonder what'll happen when we put 500,000 troops into Iraq and comb the country from one end to the other and find nothing?"[108]

On January 11, Cheney informed Rumsfeld and Saudi Arabia's ambassador to the United States that "the president has made the decision to go after Saddam Hussein."[109] Two days later, after a NSC meeting, Bush asked Powell to stay in the Oval Office. The president declared, "I really think I'm going to have to take this guy out." Powell scrambled to caution the president one more time: "Okay," he said, "we'll continue to see if we can find a diplomatic way out of this. But you realize what you're getting into? You realize the consequences of this?" Bush answered in the affirmative.[110] Bush's question for Powell was one of loyalty. "Are you with me on this?" Bush asked. "I think I have to do this. I want you with me." Powell committed himself. "Yes, sir," he said, "I will support you."[111] While the secretary clung to some hope that "things [might] break differently" with Iraq, he realized that the final countdown to war had begun.[112]

Bush's closest foreign ally, Blair, wanted a second Security Council resolution, one that explicitly authorized the use of force. The president "dreaded" the prospect of revisiting the United Nations, and Powell advised him that a second resolution, if at all possible, was unnecessary.[113] Powell considered Resolution 1441 to be "license to go to war" that granted "more than enough authority" for military action.[114] Still, both were willing to try for Blair, who wanted to bolster support in Parliament. Over the ensuing weeks, they worked behind the scenes to secure enough votes. The war hawks in the Bush administration thought that the Europeans were "full of shit" on international security, but Powell always retorted, "They're full of shit, and we've got to deal with them."[115]

On January 20, the Security Council met in New York for the purpose of discussing the global war on terrorism, not Iraq. What transpired during and after the meeting elicited Powell's anger at key European allies. In the morning session, Germany's foreign minister announced his government's total opposition to a military assault on Iraq and predicted "disastrous consequences" if one occurred.[116] The Russian and Chinese foreign ministers supported the German view. Annoyed by the focus on Iraq, Powell and the British foreign minister countered, arguing that it was dangerous to delay action much longer. On his way back to Washington, Powell learned that the French foreign minister had convened a press conference to state his government's complete opposition to the use of force in Iraq. "Nothing," Dominique de Villepin said, "justifies cutting off inspections to enter into a war and uncertainty."[117] Powell was livid; he felt betrayed and humiliated by his counterparts. After being "screwed," he realized that the chances of securing a new resolution and a broad-based war coalition were doomed.[118]

Powell channeled his rage. Four days later, in his speech at the World Economic Forum in Switzerland, he lectured his international audience on American history from World War II and the Cold War to the Persian Gulf War and Afghanistan. He spoke of the nation's judicious use of political, military, and economic power and asserted that the United States leads when "we feel strongly about something" and works to build consensus when other nations have differing positions. In the end, he cautioned, "multilateralism cannot become an excuse for inaction." Powell then condemned Iraq for failing to disclose the extent of its biological, chemical, nuclear, and missile programs. "This is not about inspectors finding smoking guns. It's about . . . Iraq's failure to tell the inspectors where to find its weapons of mass destruction."[119]

Powell's unusually blunt address, which included highly questionable references to Iraq's ties to al Qaeda and its attempts to procure uranium, could have been written by Cheney himself. "The United States believes that time is running out," Powell said. "We will not shrink from war if that is the only way to rid Iraq of its weapons of mass destruction." In an extended Q&A session, Powell fielded a question from George Carey, the former archbishop of Canterbury, who asked if U.S. foreign policy relied disproportionally on its military power. In response, Powell reminded Carey that it was not "soft power" that had liberated Europe and added, defensively, "I don't think I have anything to be ashamed of or apologize for with respect to what America has done for the world."[120] The State Department's Richard Haass, who was with Powell in Switzerland, thought his boss had given a superb speech, one that "came closest to articulating an approach to American foreign policy that he [Powell] agreed with (emphasizing diplomacy and multilateralism) while still managing to be a reflection of administration policy"[121]

Powell returned to the United States glad to have blown off some steam. He had no regrets about the tenor of the speech, especially when on January 27, Blix reported that "Iraq appears not to have come to a genuine acceptance—not even today—of the disarmament which was demanded of it."[122] The Bush administration seized upon Blix's negative report like "seagulls after sardines."[123] Powell held a press conference after the inspectors' report and proceeded to repeat Blix's line twice. He also asked, emphatically, "Where are the chemical and biological munitions? Where are the mobile biological laboratories?" "If the Iraqi regime was truly committed to disarmament, we wouldn't be looking for these mobile labs. They'd drive them up and park them in front of the U.N. inspectors."[124]

While Blix and his team continued the inspections, Bush determined that the Iraqi danger warranted a bold, evidentiary hearing in the court of world opinion. He asked Powell to prepare a final comprehensive brief against Iraq, one that publicly justified a preventive war to remove Saddam Hussein from power. A few days later, in a private meeting with Blair in the Oval Office, the president talked as if war was inevitable, saying "the start date for the military campaign was now penciled in for 10 March." Rice assured the prime minister that "aftermath planning . . . was now in hand."[125]

Once again, the president sought to leverage Powell's popularity and credibility, which far exceeded his own and that of all other cabinet members. On September 30, 2002, Gallup had reported that Powell "remains the most popular political figure in America" and that his 88 percent favorable rating "is in fact one of the highest such ratings in Gallup Poll history."[126] The president's strategy was obvious to State Department personnel. According to Lawrence Wilkerson, Powell's chief of staff,

"No one [else] in the Bush administration had high poll ratings amongst the American people or the international community. Colin Powell's ratings were up there with Mother Teresa at the time."[127]

Moreover, it was invaluable to have the secretary of state plead the administration's case because, as Bush later wrote, Powell was "known to be reluctant about the possibility of war."[128] "We've really got to make the case," the president told Powell, "and I want you to make it. You have the credibility to do this. Maybe they'll believe you."[129] Cheney added, "You've got high poll ratings, you can afford to lose a few points."[130] One of Powell's deputies characterized the president's order as "Go up there and sell it, and we'll [the administration will] have moved ahead a peg or two. Fall on your damn sword and kill yourself."[131]

Powell was up to the president's directive. He was the ideal subordinate to prepare and present the case against Iraq. Effective public prosecutors must have capability and believability, and the retired general possessed both, in surplus. His sterling reputation for integrity was matched by his capacity to construct and deliver persuasive and compelling briefings. The U.N. presentation would mark the zenith of Powell's extraordinary forty-year career in government service, and it was as if he had been preparing for the moment all of his life.

The address was scheduled for February 5 at a televised meeting of the Security Council. Powell was informed that he would not have to prepare his speech from scratch. During the prior month, the president had instructed the CIA to make several "marketing" presentations of their best "public case" that Iraq possessed and would use WMD.[132] Despite Tenet's infamous claim that making the case was as sure as a "slam dunk," Bush did not find any of the briefings compelling enough to persuade the public.[133] He asked the NSC staff and Cheney's office, led by I. Lewis "Scooter" Libby, to redesign the presentation as a dramatic legal "closing argument" against Saddam Hussein.[134] While Powell was in Switzerland, Armitage had witnessed a

ADVISER

rehearsal of Libby's presentation. He described it to Powell as "bizarre," with "hyperbole . . . flashing in neon lights."[135]

Powell approached his mission with the zeal and thoughtfulness of an excellent subordinate. His first decision was to reject a White House proposal that he present over three days, covering three topics: Iraq's nexus with terrorism, its human rights violations, and its WMD programs.[136] Instead, Powell insisted upon building a concise ninety-minute presentation that focused predominantly on WMD delivery systems, production programs, and inventories.[137]

The secretary sought to draw only incontrovertible conclusions from "solid evidence" backed by the CIA and to discard any intelligence "that seemed a stretch or wasn't multisourced."[138] "The fact that he [Powell] understood his reputation was on the line," Haass later wrote, "made this naturally cautious and rigorous person even more so."[139] When the secretary received a fifty-page WMD draft speech from Cheney's office, Powell assigned it to a trusted and loyal aide, Chief of Staff Wilkerson. The vice president had told Powell that the document had "good material in it."[140] Powell told Wilkerson and a few other staff officers to carve out a credible address; there was no time to waste.

Wilkerson and his team, which was joined by Powell and sometimes Rice, camped out at CIA headquarters in Langley, Virginia. Along with Tenet, Deputy Director John McLaughlin, and a group of intelligence analysts, they began scrutinizing Libby's working draft. From the beginning, there were documentation and sourcing problems. CIA officer Michael Morell, who had been Bush's daily briefer and was now assisting Powell, concluded that Libby's document "contained information of unknown origin" and made judgments that went "well beyond CIA analysis."[141] Powell, his staff, and the CIA leadership quickly determined that Libby's work was "crap," "garbage," "incoherent," "unusable," "worthless," and "a disaster."[142] They decided to scrap it altogether and adopt Tenet's recommendation to base Powell's speech on CIA documentation and the classified

National Intelligence Estimate on Iraq that had been delivered to Congress in October 2002.

Powell, who spent "dozens of hours" at Langley, led a rigorous vetting process. Each draft of the speech was scrutinized and amended by a team of CIA analysts, and then Powell reinspected the document and posed new inquiries, which led to further modifications. According to Morell, the secretary methodically scoured each draft, examining it "word by word, sentence by sentence," and asking "question after question."[143]

As a result of this process, even some judgments of the October National Intelligence Estimate now seemed untenable because Powell determined they were based on "a single source or just didn't sound right."[144] One significant example was his refusal to include Iraq's supposed attempt to acquire uranium from Niger. The intelligence "did not rise to his standards."[145] Powell was also loath to include intelligence knowingly provided by the Iraqi National Congress, an exile group that the CIA and State Department considered highly unreliable.[146] "Point by point," Morell later wrote, "Powell would ask us for backup information on the assertions, and as we dug into them, many seemed to fall apart before my eyes. . . . What was collapsing was some of the facts used in the NIE to support the judgments there."[147]

Throughout the speech-crafting process, Powell and CIA analysts fended off Cheney's staff, who attempted to insert claims against Iraq that could not be substantiated. The vice president seemed especially keen to "beef up" the evidence of Iraq's nuclear program and Saddam Hussein's supposed connections to 9/11 and al Qaeda.[148] When asked by a Cheney staffer, for example, why the speech did not make reference to Iraq's attempt to acquire uranium in Africa, a CIA analyst answered, "[We] do not believe the information to be true."[149] Likewise, much to Cheney's consternation, Powell was reluctant to accept any direct connection between Iraq and 9/11, including a supposed meeting in Prague between one of the 9/11 hijackers, Mohamed Atta, and Iraqi intelligence operatives.[150] "George, you don't believe this crap," Powell said to the CIA director, "about Iraq and al Qa'ida, do you?" Tenet responded, "No, Mr. Secretary, we do not. I do not know where that came from, but we will fix it."[151] "What was impressive to me," Haass wrote later, "was what did not get into his Security Council presentation. All the things that people pressed him to include which he said 'no' to."[152]

After four days and nights of analysis and composition, Powell, Tenet, McLaughlin, and Rice were satisfied that they had constructed a highly credible—indeed, airtight—briefing that proved the president's contention that Iraq, with its WMD and association with terrorists such as al Qaeda, represented a clear and present danger in the post-9/11 era. "After all the back-and-forth," Tenet later wrote, "we believed we had produced a solid product."[153] In fact, he personally assured Powell that the information in the U.N. presentation was "ironclad."[154] Rice, too, was reassured about going to war and "couldn't have felt more confident about the case he [Powell] would make."[155] General Myers, the chairman of the Joint Chiefs of Staff, was especially glad that Powell had gone to the CIA to satisfy himself that the WMD intelligence was reliable.[156]

On February 3, before Powell and his team left for New York, he joined a scheduled luncheon at the Pentagon. There, he, Rumsfeld, Rice, and McLaughlin assured a group of Republican and Democratic foreign policy elder statesmen, including Henry Kissinger, Robert McNamara, and Madeleine Albright, that the administration was absolutely certain about its case against Iraq. Former Carter national security adviser Zbigniew Brzezinski, who, twenty-six years earlier, had interviewed Powell for an NSC position, left the meeting much less skeptical than when he had entered. "Your doubts, honestly, tend to shrink," he later said, "when three people you respect, whom you trust, whom you have known for years, tell you they *know*. . . . Well, if they *know*, it must be so."[157] That same day, Powell wrote an op-ed for the *Wall Street Journal* that foreshadowed his U.N. address.

In it he stated, "While there will be no 'smoking gun,' we will provide evidence . . . offer a straightforward, sober, and compelling demonstration that Saddam is concealing the evidence of his weapons of mass destruction, while preserving the weapons themselves." He concluded with a threat to Saddam Hussein: "We will not shrink from war if that is the only way to rid Iraq of its weapons of mass destruction."[158] Two days later, a new *USA Today*/CNN/Gallup Poll showed that the American people trusted Powell over Bush on U.S-Iraq policy by a margin of 63 to 24 percent.[159]

On the morning of February 5, before a worldwide television audience, Powell delivered his address for war to the United Nations Security Council. It had been three months since his championing of Resolution 1441 and the subsequent reentry of U.N. weapons inspectors in Iraq. Knowing his and the president's reputations were at risk, Powell made certain that the CIA director was seated visibly and immediately behind him. "There I was," Tenet later recalled, "on international TV, a prop on the set."[160] The seventy-six-minute briefing, titled "Iraq: Failing to Disarm," was a multimedia event that featured symbolic vials of fake anthrax, satellite imagery, videos, maps, intercepted audiotapes, photographs, and renderings of mobile biological weapons laboratories.

Powell's approach was sober and methodical, and he spoke throughout with supreme confidence. "Every statement I make today," he declared, "is backed up by sources, solid sources. These are not assertions. What we are giving you are facts and conclusions based on solid evidence." No fewer than sixteen times, Powell employed the definitive phrase *We know*. The briefing was saturated with statements of certitude: "These are facts corroborated by many sources," "the facts speak for themselves," "this conclusion is irrefutable and undeniable," "there are real and present dangers," "This is evidence, not conjecture. This is true. This is all well documented," "there can be no doubt," and "there is no doubt in my mind," Powell said.[161]

For the first hour, Powell described "the real and present dangers" of Iraq's "vast" WMD programs, stockpiles, and delivery systems and how Saddam Hussein had concealed them from the international community. The secretary asserted that there was absolutely "no doubt" about Iraq's possession of biological weapons, mobile production facilities, and the means of delivery, all of which could "cause massive death and destruction." Powell emphasized that the intelligence came from human eyewitnesses, most importantly from an Iraqi chemical engineer who had defected and was hiding in a foreign country. "Equally chilling," he argued, were Iraq's "vast amounts" of chemical weaponry, including mustard gas, which had never been accounted for.[162]

Regarding Iraq's nuclear program, Powell stated, "There is no doubt in my mind" that Saddam Hussein was "very much focused" on developing weapons and "already possesses two out of the three key components needed to build a nuclear bomb." The secretary of state pointed to Iraq's attempts to acquire high-tolerance aluminum tubes. He admitted that experts disagreed about the tubes' purposes, with "most" saying they had capacity to enrich uranium, while a minority had concluded they were apt for conventional weapons. But Powell stated assuredly, with his storied credentials as "an old army trooper," that he believed that the tubes and other Iraqi activities evidenced Iraq's ongoing "attempt to reconstitute its nuclear weapons program."[163]

The secretary of state also invested twelve minutes in explaining Iraq's "decades-long" association and "understanding" with terrorist groups. While he did not directly implicate Saddam Hussein in the 9/11 attacks, Powell did provide a detailed description of a "sinister nexus" between Iraq and al Qaeda. Accordingly, Iraq knowingly harbored a "network" of terrorists and "poison cell plotters" such as Abu Musab al-Zarqawi, a known "associate and collaborator of Osama bin Laden." Powell made no less than twenty references to al-Zarqawi, who heretofore was a low-level terrorist.[164]* Citing the confession of a "senior" al Qaeda operative, the secretary also contended that Iraq actively trained members of al Qaeda in biological and chemical weapons manufacturing. That an operative relationship between al Qaeda and Baghdad existed, Powell said, should not "come as a surprise to any of us."[165]

In his closing statement, Powell argued that the risks of inaction against Iraq were unbearable. The combination of Saddam Hussein, WMD, and terrorism was simply intolerable. Hussein's history of aggression, including his use of WMD, his ties to terrorists, and his hatred of other nations all but guaranteed that he would again deploy devastating weaponry. In other words, Iraq was on the brink of launching WMD or proliferating them among terrorist groups. Leaving Hussein in possession of WMD was "not an option, not in a post-September 11th world." The United States, Powell said, "will not and cannot run that risk," and he hoped that the United Nations, which had passed Resolution 1441 in hopes of staving off war, would now "not shrink from whatever is ahead of us."[166]

After the briefing, Powell and others in the administration believed that he had made the casus belli argument effectively. "My feeling," the secretary later wrote, "was that the presentation went well. . . . On balance, we seemed to have made a powerful case."[167] Tenet thought Powell had given "an extraordinary performance."[168] Rice considered it "a tour de force."[169] Bush concurred, describing the presentation as "exhaustive, eloquent, and persuasive."[170] The president's senior political adviser, Karl Rove, later wrote that Powell's "extremely significant" speech had "perfectly captured our thinking."[171]

*In his definitive account of the rise of ISIS, Joby Warrick writes that Powell's speech "transformed Zarqawi from an unknown jihadist to an international celebrity and the toast of the Islamist movement." See *Black Flags*, 97.

Foreign responses to Powell's presentation were mixed, and most significantly, he had failed to convert any of the reluctant members of the Security Council. After the secretary's presentation, Secretary-General Annan hosted a luncheon for the council members. The tension between the American secretary of state and the French foreign minister, Dominique de Villepin, was especially acute. According to Annan, Powell "brought the gravity of the moment firmly into the room" when he assured his council colleagues that he understood the agony and costs of war and had attempted to avoid one in Iraq.[172] "My credentials are solid with this group. I have looked here for a peaceful solution. . . . I know more about war than anyone in this room," he said. "I've lost friends in war; I've fought in two wars; I've commanded wars. The last thing I want is another war."[173] Powell also reminded his colleagues that wars can lead to very positive outcomes, and that if it came to war with Iraq, then the United States would embrace its leadership responsibilities. "I don't accept the premise that wars always lead to bad results. . . . If conflict comes," he said, "we [the United States] will not look away, and Iraq and the region will be better off."[174]

In contrast to the foreign reaction, response to Powell's address in the United States was decidedly in his favor.[175] Columnist George Will wrote, "Powell's presentation, its power enhanced by the avoidance of histrionics, will change all minds open to evidence."[176] Indeed, Powell's argument converted many skeptics in Congress and across the nation. Senator Dianne Feinstein was representative. The California Democrat had previously challenged the president on Iraq, but after Powell's presentation she confessed, "I no longer think inspections are going to work."[177] If not yet ready for war, both the *Washington Post* and the *New York Times* editorialized that Powell had made the single most serious and convincing case against Iraq.[178] Liberal columnist Mary McGrory wrote that "the cumulative effect" of Powell's presentation "was stunning," and, as a result, he "persuaded me, and I was as tough as France to convince."[179] Jim Hoagland, a Pulitzer Prize–winning journalist and columnist, asserted, "To continue to say that the Bush administration has not made its case, you must now believe that Colin Powell lied in the most serious statement he will ever make, or was taken in by manufactured evidence. I don't believe that. Today, neither should you."[180]

The high point of the positive reaction to Powell's U.N. speech came on February 6, when the secretary testified before the Senate Foreign Relations Committee. Democrat Joe Biden quipped, "I'd like to move for the nomination of Secretary of State Powell for President of the United States."[181] Understandably, Bush was very pleased with the secretary's "profound impact on the public debate."[182] Powell himself recognized that his presentation "had enormous impact and influence in this country and worldwide."[183]

Before it was known that Iraq no longer possessed WMD, Powell's conduct in both the preparation and delivery of the U.N. briefing, appeared a model of exemplary followership in service to the president. Bush had given his secretary of state an important and challenging assignment, one that not only tested Powell's abilities, but also mortgaged his enormous prestige. He responded to the mission with utter dedication and considerable skill. Moreover, Powell demonstrated his initiative, caution, and resourcefulness and exercised his capacities for critical judgment and masterful communication. Above all, perhaps, Powell had acted honorably. He believed what he said. On multiple occasions while building his U.N. brief, he rejected information that he found spurious and included only intelligence that either he or the CIA leadership judged as credible and reliable. That the president and so many Americans, at the time, thought so highly of Powell's performance was completely understandable.

During the course of the next six weeks, as U.N. inspectors continued their fruitless search for WMD in Iraq, the Pentagon marshaled an impressive invasion force. By mid-March, nearly a quarter million troops were in potential striking positions.[184] On March 17 Powell gathered reporters to announce that all attempts for a new Security Council resolution had failed and the president would issue a televised ultimatum to Saddam Hussein. "I think the time for diplomacy has passed," Powell told the journalists. "I think that's pretty clear."[185] That night, Bush gave the Iraqi dictator and his two sons forty-eight hours to flee. "Their refusal to do so," he vowed, "will result in military conflict."[186]

Two days later, with Hussein still defiant, the president met with his senior advisers in the White House Situation Room. It was D-Day. First, Bush confirmed that his combat commanders supported the war strategy and possessed the resources needed to execute it. Then he ordered Rumsfeld to implement Operation Iraqi Freedom. Appearing on closed-circuit television, General Franks saluted Bush. "Mr. President," he said, "may God bless America."[187] Bush returned the salute, and his eyes welled up. "The gravity of the moment," he later wrote, "hit me."[188] As a gesture of support in this somber moment, Powell reached over and touched the president's left hand.[189] A second American war against Iraq had commenced.

By the spring of 2002, it appeared that Powell had acquitted himself exceptionally well as secretary of state. He routinely provided the president with sound foreign policy alternatives and with honest, independent counsel that frequently diverged from Bush's own inclinations and the advice of other powerful advisers. In the immediate aftermath of 9/11, Powell, more than anybody, persuaded the president to focus on the clear and present danger in Afghanistan. After coalition forces defeated al Qaeda and the Taliban, it was Powell who, seven months before the invasion of Iraq, convinced Bush, over the objections of Cheney and Rumsfeld, to pursue his strategy of coercive diplomacy through the United Nations and with congressional authorization to use force. Moreover, in America, Powell's U.N. presentation was considered a triumph, another demonstration of his remarkable powers of persuasion.

Not long after the March 2002 invasion, however, the U.N. briefing lost its luster; worse, Powell became the target of derision and ridicule. Ten months after the war began, David Kay, the CIA's chief weapons inspector, came to a definitive conclusion: "We were almost all wrong" about WMD in Iraq.[190] Eight months later Kay's successor, Charles Duelfer, concurred, and he repeated, "We were almost all wrong."[191] Beyond the absence of WMD, subsequent federal investigations also determined that there were no operational ties between Iraq and al Qaeda before, during, or after 9/11.[192] In short, the Bush administration had launched a war under false pretenses, and for many people Powell personified the failure.

Powell had made some serious mistakes in his forty-year career, but none was more consequential than his specious U.N. briefing. He had argued—with categorical conviction—that the evidence of Iraq's WMD stockpiles and programs and its collaboration with WMD-seeking terrorists, including al Qaeda, was overwhelming and incontrovertible: "Every statement I make today is backed up by sources, solid sources. These are not assertions. What we are giving you are facts and conclusion based on solid evidence." Powell's statements were, of course, fully supported by CIA leadership and the NSC. But so many of the secretary's primary assertions about WMD, which he believed were accurate, were completely erroneous. Powell, in short, had unknowingly given false—grossly false—testimony in the government's public case for war against Saddam Hussein. So often a consummate subordinate, Powell's critical judgment had failed him, the president, and his country. The U.N. speech, he later admitted, was "one of my most momentous failures."[193]

Many have claimed that the speech represented a monumental lapse of personal ethics—not in that Powell deliberately lied at the United Nations (although some do level that extreme charge), but rather in that he betrayed himself and the nation by arguing for a war that he did not support.[194] In brief, the criticism is that Powell prioritized his loyalty to the president's mission over his personal opposition to the war. In 2014 Ambassador Hill wrote, "I could not help but recall his [Powell's] strong view that the war in Iraq would be a mistake, against the light of his February 2003 speech . . . in which he used his extraordinary communication skills to make the case for war. . . . the case for something I knew he did not believe in. I wondered if I could do such a thing with such persuasiveness. I hoped not."[195] Annan wrote, "I could only be impressed by the resilience of this man [Powell], who had endured so much to argue for a war he clearly did not believe in."[196] Greg Thielmann, director of the State Department's Office of Strategic, Proliferation, and Military Affairs, came to a similar conclusion. When asked why he thought the secretary presented debatable if not dubious intelligence with such conviction, Thielmann said, "I can only assume that he was doing it to loyally support the President of the United States and build the strongest possible case for arguing that there was no alternative to the use of military force."[197]

Such criticism of Powell, which remains widespread, presumes that he opposed Bush's decision to topple Saddam Hussein by force. But having a "strong view" about an impulsive, premature rush to war without congressional authorization or a new U.N. Security Council resolution is not equivalent to opposing the war altogether. "The dissent" within the administration, Powell later said, "was over the pace at which to approach the problem and how to take it to the international community."[198]* Moreover, the secretary believed the intelligence he presented, trusted the CIA's leadership, and—like a substantial majority in Congress—supported Bush's decision to invade Iraq. In 2005 Powell said, "I am a reluctant warrior . . . but when the president decided that it was not tolerable for this regime to remain in violation of all these U.N. resolutions, I'm right there

---

*Similarly, Rich Armitage has stated, "Powell and I did not object to the prospect of taking out Saddam Hussein, but we had real questions about the timing"; see Gordon and Trainor, *Cobra II*, 82.

with him with the use of force."[199] Seven years later, he told a British journalist, "I fully supported it [the war] and you will find nothing in the record from the UN speech and onwards that I spoke against it."[200]

In the run-up to the invasion of Iraq, Powell had not been duplicitous. In fact, the secretary of state had often demonstrated the hallmarks of a stellar subordinate. He was remarkably dedicated, loyal, and thoughtful in his work as a senior counselor. Powell pressed Bush to clarify his policy objectives and strategies, and he advised the president to seek endorsements from Congress and the United Nations. He had also implored the president to consider the consequences of a war: "If you break it, you are going to own it. . . . It is what happens after you get to Baghdad. And it ain't going to be easy." When Barbara Walters asked Powell if he had put loyalty to the president "ahead of leadership" and thus implicitly ahead of his own integrity, he replied, "Well, loyalty is a trait that I value, and yes, I am loyal. And there are some who say, 'Well, you shouldn't have supported it [the war], you should have resigned.' But I'm glad that Saddam Hussein is gone."[201]

The secretary of state's U.N. briefing was less a failure of ethics and more a failure of senior subordinates, including Powell, to exercise *sufficient* critical judgment and independent thought. As noted earlier, in crafting the briefing, Powell had refused to include discredited intelligence that Saddam Hussein had sought to purchase Nigerian uranium for a nuclear bomb, nor was he willing to draw a direct connection to Iraq and 9/11. Still, Powell did not adequately challenge the reliability of key pieces of intelligence that underpinned his supposedly airtight case on Iraq's WMD programs and its relationship with al Qaeda. As the secretary's own chief of staff has recounted, "What we were all involved in—groupthink isn't the right word—it was a process of putting the data to points in the speech rather than challenging the data itself."[202]

Moreover, the secretary's U.N. presentation evidenced his willingness to discount or ignore acknowledgments within the

2002 National Intelligence Estimate that U.S. intelligence agencies lacked good, firsthand intelligence on Iraq and doubted Saddam Hussein would use WMD unless pushed to the brink of being overthrown by the American military.

The intelligence estimate definitely expressed certitude that Iraq possessed WMD and was continuing and even expanding its programs, but it also reported that the intelligence agencies had severely limited knowledge about the stockpiles and programs; the latter should have bolstered Powell's innate cautiousness. The estimate stated, "Iraq's BW [biological weapons] program . . . continues to be difficult to penetrate and access, and we do not have specific information on the types of weapons, agent, or stockpiles Baghdad has at its disposal," "We are unable to determine whether BW agent research or production has resumed," and "Our understanding of Iraq's current BW delivery systems is limited." The intelligence agencies further acknowledged, "We have little specific information on Iraq's CW [chemical weapons] stockpile" and "the paucity of detailed intelligence . . . make[s] determining the location of suspected CW stockpile and production facilities extremely difficult." The intelligence estimate even concluded that "Iraq's CW capability probably is more limited now than it was at the time of the Gulf war."[203]

The National Intelligence Estimate's accounting of Saddam Hussein's nuclear program was also obviously problematic, and it too should have suppressed Powell's certainty about the Iraqi threat. The estimate stated, "Today we have less direct access and know even less about the current status of Iraq's nuclear program than we did before the Gulf War when [there were] significant collection gaps [in the intelligence]." The estimate also included a detailed judgment by the State Department's intelligence agency that there was little evidence that Iraq had reconstituted its nuclear program, and as a result there was no "compelling reason" to project that Saddam Hussein would possess nuclear weapons in the coming decade. According to State's

Bureau of Intelligence and Research (INR), "The activities we have detected do not . . . add up to a compelling case that Iraq is currently pursuing . . . an integrated and comprehensive approach to acquire nuclear weapons." Moreover, according to the intelligence estimate, the Department of Energy, the National Laboratories, and the INR all concluded that Iraq's pursuit of high-strength aluminum tubes—which was viewed as "central to the argument that Baghdad is reconstituting its nuclear weapons program"—was not part of a nuclear program, but rather meant for conventional weaponry.[204]

As for a nexus between the Iraq government and terrorists such as al Qaeda, the intelligence estimate stated that reliable intelligence was limited and that Saddam Hussein was not inclined to support such groups, although there were reports of "some contacts." It stated, "Saddam has not endorsed al-Qa'ida's overall agenda and has been suspicious of Islamist movements in general," and there was "no solid evidence that Iraq has ever provided CBW [chemical biological weapons] or materials to any terrorist group." And while one captured al Qaeda operative, Ibn al-Shaykh al-Libi, "told us" that Iraq provided WMD training to two members of his organization, "none" of the prisoners from the Afghanistan War claimed they had been trained by Iraqis. "As with much of the information on the overall relationship," the National Intelligence Estimate admitted, "details on training and support are second-hand or from sources of varying reliability." The estimate did note the presence of some "extremists with al-Qa'ida ties" in Iraq, but stated, "We do not know to what extent Baghdad may be actively complicit in this use of its territory for safehaven and transit."[205]

Notwithstanding the tenuous "possible" connections between Iraq and terrorists, the intelligence estimate projected that it was highly improbable that Iraq would share WMD with groups such as al Qaeda. Moreover, the intelligence agencies believed that Saddam Hussein was also unlikely to use WMD at all unless forced into a desperate situation. Such thinking about

Hussein's intentions ran contrary to the supposed imminent threat perpetuated by Powell at the United Nations. The intelligence agencies opined that Iraq was *not* likely to conduct offensive terrorist-style operations against the United States or its allies (with conventional weapons or WMD), because it would prompt a severe retaliation. According to the National Intelligence Estimate, Saddam Hussein was likely to use terrorist tactics and WMD only as an extreme final defensive measure to prevent his overthrow: "He probably would use CBW when he perceived he irretrievably had lost control of the military and security situation" or "feared an attack that threatened the survival of the regime were imminent or unavoidable." Furthermore, the intelligence agencies believed that Hussein would "most likely" deploy the Iraqi Intelligence Service in these defensive operations, not foreign terrorists. According to the estimate, Saddam Hussein would only take "the extreme step" of providing Islamist terrorists with WMD if it was his "last chance to exact revenge by taking a large number of victims with him."[206]

In preparing his U.N. presentation, Powell had more often than not accepted those assertions in the National Intelligence Estimate that incriminated Saddam Hussein as representing a dire threat. The secretary later wrote that "the NIE's evidence was persuasive."[207] By comparison, he depreciated the intelligence community's many qualifications about the scarceness of reliable information and its belief that Saddam Hussein would be disinclined to deploy or share WMD. The secretary also rejected his own State Department's lengthy dissenting judgment about Iraq's nuclear weapons program, even though the INR's position on the aluminum tubes was supported by technical experts at the Department of Energy and the National Laboratories.

After reading a draft version of Powell's U.N. speech, INR analysts expressed serious concern about the secretary's "reporting as fact" intelligence from numerous unproven human sources who were Iraqi exiles or defectors with "an ax to grind." More specifically, the analysts found "highly questionable" the speech's assertion that Saddam Hussein had deployed biological weap-

ons warheads and missiles to western Iraq.[208] Director Thielmann was personally distressed by many aspects of Powell's
speech and considered the secretary's presentation on the aluminum tubes "one of the most disturbing parts."[209]

In short, the secretary was exceedingly trustful of the assurances made by the CIA leadership. For example, at one point in
preparing the U.N. briefing, after having rejected much of the
"bullshit" about a supposed close relationship between Iraq and
al Qaeda, Powell reversed course and agreed to make an assertive case for a "sinister nexus" between them. According to State
Chief of Staff Wilkerson, Tenet told Powell that new intelligence
had arrived from "a high-level al-Qaeda" detainee, who "not
only confirmed substantial contacts . . . but also . . . [the] training [of] al-Qaeda operatives in the use of chemical and biological weapons." Powell did not demand details about the
origins of the "bombshell" information, nor did he ask if it had
been corroborated.[210] Had he done so, he would have learned
that the intelligence stemmed from a single human source, one
already mentioned in the intelligence estimate. He would also
have learned that the informant's reliability was suspect.

This source was al Qaeda trainer al-Libi, who had been rendered to an Egyptian prison by the CIA in January 2002 for coercive interrogation. His forced statement that Iraq had trained
al Qaeda operatives came only after being tortured. Had Powell
inquired further, he might also have learned that the U.S. Defense Intelligence Agency had previously determined that al-Libi
was "a probable fabricator."[211] Instead, Powell accepted Tenet's
assurances that this unnamed, untested source was completely
credible.

Similarly, Powell did not press the CIA leadership extensively enough on intelligence related to Iraq's supposed mobile
facilities for producing biological weapons. Had he done so, he
would have learned that "by far the most important source on
the subject," a controversial Iraqi defector codenamed "Curveball," had never been interrogated by U.S. officials.[212] American
intelligence agencies did not even know his real name. In the

process of seeking asylum in Germany, Rafid Ahmed Alwan al-Janabi, a chemical engineer, had told German intelligence services that he worked at an Iraqi plant that manufactured mobile biological weapons labs. The Germans determined that Curveball was unstable and they could not verify his information. This was conveyed to the U.S. Defense Intelligence Agency, and in January 2003, the CIA's chief for clandestine operations in Europe, Tyler Drumheller, warned Deputy Director McLaughlin that Curveball was "probably a fabricator."[213] Powell did not uncover any of this information.

Put in terms of the U.S. Army Leadership Requirements Model, the U.N. briefing had been a failure not of Powell's "character," but rather of "sound judgment" and "mental agility."[214] Yes, he had effectively weeded out some of the bad intelligence, but he knew that the remaining bed of information concerning Iraq's WMD, its relationship with al Qaeda, and Saddam Hussein's intentions was fraught with uncertainty. The intelligence was, to use Powell's own words, "mostly circumstantial and inferential," but still he presented it to the public as absolutely conclusive proof of a clear and present danger to national security.[215]

Powell and other government leaders suffered from a classic—indeed, catastrophic—case of "confirmation bias," whereby they largely dismissed information in the National Intelligence Estimate that conflicted with what they believed to be true about Iraq and amplified information that seemed to confirm their dire and erroneous beliefs.[216] The hard lesson learned, Powell later admitted on *The Daily Show with Jon Stewart*, was "you really, really have to bore down far more deeply than we did at that time with respect to the intelligence."[217] Similarly, he wrote, "I learned to be more demanding of intelligence analysts. I learned to sharpen my own natural skepticism toward apparently all-knowing experts."[218]

In the end, Powell judged that if the CIA leadership "*believed* what we were presenting then we had to believe it. Because they were the experts."[219] All along, he and leaders in the intelligence community, as well as other senior administration officials, wrongly assumed that Saddam Hussein would never dismantle his WMD and would always develop new ones to the fullest extent possible. These mistaken assumptions and poor judgments led to unwarranted certitude and a disastrous war that cost trillions of dollars and killed hundreds of thousands of people.[220]

To his credit, Powell eventually took responsibility for his part in the catastrophic intelligence failure. In his first public interview after leaving the Bush administration, Powell told Barbara Walters that his U.N. briefing marked a "painful" and permanent "blot" on his record of distinguished public service. In his 2012 book *It Worked for Me*, Powell reflected on the U.N. speech. "And yes," he wrote, "a blot, a failure, will always be attached to me and my UN presentation. But I am mad mostly at myself for not having smelled the problem. My instincts failed me. . . . It was by no means my first, but it was one of my most momentous failures, the one with the widest-ranging impact."[221]

The U.N. speech and the decision to invade Iraq demoralized many of Powell's devoted followers at the State Department. They did not blame Powell for the war, but some thought that he had been overconfident in his ability to prevent one and in his ability to rally the international community in support of an invasion. The secretary "convinced all of us," one senior official said, "to believe that this would come out our way in the end. And it didn't."[222] Other State officials faulted Powell for his unwillingness to leverage his personal stature and render a different administration policy. "The guy . . . had everything he needed to be a great secretary of state," concluded one official about Powell. "If he had wanted to, he could have used all of his clout to steer policy in a different direction."[223] For still others in the department, Powell's singular weakness was his unswerving loyalty to the president and his policies. In an open letter of resignation printed in the *New York Times*, veteran Foreign Service officer John B. Kiesling expressed tremendous admiration for Powell's "character and ability" and for his preservation of "more international credibility for us than our policy deserves."[224] But, in the end, Kiesling concluded that the secretary's "loyalty to the President goes too far."[225]

Nevertheless, in March 2003, when the "shock and awe" invasion of Iraq began, the horrendous intelligence failure was not yet known. The large majority of people in the State Department were still very pleased to have Powell as their leader and defender, and they hoped that he would never resign in protest of or out of frustration with the administration. "The feeling in the building was very, very clear," said one assistant secretary. "Pray to God that he doesn't resign, because he is preventing much worse stuff from happening."[226] Worse stuff was right around the corner.

Whether the going was rough or smooth,
I always tried to do my best and to be loyal
to my superior and the mission given to me.

—COLIN POWELL

CHAPTER NINE

Defender in Chief

(2003–2004)

Colin Powell's final two years as secretary of state were equal parts stressful and exhausting. As anticipated, the U.S. military swiftly toppled Saddam Hussein's regime, but the Bush administration was woefully unprepared to manage the chaos and violence that followed. In the two years after the launch of Operation Iraqi Freedom, more than a thousand Americans were killed in action and over ten thousand wounded; the Iraqis suffered twice as many casualties. Before the war, Powell and several American generals had expressed prescient concern that the United States was not deploying sufficient ground troops for the Iraq campaign. Moreover, in the aftermath of the invasion, it became increasingly apparent that the primary justification for the war—Iraq's possession of WMD—had been based on grossly inaccurate intelligence. Indeed, Iraq no longer possessed WMD. Powell, who had staked his personal reputation on the quality of the prewar intelligence, was slow to accept that he and the administration had committed a horrendous foreign policy blunder. Instead, he emerged as the most ardent defender of the president's ill-fated decision to remove Saddam Hussein from power.

During the spring 2003 invasion, nobody on the NSC, including Powell, anticipated protracted combat with the Iraqi army. While U.S. military and intelligence leaders feared that a desperate Saddam Hussein might deploy chemical and biological weapons, it was widely believed that the war would be won in two or three months. The Pentagon's planning called for a quick drawdown after major combat operations and a residual stabilization force of some thirty thousand troops.[1]

Months before the war, Powell and others questioned the relatively small size of the invasion force.[2] The obvious point of comparison was Desert Storm, for which five hundred thousand troops had been deployed, and unlike the new war being planned by Rumsfeld and his generals, the 1990–1991 operation did not include a march to Baghdad, engagement with the entire Iraqi army, or the reconstitution of the Iraqi government. Powell began to have serious reservations in early August 2002, when General Tommy Franks, the CENTCOM commander, briefed the NSC on the Pentagon's detailed war plan, which predicted that nearly all U.S. forces would be withdrawn from Iraq by December 2006.[3] Although Powell did not challenge the planning at that moment, "it was obvious" to Franks that "there was something on his mind." A month later, just before another round of NSC briefings, Powell called Franks to give him a heads-up. "I am going to critique your plan at Camp David," the secretary of state said. "I've got some problems with force size and support of that force, given such long lines of communication."[4] Franks thanked the secretary for providing advance warning.

Franks respected Powell's tip-off, but he considered the secretary's war strategy to be antiquated. Powell, he thought, was "from a generation of generals who believed that overwhelming force was found in troop strength—sheer numbers of soldiers and tanks on the ground."[5] Franks and Rumsfeld both had determined that the Powell Doctrine and "the days of half-million-strong mobilizations" had long passed.[6] In fact, only two weeks after the terrorist attacks on 9/11, Rumsfeld had penned an op-ed in the *New York Times* that essentially declared the death of the Powell Doctrine. "Forget about 'exit strategies,'" he wrote, "we're looking at a sustained engagement that carries no deadline. We have no fixed rules about how to deploy our troops."[7]

Immediately after Powell's call, Franks telephoned the defense secretary, reporting, "I appreciate his call, but I wanted to tell him that the military has changed since he left it." According to Franks, Rumsfeld "chuckled."[8] Years later, in his memoirs, the defense secretary ridiculed Powell's concerns about force size and criticized the "Weinberger or Powell Doctrine" as ill-fitted to "complex operations in the real world."[9]

Powell aired his concerns on September 7, 2002, at a gathering of the NSC. He asked the group to consider whether the planned deployment of approximately 150,000 ground troops was adequate to wage a nationwide campaign against the entire Iraqi military. According to Franks, Powell "questioned the friendly-to-enemy force ratios, and made the point rather forcefully that the Coalition would have 'extremely long' supply lines."[10] Franks's response was, in short, that the force size was more than sufficient to meet the mission, and that the military was "moving into a new strategic and operational paradigm."[11] Powell did not debate the issue, which left Franks wondering whether he had satisfied the secretary's concerns.

Powell had not been persuaded. Moreover, he was not the only senior official worrying about troop levels. In December 2002, the *Washington Post* reported that both General Eric Shinseki, the army's chief of staff, and General James L. Jones, commandant of the marine corps, had reservations about the Rumsfeld-Franks war plan, which the newspaper described as "a fast-moving ground attack without an overwhelming number of reinforcements on hand." The generals believed the war plan was "riskier than usual U.S. military practice." As America's "ground forces chiefs," Thomas E. Ricks reported, they wanted "more attention to planning for worst-case scenarios" and "the burden of postwar peacekeeping in Iraq."[12] The next month, the Pentagon's top generals met with Bush and Cheney to discuss the war plans. While Shinseki did not formally propose a change to the war planning, he took the opportunity to share his trepidations. He thought the "light-footprint" strategy might create operational problems in "force flows" and "supply lines."[13] The critique caught Bush and Cheney off guard, but neither chose to engage the general's concerns.

Four weeks later, on February 25, Shinseki sparked a controversy while giving testimony before the Senate Armed Services Committee. Senator Carl Levin asked the general to estimate "the Army's force requirement for an occupation of Iraq following a successful completion of the war." Shinseki was prepared, as he had recently spoken with Brigadier General Steven Hawkins, who was studying the issue. Hawkins told the army chief that stability operations would require three hundred thousand troops.[14] As a result, Shinseki informed Levin, "Something on the order of several hundred thousand soldiers are probably a figure that would be required. We're talking about post [war] hostilities, control over a piece of geography that's fairly significant with the kinds of ethnic tensions that could lead to other problems and so it takes a significant ground force presence to maintain a safe and secure environment."[15]

Rumsfeld, Cheney, and Deputy Secretary of Defense Paul Wolfowitz were appalled at Shinseki's large estimate. The next morning, Wolfowitz called Secretary of the Army Thomas E. White to complain. But White, a Vietnam veteran and supporter of the Powell Doctrine, defended Shinseki's "expert" estimate as "perfectly reasonable."[16] Retired Army Lieutenant General Jay Garner also instructed Wolfowitz and Rumsfeld that Shinseki's informed estimate was "probably [in] the ballpark."[17] Nevertheless, Wolfowitz publicly contradicted White and Shinseki's position. At a hearing of the House Budget Committee, the deputy secretary said, "the notion that it will take several hundred thousand U.S. troops to provide stability in post-Saddam Iraq" was "wildly off the mark" because American forces would be greeted by the Iraqi people "as liberators, and that will help us to keep requirements down."[18] On February 28, Rumsfeld told reporters that Shinseki's estimate "will prove to be high."[19] Two weeks later, Cheney appeared on *Meet the Press*. He told Tim Russert, "I really do believe that we will be greeted as liberators. . . . To suggest that we need several hundred thousand troops there after military operations cease, after the conflict ends, I don't think that is accurate. I think that's an overstatement."[20]

In the end, Bush trusted in the Rumsfeld-Franks war plan despite the concerns raised by Shinseki and Powell. The president, too, believed that Powell's strategy of massive ground deployments belonged to a bygone era. In his memoirs, Bush wrote, "Colin had the deepest reservations. In a one-on-one meeting in early 2003, he had told me . . . we could manage the threat of Iraq diplomatically. He also told me he was not fully comfortable with the war plans. That did not surprise me. The operation Tommy Franks had conceived would use about a third as many troops as we had in the Gulf War. It marked a stark departure from the belief that America could win wars only by deploying massive, decisive force—commonly known as the Powell Doctrine."[21] In the same conversation, Bush told Powell that he still hoped that diplomacy would work with Iraq, but if it did not, he wanted to know if his secretary of state would fall into line and support a decision for war. "If this is what you have to do," Powell said, "I am with you, Mr. President."[22] Once again, the secretary adhered to his conception of the consummate subordinate by "disagreeing strongly" and then "executing faithfully."[23]

Powell did agree with Bush's decision to have the Defense Department, rather than the State Department, oversee Iraq's postwar transition to a new government.[24] Only Defense had the resources to guarantee security and stability. There were good reasons, Powell thought, why it was *General* Douglas MacArthur and not "*Ambassador* MacArthur" who presided over postwar Japan.[25] The State Department's Richard Haass detected an additional rationale, "a sense that Defense, having advocated for the war, should now sleep in the bed of its own making."[26] The decision to put Rumsfeld in charge of administering Iraq and rebuilding its civil and military institutions was uncontroversial at the time. But later, it was judged "one of the most critical and ultimately disastrous decisions . . . made on the march to Baghdad."[27] Years after the war, Rice remained critical of Rumsfeld's leadership. In a personal email to Powell, she wrote, "If Don and the Pentagon had done their job (after claiming the rights to lead post-war rebuilding)—things might have turned out differently."[28]

Before the invasion of Iraq, the State Department, the Defense Department, and the CIA all engaged in various post-conflict planning exercises, but they largely worked in isolation from one another.[29] A year before the war, State's Bureau of Near East Affairs (NEA) launched the Future of Iraq project, which organized two hundred Iraqi expatriate scholars, lawyers, doctors, engineers, business leaders, and other experts to explore a broad range of issues to be addressed if regime change occurred in Baghdad.[30] After multiple conferences with Iraqi opposition groups in the United States and London, the Future of Iraq project, led by Tom Warrick, produced around a thousand pages of analysis, predictions, and proposals loosely assembled in thirteen volumes.[31] The project represented a wealth of knowledge about Iraqi society, but it was not a coherent plan to rebuild Iraq after an invasion.[32] The Future of Iraq project work was submitted to the Pentagon in December 2002. Rumsfeld, who sought to minimize the State Department's influence, dismissed the effort as "not on its face a seminal achievement," and as a result the extensive effort was never utilized.[33] That, according to historian Gordon W. Rudd, was "an avoidable tragedy" in the Pentagon's derelict planning for Iraq's reconstruction.[34]

As war became more imminent, Powell started to think more deeply about the consequences of deposing Saddam Hussein. As the administration's senior foreign policy adviser, he felt "an obligation to point out some of the problems one might run into."[35] Powell distributed a fifteen-page memorandum to Rumsfeld,

Cheney, and Rice on the tremendous challenges of postwar reconstruction based on historic lessons learned in Japan, South Korea, Greece, and Italy. The memo's first sentence read, "If we end up going to war with Iraq, we need to be prepared to win the ensuing peace."[36] Prepared by the State Department's Policy Planning Staff, the paper argued for a comprehensive postwar plan and a steadfast commitment to it because "in post-conflict reconstruction, you usually get what you pay for. . . . Our commitment in time and resources must be calibrated to both the scale of our ambitions and the situation we inherit."[37]

Powell also charged his NEA bureau with providing an assessment of a worst-case scenario in a post-Saddam Iraq. The classified white paper was dubbed "The Perfect Storm."[38] One of its principal authors, William J. Burns, later recalled that "Powell was trying to be thorough and thoughtful about—in the run-up to the war in 2003—about thinking through the second- and third-order consequences of that kind of action, and had asked us at one point to try to think through everything that could go wrong."[39] The CIA had completed a similar document bearing the exact same name in August 2002, only to have it buried in the back of a dense briefing book. "Had we felt strongly that these were likely outcomes," Tenet later wrote, "we should have shouted our conclusions. There was, in fact, no screaming, no table-pounding."[40]

Meanwhile, the Pentagon made its plans for the post-conflict stabilization mission. In January 2003, only two months before the invasion, the Defense Department created the Office for Reconstruction and Humanitarian Assistance (ORHA), which, under the leadership of retired Army Lieutenant General Jay Garner, was designed as a short-lived, caretaker administrator for Iraq. The planning seemed extraordinarily hasty to the general, who told Rumsfeld, "George Marshall started [postwar planning] in 1942 working on a 1945 problem. You're starting in February working on what's probably a March or April problem."[41] But the civilian leadership at the Pentagon anticipated a rapid transfer of power to an interim Iraqi governing authority, and Garner was "assured" that "his mission would not last more than a few months."[42]

A related point of contention between Defense and State concerned the role that Iraqi exiles should play in the postwar government.[43] The Pentagon wanted them to assume a lead role and favored Ahmed Chalabi of the London-based Iraqi National Congress (INC). The State Department and the CIA, on the other hand, distrusted Chalabi, whom Tenet described as "a most unreliable partner."[44] Moreover, Tenet and Powell thought that the Iraqi people, not the United States, should select the first post-Saddam administration. Powell and Rumsfeld's sparring on the subject of the INC was occasionally heated.[45] Years after the war, Powell emailed Rice, describing the Pentagon's postwar plan as "(turn Iraq and our Army over to Chalibi [*sic*]) and leave."[46]

By April 1, 2003, Bush had sided with Powell and the State Department on the importance of establishing a legitimate government in Iraq, not one of exiles appointed by Washington.[47] Powell later wrote that the Pentagon's civilian leaders "were brain dead" on the issue, while "43 [Bush] knew what had to be done, specifically rejected the Chalibi [*sic*] crowd."[48] Nevertheless, with U.S. forces moving rapidly toward Baghdad, Rumsfeld continued to urge the president to create an interim Iraqi government, led by Chalabi and the INC.[49] Powell considered it an absolutely "stupid" idea, and Bush agreed with him.[50] On April 4, the Defense Department flew Chalabi and his six-hundred-man militia into the liberated city of Nasiriyah, Iraq, to demonstrate that the United States was a liberating, not occupying force.[51] Powell and Tenet were "stunned" when they learned about the "crazy" operation, which proved wholly ineffectual.[52]

The State Department's opposition to Chalabi and an exile-dominated Iraqi government elicited public criticism from Republican conservatives. Former Speaker of the House Newt Gingrich gave a biting speech at the American Enterprise Institute that assailed State for supposedly resisting Bush's foreign policies. Under Powell's leadership, Gingrich said, the department had been "deliberate and systematic" in its attempts to undercut the president, including his hardline against Saddam. Now, he said, the "ineffective and incoherent" State Department "threatens to undo" the positive effects of an assured military victory in Iraq.[53]

Gingrich's attack did not catch Powell or Deputy Secretary Armitage by surprise. To mitigate press coverage of the speech, the deputy secretary telephoned a journalist that afternoon to express his bewilderment that Gingrich would oppose Bush's position on exiles in the new Iraqi government. For good measure, Armitage added, "It's clear that Mr. Gingrich is off his meds and out of therapy."[54]

Likewise, Powell defended himself and the State Department when testifying at a Senate Appropriations Committee meeting. He stated that it was not uncommon for secretaries of state to be criticized for seeking peaceful solutions to knotty problems or for them to build international friendships and alliances. "That's what we do," Powell said. "We do it damn well. I am not going to apologize to anybody. I'm on the offensive for the people who work in my Department doing a great job, and if you come after them, come after them with legitimate criticism. We'll respond to that. We're not above criticism. But if you come after us just to come after us, you're in for a fight, and I am going to fight back."[55]

On April 9, U.S. forces reached downtown Baghdad, causing Hussein and his sons to flee. The "shock and awe" invasion plan had been executed with minimal American casualties. General Franks told Rumsfeld, "There's a lot of work to be done over here, but major combat operations are over."[56] The victorious field commander would soon announce his retirement. Unlike Rumsfeld, Franks believed that the postwar phase of the Iraq mission would last several years, and he could not "imagine staying . . . for that long." For that reason, Franks was eager to turn over control to Jay Garner and the ORHA team.[57]

Many Iraqis appeared jubilant about the American victory. The televised razing of Saddam Hussein's massive statue in

Firdos Square inspired genuine revelry. But with the arrival of thousands of U.S. troops, the local police and army forces scattered, which allowed chaos and lawlessness to erupt. With the exception of securing the Iraqi Ministry of Oil, American troops stood by while Iraqis pillaged government buildings. By the time the Pentagon's ORHA group arrived in mid-April, the large majority of Iraq's government ministries had been ransacked and most civil servants displaced. "The war, in short, went great," Tenet later wrote, "but peace was hell."[58]

Garner had experienced the friction between the State and Defense Departments from the beginning of his assignment.[59] While he was still in Washington, Powell had told him that he wanted to support ORHA, but that Rumsfeld and his deputies were "stiff-arming" the State Department to maintain tight control of the operation. Garner knew that this was true.[60] He had recruited to ORHA diplomat Thomas Warrick, the regional expert who had directed State's Future of Iraq project. But, with Cheney's approval, Rumsfeld insisted that Garner dismiss Warrick.[61] "The Pentagon just liberated Iraq," the vice president cracked. "What has the State Department done?"[62]

Later, when Powell volunteered seven ambassadors with regional expertise to bolster ORHA's staff as advisers to various Iraqi ministries, the offer was rebuffed. Rumsfeld told Garner that he wanted "his people" in senior positions, not the State Department's.[63] Powell was informed that ORHA required personnel who "are really committed and believe in what we are doing."[64] Outraged over this "bullshit" move, Powell telephoned Rumsfeld and declared, "You are going to need a lot of help, and I am pulling these guys from embassies and I am pulling anybody who is not in an embassy but can help. But if you are blackballing my seven ambassadors, then I am not sending anybody."[65] Even Rumsfeld's sycophantic undersecretary for policy, Douglas Feith, sympathized with Powell's "unhappiness."[66] National Security Adviser Rice took the "affront to Colin" to the president, but Bush refused to intervene, saying it was "the Defense Department's show."[67]

The issue of prewar planning, including the size of the occupation force, demonstrates both Powell's sound critical thinking on the risks involved and the limits of his influence as a senior subordinate. The president agreed with him that Iraq's new government should not be dominated by Iraqi exiles underwritten by the United States. But, more generally, Bush deferred to Rumsfeld and Cheney's judgments about force size and plans for managing postwar Iraq.

Rumsfeld eventually accepted some of Powell's diplomats for the reconstruction effort, but after the invasion, with the fabric of Iraqi society starting to unravel, the defense secretary lost confidence in Garner's leadership and ORHA's capacity to bring stability and establish a viable government. On Rumsfeld's initiative, Garner was quickly replaced with L. Paul "Jerry" Bremer III, a strong-willed, nonideological retired diplomat with counterterrorism experience.[68] Under his leadership, the postwar administration of Iraq was renamed the Coalition Provisional Authority (CPA), and Bremer was empowered by Bush and Rumsfeld with "all executive, legislative, and judicial" authority.[69]

Powell was elated by Bremer's selection. He told the envoy, "I flat-out whooped for joy" after hearing the news.[70] But the secretary soon developed serious reservations. Supported by Rumsfeld, Bremer abruptly announced that he was disbanding the Iraqi army, removing the Ba'ath Party from government, and firing Zalmay Khalilzad, an Arabic-speaking American on the NSC staff whom Bush had appointed as special envoy and ambassador at large to work with Iraq's disparate regional leaders. Neither Powell nor Rice had been consulted on these critical decisions.[71]* Khalilzad was the highest-ranking Muslim in the

---

*Years after the war, former Deputy Defense Secretary Paul Wolfowitz claimed that it had been the State Department's decision to disband the Iraqi Army and dispel the Baathists. Powell responded to this claim in a private email, "He is a fucking liar. . . . Bremer worked for him." Rice characterized Wolfowitz's

Bush administration and, according to Powell, "was the one guy that knew [the Iraqi people] better than anyone. I thought this [Khalilzad] was part of the deal with Bremer. But with no discussion, no debate, things changed. I was stunned."[72] Thinking the administration had committed a "major, massive strategic error," Powell immediately contacted Rice, who was not aware of Bremer's decision to disband the Iraqi army. She later informed Powell that the president would not overrule the Pentagon.[73] "I was shocked," Khalilzad himself recounted, "that senior leaders were as out of the loop as I was."[74] Bush later expressed regret for not having the NSC deliberate these fundamental issues, and even Rumsfeld admitted that "the failure to fashion a deliberate, systematic approach . . . [to] U.S. policy on the political transition in post-Saddam Iraq was among the more consequential of the administration."[75]

Beyond the challenges of Iraq's reconstruction, there remained the question of Saddam Hussein's WMD. No Iraqi chemical or biological weapons had been used or found during the invasion. Shortly after Bush's May 1 declaration that major combat operations had ended in Iraq, he assigned Tenet the responsibility, in coordination with the Pentagon, for finding Iraq's WMD. The CIA director hired former U.N. weapons inspector David Kay to lead the Iraq Survey Group. Tenet's orders were "find the truth" and "don't fuck up."[76] Kay, like Powell and all members of Bush's national security team, thought it was only a matter of time before the illicit weapons were found.

For many months after the invasion, Powell and CIA officials asserted that evidence of Saddam's WMD programs was being uncovered. In late May, after several suspect vans had been located, CIA analysts concluded that the vehicles were

---

statement as an "amazing rewriting of history!" See Powell, Personal Emails, Colin Powell to Larry Wilkerson, August 28, 2016, and Condoleezza Rice to Colin Powell, August 29, 2016.

mobile biological weapons laboratories of the type Powell had warned about in his U.N. speech. The secretary was elated when shown a photograph of the vehicles. He quickly informed U.N. Secretary-General Annan of the find. Annan later noted that Powell's "relief—and the exhaustion—was palpable. . . . The war had been justified; the cause affirmed."[77] "You should have seen the smile on my face," Powell told reporters, when the CIA informed him about finding "those vans."[78] Soon thereafter, however, the State Department's own intelligence branch determined that the vans were not weapons facilities. When the secretary questioned Tenet on the matter, the director expressed complete confidence that they had found weapons labs. Powell accepted the CIA's judgment and "kept sailing along, sticking with the story."[79]

By May, with no WMD stockpiles found, the press began to raise serious questions about the prewar intelligence used to justify the invasion.[80] On June 1, *Time* magazine's Michael Duffy wrote that a growing number of experts doubted that WMD would be found, and thus the acronym should stand for "Weapons of Mass Disappearance."[81] Eleven days later, a front-page story in the *Washington Post* reported that a CIA mission to Niger in 2002 had discredited intelligence reports that Iraq had attempted to acquire uranium.[82] On June 19, the *New Republic* published a similar piece.[83] Joseph C. Wilson, a retired diplomat and Clinton-era NSC staffer, had been a key source for the articles. A year before the war, the CIA, prompted by an inquiry from Cheney, had sent Wilson to Africa to determine the veracity of a claim that Iraq had attempted to acquire five hundred tons of uranium from Niger.[84] Wilson and the State Department's intelligence bureau, and eventually the CIA, concluded that the claim was not credible.[85] Nevertheless, Bush cited the Niger uranium story in his January 2003 State of the Union speech. Other senior administration officials also made public references to the Niger-Iraq nexus. Even Powell had mentioned it, in his Switzerland speech, though he later refused to include it in his U.N. address.

On July 7, Wilson wrote an op-ed in the *New York Times* that was highly critical of the Bush administration. Based on his firsthand experience, the ambassador stated that he had "little choice but to conclude that some of the intelligence related to Iraq's nuclear weapons program was twisted to exaggerate the Iraqi threat."[86] The accusation angered White House officials. Cheney and Libby, his trusted chief of staff, mounted a behind-the-scenes campaign to discredit the former ambassador.[87] On July 11, Tenet issued a public statement taking responsibility for the error in the president's State of the Union address, but he also underscored that the Niger claim was not one of the Key Judgments of the October 2002 National Intelligence Estimate, which was the primary basis of Bush's speech and Powell's U.N. presentation.[88]

The beltway controversy was exacerbated on July 14. In his reporting on the Nigerian uranium story, columnist Robert Novak mentioned that Ambassador Wilson's wife, Valerie Plame, was a CIA "operative" who worked on WMD.[89] Under certain circumstances, the public outing of a CIA agent can be a federal crime, and thus the Justice Department intervened. A long, complicated political and legal scandal ensued, one that enveloped Powell and Armitage.

Powell, Armitage, Cheney, and Libby had learned about Plame and her connection to Wilson in various ways in June. Tenet had told the vice president.[90] Powell and Armitage were informed by a State Department intelligence memorandum, which detailed Wilson's 2002 trip to Niger and his skepticism about Iraq's supposed attempt to acquire uranium. Libby, who learned of Plame from Cheney and from several CIA and State Department briefers, discussed the information with presidential adviser Karl Rove. By July 12, before Novak's column, Armitage, Libby, and Rove had each mentioned Plame's name to multiple journalists.[91]

Armitage had been interviewed by Bob Woodward on June 13 and by Novak on July 8. Both reporters asked him why the

CIA would send Wilson to Niger. Armitage, who thought Plame was an analyst rather than a covert operative, casually explained to both journalists that Wilson had been selected because of his knowledge of Africa and because, as he told Woodward, "His wife's a fucking analyst at the agency. It—it's perfect."[92] Like Woodward, Novak later stated that Armitage's idle mention of Plame "was not a planned leak but came out as an offhand observation."[93]

Powell did not learn that Armitage was one of Novak's three sources until October 1, 2003, when his deputy called in a panic. Novak had just published another article in which he said Plame's CIA identity was common knowledge and that he had not received "a planned leak."[94] "I may have been the leaker," Armitage confessed to Powell. "I talked to Novak." Armitage was ashamed of himself. He had "fucked up" and offered to resign.[95] Powell thought his friend was probably overreacting and called Will Taft, the senior State Department lawyer. They agreed that Armitage should immediately disclose his conversation with Novak to the Department of Justice, which had launched an official investigation.[96]

Taft called the Justice Department. Next, he telephoned White House Counsel Alberto Gonzales to inform him that the State Department possessed information pertinent to the CIA leak case and that he had contacted federal investigators. Taft asked if the White House wanted any of the details. Gonzales said no.[97] By not directly informing the president, Powell had in essence chosen loyalty to a friend, his subordinate, over complete candor with his superior. This reflects the limited nature of the secretary's relationship with President Bush. By comparison, it is difficult to imagine Powell withholding such information from President George H. W. Bush.

The next day, an FBI agent and a Justice Department official interviewed Armitage in his office with Taft present.[98] Armitage swore that he did not know Plame was a covert operative. Taft disclosed that he had contacted Gonzales. From there, neither

Powell, Taft, nor Armitage discussed the case with the White House, which had its own leakers, Libby and Rove, who were actively trying to discredit Wilson.

A year later, after having been interviewed by the Justice Department and the FBI, Powell appeared before the grand jury considering the Plame case. When a reporter asked a State Department spokesman if the secretary had been Novak's source, he barked, "Of course not!"[99] It was not until November 2005 that Armitage finally learned that no charges would be brought against him. His role in the Plame affair was not even made public until September 2006.[100] The following year, Libby, the vice president's most trusted senior adviser, was convicted of perjury, obstruction of justice, and making false statements in a federal investigation. Libby's conviction "left a cloud" over Cheney and his role in the sordid affair.[101] Not since the Iran-Contra scandal had such a high-ranking White House official been convicted of a felony.

In early October 2003, Kay returned to Washington, DC, to update Congress on the search for WMD in Iraq. In his testimony before the Senate Select Committee on Intelligence, Kay reported finding equipment, labs, and documentation that might be related to WMD research and production, but he needed more time to reach definitive conclusions. He also testified that there was no evidence of a meaningful nuclear program, but Iraq was attempting to develop banned long-range missile technology. Kay asserted that Iraq's various activities violated U.N. resolutions and that Saddam Hussein had intended to restart a WMD program, but he and his team had not unearthed any stockpiles of unconventional weapons.[102] Republican senator Pat Roberts, chair of intelligence committee, was upset that seven months after the invasion no WMD had been found. "I am not pleased by what I heard today," he said. "There has not been a breakthrough."[103] Democratic senator Nelson Rockefeller was angry. "I just think it's extraordinary," he said, "that a decision was made to go to war, and that we were told by our highest policymakers that there was, you know, an imminent threat."[104]

Press coverage of Kay's interim report accentuated the ongoing failure to discover WMD in Iraq.[105]

Bush was "shocked" by the paltry results of Kay's investigation, but he relied on Powell to defend the administration's decision to oust Saddam Hussein, even if WMD were never found.[106] On October 7, in an op-ed published by the *Washington Post*, the secretary of state underscored everything that Kay *had* found, including "a host of activities related to weapons of mass destruction" that put Iraq in material breach of U.N. Resolution 1441.[107] Powell also highlighted Kay's estimation that Saddam Hussein "had every intention of continuing his work on banned weapons," which would have led to WMD deployment or proliferation. Therefore, the secretary argued, the United States was justified in eliminating the dangerous regime.[108] Powell concluded that Bush was correct in his decision to invade Iraq: "This was an evil regime, lethal to its own people, in deepening material breach of its Security Council obligations, and a threat to international peace and security. Hussein would have stopped at nothing until something stopped him. It's a good thing that we did."[109]

In the absence of WMD, Powell had begun to pivot from the premise of his February presentation at the United Nations, in which he had argued for a *preemptive* war against clear and present danger. Now, with no stockpiles found, he was providing a justification for a *preventive* war against a known but not immediate threat. Tenet, like Powell, thought Kay's findings were substantive and incriminating of Saddam Hussein. Still, he later admitted, "None of it . . . was the 'smoking gun' that would justify our NIE estimates and validate the allegations in Powell's UN speech."[110]

The political controversy over undiscovered WMD in Washington paled in comparison to the chaotic and increasingly violent situation in Iraq. Occupation forces were under assault from an expanding insurgency, and the number of American casualties had escalated significantly since the end of "major combat operations."[111] The Pentagon was not prepared to provide post-conflict security. By early fall 2003, Powell concluded that "we were in trouble."[112]

Bush responded by shifting more command and control from the Defense Department to the White House. He approved the creation of the Iraq Stability Group, which was coordinated by Rice and her NSC staff.[113] Earlier, she had telephoned Bremer in Baghdad to convey a sense of urgency. "Colin and I are convinced," Rice said, "that Iraq has become the decisive theater in the war on terrorism and that if we win in Iraq, Islamic terrorism can be defeated."[114] Meanwhile, upset over his diminished control and the "confused chain of command," Rumsfeld sourly suggested that Bremer begin reporting directly to Rice or Powell.[115] Years later, Powell would write in a private email that Rumsfeld had "abdicated" his position as steward of the postwar occupation and "should have been fired."[116] Bremer officially worked for the Pentagon, but he never really considered the defense secretary his boss. From the outset, the former ambassador saw himself as "neither Rumsfeld's nor Powell's man," but rather "the president's man."[117]

By mid-November, with conditions in Iraq deteriorating under the CPA, the Bush administration sought to expedite the transfer of political authority to the Iraqis.[118] While in agreement, Powell continued to argue for a legitimate process and warned of the risks associated with moving hastily on the political front without solving the security problem.[119] "Given the mounting popular discontent with occupation," the secretary wrote, "we cannot sustain the current CPA arrangement long enough to allow completion of the complicated process of drafting a Constitution and holding full-fledged elections. . . . A credible political process leading to an early transition of power is critical to subduing the growing insurgency."[120] Rumsfeld balked at Powell's use of the term *insurgency* and continued to insist that "we had enough troops on the ground."[121] Regardless, Bush's national security team agreed that Bremer must relinquish administrative control of Iraq to a credible interim government by June 30, 2004.[122]

Amid the turmoil in Iraq, the Bush administration received two early Christmas presents in 2003. On December 14, U.S. troops captured Saddam Hussein. Officials hoped that this would be a turning point in Iraq's reconstruction. Two days later, Libya announced that it would abandon its WMD programs and invite weapons inspectors to verify its disarmament. Interviewed on a national radio show, Powell admitted that it had been a "terrific week" but also cautioned that Iraq's road to stability and democracy was fraught with obstacles. "We still have a lot of work ahead us," he said. When asked whether he would serve in a second Bush term, Powell dodged, saying merely that he served at the pleasure of the president.[123]

One week into the New Year, Powell met with reporters to offer his reflections and to field questions on the state of international affairs. He aimed to accentuate the positive. Powell said that U.S. foreign policy was based on the principles of human rights, democracy, and free markets, and he pledged that the administration would "to do everything we can" to achieve world peace and expand economic opportunity. While acknowledging that significant challenges lay ahead, the secretary emphasized constructive developments in countries such as Afghanistan, Pakistan, and Libya.[124]

The press pool, however, wanted Powell to discuss "something a little less rosy": the accusation that the administration had "vastly exaggerated" the Iraqi threat. A reporter asked the secretary if he would like to go back in time and modify his February speech to the U.N. Security Council. Powell responded with an emphatic "No" and launched into a well-considered self-defense. He said he always knew that the U.N. speech would be scrutinized, and that is why he had invested so much time "with the experts" to build a case against Iraq based on "solid and multi-sourced" evidence. "I am confident of what I presented last year," he said, and so, he added, was the intelligence community. Powell also recounted Saddam Hussein's appalling record of deploying WMD and his history of flouting U.N. resolutions and weapons inspectors. Nor was there any disputing

Hussein's desire to produce more WMD or his "intact" programs and "infrastructure." The only debate remaining, the secretary said, was whether large stockpiles of WMD would be found. On that score, he recommended that everybody let the weapons inspectors complete their work.[125]

Two weeks later, Kay, soon to depart his role as leader of the Iraq Survey Group fact-finding mission, announced that no WMD had been found in Iraq. "I don't think they existed," he told reporters.[126] Nevertheless, the CIA continued the search under Charles Duelfer, another former U.N. weapons inspector. On January 25, aboard an airplane bound for Europe, a journalist asked Powell who was right about WMD in Iraq, him or Kay. The secretary responded honestly, "I think the answer to the question is I don't know yet." Powell then returned to his familiar defense of the administration: his "good solid comprehensive" U.N. presentation had been based on "the best intelligence," which not only reflected the credible National Intelligence Estimate submitted to Congress, but was also "consistent with the views of other intelligence agencies of other governments." Powell recounted Saddam Hussein's history with WMD and U.N. inspectors and said that the prewar intelligence had been proven "correct with respect to intention, with respect to capability to develop such weapons, with respect to programs." The only outstanding question, Powell reiterated, was whether Iraq actually had any stores of WMD. "And if they had any, where did they go? And if they didn't have any, then why wasn't that known beforehand?" The answer, he said, would be provided by the new chief weapons inspector, Duelfer.[127]

In his midflight conversation with reporters, Powell had unwittingly made headline news.[128] He was the first member of Bush's national security team to admit that there might not be WMD in Iraq. Rice telephoned to complain. Powell was flummoxed. It had been ten months since the invasion, and no weapons had been found. He thought it ludicrous not to admit the possibility that stockpiles might not be discovered. "The fact of the matter is," he told Rice, "you can't ignore the possibility, since the guy [Kay] we sent there for eight months as *our guy* says there's nothing there."[129]

On January 28, Kay, who had long believed that Iraq did possess WMD stockpiles, delivered distressing news to the Senate Armed Services Committee. "Let me begin," he said, "by saying, we were almost all wrong, and I certainly include myself here." By *we,* Kay meant not just the United States, but also other major powers, including France and Germany. By "almost all wrong," Kay meant that there was evidence that Iraq had been engaged in "activities prohibited" by the United Nations, but it was not manufacturing or in the possession of WMD. "It turns out," he reiterated, "that we were all wrong [about stockpiles] . . . and that is most disturbing." Kay further argued that he did *not* believe that the faulty prewar intelligence, which was based on "limited data," had been politicized by the White House.[130]

Kay's testimony decimated the Bush administration's primary rationale for going to war. There had been no imminent threat because there were no WMD. The president's reaction shifted from "shock" to "anger."[131] Powell, once again, prepared the administration's defense. He pored over Kay's senate testimony to locate any evidence that might justify a preventive war against Iraq. At a White House cabinet meeting, the secretary outlined the parameters of his analysis, extrapolating Saddam Hussein's clear "intent" and "capabilities" related to WMD. Thereafter, he took his case, including an annotated and highlighted transcript of Kay's testimony, to two dozen editors and reporters at the *Washington Post.*[132]

At the outset of the meeting, Powell was asked whether he remained confident that war with Iraq had been warranted. He was adamant. "Yes. I think it was the right thing to do," he said, "and I think history will demonstrate that." The secretary then gave a lengthy exposition on an "intent" and "capabilities" "formula" for going to war, a formulation, he argued, that was vindicated by Kay's testimony. Powell's thesis was that if an enemy had both intent and capability to develop and deploy WMD, then a preventive war was justified. There could be no doubt, Powell stated, that Saddam Hussein intended to develop and deploy WMD, based on the evidence of his previous use of banned weapons and his many denials and deceptions.[133]

As for WMD programs, Powell outlined five levels of capability that must be examined. "There is no question," he said, that Iraq possessed level-one capability, the engineers and scientists with "intellectual ability" to develop WMD. Iraq also kept in place, he argued, dual-use scientific laboratories, the "technical infrastructure" that represented level-two capability. As for level three, did Hussein have the "actual facilities" to produce weapons? Powell equivocated, saying, "I think there is evidence to suggest that he was keeping a warm base, that there was an intent on his part to have that capability." Level-four capability, the secretary said, was the creation of "delivery systems," and the Iraqis were clearly attempting to "develop longer-range missiles." Powell quoted Kay's testimony on the discovery of "hundreds of cases" of Iraqi violations of U.N. Resolution 1441, which demonstrated "the intent of Saddam Hussein to retain [WMD] capability and that there was capability." As for Iraq's level-five WMD capability—"an actual stockpile"—Powell said the final verdict had not yet been rendered, and thus it was only "prudent" to let the weapons inspectors complete their work. Regardless of what they found, Powell contended, "the American people will understand . . . that with that body of evidence—that information and intelligence—that was available to the President at that time, the President made a prudent decision."[134]

The *Post* reporters wanted to determine whether Powell's belief in WMD stockpiles had been the critical factor in his support of the war. He was asked a hypothetical question, one that contrasted a decision for a preemptive war against an imminent threat with a preventive war against a gathering threat. If, in February 2003, the CIA had concluded that there were no stockpiles in Iraq, would the secretary still have "recommended the invasion" to the president? "I don't know," Powell said candidly.

"I don't know because it was the stockpiles that presented the final little piece that made it more of a real and present danger and threat to the region and to the world." To clarify, a reporter asked whether the absence of stockpiles would have lessened the immediacy of the Iraqi danger? "The absence of a stockpile," Powell answered, "changes the political calculus. It changes the answer you get with the little formula I laid out."[135]

Even if Iraq did not have stockpiles, Powell was convinced that Saddam Hussein would have eventually obtained them. Without the threat of a military invasion, he said, Hussein would have dodged U.N. weapons inspectors and eventually broken free of sanctions, and then, absent such "constraints," would have resumed the manufacture of WMD caches. This belief, Powell asserted, was shared by Kay. "There is no doubt in my mind," he said, "that intention and capability would be married up again and they would have gone to the next level and reproduced these weapons. Why wouldn't they? That was always his intention."[136]

Powell was then asked whether, in preparation of his U.N. speech, he had challenged the CIA "hard enough" to disclose its intelligence sources on WMD and if he received "forthright answers" to his questions. The secretary expressed absolute satisfaction with the process of crafting his address at CIA headquarters—"we really went through it"—and he remained confident that every claim he made was supported by the credible and unpoliticized views of Tenet and his analysts. He admitted that intelligence reports were imperfect, but "there wasn't a word that was in that presentation that was . . . not totally cleared by the intelligence community. It wasn't shaped, it wasn't added to by anyone else in the government."[137]

A summary of Powell's extended interview was published by the *Washington Post* on February 3 and instantly covered by the major wire services and television news networks.[138] In addition to his robust defense of the decision to invade Iraq, press coverage emphasized the secretary's uncertainty on whether he would have recommended war if he believed Iraq had no WMD stock-piles. Predictably, Rice telephoned to complain. The administration was not pleased with Powell's willingness to entertain hypothetical questions because the search for WMD was still ongoing. He was seen as undercutting Bush's decision to overthrow Saddam. "I think the whole White House operation was mad," the secretary recounted, ". . . the NSC, the president—everybody was annoyed."[139] But since he did not think he had erred or said anything "particularly startling," Powell ordered the State Department to release the full transcript of the *Washington Post* interview.[140]

Soon after talking to Rice, Powell was on television vigorously defending himself and the administration. No less than three times, he stated that the president had made the correct decision to invade Iraq, and for further stark emphasis, he added, "I think it was clear that this was a regime with intent, capability, and it was a risk the president felt strongly we could not take, and it was something we all agreed to and would probably agree to it again under any other set of circumstances."[141] The *New York Times* noted how Powell had "scrambled . . . to present a united front about the war in Iraq."[142]

The media spotlight turned next to George Tenet. On the heels of Kay's testimony, the embattled CIA director chose to give a comprehensive address at Georgetown University to educate "the American people" on how the U.S. intelligence community had evaluated Iraq's WMD programs and how that evaluation led to the now-controversial National Intelligence Estimate of October 2002. The detailed address, delivered on the one-year anniversary of Powell's U.N. speech, included new admissions about "discrepancies" in "some intelligence claims" and possible overestimations about Iraq's WMD programs, but it was largely a vigorous defense of the CIA's prewar WMD intelligence, which he presented as a well-grounded "objective assessment . . . of a brutal dictator who was continuing his efforts to deceive and build programs that might constantly surprise us and threaten our interest." Moreover, Tenet argued that CIA analysts had actually been moderate in their briefings on Iraq and had "never said there was an 'imminent' threat." Like Powell, Tenet also asserted that Kay's investigation, even without uncovering WMD, had vindicated much of the intelligence that underpinned Bush's decision to invade Iraq.[143]*

A few days later, the president appeared on NBC's *Meet the Press*. Bush defended his decisions and the policy of preventive war: going to war when threats to national security were clear but not immediate. "I believe it is essential—that when we see a threat," he told Tim Russert, "we deal with those threats before they become imminent. It's too late if they become imminent. It's too late in this new kind of war, and so that's why I made the decision I made."[144]

During the next three weeks, Powell appeared on scores of television and radio programs and before the House International Relations Committee, where he robustly defended the intelligence community and Bush's decision to invade Iraq. On the *Sean Hannity Show,* Powell said three times that Bush, with the full support of his advisers, had made the right choice, and that the debate over undiscovered WMD stockpiles did nothing "to take away from the rightness, the correctness, of the president's decision."[145] At every opportunity Powell reiterated his intent and capability formula that, he said, justified preventive warfare and the overthrow of a sovereign foreign government.

The secretary's testimony before the House committee mirrored his exposition at the *Washington Post* office, including his use of Kay's report to bolster his argument that the war had been just. Powell told the committee that the weapons inspectors had proved "there was no question about [Iraq's] intent, no question about capability, no question about infrastructure, and no question . . . that Saddam Hussein was in material breach of his obligation. . . . And there was no question in Dr. Kay's mind,

---

*Powell's reaction to Tenet's public admission of "discrepancies" in the intelligence on Iraq amounted to "Holy Shit!" See Woodward, *Plan of Attack*, 440.

just as there was no question in my mind or any of the president's advisers, that this was something that had to be dealt with." As for the absence of WMD, Powell admitted the administration's great surprise. Still, he argued that Bush did not take the country to war under false pretenses because the intelligence professionals believed that Iraq possessed banned weapons. "We believed it at the time," Powell said. "And we believed it because the intelligence information available to us said the stockpiles were there.[146]

Over the course of numerous public appearances, Powell had defended the president's war decision without stirring more controversy. But on February 27, he became ensnared in another hypothetical question of whether he would have recommended war had he known that Iraq did not possess WMD. Referring to Powell's *Washington Post* interview, Paula Zahn asked the secretary if the absence of stockpiles meant that there had been no clear and present danger to the United States. Powell replied, "If we had known at the time we were going through the run-up to the war that there were no stockpiles, we would have taken that into account. Might we still have gone ahead? Perhaps. Would we have seen it as a serious or a present danger? Maybe not. All I was saying [to the *Washington Post*] is that reasonable people when faced with the new information should put that into their calculation and think it through again."[147]

Not satisfied, Zahn pressed on. Knowing what he knew about WMD in February 2004, would Powell still have supported the war in February 2003? At first Powell deflected. He said that the weapons inspectors were still reviewing documents, still interviewing people, and still searching for banned weapons. But then he came back to the question. "And whether I would have come to the same conclusion or not," he told Zahn, "that was the question I was asked [by the *Washington Post*], and the answer was: I don't know. Because I would have had to take a whole situation, once again, into account, and I think the President would have as well." Regardless, Powell said, the administration had made the decision for war based on the best information available. "The fact of the matter is," he concluded, "we did the right thing. This regime is no longer a danger. Whether they had stockpiles or not, they will never have stockpiles in the future."[148]

For Powell, the press's fixation on prewar WMD intelligence was an exhausting distraction from the immediate challenge of reconstructing Iraqi society, including the formation of a legitimate government. "Now what we have to do," he told one interviewer in mid-February, "is focus not on the past, but on the future. We have to focus on building a democracy in Iraq."[149] The administration was clinging to the plan it made in November to establish an Iraqi transitional administration and assembly by June 30, 2004. In Iraq, Jerry Bremer was brokering the means by which the new government would be brought to power. Meanwhile, Powell pressured Secretary-General Annan to support the administration's timetable and play a central role in Iraq's reconstruction.

By early March 2004, there was demonstrable progress in Iraq despite the ongoing violence. In a major step toward the transfer of political sovereignty, the Iraqi Governing Council approved the Transitional Administrative Law.[150] This interim constitution guaranteed freedom of expression and religion, and the right to assemble and to organize political parties, and prohibited discrimination based on religion, nationality, or gender. Moreover, it called for Iraq's political independence by the end of June. Powell considered it "a remarkable milestone" on Iraq's road to constitutional democracy.[151] "We are now starting to see democracy take root in a country that has never known it before," he said. "And so when people see that happening, I think they will see, over time, this [the war] was the right thing to do."[152]

By the end of the month, however, American troops were engaged in full-fledged combat with the militia of radical Shiite cleric Muqtada al-Sadr. Moreover, four American security contractors were killed in Fallujah by insurgents who hung two of their mutilated bodies on a bridge spanning the Euphrates River. Rumsfeld ordered a major reprisal against the extremists. But, on April 9, Bush terminated the Fallujah offensive because the Iraqi Governing Council threatened to resign if he failed to do so. The council's resignation would have jeopardized the transfer of sovereignty.[153]

A week later, the publication of a new book by Bob Woodward provoked more controversy in Washington. *Plan of Attack* detailed the sixteen-month ramp-up to the invasion and depicted the Bush administration as plotting for war as early as November 2001. Among the book's other disclosures was Tenet's infamous statement to the president that the WMD case against Iraq was a "slam dunk."[154] Powell, on the other hand, was portrayed sympathetically as the only senior adviser who had expressed misgivings about going to war. According to Woodward, Powell warned the president about the dire consequences of overthrowing Saddam Hussein's regime: "You will become the government until you get a new government. You are going to be the proud owner of 25 million people. You will own all their hopes, aspirations and problems."[155]

After months of Powell's loyal defense of the administration's decision to go to war, Woodward's narrative was hotly debated in Washington and the national media. Press accounts of *Plan of Attack* frequently placed Powell at the center of the story. Not only had he been the most independent-minded presidential adviser, but his prewar admonitions seemed especially prescient just when "the American occupation has met with new perils."[156] Bush's critics cited Powell's warnings as evidence of the president's hubris and failure to adequately prepare for the instability created by the invasion. "The strongest criticism of Bush," said Democratic campaign manager Steve Murphy, "is that he did not have a plan for the aftermath of the war. And that was exactly what Powell was pointing out to him. He is a credible source."[157]

Powell waited several days before commenting on the book and clarifying his role in prewar decision making. He told reporters that he was proud of his performance as a senior adviser to the president. It was true that he had wanted the administration to consider "all the options" regarding Iraq and that he had made the president understand "that it was going to be a difficult mission in the aftermath" of major combat operations. "I will always plead guilty to being cautious about matters of war and peace," Powell stated, but he also acknowledged his participation in the military planning and preparations for war. "[After] going down the United Nations path," Powell said, his support for the president's decision was "willing and it was complete, no matter how others might try to impose their policy wishes on . . . my body."[158] A month later, appearing on CNN, Powell was asked if Woodward's portrayal of him was accurate. He answered, "Yeah, it's an interesting book, and anybody who is interested in politics and how things work in Washington and the White House would learn a lot from reading it. . . . I don't think I was surprised by anything in the book."[159]

Many political commentators concluded from Woodward's account that Powell had been against the war with Iraq. As a result, they excoriated him for lacking the moral courage to forcefully oppose the war and for being excessively loyal to Bush. Columnist Maureen Dowd derided the secretary of state's behavior as a "profile in cravenness" for not standing up to the president.[160] Likewise, Clarence Page of the *Chicago Tribune* lamented that Powell had not resigned in protest before the invasion. "By now," Page wrote, the secretary of state "might be seen as some sort of principled hero," but instead, "Super-Colin looks more like a semi-Colin."[161] Sidney Blumenthal, a former senior adviser to Bill Clinton, disparaged Powell for playing "the good soldier, not taking his qualms and knowledge to the Congress or the American people. The most popular man in the country, he never used his inherent veto power to promote his position."[162]

The editorial board of the *New York Times* was equally harsh. Powell was denounced as a timid foreign policy leader who had failed to fulfill "his promise of being the powerful voice of reason" within a highly ideological administration. According to the *Times*, an all-too-familiar Colin Powell had reemerged, the dutiful follower—that "faithful soldier who prized loyalty, sometimes too much, and had an overly refined sense of the governmental feeding chain." Powell was chastised for trying to "have it both ways," to portray himself in public as the president's always dependable and loyal subordinate, but act in private as the independent "wise man" who knew that war with Iraq was a horrible idea. "Knowing that Mr. Powell thought the invasion was a bad idea doesn't make him look better," the editorial concluded, "it makes his inaction puzzling and disappointing."[163]

The controversy over Woodward's book paled in comparison to a crisis that erupted over a U.S. military prison in Abu Ghraib, Iraq. On April 28, 2004, the television news program *60 Minutes II* broadcast damning photographs of American soldiers humiliating and abusing Iraqi prisoners. The chairman of the Joint Chiefs of Staff and the secretary of defense had been informed of these violations of the Geneva Conventions three months prior.[164] In January 2004, the army had launched a preliminary criminal inquiry; two officers, a captain and a colonel, were quickly suspended from duty.[165] Soon afterward, a second, wider investigation was initiated under Major General Antonio M. Taguba. In February, as the investigation continued, an army official announced that seventeen military personnel had been suspended.[166] Moreover, the army admitted that three months earlier senior commanders in Iraq had received an incriminating report of prisoner abuse from the International Committee of the Red Cross.[167] Taguba's chilling report, which was dated March 2004, chronicled the "systemic and illegal abuse of detainees" with "numerous incidents of sadistic, blatant, and wanton criminal abuses."[168] He recommended further investigation and disciplinary action against a dozen officers and civilian contractors.

Bush and Powell had some knowledge of the problems at Abu Ghraib before the *60 Minutes II* broadcast, but unlike military and civilian leaders at the Pentagon, neither had seen the vivid photographic evidence until it appeared on national television.[169] In mid-April, Chairman of Joint Chiefs of Staff Richard

Myers had learned that CBS planned to show the "so disgusting" Abu Ghraib photographs.[170] On two separate occasions, he convinced reporter Dan Rather to "sit on this blockbuster story."[171] When the pictures were finally broadcast, Bush felt "blindsided," and he considered the ensuing crisis "a low point" in his presidency.[172] A week after the scandal broke, Powell appeared on *Larry King Live* and compared his own shocked reaction to when he first learned of the My Lai massacre in Vietnam.[173] "Nobody," the secretary said later, "was prepared for that CBS show that night."[174]

Rumsfeld, however, thought Powell and others were overreacting. He determined that the abuses at Abu Ghraib were merely "the senseless crimes of a small group of prison guards who ran amok in the absence of adequate supervision."[175] An independent review panel, commissioned by Rumsfeld himself, disagreed. The so-called Schlesinger Report of August 2004 concluded that the physical and psychological prisoner abuses in Iraq "were not just the failure of some individuals to follow known standards, and they are more than the failure of a few leaders to enforce proper discipline. There is both institutional and personal responsibility at higher levels."[176]

More than a year before the Abu Ghraib scandal, Bush, Rumsfeld, Cheney, Rice, and Tenet had decided that in the post-9/11 era, traditional prisoner interrogation techniques were inadequate to protect the nation. Attorney General John Ashcroft agreed with them. In summer 2002, the Justice Department, working secretly with the CIA and White House lawyers, opined in the infamous "torture memo" of August 1, 2002, that enhanced interrogation techniques (EIT) were legal and free of congressional interference.[177] Later that year at the Defense Department, Rumsfeld skirted the Geneva Conventions and the Uniform Code of Military Justice by authorizing a new list of coercive interrogation methods. While he forbade the use of the most egregious torture practices, including waterboarding, the CIA readily adopted extreme tactics.[178] "When Secretary Rumsfeld approved the use of abusive techniques against detainees,"

Senator Carl Levin of the Armed Services Committee later concluded, "he unleashed a virus which ultimately infected interrogation operations conducted by the U.S. military in Afghanistan and Iraq."[179]

Under orders from the White House, the new, expansive guidelines for military and CIA interrogations were initially kept secret from the State Department's leadership. According to the head of the Justice Department's Office of Legal Counsel, this highly unusual decision was made for two reasons. First, because the secretary of state and his lawyers "would have strenuously objected," and second, because of fear that the State Department would leak the information to the press.[180] By the summer of 2003, several al Qaeda prisoners, including Abu Zubaydah and Abd al-Rahim al-Nashiri, had been tortured by the CIA at a secret black site. In July 2003, a CIA officer wrote in an email that the White House was "extremely concerned Powell would blow his stack if he were to be briefed on what's been going on."[181] It appears that Powell and his staff learned the full details of the Justice Department's "torture memo," which sanctioned the CIA's program, only when they read about them in the press shortly after the Abu Ghraib scandal broke.[182]

The undisclosed legal opinions aside, Powell was not oblivious to the CIA's mistreatment of Afghan War prisoners. He was aware that Bush's February 2002 order for the general humane treatment of detainees pertained only to the U.S. military, not the CIA. Powell also knew of press reports about secret CIA detention facilities and their use of coercive interrogation techniques.[183] Furthermore, on January 16, 2003, the CIA's general counsel, Scott Muller, reminded Powell, Rice, Rumsfeld, and Cheney that the agency had been authorized to use interrogation techniques "inconsistent with the humane treatment of detainees." According to Muller's meeting notes, "Everyone in the room evinced understanding of the issue. CIA's past and ongoing use of enhanced techniques was reaffirmed and in no way drawn into question."[184]

By fall 2003, seven months before the Abu Ghraib scandal, Powell and Rumsfeld had learned the intricate details of the CIA's torture program. Attorney General Ashcroft had argued that the president's senior advisers should not be discussing such particulars, and after one meeting he conveyed his dismay, asking, "Why are we talking about this in the White House. History will not judge this kindly."[185] Nevertheless, in September 2003 an increasingly anxious Rice had decided that Rumsfeld and Powell should be fully aware of the harsh interrogations before the administration reaffirmed the secret policy. This torture briefing occurred on September 16; it was the first in a series of subject-matter meetings among Bush's principal advisers, including Powell. According to a subsequent investigation by CIA Inspector General John L. Helgerson, "none of those involved in these briefings expressed any reservations about the program."[186] Powell was, however, visibly uneasy with EIT. The CIA's chief legal officer, John Rizzo, who was present at the torture briefings, later wrote of Powell's obvious discomfort: "The most interesting figure of all at these meetings was Colin Powell. Now, there was a man giving off an unmistakable vibe of being there out of a sense of duty but intensely uncomfortable about it. At the end of each EIT update session, Powell would bolt out of the Situation Room as fast as he could."[187]

Thus, in spring 2004, when the Abu Ghraib prison scandal flared, Powell was completely aware of the CIA's secret brutal interrogations of captured terrorists. Nevertheless, he, like the president, was caught off guard by the public airing of the graphic photographs from Iraq. Unlike the al Qaeda terrorists, Iraqi prisoners were obviously covered under the Geneva Conventions. Powell was asked repeatedly by the press to comment on the U.S. abuse of wartime detainees, and he tried—not always successfully—to specifically condemn the Defense Department's (not the CIA's) maltreatment of prisoners. The secretary said that he had seen the army's initial investigation report on Abu Ghraib in March and trusted that all responsible personnel in the chain of command would be punished appropriately.

Throughout, Powell consistently underscored his personal support for international laws, especially the Geneva Conventions, that govern the treatment of prisoners. Given his long acquiescence to the CIA's torture program, however, his public statements were sometimes deceitful. "Torture is torture is torture," he said on Fox News. "It is unacceptable. It is not the way you deal with human beings who are entrusted to your care . . . and you are totally responsible for their welfare. We have international standards that have to be maintained."[188] Even if prisoners were designated as unlawful combatants "not directly under the Convention," he told NBC's Tim Russert, "we should treat them, nevertheless, in a humane manner, in accordance with what is expected of us by international law and by the Geneva Convention."[189] When asked about U.S. interrogation techniques, Powell regularly referred reporters to the Defense Department—not the CIA—saying, "I don't know about the details of the interrogation rules" and "I can't comment on a specific set of interrogation rules. I'll have to yield to my friends at the Pentagon."[190]

On May 5, 2004, Rumsfeld expressed his willingness to resign over the Abu Ghraib scandal. Indeed, the president was furious and wanted "someone's head . . . to roll on this one."[191] But Bush regained his composure, and he eventually ordered an innocuous punishment. The president allowed his dissatisfaction with his "crusty old" defense secretary to be leaked to the press.[192] As the prison controversy swirled, Rumsfeld was forced to take responsibility at a congressional hearing; on May 10 he actually submitted a letter of resignation to the president. Bush rejected it.

In the end, the Abu Ghraib scandal resulted in nearly a dozen courts-martial. The prison's commanding officer was demoted and its head of military intelligence reprimanded and relieved of command. Major General Taguba, who had conducted the first major investigation of the scandal, did not think the punishment went high enough up the chain of command. He ultimately concluded that the abuse of Iraqi prisoners had transpired because "the Commander-in-Chief and those under him authorized a systemic regime of torture."[193]

Even after Abu Ghraib, the Justice Department issued new opinions that the CIA torture program was legal, and as a result enhanced interrogations continued with the consent of Bush's senior advisers, including Powell. According to the CIA's chief legal officer, "The Agency's posture in this regard did not endear us to the rest of the Bush national security team. A series of testy Principals Committee meetings in the White House Situation Room ensued that summer. . . . Secretary of State Colin Powell, for his part, mostly just glowered. He had never hidden his unhappiness about having to attend any meetings on the EIT program, and by now he seemed totally fed up with the Agency in general, angry—understandably, to be sure—that the CIA's faulty assessments on the Iraq WMD issue had caused this proud and revered public servant to look like a fool in the wake of his high-profile speech at the UN the year before."[194]

Although the president refused to accept Rumsfeld's resignation over Abu Ghraib, he readily took George Tenet's. On June 3, Bush announced the CIA director's decision. Tenet had felt increasingly estranged from the administration. After the intelligence behind Powell's U.N. speech began to collapse, he knew that he was in serious jeopardy. Indeed, the secretary of state was furious with him.[195] "I am so fucked," Tenet told a subordinate.[196] The director believed that the White House made him the scapegoat for the decision to invade Iraq and for the failure to find WMD. He was especially piqued by Woodward's *Plan of Attack* and the related press coverage that accentuated his "slam dunk" statement at the White House. "Woodward's book," Tenet later wrote, "had ignited a media bonfire, and I was the guy . . . burned at the stake."[197]

Tenet never apologized to Powell for the gross intelligence failure, but one of his CIA subordinates eventually did. In his 2015 book *The Great War of Our Time*, Michael Morell expressed sorrow "for putting his [Powell's] well-deserved reputation for probity at risk by arming him with bad intelligence to use as the basis of his UN speech. . . . CIA and the broader intelligence community clearly failed him and the American public."[198] When Powell learned of the belated public apology he dismissed it as a crass attempt to garner press attention and sell books.[199]

Tenet's departure from the Bush administration renewed speculation about Powell's future. The previous summer, the *Washington Post* had reported that the secretary and his chief deputy, Rich Armitage, had informed Rice that they planned to serve only one term with the Bush administration.[200] The White House overreacted to the story, disturbed by the implication that Powell was protesting the president's foreign policy. The following day, Powell and his deputy flew to Texas to see Bush at his ranch. There, the trio discussed policy but never the issue of resignation. In short, their meeting was a public relations ploy to demonstrate administration unity. The truth was that Powell and Armitage had no inclination to serve a second tour of duty, and the president was disinclined to have them stay on.[201]

By the spring of 2004, Powell, like Tenet, was feeling like a "casualty of war," and he did not discourage senior aides or his friends from talking to journalists about the trials and tribulations of being Bush's secretary of state.[202] A profile in *GQ* magazine concluded, "Powell was finished. . . . Exhausted. Frustrated. Bitter."[203] U.N. Secretary-General Kofi Annan later wrote that no political figure endured the Iraq War "more painfully or publicly than Colin Powell. . . . The Bush administration had exploited, and exhausted, his stature."[204]

Around that time, Powell met privately with Bush to convey his frustration with the administration's policy-making process and his intention to resign after the November election. "Your system is not working well," he told Bush. "We are too many different philosophical views, and we are not reconciling them."[205] The president disagreed, saying that "different views are essential" for an effective administration, just as they had been with Weinberger and Shultz in the Reagan era. Powell considered that a poor comparison. "Mr. President," he said, "I lived through Weinberger and Shultz. I was there. And yes, they had their differences. But they had a system for resolving them. We don't now. We sort of each go our own way and go around." Should there be a second term, Powell encouraged the president to devise a better process for reconciling competing views among his principal advisers. Moreover, he recommended that the president "get a whole new team, and it begins with my departure because I am so different from the rest of your team."[206]

The president sympathized with Powell's frustrations, and he readily accepted his decision to resign at the end of the year. Bush later wrote, "He had served three tough years and was naturally fatigued. He was also a sensitive man who had been wounded by the infighting and discouraged by the failure to find weapons of mass destruction in Iraq. . . . I admired Colin, but it sometimes seemed like the State Department he led wasn't fully on board with my philosophy and policies. It was important to me that there be no daylight between the president and the secretary of state."[207]

In his final months as secretary of state, Powell's top priority was the successful transfer of political power in Iraq from the CPA to a legitimate interim government. By mid-March 2004 there had been meaningful progress, with the United Nations agreeing to play a substantial role in Iraq's political reconstruction. Moreover, the Iraqi Governing Council had approved the Transition Administrative Law, which laid the groundwork for a new Iraqi constitution and set deadlines for a new temporary government by June 30, 2004, and the election of a national assembly by January 31, 2005.[208] This momentum was jeopardized, however, when factions of the Shia and Sunni communities rose up against the U.S.-led occupation.

By May the State Department, which was exerting increased influence on Iraq's reconstruction, had made major strides in setting up a new, four-thousand-person American embassy in Baghdad. With only six weeks remaining as the administrative leader of the occupation, Bremer recommended the deployment of an additional twenty-five to forty thousand U.S. troops to bolster security and stability. Rumsfeld resisted.[209] Meanwhile, Bush accepted Powell's recommendation that John Negroponte, a career diplomat and then U.S. ambassador to the United Nations, become the new ambassador to Iraq.[210]

On May 28 the Iraqi Governing Council announced that Ayad Allawi had been chosen to become the country's interim prime minister. During the next few days, members of the governing council and its cabinet were appointed to leadership positions in various ministries. On June 2 Iraq's new government was inaugurated with great fanfare. A week later, the U.N. Security Council passed a resolution in support of the provisional administration and its plans to hold democratic elections in January. On June 28, with Negroponte's arrival in Baghdad and the opening of the U.S. embassy, the CPA was dissolved and Iraq's sovereignty restored.[211] The establishment of the interim government was "another huge milestone," Bremer later wrote, but "security remained a big problem."[212]

Developments in Iraq, both political progress and in the seething insurgency, were central issues in the 2004 U.S. presidential contest between Bush and Democrat John Kerry. Many were surprised when the White House announced that neither Powell nor Rice would give speeches at the Republican convention. Powell, who had given keynote addresses at the two previous conventions, remained the party's most admired leader. A May NBC-*Wall Street Journal* poll indicated that 69 percent of Americans viewed Powell favorably, compared to only 49 percent for Bush and 39 percent for both Cheney and Rumsfeld.[213] The White House asserted that it was customary for national security officials not to attend political conventions, and Powell hewed to that line. "As secretary of state," he told a group of journalists, "I am obliged not to participate in any way, shape, fashion, or form in parochial, political debates."[214] In truth, the secretary chose not to attend the Republican convention, knowing full well that Secretaries of State George Shultz and James Baker had attended in 1984 and 1992, respectively. Unlike Rice, Powell wanted no part in Bush's reelection campaign.[215] Some interpreted his decision as a snub to the administration's "hawks over the war in Iraq," while others merely saw him sidestepping partisan politics. The secretary, his friends said, was hardly "devastated about staying home."[216]

The Bush reelection campaign suffered a serious blow in early October when the CIA's chief weapons inspector in Iraq delivered a thousand-page report to Congress. Like his predecessor, Charles Duelfer announced, "We were almost all wrong" about WMD in Iraq.[217] He concluded that Saddam Hussein wanted to avoid U.N. sanctions, and while he dreamed of reconstituting WMD and long-range missile programs, Iraq's unconventional weapons programs and stockpiles had been destroyed years before the U.S. invasion. Moreover, Iraq had "no formal written strategy or plan for the revival of WMD after sanctions."[218] The *New York Times* editorialized, "Nothing in the voluminous record provides Mr. Bush with the justification he wanted for a preventative war because the weapons programs did not exist."[219]

After Duelfer's report, the promotion of democracy in Iraq and the January 31 national assembly election became increasingly important to Powell and the entire Bush administration. The biggest threat to a successful election was the dramatic rise in violence in the late summer and fall of 2004. "The danger we have to worry about," Powell had told Matt Lauer on NBC's *Today Show*, "is this insurgency. And we must not lose heart. We must not fall faint now because we can prevail. . . . We cannot go into the future with these places under the control of these dissident elements."[220] In August U.S. forces had battled with the Mahdi Army in Najaf until the Shia religious leader Ali al-Sistani intervened and negotiated a truce. The next month, U.S. soldiers from the First Infantry Division, together with Iraqi soldiers and national guardsmen, captured the insurgent stronghold of Samarra.

The death toll was mounting. From the time that Iraq had regained its political sovereignty in June to the end of September 2004, 162 Americans were killed. That was more than had died during the major combat operations of the invasion. Since March 2003, more than 1,000 U.S. troops had been killed and some 7,000 wounded.

On November 7, 2004, just weeks before Iraq's national elections, U.S. marines and soldiers, along with Iraqi troops, launched Operation Phantom Fury, a bloody and destructive campaign. The mission was to take Fallujah. In an interview with the *Financial Times*, Powell described the city as "a hotbed of the insurgency, a magnet for terrorists and a source of instability in the Sunni Triangle."[221] The mission was partially successful: two thousand insurgents were killed or captured, but many others escaped the city. Ninety-two more Americans died.[222]

The assault on Fallujah had begun five days after the U.S. elections, in which Bush defeated Kerry in both the Electoral College and the popular vote. Republicans also made gains in the House and the Senate. Powell interpreted the outcome as affirmation, if not vindication, of his and the president's foreign policy, a mixture of unilateralism and multilateralism in defense of national interests. "The President took that message to the American people," Powell said, "and the American people accepted that message and gave him more than a marginal mandate to keep moving forward."[223]

On November 4, Bush informed his principal advisers that cabinet changes were forthcoming. Despite what the president had told Powell earlier, he, too, had grown tired of the infighting on his national security team and of the press's portrayal of an administration in disarray. "What started as creative tension," Bush later wrote, "had turned destructive."[224] The next day, unbeknownst to Powell, Bush offered the position of secretary of state to Condoleezza Rice. White House Press Secretary Scott McClellan thought it was a monumental mistake. He considered Powell the president's most valuable senior subordinate. "Like much of the country," McClellan wrote, "I was sorry to see Powell go. I always knew him to offer straight, unvarnished advice based on his years of experience as a military and foreign policy leader. What's more, he never hesitated to make his position clear. . . . I think he exemplified what it means to be a team player. He looked out for the interests of the man he served, as well as the country to whom both had sworn allegiance, with great care and wisdom. It was a mistake not to find a way to keep him around."[225]

Five days after Bush's offer to Rice, his chief of staff, Andrew Card, telephoned Powell. Card asked for the secretary's letter of resignation. There had been some discussion of Powell staying on, at least until the January Iraqi election. Some of the secretary's top aides thought their boss actually wanted an invitation to stay and that he probably would have accepted it. Thus, Powell was caught off guard by Card's call. "I thought we were going to talk about it," he said.[226] The secretary then inquired if Rumsfeld had been asked to resign. Card said that he did not know. "If I go, Don should go," he instructed Card.[227] When Card relayed the conversation to the president, Bush was surprised to hear of Powell's "second thoughts about leaving."[228]

Powell delivered a concise letter of resignation on Friday, November 12. In it, he extolled Bush's determined leadership and the administration's achievements in international affairs. "I am pleased to have been part of a team," he wrote, "that launched the Global War Against Terror, liberated the Afghan and Iraqi people, brought the attention of the world to the problem of proliferation, reaffirmed our alliances, adjusted to the post-Cold War World and undertook major initiative to deal with the problem of poverty and disease in the developing world."[229]

Powell did not inform the majority of his staff until the following Monday, just before the White House issued a formal statement. In the press release, Bush described the secretary as "one of the great public servants of our time . . . a soldier, a diplomat, a civic leader, a statesman, and a great patriot."[230] Powell also received a handwritten letter from the president, who praised his wise counsel and their collective achievements. "I value our friendship, and I value your advice," Bush wrote. "A president must listen to experienced leaders. And by listening to you I became a better President. History will judge your tenure well because we accomplished a lot and the world is better off."[231]

Later that afternoon, Powell met with reporters at the State Department. They were eager to learn the details of his resignation. The secretary announced that he would continue to lead the department until Congress confirmed his successor, and he insisted that he had always intended to stay on for a single term. "We knew," Powell said about himself and the president, "where we were heading."[232] The secretary served until January 26, 2005.

★ ★ ★ ★

Newspaper editorials assessing Powell's tenure as secretary of state were decidedly mixed. Some faulted him for not fully utilizing his domestic popularity and international credibility to shape administration policy, and for being too obedient to a misguided president. Most assessments focused on the Iraq War. The *New York Times* reproached Powell for squandering his "enormous stature," for betraying his own misgivings about the war, and for defending Bush's invasion without broader support from traditional U.S. allies. "Mr. Powell," the editorial claimed, "long ago chose loyalty over leadership," and rather than resigning in protest over the war, "he soldiered on, [only] leaving when it was safe and convenient for his boss."[233] Similarly, Richard Cohen of the *Washington Post* castigated Powell for not resigning once he realized that Bush was bent on a war that did not meet the requirements of the Powell Doctrine. "He should have used his immense standing," Cohen wrote, "to oppose a war he knew was unwise and was being fought in ways he knew were wrong. He was, paradoxically, in violation of his own doctrine: caught in a quagmire and with no exit strategy."[234]

While many commentators bemoaned Powell's bad followership, others defended the secretary as an exemplary subordinate who had honorably served his president and country by offering thoughtful, independent, and cautionary counsel. According to the *Washington Post*'s editorial board, Powell was "less a trouper than a dissident," someone who sought to "brake"

Bush's decisions by moderating policies advocated by hard-liners such as Cheney and Rumsfeld. And, while not uncritical of Powell, the editorial board was dumbfounded that "it is Mr. Powell who leaves, while the architects of the failed and even disastrous policies he opposed from postwar Iraq to Guantanamo Bay and Abu Ghraib, remain in office."[235] London's *Daily Mail* also mourned Powell's resignation, as he was "one of the few voices of sanity in the U.S. administration." Paris's *Le Figaro* concluded that the secretary's departure "will leave an immense void and it will worry all of America's allies."[236]

Perhaps Powell's foremost public champion at the time was Walter Isaacson, the former CEO of CNN. Isaacson argued that Powell had performed nobly as secretary of state, serving his boss exceptionally well by following his own conscience and giving the president sound advice and unqualified support. Isaacson assumed that the secretary did not oppose the Iraq War outright and as a result was never deceitful or deserving of scorn for not resigning earlier. Instead, Powell had shined through the morass of the Bush administration's foreign policies. According to Isaacson, he had justly provided his superior with unpopular "cautions and reservations" regarding Iraq, argued for a broad coalition of allies, and advised more careful planning for the postwar occupation. Powell, Isaacson wrote, deserved "an honored place in history's pantheon for statesmen whose ideas and instincts turned out to be right—even though they are ignored."[237]

Indeed, there is much to admire in Colin Powell's performance as secretary of state. His commitment, ability, and independent judgment were readily apparent throughout his four-year tenure. Powell's most unadulterated achievement was his transformational leadership at the State Department. Drawing upon his stature, popularity, and charisma, the secretary inspired the once-demoralized staff and persuaded Congress to underwrite sweeping improvements in facilities, technology, security, recruitment, and training.

Much of Powell's record as the president's principal foreign policy adviser is also commendable. Benefiting from years of experience in national security affairs, the secretary provided Bush with well-considered independent assessments, policy alternatives, and honest counsel—which frequently ran contrary to the inclinations of the president and the recommendations of other influential senior advisers. Some of Powell's notable successes were the peaceful resolution of the South China Sea crisis, the implementation of a multi-billion-dollar initiative in international health care, and the organization of a broad coalition to fight al Qaeda and the Taliban and to establish the basis for a democratic Afghan government.

Powell's influence on Iraq policy was also significant, most notably during the run-up to the war. In the immediate aftermath of 9/11, he persuaded Bush to focus on al Qaeda and reject Cheney and Rumsfeld's counsel to launch a precipitous attack against Iraq. In 2002 Powell, "the reluctant warrior," pressed the president to clarify his policy objectives and to contemplate the precarious consequences of removing Saddam Hussein from power. The secretary offered Bush a viable policy alternative through the United Nations with potential to achieve the administration's goals without incurring a costly war in the Middle East. Powell further advised the president on the importance of obtaining congressional authorization, should military force be deemed necessary, and pressed for the deployment of adequate ground forces to ensure a lasting victory.

Powell's fidelity to the president's ultimate decision to invade Iraq can also be respected. Those who criticize the secretary for excessive loyalty and for failing to resign in protest before the war wrongly presume that he opposed the overthrow of the Iraqi government. He did not. Over time, Powell came to perceive Saddam Hussein as a clear and present danger, so to resign or to threaten resignation would have been self-contradictory. The secretary's advocacy of coercive diplomacy, his formidable presentation at the United Nations, and his vigorous defense of the war were manifestations of his genuine support for his superior and the decision—with congressional sanction—to topple the Iraqi regime. "Since I set the President on this diplomatic path," he wrote, "I told him if he chose war I would support."[238]

Still, Powell's followership as secretary of state was not without gross failings, both intellectual and ethical. As he admits, the U.N. speech was a monumental failure of discernment, one that had, to use his words, "enormous impact and influence in this country and worldwide."[239] At a crucial juncture in the history of U.S. foreign relations, Powell's judgments on Iraq's WMD programs and its ties to terrorists failed him, the president, and the country. Kenneth R. Hammond, a prominent scholar of human decision making, aptly characterized Powell's U.N. presentation as "a classic example of innocent judgmental incompetence."[240]

Years before becoming secretary of state, Powell had regularly lectured audiences to "challenge the pros," to look "beneath surface appearances," and not to be "buffaloed by experts and elites."[241] Yet, in early 2003, as secretary of state, he too-readily accepted as fact and presented as truth limited and questionable intelligence from dubious sources. While *many* people were to blame for the U.N. speech fiasco, Powell later wrote, "I am mostly mad at myself for not having smelled the problem. My instincts failed me."[242]

Even more problematic and less forgivable was Powell's willingness to claim with utter certainty that Iraq presented an imminent danger to national and international security. He did so despite knowing that the U.S. intelligence community, including the State Department's Bureau of Intelligence and Research, did not believe that Iraq was on the brink of using or sharing WMD. In fact, the 2002 National Intelligence Estimate stated clearly that Saddam Hussein was not likely to deploy WMD unless he was forced into a desperate situation, one that threatened his survival. And only then, as a last-ditch reprisal, the intelligence estimate concluded, would Hussein even consider providing such weapons to terrorist groups. In 2012, even Powell finally acknowledged that the evidence against Iraq as presented in the intelligence estimate was "mostly circumstantial and inferential."[243] Later, in 2017, he stated that he could not even recall if he had studied the entire estimate before making his presentation to the United Nations. "I read it . . . in great detail," he wrote, "after it fell apart [and the WMD were not found]."[244]

Equally troubling in Powell's performance as secretary of state was his acquiescence to Bush's policies on the treatment of war captives. As a combat veteran and retired four-star general who understood the necessity of Geneva prisoner-of-war protections, the secretary should have, at a minimum, been adamant that all Afghan War prisoners, al Qaeda and Taliban, receive humane treatment, even if not granted Geneva status. Bush's November 2001 order, which directed the U.S. military to generally treat its captives humanely, also permitted the armed forces to abuse detainees if "appropriate and consistent with military necessity."[245] Powell did not contest that gaping contingency clause, which Rumsfeld and the Pentagon swiftly used to their advantage. Moreover, Powell accepted that CIA interrogators were entirely exempt from this presidential directive, and when he became intimately familiar with the agency's secret torture program, he did not object to it. Worse still, Powell gave the false impression in public that he was a champion of Geneva protections for all detainees, including so-called illegal enemy combatants, and that he vigorously opposed torture and harsh coercive interrogations. In the end, Powell's service as secretary of state featured superlative leadership of the State Department, but a decidedly mixed record of good and bad followership as the president's senior counselor on American foreign relations.

Leadership is all about followership.

—COLIN L. POWELL

Epilogue

Colin Powell's American journey from a working-class immigrant neighborhood in the South Bronx to the highest echelons of military, political, and diplomatic power was truly remarkable. Once a boy without ambition or direction, a young man who barely graduated from college, he became the most trusted leader in the United States and might have become president.

Powell discovered his raison d'être in the army, and from the beginning of his career he demonstrated tremendous leadership potential. After two tours of duty in Vietnam, Powell dispelled all lingering self-doubt and fully proved his leadership mettle in the 1970s as a battalion commander stationed in South Korea. "Goddamn, this son of a bitch can command soldiers," his superior declared.[1] By 1989, at the age of fifty-one, Powell had become a four-star general. As the chairman of the Joint Chiefs of Staff, he oversaw the planning and prosecution of victorious wars in Central America and the Middle East, which prompted Senator John McCain, himself a Vietnam War hero, to proclaim the chairman America's greatest military leader since World War II.[2] Seven years after retiring from the army, Powell once again demonstrated immense talents as a transformational leader of the State Department.

Powell's impressive leadership notwithstanding, his effective followership was even more essential to his rise to national and international prominence. He was, as Defense Secretary Frank Carlucci once said, the quintessential "right hand man" who consistently delivered results for his superiors.[3] Throughout his four decades of government service, Powell was always somebody's subordinate, and most often he served as a staff officer, an adviser, or student, not as a field commander. As a senior ranking military officer, his job titles frequently marked the persistence of his follower status: assistant, deputy assistant, executive assistant, military assistant, deputy military assistant, and senior military assistant. Even while serving as national security adviser, as chairman of the Joint Chiefs of Staff, and as secretary of state, Powell's principal duties were to provide expert counsel to his superiors and to ensure the execution of their decisions and the realization of their visions. As a result, Powell's career presents a revealing case study of followership and its central role in the leadership process.

Powell's story is informative on multiple levels. At different times, he personified many principal qualities of both good and bad followership. His career also demonstrates that effective and ethical followership, as with good leadership, is learned and developed over time and is reliant on the influence of others, including mentors, role models, and superiors. Moreover, Powell's career illustrates the considerable power that followers can wield on leaders, organizations, and outcomes, while also epitomizing the paradox that most leaders serve simultaneously as followers of others.

During his army career, Powell frequently exhibited central characteristics of an exemplary follower. His overall effectiveness stemmed partly from his congenial and equanimous personality, but more importantly, his motivation and dependability never flagged. Furthermore, Powell worked continuously to develop his professional competencies, demonstrated bravery on the battlefield, and consciously sought to learn from personal experience and from others, especially his military and civilian mentors. Over time, he displayed increased capacity for critical thinking and a related proclivity for independent expression and action. Almost without exception, his superiors lauded his temperament and ability, and they consistently recommended him for accelerated promotion.

Two prime examples of Powell's exemplary followership include his performance as a brigade commander with the 101st Airborne and his subsequent service on Ronald Reagan's NSC. At Fort Campbell, Kentucky, Colonel Powell faced a brusque and demanding assistant division commander and the challenge of leading a floundering brigade. With composure and determination, he seized the initiative, boosted standards, and ultimately transformed the underachieving unit. Powell's supervisors extolled his independence and sound judgment, with one commander recalling how the colonel was "very reassuring to those above him also. He didn't seem to have an agenda, and he got results."[4]

Similarly, amid the historic challenges of the Iran-Contra scandal, Powell demonstrated absolute competency and dedication, first as the deputy to Carlucci and thereafter as President Reagan's sixth national security adviser. Throughout, Lieutenant General Powell displayed exceptional managerial skill in overhauling the NSC staff and mission, including his revitalization of a transparent interagency process for policy making. According to David Rothkopf's history of the NSC, Powell demonstrated "a knack for keeping the interagency team together" and played an indispensable role in redeeming for the president the once "undersupervised, underproductive, ingrown system that [had] collapsed on itself and almost brought the administration down with it."[5]

By the time Powell became chairman of the Joint Chiefs of Staff, he had evolved into the consummate subordinate. Drawing upon well-developed competencies and three decades of experience, he regularly pressed his superiors to articulate well-defined objectives and consistently advised that military force be used as a last resort. Aiming to provide his bosses with clear-cut options and judicious recommendations, Powell performed as a self-determined and anticipatory thinker. "Colin kept thinking,"

National Security Adviser Brent Scowcroft said, "longer than I did or Dick Cheney did, and probably longer than the president."[6] Again and again as chairman, Powell demonstrated determination and moral courage by raising concerns and staking out unpopular policy positions—being the proverbial skunk at the picnic—and when it was important enough, he openly disagreed with his superiors. All the while, Powell recognized his subordinate position in the chain of command and loyally and effectively executed his superiors' final decisions.

There were also points in Powell's career when his followership was ineffective and he failed to achieve intended results. As a young, inexperienced officer in West Germany, for example, Powell committed multiple infractions, including the misplacement of his sidearm and the loss of his platoon's train tickets. Many years later, while at Fort Carson, then Brigadier General Powell clashed with his superior. He failed to argue persuasively for needed reforms, and he botched an attempt to play the honest broker between his commander and the post's demoralized troops. A more significant failing came as secretary of state. As Powell readily admits, his presentation to the U.N. Security Council represented an abject failure of critical judgment, a failure that left a permanent and prominent blot on his decorated record of government service.[7]

At times, Powell's followership also suffered from severe ethical lapses. As both a junior and field-grade officer, he readily embraced the army's self-deceptive, self-promoting, and deleterious culture of "breaking starch," wherein soldiers were amply rewarded for short-term expediency, style over substance, and blind obedience. Consequently, ambitious officers such as Powell were slow to develop their capacity and inclination for independent reasoning and ethical discernment. One extreme result was the willingness of the army officer corps to participate in the cover-up of atrocities committed against defenseless Vietnamese POWs and civilians, including women, children, and the elderly. As Powell confessed in his memoirs, "I broke starch with the best of them. It was tradition"; he wrote further, "That was Vietnam as experienced by the career lobe of my brain. . . . We had lost touch with reality."[8]

A decade after the Vietnam War, Major General Powell became entangled in the Iran-Contra scandal. Aspects of his followership, both during and after the illegal Iranian arms-for-hostages operations, amounted to a dereliction of duty. In 1985, as the defense secretary's chief confidant and action officer, he had contemporaneous knowledge of the illicit arms shipments to Iran—a declared state sponsor of terrorism—and of the need to replenish Israeli stockpiles. Powell also understood that the transfer of American-made missiles from one foreign government to another mandated congressional notification. Then, in 1986, working under direct presidential instruction, Powell himself orchestrated a large shipment of missiles from U.S. stockpiles to Iran, again knowing that the action required communication with Congress.

As a senior government official who swore an oath to support and defend the Constitution, Powell possessed a duty to report the unlawful Iranian transactions to army leadership, congressional leadership, or the Justice Department. To make matters worse, Powell wittingly participated in the subsequent cover-up of the Iranian operation. In the process, he obstructed justice by deceiving and misleading federal investigators in order to protect himself and his superiors.

To this day, Powell remains angry and defiant about Iran-Contra. He insists that Weinberger was a courageous hero for expressing opposition to the Iranian initiative. Moreover, Powell still believes that he and Weinberger were innocent victims of an "out-of-control independent counsel."[9] Thus, it is intriguing to compare this strident perspective to Robert Gates's recent reflections on his own role in the scandal. In his 2016 book, *A Passion for Leadership*, Gates confesses that, as the CIA deputy director,

> *I hadn't done enough right.* . . . I didn't go to the White House counsel, to the chairmen of the congressional oversight committees, or to the attorney general. I told myself for

years that I only knew part of the story, I was no lawyer. . . . But when it was all over, I knew, in my heart of hearts, by my own standard of conduct, I had somehow fallen short. I swore it would never happen again. For most at or near the top of the bureaucratic heap, it is not the great crime that undermines integrity but the little things that erode it.[10]

Powell's tenure as secretary of state, while featuring some notable successes, was also marred by poor ethical acuity. As a combat veteran with a vested interest in the Geneva Conventions, it was surprising and disheartening that the secretary did not rise to champion minimum standards of humane treatment for all captives in the war against al Qaeda and the Taliban. Instead, Powell argued the technical point that the detainees deserved due process to determine if they warranted prisoner-of-war protections. The secretary did not personally believe that al Qaeda fighters deserved POW status, although the Taliban might. Regardless, Powell never seriously advocated giving *any* of the Afghan detainees ironclad Geneva protections from physical and psychological abuse. Nor did the secretary protest the gaping contingency clause in the president's directive to U.S. armed forces that allowed for and quickly led to the purposeful mistreatment of detainees.

Furthermore, Powell did not object to the CIA's clandestine program of rendition and torture, which Senator John McCain, a former POW, condemned as a "disgraceful program" that contributed to "one of the darkest chapters in American history."[11] To make matters worse, Powell gave the false impression in public that he opposed the mistreatment of *all* captives, including so-called unlawful enemy combatants. As secretary of state, for example, he assured Fox News's Chris Wallace that "Torture is torture is torture. It is unacceptable" and "Even if the Geneva Convention does not directly apply in terms of individuals being illegal combatants and not prisoners of war, we still have an obligation to treat them humanely, consistent with international standards. And that's been my position."[12] For years in retirement, Powell perpetuated the myth of his opposition to detainee abuse, falsely telling CNBC's Rachel Maddow in 2008, "We had no meetings on torture" and "It was always the case that, at least from the State Department's standpoint, we should be consistent with the requirements of the Geneva Convention."[13]

In May 2009 Powell finally admitted the truth about supporting the Bush administration's torture program and attempted to justify his utilitarian ethics. On CBS's *Face the Nation*, he told Bob Schieffer,

> When we started to examine these techniques I was in some meetings where they were discussed. . . . You had to give some—some flexibility to the CIA. . . . But . . . it's easy now in the cold light of day to look back and say, you shouldn't have done any of that. But . . . nobody would have forgiven us for not doing everything we could. And the CIA thought we needed those kinds of techniques but now we see that these are not appropriate. . . . And remember waterboarding comes out of your Survival, Evasion and Escape techniques. And those were intended to be torture to show our guys what they should be subjected to.[14]

One can be sympathetic to Powell's position that in the chaotic aftermath of September 11, 2001, the Bush administration had to do everything it could to prevent another assault on the homeland. But more than a year later, after security protections had been strengthened and no follow-up attacks had occurred, some of the extraordinary reactive policies, including the state-sponsored torture program that violated the Geneva Conventions, should have been shuttered. As secretary of state, Powell himself recognized that by March 2003 homeland security conditions had improved significantly and thus warranted a relaxation of the country's stringent visa restrictions. In 2009 Powell recalled,

In the first year after 9/11, we did everything we could to stop the possibility of another 9/11. We put in place the Patriot Act. We used enhanced interrogation techniques. I shut down for the most part the visa system until we could fix it. But after about a year and a half when it looked like things were relatively secure and we were doing a better job, then we started to relax the visa system once we fixed it because we can't keep moving in that direction with putting people in jail forever without resolving their cases. We were not letting people come to our country. So it was natural to start shifting back to our more normal ways of doing business and dealing with the rest of the world after we had achieved a level of security.[15]

That the secretary of state did not also see the need to terminate the CIA torture program represented a momentous ethical failure.

Powell's episodic bad followership, from breaking starch to condoning state-sponsored torture, signals the dangers of misguided ethics, extreme ambition, strict conformity, and unswerving obedience. By contrast, the best subordinates consciously develop and exercise their capacities for critical independent judgment. They also adhere to codes of ethical conduct that prioritize core moral principles over pragmatism, self-interest, and loyalty to authority figures. Of course, expressions of self-determined thought and sound ethical judgment require moral courage, the willingness to endure negative consequences for doing what is right. And while one might sympathize with an ambitious young major's willingness to conform to a corrupt army culture and obey unethical superiors, our expectations of a forty-eight-year-old major general and a sixty-five-year-old secretary of state must be substantially higher.

Colin Powell remains one of the most admired and respected people in the United States, and there are just reasons for his enduring popularity. But, as with America's most revered presidents, George Washington, Abraham Lincoln, and Franklin Roosevelt, Powell proved a fallible patriot, who, in the course of a long and often distinguished career, made some grave and consequential errors in judgment. While those blunders do not erase the significance of his commendable achievements and decades of public service, they are failures nonetheless, and we can learn from both his good and bad followership.

NOTES

INTRODUCTION

1. Powell, "Remarks to the United Nations Security Council," February 5, 2003, in Speeches and Remarks as Secretary of State, State Department Archive (hereafter Speeches and Remarks).

2. DeYoung, *Soldier*, 439.

3. Powell, *It Worked for Me*, 220.

4. Powell, *It Worked for Me*, 219; Tenet, *At the Center of the Storm*, 374.

5. National Intelligence Council, "National Intelligence Estimate," October 2002.

6. Morell, *The Great War of Our Time*, 95–96.

7. Powell, *It Worked for Me*, 220; Tenet, *At the Center of the Storm*, 374; Rice, *No Higher Honor*, 200.

8. Powell, "Remarks to the United Nations Security Council," February 5, 2003, in Speeches and Remarks.

9. Ibid.

10. Powell, *It Worked for Me*, 220.

11. Tenet, *At the Center of the Storm*, 375.

12. Rice, *No Higher Honor*, 200.

13. Bush, *Decision Points*, 245.

14. Nick Anderson, "Much of the Skepticism among Lawmakers Appears to Buckle," *Los Angeles Times*, February 5, 2003.

15. "Irrefutable," *Washington Post*, February 6, 2003; "The Case against Iraq," *New York Times*, February 6, 2003.

16. "Officer Efficiency Report," July 1959, in Powell, Papers of General Colin L. Powell (Ret.). (hereafter Powell Papers).

17. "Officer Efficiency Report," October 1968, Powell Papers.

18. "Officer Efficiency Report," December 1968, Powell Papers.

19. "Officer Efficiency Report," May 1981, Powell Papers.

20. "Officer Efficiency Report," July 1985, Powell Papers.

21. Harari, *The Leadership Secrets of Colin Powell.*

22. "Officer Efficiency Report," October 1961, Powell Papers.

23. Means, *Colin Powell*, 181.

24. Rudy Abramson and John Broder, "Four-Star Power: Colin Powell's Career Has Proceeded with the Certainty of a Laser-Guided Missile. How Much Higher Will He Go?" *Los Angeles Times*, April 7, 1991.

25. *National Journal,* "Managing the Departments: Grades for Bush's Cabinet Secretaries," *Government Executive*, January 27, 2003.

26. Felice, *How Do I Save My Honor?*, 65–96.

27. Powell, *It Worked for Me*, 222–23.

28. Among the seminal works on followership are: Kellerman, *Followership*; Riggio, Chaleff, and Lipman-Blumen, *The Art of Followership*; Kelley, "In Praise of Followers"; Kelley, *The Power of Followership*; Kelley, *How to Be A Star at Work*; Chaleff, *The Courageous Follower*; Lipman-Blumen, *The Allure of Toxic Leaders*; and Hollander, "Leadership, Followership, Self, and Others." For the origins of followership research, see Baker, "Followership."

29. Burns, *Transforming Leadership*, 172.

CHAPTER 1   Obedient Son (1937–1957)

1. George Frank, "A Sister's Salute: Family: Marilyn Berns Recalls Her Sibling as an Average Boy," *Los Angeles Times*, February 17, 1991.

2. Powell, *My American Journey*, 12.

3. Ibid., 9.

4. Henke, *The West Indian Americans,* 41, 129–33, 146.

5. Frank, "A Sister's Salute"; Adler, *The Generals*, 19.

6. Powell, *My American Journey*, 37.

7. Means, *Colin Powell*, 71.

8. Powell, *My American Journey*, 9.

9. Colin L. Powell, interview with the author, June 22, 2017. (Hereafter Colin L. Powell, author interview.)

10. Powell, *My American Journey*, 9.

11. Hughes, *Colin Powell*, 39.

12. DeYoung, *Soldier*, 24.

13. Powell, *It Worked for Me*, 85.

14. Powell, *My American Journey*, 15.

15. Ibid., 8.

16. Ibid., 16.

17. Ibid., 12.

18. Powell, *It Worked for Me*, 85; Colin L. Powell, author interview.

19. Means, *Colin Powell*, 52.

20. Colin Powell, "Remarks to Morris High School," April 15, 1991, Powell Papers.

21. Powell, *My American Journey*, 12.

22. Academy of Achievement, "General Colin L. Powell, USA," *What It Takes,* May 23, 1998, http://www.achievement.org/achiever/general-colin-l -powell/.

23. Powell, *My American Journey*, 18.

24. Alder, *The Generals*, 17.

25. Hughes, *Colin Powell*, 26–27.

26. Means, *Colin Powell*, 50.

27. Powell, *My American Journey*, 12, 17.

28. Means, *Colin Powell*, 61.

29. Powell, *It Worked for Me*, 33.

30. Powell, *My American Journey*, 12.

31. Ibid., 20.

32. Adler, *The Generals*, 20.

33. Powell, *My American Journey*, 20.

34. Ibid., 20, 18.

35. Ibid., 17.

36. Powell, *It Worked for Me*, 32.

37. Colin Powell to Hank Cohen, October 7, 1988, Powell files, Reagan Presidential Library.

38. Roth, *Sacred Honor*, 32.

39. Powell, *My American Journey*, 24.

40. Colin L. Powell, Civil Engineering Essay, February 23, 1954, Powell Papers.

41. "Remarks by General Colin L. Powell," Marshall ROTC Awards Seminar, Virginia Military Institute, Lexington, Virginia, April 14, 1993, Powell Papers.

42. Powell, *My American Journey*, 25.

43. Powell, Civil Engineering Essay, February 23, 1954, Powell Papers.

44. Means, *Colin Powell*, 81.

45. Powell, *It Worked for Me*, 89.

46. Means, *Colin Powell*, 81.

47. Frank, "A Sister's Salute," *Los Angeles Times*, February 17, 1991.

48. Powell, *My American Journey*, 28.

49. Ibid., 25–28; Roth, *Sacred Honor*, 36.

50. Means, *Colin Powell*, 82.

51. Powell, *My American Journey*, 29.

52. Ibid.; Means, *Colin Powell*, 54.

53. Powell, *My American Journey*, 34.
54. Powell, *It Worked for Me*, 273.
55. Ibid., 273.
56. DeYoung, *Soldier*, 31–32.
57. Powell, *My American Journey*, 38.
58. Ibid., 38.
59. Means, *Colin Powell*, 88.
60. Powell, *My American Journey*, 20.
61. Ibid., 37.
62. Means, *Colin Powell*, 81–82.

CHAPTER 2   Dutiful Soldier (1958–1969)

1. Powell, *My American Journey*, 39.
2. DeYoung, *Soldier*, 35.
3. Powell, *My American Journey*, 51–52.
4. Powell, *It Worked for Me*, 9.
5. Means, *Colin Powell*, 111.
6. Powell, *My American Journey*, 46.
7. Ibid., 46.
8. Powell, *It Worked for Me*, 50.
9. Ibid., 265.
10. DeYoung, *Soldier*, 38.
11. "Officer Efficiency Report," November 1960, Powell Papers.
12. "Officer Efficiency Report," November 1959, Powell Papers.
13. "Officer Efficiency Report," December 1960, Powell Papers.
14. Powell, *My American Journey*, 56.
15. Ibid., 59.
16. "Officer Efficiency Report," April 1961, Powell Papers.
17. "Officer Efficiency Report," October 1961, Powell Papers.
18. Powell, *My American Journey*, 41–42.
19. Ibid., 82.
20. Powell, *It Worked for Me*, 26.
21. Powell, *My American Journey*, 88.
22. Ibid., 89.
23. Nguyen Dang-So to Colin Powell, not dated, Powell Papers.
24. Powell, *My American Journey*, 94.
25. Ibid., 95.
26. Ibid., 97.
27. Ibid., 87.
28. Ibid., 97–98.

29. Academy of Achievement, "General Colin L. Powell, USA," *What It Takes,* May 23, 1998, http://www.achievement.org/achiever/general-colin-l-powell/.

30. "Citation" Colin L. Powell, Bronze Star Medal, Powell Papers.

31. Powell, *My American Journey,* 99–102.

32. Colonel Tri, "Letter of Appreciation," May 17, 1963, Powell Papers.

33. "Officer Efficiency Report," June 1963, Powell Papers.

34. Ibid.

35. Powell, *My American Journey,* 103.

36. Ibid., 108.

37. Ibid., 109.

38. Roth, *Sacred Honor,* 74.

39. "Officer Efficiency Report," March 1966, Powell Papers.

40. Powell, *My American Journey,* 112.

41. Roth, *Sacred Honor,* 75–76.

42. "Officer Efficiency Report," May 1965, Powell Papers.

43. Powell, *My American Journey,* 113.

44. Ibid., 117.

45. Powell, *It Worked for Me,* 244.

46. Powell, *My American Journey,* 116; "Officer Efficiency Report," June 1967, Powell Papers.

47. "Officer Efficiency Report," March 1967, Powell Papers.

48. DeYoung, *Soldier,* 71.

49. Powell, *My American Journey,* 122.

50. Ibid., 126.

51. Colin L. Powell, "Remarks at the Elliot School of International Affairs," George Washington University, September 5, 2003, in Speeches and Remarks.

52. Powell, *My American Journey,* 136.

53. Ibid., 131.

54. Means, *Colin Powell,* 147.

55. Powell, *My American Journey,* 134.

56. "Officer Efficiency Report," October 1968, Powell Papers.

57. Means, *Colin Powell,* 147.

58. Powell, *It Worked for Me,* 35; Powell, *My American Journey,* 29.

59. Powell, *My American Journey,* 135.

60. Adelman, "Ground Zero," 71; Means, *Colin Powell,* 156.

61. Colin L. Powell, "Diary, 68–69 VN," November 16, 1968, Powell Papers.

62. "Award of the Soldier's Medal," General Orders Number 9285, Department of the Army, December 3, 1968, Powell Papers.

63. "Officer Efficiency Report," July 1969, Powell Papers.

64. Means, *Colin Powell*, 147, 152.

65. Powell, *My American Journey*, 54, 57.

66. Ibid., 102.

67. Ibid., 87.

68. Ibid., 144–46.

69. Jones, *My Lai*, 127–36.

70. Ibid., 139.

71. Ibid., 157–59.

72. "Col. Henderson's Report of Investigation (April 24, 1968)" in Peers, *The My Lai Inquiry*, 272–73; Jones, *My Lai*,125, 166, 171–72; Bilton and Sim, *Four Hours in My Lai*, 182.

73. Belknap, *The Vietnam War on Trial*, 94.

74. Jones, *My Lai*, 161.

75. DeYoung, *Soldier*, 88.

76. Bilton and Sim, *Four Hours in My Lai*, 175.

77. Tom Glen to General Creighton Abrams, November 27, 1968, My Lai Investigation Files, National Archives.

78. Albert L. Russell to Commanding General, American Division, December 11, 1968, My Lai Investigation Files, National Archives.

79. Colin L. Powell, author interview.

80. Colin L. Powell to Adjutant General, December 11, 1968, My Lai Investigation Files, National Archives.

81. Colin L. Powell to Adjutant General, December 11, 1968, My Lai Investigation Files, National Archives.

82. Bilton and Sim, *Fours Hours in My Lai*, 213.

83. DeYoung, *Soldier*, 88–89.

84. Jones, *My Lai*, 183.

85. "Officer Efficiency Report," October 1968, Powell Papers.

86. Howard H. Cooksey to Thomas B. Glen Jr., December 13, 1968, My Lai Investigation Files, National Archives.

87. Powell, *My American Journey*, 87.

88. Turse, *Kill Anything That Moves*, 203.

89. Ibid., 200; Parry, Parry, and Parry, *Neck Deep*, 95–96.

90. "Officer Efficiency Report," July 1969, Powell Papers.

91. Lieutenant Colonel Colin L. Powell, sworn statement, August 10, 1971, Powell Papers.

92. DeYoung, *Soldier*, 90.

93. Powell, *My American Journey*, 143.

94. Ibid., 144.

95. Bilton and Sim, *Four Hours in My Lai*, 219–20.

96. Robert M. Cook, Inspector General to Chief of Staff, July 12, 1969, Military Assistance Command Vietnam, Inspector General, Investigations Division, National Archives.

97. Powell, *My American Journey*, 142.

98. "Testimony of MAJ Colin L. Powell," May 23, 1969, Military Assistance Command Vietnam, Inspector General, Investigations Division, National Archives.

99. Ibid.

100. Ibid.

101. Ibid.

102. Powell, *My American Journey*, 143. The official interview transcript does not indicate that Powell stopped the interview.

103. "Testimony of MAJ Colin L. Powell," May 23, 1969.

104. Powell, *My American Journey*, 143.

105. Ibid., 142.

106. DeYoung, *Soldier*, 91.

107. "Officer Efficiency Report," December 1968, Powell Papers.

CHAPTER 3   Follower and Commander (1970–1982)

1. Means, *Colin Powell*, 18–19.

2. Powell, *My American Journey*, 141; Colin L. Powell, author interview.

3. Roth, *Sacred Honor*, 91.

4. Colin L. Powell, author interview; Colin Powell, "Remarks at the Elliot School of International Affairs," George Washington University, September 5, 2003, in Speeches and Remarks.

5. DeYoung, *Soldier*, 93.

6. Colin Powell, "Commencement Address at the George Washington University," February 18, 1990, Powell Papers.

7. Colin L. Powell, author interview.

8. "Officer Efficiency Report," August 1971, Powell Papers.

9. Ricks, *The Generals*, 335–53; Gole, *General William E. DePuy*; Kitfield, *Prodigal Soldiers*, 156–61.

10. Powell, *My American Journey*, 156.

11. Kitfield, *Prodigal Soldiers*, 127.

12. Colin L. Powell, author interview.

13. Gole, *General William E. DePuy*, 226.

14. Powell, *My American Journey*, 157.

15. Ibid.

16. Ibid., 158.

17. DeYoung, *Soldier*, 99; "Officer Efficiency Report," August 1972, Powell Papers.

18. Rudy Abramson and John Border, "Four-Star Power: Colin Powell's Career Has Proceeded with the Certainty of a Laser-Guided Missile. How Much Higher Will He Go?," *Los Angeles Times*, April 7, 1991; Means, *Colin Powell*, 166.

19. George Frank, "A Sister Salutes," *Los Angeles Times*, February 17, 1991.

20. Rudy Abramson and John Border, "Four-Star Power: Colin Powell's Career Has Proceeded with the Certainty of a Laser-Guided Missile. How Much Higher Will He Go?," *Los Angeles Times*, April 7, 1991.

21. Powell, *My American Journey*, 161.

22. Means, *Colin Powell*, 175.

23. Powell, *My American Journey*, 166.

24. Ibid., 166.

25. Ibid., 166.

26. Ibid., 167, 173.

27. Ibid., 167.

28. Means, *Colin Powell*, 174–75.

29. Kitfield, *Prodigal Soldiers*, 125.

30. Powell to Roosevelt Martin, February 24, 1981, Powell Papers.

31. Powell, *My American Journey*, 182.

32. Ibid., 181.

33. Ibid., 186.

34. Roth, *Sacred Honor*, 99.

35. Powell, *My American Journey*, 191.

36. "Officer Efficiency Report," July 1974, Powell Papers.

37. Ibid.

38. Powell, *My American Journey*, 202.

39. Means, *Colin Powell*, 181.

40. Ibid., 181.

41. Powell, *My American Journey*, 202–3.

42. Ibid., 206.

43. Ibid., 206.

44. Ibid., 206.

45. Ibid., 206.

46. "Citation . . . Joint Service Commendation Medal," Powell Papers.

47. Becton, *Becton*, 110–11.

48. Powell, *My American Journey*, 207.

49. Ibid., 207.

50. Ibid., 207–8.

51. Ibid., 208.

52. Ibid., 207.

53. "Permanent Faculty Advisor's Midyear Evaluation of Advisee," January 12, 1976, Powell Papers.

54. "Permanent Faculty Advisor's End of the Year Evaluation of Advisee," May 21, 1976, Powell Papers.

55. Ibid.

56. DeYoung, *Soldier*, 111.

57. "Service School Academic Evaluation Report," July 23, 1976, Powell Papers.

58. DeYoung, *Soldier*, 110–11.

59. Powell, *My American Journey*, 211.

60. Ibid., 211.

61. Ibid., 214.

62. "Officer Efficiency Report," April 1977, Powell Papers.

63. Ibid.

64. Ibid.

65. Roth, *Sacred Honor*, 103.

66. DeYoung, *Soldier*, 114.

67. Powell, *My American Journey*, 233.

68. Rudy Abramson and John Border, "Four-Star Power: Colin Powell's Career Has Proceeded with the Certainty of a Laser-Guided Missile. How Much Higher Will He Go? *Los Angeles Times*, April 7, 1991; Means, Colin Powell, 192–94.

69. Unnamed letter writer to Powell, March 14, 1978, Powell Papers.

70. Powell, *My American Journey*, 238.

71. "Officer Efficiency Report," January 1979, Powell Papers.

72. Powell, *My American Journey*, 244.

73. Ibid., 243, 244.

74. Ibid., 240–42.

75. Ibid., 242.

76. Means, *Colin Powell*, 197.

77. "Officer Efficiency Report," October 1979, Powell Papers.

78. Kitfield, *Prodigal Soldiers*, 217–30.

79. Powell, *My American Journey*, 249.

80. Ibid., 249.

81. "Officer Efficiency Report," December 1980, Powell Papers.

82. DeYoung, *Soldier*, 124.

83. "Officer Efficiency Report," May 1981, Powell Papers.

84. Powell, *My American Journey*, 260.

85. "Officer Efficiency Report," May 1981, Powell Papers.

86. Powell, *My American Journey*, 260.

87. Powell to John G. Kester, October 2, 1981, Powell Papers.

88. Powell, *My American Journey*, 260–61; Felix, *Wesley Clark*, 105; Halberstam, *War in a Time of Peace*, 432–33; Bob Woodward, "The Powell Predicament," *Washington Post Magazine*, September 24, 1995.

89. Charles W. Dyke to Powell, May 4, 1981, Powell Papers.

90. Powell, *My American Journey*, 265.

91. Ibid., 272.

92. Colin L. Powell, author interview.

93. Powell, *My American Journey*, 269.

94. "Officer Efficiency Report," May/June 1982, Powell Papers.

95. Ibid.

96. Bob Woodward, "The Powell Predicament," *Washington Post Magazine*, September 24, 1995.

97. Ibid.

98. Powell, *My American Journey*, 271.

99. Ibid., 281, 273.

100. Becton, *Becton*, 172.

101. Julius W. Becton Jr. to Powell, November 19, 1982, Powell Papers.

102. "Officer Efficiency Report," May 1983, Powell Papers.

103. James V. Hartinger to Powell, November 19, 1982, Powell Papers.

104. "A Transition Report to General John A. Wickham Jr.," May 27, 1983, Powell Papers.

105. John A. Wickham Jr. to Colin L. Powell, July 12, 1983, Powell Papers.

106. Powell, *My American Journey*, 279.

107. John A. Wickham Jr. to Colin L. Powell, July 12, 1983, Powell Papers.

108. Bob Woodward, "The Powell Predicament," *Washington Post Magazine*, September 24, 1995.

109. Powell, *It Worked for Me*, 10.

CHAPTER 4   Loyalist (1983–1988)

1. Woodward, *The Commanders*, 108.

2. "The Testimony of Colin Powell," April 22, 1992, Records of the Independent Counsel Lawrence Walsh, National Archives.

3. Powell, *My American Journey*, 289.

4. Ibid., 298.

5. Timberg, *The Nightingale's Song*, 342.

6. Weinberger, *Fighting for Peace*, 147, 150.

7. Shultz, *Turmoil and Triumph*, 108.

8. Powell, *My American Journey*, 291.

9. Weinberger, *Fighting for Peace*, 174.

10. Timberg, *The Nightingale's Song*, 344.

11. Reagan, *An American Life*, 458.

12. Western, *Selling Intervention and War*, 94–132.

13. Weinberger, *Fighting for Peace*, 105–6.

14. Shultz, *Turmoil and Triumph*, 323–34; Weinberger, *Fighting for Peace*, 101–33; Crandall, *Gunboat Democracy*, 105–68.

15. Shultz, *Turmoil and Triumph*, 328–29.

16. Weinberger, *Fight for Peace*, 111.

17. Andy Pasztor and Gerald F. Seib, "Cool Commander," *Wall Street Journal*, October 15, 1990.

18. Crandall, *Gunboat Diplomacy*, 105–68.

19. Powell, *My American Journey*, 314.

20. Ibid., 292.

21. DeYoung, *Soldier*, 141.

22. Weinberger, "The Uses of Military Power."

23. Powell, *My American Journey*, 303.

24. "Officer Efficiency Report," May 1984, Powell Papers; Powell, *My American Journey*, 252, 256, 313.

25. Powell, *My American Journey*, 293.

26. Jacqueline Trescott, "Colin Powell, Before History Tapped," *Washington Post*, February 25, 1991.

27. "Officer Efficiency Report," May 1985, Powell Papers.

28. Powell, *My American Journey*, 298.

29. Ibid., 298–99.

30. Byrne, *Iran-Contra*, 60–61.

31. Powell, *My American Journey*, 304.

32. Weinberger to Powell, June 18, 1985, Records of the Independent Counsel Lawrence Walsh, National Archives.

33. Weinberger to McFarlane, "U.S. Policy toward Iran," July 16, 1985, Records of the Independent Counsel Lawrence Walsh, National Archives.

34. Byrne, *Iran-Contra*, 61.

35. "Deposition of General Colin L. Powell," June 19, 1987, Records of the Independent Counsel Lawrence Walsh, National Archives; Byrne, *Iran-Contra*, 68.

36. "Interview with Major General Colin Powell," April 17, 1987, Records of the Independent Counsel Lawrence Walsh, National Archives; Powell, *My American Journey*, 305.

37. Byrne, *Iran-Contra*, 69.

38. Ibid., 70–71.

39. Ibid., 71.

40. Ibid., 70–71.

41. McFarlane, *Special Trust*, 28, 32.

42. Powell, *My American Journey*, 308.

43. Reagan, *An American Life*, 506.

44. McFarlane, *Special Trust*, 35.

45. Byrne, *Iran-Contra*, 72.

46. Ronald Reagan, "Remarks Announcing the Release of the Hostages from the Trans World Airlines Hijacking Incident," June 30, 1985, American Presidency Project; Byrne, *Iran-Contra*, 75–76, 156.

47. Byrne, *Iran-Contra*, 75–76, 104–5.

48. Ibid., 75–76, 104–5, 156.

49. "Deposition of General Colin L. Powell," June 19, 1987, Records of the Independent Counsel Lawrence Walsh, National Archives.

50. Walsh, *Final Report of the Independent Counsel for Iran/Contra Matters,* volume I, part 8, August 4, 1993.

51. Ibid.

52. Brinkley, *The Reagan Diaries*, 350.

53. "The Testimony of Colin Powell," April 22, 1992, Records of the Independent Counsel Lawrence Walsh, National Archives.

54. Walsh, *Final Report of the Independent Counsel for Iran/Contra Matters,* volume I, part 8, August 4, 1993.

55. Ibid.

56. Powell, "Record of Interview," July 18, 1987, Records of the Independent Counsel Lawrence Walsh, National Archives.

57. Powell, *My American Journey*, 308.

58. Byrne, *Iran-Contra*, 73–74.

59. Ibid., 75.

60. Walsh, *Final Report of the Independent Counsel for Iran/Contra Matters,* volume I, part 8, August 4, 1993.

61. Woodward, *Veil*, 414.

62. Walsh, *Final Report of the Independent Counsel for Iran/Contra Matters,* volume I, part 8, August 4, 1993; Byrne, *Iran-Contra*, 75.

63. Powell, *My American Journey*, 308.

64. Byrne, *Iran-Contra*, 94.

65. Oliver North, Congressional Testimony, July 7, 1987, Records of the Independent Counsel Lawrence Walsh, National Archives.

66. "The Testimony of Colin Powell," April 22, 1992, Records of the Independent Counsel Lawrence Walsh, National Archives; Byrne, *Iran-Contra*, 94.

67. Ibid.

68. Byrne, *Iran-Contra*, 95.

69. Ibid.

70. Walsh, *Final Report of the Independent Counsel for Iran/Contra Matters,* volume I, part 8, August 4, 1993; Byrne, *Iran-Contra,* 95.

71. Byrne, *Iran-Contra,* 96; Powell, *My American Journey,* 310.

72. "Interview with Major General Colin Powell," April 17, 1987, and "Powell Outline: Weinberger's Notes," Records of the Independent Counsel Lawrence Walsh, National Archives.

73. Walsh, *Final Report of the Independent Counsel for Iran/Contra Matters,* volume I, part 8, August 4, 1993.

74. Ibid.

75. Byrne, *Iran-Contra,* 96.

76. Gates, *From the Shadows,* 399–400.

77. Walsh, *Final Report of the Independent Counsel for Iran/Contra Matters,* volume I, part 8, August 4, 1993.

78. Byrne, *Iran-Contra,* 101–5.

79. Walsh, *Final Report of the Independent Counsel for Iran/Contra Matters,* volume I, part 8, August 4, 1993.

80. Reagan, *An American Life,* 512.

81. Brinkley, *The Reagan Diaries,* 374.

82. Walsh, *Final Report of the Independent Counsel for Iran/Contra Matters,* volume 1, part 8, August 4, 1993.

83. Ibid.

84. McFarlane, *Special Trust,* 46.

85. Byrne, *Iran-Contra,* 106.

86. Walsh, *Final Report of the Independent Counsel for Iran/Contra Matters,* volume 1, part 8, August 4, 1993.

87. Reagan, *An American Life,* 510.

88. Byrne, *Iran-Contra,* 107, 325.

89. Walsh, *Final Report of the Independent Counsel for Iran/Contra Matters,* volume I, part 8, August 4, 1993.

90. Walsh, *Firewall,* 347.

91. "The Testimony of Colin Powell," April 22, 1992, Records of the Independent Counsel Lawrence Walsh, National Archives.

92. Hamilton and Inouye, *Report of the Congressional Committees Investigating the Iran-Contra Affair,* 206.

93. Walsh, *Final Report of the Independent Counsel for Iran/Contra Matters,* volume I, part 8, August 4, 1993.

94. Ibid.

95. Byrne, *Iran-Contra,* 158.

96. Ibid., 372; Draper, *A Very Thin Line,* 250–51; Walsh, *Final Report of the Independent Counsel for Iran/Contra Matters,* volume I, part 8, August 4, 1993.

97. Powell, *My American Journey*, 311.

98. Crowe, *The Line of Fire*, 300.

99. Powell, *My American Journey*, 311; Means, *Colin Powell*, 218.

100. Means, *Colin Powell*, 219.

101. Parry, *America's Stolen Narrative*, 176–79; Parry, Parry, and Parry, *Neck Deep*, 102–6.

102. Powell FBI Interview "Transcript," December 4–5, 1986, and "Testimony of Colin L. Powell," December 22, 1986, Records of the Independent Counsel Lawrence Walsh, National Archives.

103. Byrne, *Iran-Contra*, 165–67.

104. Ibid., 163, 277.

105. Powell FBI Interview "Transcript," December 4–5, 1986, Records of the Independent Counsel Lawrence Walsh, National Archives.

106. Powell, *My American Journey*, 336.

107. Ibid., 311.

108. Powell FBI Interview "Transcript," December 4–5, 1986, Records of the Independent Counsel Lawrence Walsh, National Archives.

109. Hamilton and Inouye, *Report of the Congressional Committees Investigating the Iran-Contra Affair*, 615; Parry, *America's Stolen Narrative*, 178; Parry, Parry, and Parry, *Neck Deep*, 104.

110. Hamilton and Inouye, *Report of the Congressional Committees Investigating the Iran-Contra Affair*, 652–53.

111. Powell, *My American Journey*, 312.

112. "Deposition of General Colin L. Powell," June 19, 1987, and "Memorandum for Vice Admiral Poindexter," March 12, 1986, Records of the Independent Counsel Lawrence Walsh, National Archives.

113. Parry, *America's Stolen Narrative*, 178.

114. Colin Powell "Affidavit," April 21, 1992, Records of the Independent Counsel Lawrence Walsh, National Archives.

115. Powell, *My American Journey*, 312.

116. "Officer Efficiency Report," May, 1986, Powell Papers.

117. Colin L. Powell, author interview.

118. Colin Powell "Affidavit," April 21, 1992, Records of the Independent Counsel Lawrence Walsh, National Archives; Powell, *My American Journey*, 314.

119. Powell, *My American Journey*, 326.

120. Gates, *From the Shadows*, 390.

121. DeYoung, *Soldier*, 157.

122. Powell, *My American Journey*, 329, 331.

123. Ibid., 329.

124. Powell, *My American Journey*, 329; DeYoung, *Soldier*, 148.

125. Andrew Rosenthal, "Military Chief: Man of Action and of Politics," *New York Times*, August 16, 1990; Powell FBI Interview "Transcript," December 4–5, 1986, Records of the Independent Counsel Lawrence Walsh, National Archives.

126. Parry, *America's Stolen Narrative*, 180.

127. Powell, *My American Journey*, 330.

128. Ibid., 330.

129. Ibid., 331–32.

130. Ibid., 334.

131. Ibid., 334.

132. Daalder and Destler, "The National Security Council Project," 3.

133. Powell, *It Worked for Me*, 76.

134. Daalder and Destler, "The National Security Project," 54, 33.

135. DeYoung, *Soldier*, 158.

136. Melissa Healy and James Gerstenzang, "Security Adviser: Gen. Powell—Quest for Compromise," *Los Angeles Times*, June 27, 1988.

137. Richard Halloran, "National Security Council; Case of the Reluctant General," *New York Times*, October 5, 1987. Despite turf wars between the NSC and the State Department, Michael R. Gordon described Powell as "well-respected throughout the Administration"; see "At Foreign Policy Helm: Shultz vs. White House," *New York Times*, August 26, 1987.

138. Shultz, *Turmoil and Triumph*, 991.

139. Melissa Healy and James Gerstenzang, "Security Adviser: Gen. Powell—Quest for Compromise," *Los Angeles Times*, June 27, 1988.

140. Powell, *My American Journey*, 352.

141. Gates, *Thirteen Ways of Looking at a Black Man*, 78.

142. Byrne, *Iran-Contra*, 165–67; Gates, *A Passion for Leadership*, 163.

143. Rothkopf, *Running the World*, 255–57; Daalder and Destler, *In the Shadow of the Oval Office*, 165–67.

144. Daalder and Destler, "The National Security Council Project," 54.

145. Carlucci, "Frank C. Carlucci Oral History, Assistant to the President for National Security Affairs; Secretary of Defense."

146. Powell, *My American Journey*, 380.

147. Ibid., 375.

148. Reagan, *An American Life*, 535, 540.

149. Melissa Healy and James Gerstenzang, "Security Adviser: Gen. Powell—Quest for Compromise," *Los Angeles Times*, June 27, 1988.

150. Powell, *My American Journey*, 388–89.

151. Weinberger, *In the Arena*, 294.

152. "Officer Efficiency Report," July 1984 and May 1986, Powell Papers.

153. "Officer Efficiency Report," May 1985, Powell Papers.

154. Colin L. Powell, author interview.

155. Powell, *My American Journey*, 320.

156. Powell, *It Worked for Me*, 10.

157. Walsh, *Firewall*, 395.

158. "Deposition of General Colin L. Powell," June 19, 1987, Records of the Independent Counsel Lawrence Walsh, National Archives; "Interview with Major General Colin Powell," April 17, 1987, Records of the Independent Counsel Lawrence Walsh, National Archives.

159. Walsh, *Firewall*, 342.

160. Powell, *My American Journey*, 306; Colin Powell "Affidavit," April 21, 1992, and "The Testimony of Colin Powell," April 22, 1992, Records of the Independent Counsel Lawrence Walsh, National Archives.

161. Walsh, *Firewall*, 388.

162. Ibid., 389.

163. Ibid., 387.

164. "Interview with Major General Colin Powell," April 17, 1987, Records of the Independent Counsel Lawrence Walsh, National Archives.

165. "Deposition of General Colin L. Powell," June 19, 1987, Records of the Independent Counsel Lawrence Walsh, National Archives.

166. "Record of Interview with General Colin L. Powell," July 6 and July 9, 1987, Records of the Independent Counsel Lawrence Walsh, National Archives.

167. Colin Powell "Affidavit," April 21, 1992, Records of the Independent Counsel Lawrence Walsh, National Archives.

168. Walsh, *Final Report of the Independent Counsel for Iran/Contra Matters,* volume I, part 8, August 4, 1993.

169. "The Testimony of Colin Powell," April 22, 1992, Records of the Independent Counsel Lawrence Walsh, National Archives.

170. "OIC Interview of General Colin Powell," November 5, 1992, Records of the Independent Counsel Lawrence Walsh, National Archives.

171. Walsh, *Firewall*, 406.

172. David Johnston, "Weinberger Face 5 Counts in Iran Contra Indictment, *New York Times,* June 16, 1992; Walsh, *Final Report of the Independent Counsel for Iran/Contra Matters,* volume I, part 8, August 4, 1993.

173. Walsh, *Firewall*, 403.

174. Walsh, *Final Report of the Independent Counsel for Iran/Contra Matters,* volume I, part 8, August 4, 1993.

175. Ibid.

176. Ibid.

177. Colin Powell, author interview; Walsh, *Final Report of the Independent Counsel for Iran/Contra Matters,* volume III, Responses, August 4, 1993; Powell, *My American Journey*, 341–43.

178. Parry, *America's Stolen Narrative*, 148.

179. David Johnston, "Bush Pardons 6 in Iran Affair, Aborting a Weinberger Trial; Prosecutor Assails 'Cover-Up,'" *New York Times*, December 25, 1992.

180. Liman, *Lawyer*, 348.

181. Powell, *My American Journey*, 308.

182. Thomas Oliphant, "Eight Who Still May Be Judged Harshly in Iran-Contra," *Boston Globe*, April 11, 1990.

CHAPTER 5 Chairman (1989–1993)

1. Cheney, "Richard B. Cheney Oral History, Secretary of Defense."

2. Meacham, *Destiny and Power*, 376–77.

3. Ibid., 377.

4. Cheney, "Richard B. Cheney Oral History, Secretary of Defense."

5. Andrew Rosenthal, "Man in the News: Colin Luther Powell; A General Who Is Right for His Time," *New York Times*, August 10, 1989.

6. Meacham, *Destiny and Power*, 377.

7. Rudy Abramson and John Broder, "Four-Star Power; Colin Powell's Career Has Proceeded with the Certainty of a Laser-Guided Missile. How Much Higher Will He Go?" *Los Angeles Times*, April 7, 1991.

8. Albright, *Madam Secretary*, 182; Rothkopf, *Running the World*, 322.

9. Powell, *My American Journey*, 415.

10. Lou Cannon, "Anti-Noriega Sanctions Are Having 'Telling Effect' White House Says," *Washington Post*, April 6, 1988; Melissa Healy and James Gerstenzang, "Security Adviser: Gen. Powell—Quest for Compromise," *Los Angeles Times*, June 27, 1988; Crandall, *Gunboat Diplomacy*, 84.

11. Locher, *Victory on the Potomac*.

12. Powell, *My American Journey*, 411.

13. Baker, *The Politics of Diplomacy*, 185.

14. Woodward, *The Commanders*, 121.

15. Donnelly, Roth, and Baker, *Operation Just Cause*, 198.

16. Clancy, with Stiner and Koltz, *Shadow Warriors*, 310–11; Woodward, *The Commanders*, 121–22, 129.

17. Baker, *The Politics of Diplomacy*, 185–88; Sparrow, *The Strategist*, 329–33.

18. Cheney, *In My Time*, 172.

19. Woodward, *The Commanders*, 129.

20. Cole, *Operation Just Cause*, 17, 21–22.

21. Powell, *My American Journey*, 420–21.

22. Crandall, *Gunboat Democracy*, 200.

23. Clancy, with Stiner and Koltz, *Shadow Warriors*, 329–30.

24. Cheney, *In My Time*, 175.

25. Powell, *My American Journey*, 422–25; Woodward, *The Commanders*, 160–67.

26. Cheney, "Richard B. Cheney Oral History, Secretary of Defense."

27. Cole, *Operation Just Cause,* 29–30.

28. Baker, *The Politics of Diplomacy*, 189.

29. Powell, *My American Journey*, 425; Cole, *Operation Just Cause,* 12; Crandall, *Gunboat Diplomacy*, 201.

30. Powell, *My American Journey*, 427.

31. Clancy, with Stiner and Koltz, *Shadow Warriors*, 341–69.

32. Crandall, *Gunboat Diplomacy*, 206, 214–15.

33. Ibid., 209; Powell, *My American Journey*, 433–34.

34. Powell, *My American Journey*, 418.

35. Daadler and Destler, "The National Security Council Project," 57.

36. Powell, *My American Journey*, 426.

37. Ibid., 425.

38. Ibid., 429, 432; Cheney, "Richard B. Cheney Oral History, Secretary of Defense."

39. Daadler and Destler, "The National Security Project," 56–57.

40. Powell, *My American Journey*, 426.

41. Ibid., 430.

42. Friedman, "Four Star Warrior," 10.

43. "Fighting in Panama: The Chief of Staff; Vital for the Invasion: Politically Attuned General, *New York Times*, December 25, 1989; Woodward, *The Commanders*, 168–71.

44. Powell, *My American Journey*, 429, 431–33.

45. Ibid., 434.

46. Andy Pasztor and Gerald Seib, "Cool Commander," *Wall Street Journal*, October 15, 1990.

47. Halberstam, *War in a Time of Peace*, 235.

48. Powell, *My American Journey*, 436.

49. Ibid., 341.

50. Colin Powell, "National Security Challenges in the 1990's: The Future Ain't What It Used to Be," May 16, 1989, Powell Papers; Jaffe, *The Development of the Base Force*, 12.

51. Powell, *My American Journey*, 540.

52. Cheney, "Richard B. Cheney Oral History, Secretary of Defense."

53. Powell, *My American Journey*, 437.

54. Jaffe, *The Development of the Base Force,* 12–13; "Statement of General Colin L. Powell, US Chairman of the Joint Chiefs of Staff before the U.S. Senate Committee on Armed Services on Dramatic Change and Enduring Realities," February 1, 1990, Powell Papers.

55. Colin Powell, "U.S. Foreign Policy in a Changing World: Keeping Democracy Alive," March 23, 1990, Powell Papers.

56. Colin L. Powell, "U.S. Forces: Challenges Ahead," *Foreign Affairs* (Winter 1992/1992): 32–45.

57. Powell, *My American Journey*, 454.

58. Powell, Personal Emails, Colin Powell to Harlan Ullman, July 27, 2016.

59. George H. W. Bush, "Rose Garden Press Conference," May 23, 1991, Powell Papers.

60. Powell, *My American Journey*, 458.

61. Woodward, *The Commanders*, 229–34.

62. Gordon and Trainor, *The Generals' War*, 32, 35–36.

63. Jeffrey Goldberg, "Breaking Ranks," 54–64.

64. Powell, "Oral History: Colin Powell."

65. Bush and Scowcroft, *A World Transformed*, 324; Powell, *My American Journey*, 464.

66. Powell, *My American Journey*, 464.

67. Woodward, *The Commanders*, 253.

68. Powell, *My American Journey*, 465–66; Powell, "Oral History: Colin Powell."

69. Powell, "Oral History: Colin Powell."

70. Powell, *My American Journey*, 464–65; Powell, "Oral History: Colin Powell."

71. George H. W. Bush, "Remarks and an exchange with reporters on the Iraqi invasion of Kuwait," August 5, 1990.

72. Haass, *War of Necessity, War of Choice*, 70; Gordon and Trainor, *The Generals' War*, 69.

73. Cheney, *In My Time*, 197.

74. Wil S. Hylton, "Casualty of War," *GQ* (June, 2004): 5.

75. Powell, "Oral History: Colin Powell"; Woodward, *The Commanders*, 299.

76. Powell, *My American Journey*, 480.

77. Ibid., 480; Hylton, "Casualty of War," 5; Powell, "Oral History: Colin Powell."

78. Woodward, *The Commanders*, 38.

79. Powell, *My American Journey*, 480.

80. Bruce Auster, "Interview of General Colin L. Powell," June 25, 1991, Powell Papers.

81. Powell, *My American Journey*, 493.

82. Ibid., 483.

83. Perry, *The Pentagon's Wars*, 21–22; Powell, *My American Journey*, 486; Bruce Auster, "Interview of General Colin L. Powell," June 25, 1991, Powell Papers.

84. Powell, *My American Journey*, 483, 485; Atkinson, *Crusade*, 111–12.

85. Baker, *The Politics of Diplomacy*, 301–4.

86. Powell, *My American Journey*, 487.

87. Schwarzkopf, *It Doesn't Take A Hero*, 367.

88. Bush and Scowcroft, *A World Transformed*, 354.

89. Powell, *My American Journey*, 498.

90. Sununu, *The Quiet Man*, 293.

91. Cheney, "Richard B. Cheney Oral History, Secretary of Defense."

92. Powell, "Oral History: Colin Powell"; Powell, *My American Journey*, 489.

93. Cheney, "Richard B. Cheney Oral History, Secretary of Defense."

94. Meacham, *Destiny and Power*, 450.

95. Gordon and Trainor, *The Generals' War*, 188.

96. Woodward, *The Commanders*, 342–43.

97. Perry, *The Pentagon's Wars*, 23.

98. "War in the Gulf: The General, Briefing by Powell: A Data-filled Showcase," *New York Times*, January 24, 1991; Dick Cheney and Colin Powell, "News Briefing," January 23, 1991, Powell Papers.

99. Michael R. Gordon, "War in the Gulf: The Ground War; The 'Move It or Lose It' Ultimatum," *New York Times*, February 9, 1991.

100. Fineman, "Powell on the March," 31.

101. Bush and Scowcroft, *A World Transformed*, 472.

102. Schwarzkopf, *It Doesn't Take A Hero*, 436.

103. Powell, *My American Journey*, 516.

104. Schwarzkopf, *It Doesn't Take A Hero*, 443.

105. Powell, *My American Journey*, 516.

106. Yant, *Desert Mirage*, 143–49; Atkinson, *Crusade*, 450–54.

107. Powell, *My American Journey*, 519.

108. Baker, *The Politics of Diplomacy*, 410, 436; Atkinson, *Crusade*, 449–54, 469–71.

109. Powell, *My American Journey*, 521.

110. Powell, "Oral History: Colin Powell"; Atkinson, *Crusade*, 449–72.

111. Powell, *My American Journey*, 521.

112. Atkinson, *Crusade*, 477.

113. Powell, *It Worked for Me*, 205.

114. Ibid., 201.

115. Haynes Johnson, "Book Says Powell Favored Containment; Image of Harmony on Gulf Policy Dispelled," *Washington Post*, May 2, 1991.

116. Colin L. Powell, author interview.

117. DeYoung, *Soldier*, 215.

118. George H.W. Bush, "Remarks Announcing the Reappointment of General Colin L. Powell as Chairman of the Joint Chiefs of Staff and a News Conference," May 23, 1991, The American Presidency Project.

119. Thomas, "The Reluctant Warrior."

120. George H.W. Bush, "Remarks Announcing the Reappointment of General Colin L. Powell as Chairman of the Joint Chiefs of Staff and a News Conference," May 23, 1991.

121. Colin L. Powell, author interview; DeYoung, *Soldier*, 216–19.

122. Barry, "The Day We Stopped the War," 16.

123. Colin Powell interview transcript, *Today Show,* NBC, January 15, 1992, Powell Papers.

124. Colin Powell interview transcript, *Good Morning America,* ABC, January 15, 1992, Powell Papers.

125. Colin Powell interview transcript, CNN and CNN International, January 23, 1992, Powell Papers; Colin Powell interview transcript, *Good Morning America,* ABC, January 15, 1992, Powell Papers.

126. Colin Powell interview transcript, CNN and CNN International, January 23, 1992, Powell Papers.

127. Ibid.

128. Torreon, "A Guide to Major Congressional and Presidential Awards"; Maureen Dowd, "For Bush a Special Day at Rushmore," *New York Times*, July 4, 1991.

129. "Awarding of Congressional Gold Medal to Gen. Colin L. Powell," Congressional Record—Senate, March 21, 1991, Powell Papers.

130. "Knighthood for Colin Powell," *The Independent*, October 1, 1993.

131. Cheney, *In My Time*, 425.

132. Cohen, *Supreme Command*, 206.

133. Schwarzkopf, *It Doesn't Take A Hero*, 325.

134. Gordon and Trainor, *The Generals' War*, 343.

135. Rudy Abramson and John Broder, "Four-Star Power: Colin Powell's Career Has Proceeded with the Certainty of a Laser-Guided Missile. How Much Higher Will He Go?" *Los Angeles Times*, April 7, 1991.

136. Ibid.

137. Powell, *My American Journey*, 561; Stephanopoulos, *All Too Human*, 129.

138. Powell, *My American Journey*, 547.

139. Colin L. Powell, author interview.

140. DeYoung, *Soldier*, 229.

141. Powell, *My American Journey*, 564.

142. Ibid., 563.

143. Thomas Friedman, "The President-Elect; Clinton Says Bush Made China Gains," *New York Times*, November 20, 1992.

144. Bill Clinton, "Remarks on the Retirement of General Colin Powell in Arlington, Virginia," September 30, 1993, The American Presidency Project.

145. Frank, *Under Friendly Fire*, 59.

146. Powell, *My American Journey*, 547.

147. *Crisis Magazine,* "Pat Schroeder v. Colin Powell."

148. John Cushman Jr., "The Transition: Gay Rights; Top Military Officers Object to Lifting the Ban," *New York Times*, November 14, 1992; "How the System Works—Civilians Will Decide about Gays in the Military, *Seattle Times*, November 19, 1992.

149. Colin Powell, interview transcript, "CNN's Newsmaker Saturday," December 5, 1992, Powell Papers.

150. General Colin Powell, "Remarks to the U.S. Naval Academy, Annapolis, Maryland," January 11, 1993, Powell Papers; "Powell Praises Gay Ban, But Says Clinton Is Boss; Conform or Quit, He Warns Officers," *Atlanta Constitution*, January 12, 1993; DeYoung, *Soldier*, 230.

151. Powell, *My American Journey*, 572.

152. Clinton, *My Life*, 484.

153. Stephanopoulos, *All Too Human*, 126.

154. Powell, *My American Journey*, 572.

155. Stephanopoulos, *All Too Human*, 126.

156. "Statement by General Colin Powell," January 29, 1993, Powell Papers.

157. Stephanopoulos, *All Too Human*, 129.

158. "Powell Defends, Nunn Praises Order on Gays," *Los Angeles Times*, July 21, 1993.

159. Stephanopoulos, *All Too Human*, 128.

160. Editorial, "Who's in Charge of the Military," *New York Times*, January 26, 1993; see also A. M. Rosenthal, "On My Mind, General Powell and the Gays," *New York Times*, January 26, 1993.

161. Lacayo, "The Rebellious Soldier."

162. Germond and Witcover, "Clinton and Powell: Who's in Charge?"

163. Powell, *My American Journey*, 573.

164. Ibid.

165. Melissa Healy, "Powell Confirms He Is Considering Leaving Office Early," *Los Angeles Times*, February 11, 1993.

166. Powell, *My American Journey*, 573–74.

167. Clinton, *My Life*, 450.

168. Aoi, *Legitimacy and the Use of Armed Force*, 42–47; Western, *Selling Intervention and War*, 133–74.

169. Gates, *Thirteen Ways of Looking at a Black Man*, 90–91.

170. Colin Powell interview transcript, "CNN's Newsmaker Saturday," November 5, 1992, Powell Papers.

171. Power, *A Problem from Hell*," 274.

172. Ibid., 276.

173. Baker, *The Politics of Diplomacy*, 648–50.

174. Power, *A Problem from Hell*," 279.

175. Powell, *My American Journey*, 291.

176. Power, *A Problem from Hell*," 273.

177. Michael R. Gordon, "Powell Delivers a Resounding No on Using Limited Force in Bosnia," *New York Times*, September 28, 1992.

178. Ibid.

179. Editorial, "At Least Slow the Slaughter," *New York Times*, October 4, 1992.

180. Powell, *My American Journey*, 558.

181. Colin Powell, "Why Generals Get Nervous," *New York Times*, October 8, 1992.

182. Power, *A Problem from Hell*," 292.

183. Ibid.

184. Clifford Krauss, "U.S. Backs Away from Charge of Atrocities in Bosnia Camps," *New York Times*, August 5, 1992.

185. Powell, *My American Journey*, 562.

186. Power, *A Problem from Hell*," 297–98.

187. Powell, *My American Journey*, 576.

188. Christopher, *Chances of a Lifetime*, 252.

189. Beinart, *The Icarus Syndrome*, 270.

190. Clinton, *My Life*, 513.

191. Powell, *My American Journey*, 576.

192. Colin Powell, "Remarks at the Naval War College, Newport, Rhode Island," June 4, 1991, Powell Papers.

193. Albright, *Madam Secretary*, 183.

194. Powell, *My American Journey*, 576; Albright, *Madam Secretary*, 183.

195. Keller, "The World According to Powell," 74.

196. Power, *A Problem from Hell*," 312–16.

197. Powell, *My American Journey*, 576.

198. Ibid.

199. Pardew, *Peacemakers*, 17–22.

200. Stephanopoulos, *All Too Human*, 159.

201. Meacham, *Destiny and Power*, 542.

202. Indyk, *Innocent Abroad*, 38.

203. Clinton, *My Life*, 526.

204. Stephanopoulos, *All Too Human*, 165.

205. Ibid.

206. Indyk, *Innocent Abroad*, 150.

207. Njoku, *The History of Somalia*.

208. Don Oberdorfer, "The Path to Intervention," *Washington Post*, December 6, 1992.

209. Western, *Selling Intervention and War*, 162–63.

210. James Gerstenzang and Melissa Healy, "U.S. to Airlift Food to Combat Somali Famine," *Los Angeles Times*, August 15, 1992.

211. Sparrow, *The Strategist*, 459.

212. Zinni, *The Battle for Peace*, 100–1.

213. Powell, *My American Journey*, 564; Poole, *The Effort to Save Somalia*, 1–2; Cohen, *Intervening in Africa*, 211–14.

214. Powell, *My American Journey*, 565.

215. Annan, *Interventions*, 42.

216. Powell, *My American Journey*, 565.

217. Dick Cheney and Colin Powell "News Briefing" transcript, December 4, 1992, Powell Papers.

218. Ibid.

219. "Stephen S. Rosenfeld, "Colin Powell's Somalia Operation," *Washington Post*, December 11, 1992.

220. Editorial, *New York Times*, December 5, 1992.

221. Powell, *My American Journey*, 580.

222. Haulman, "A Country Too Far."

223. Baxter, *Somalia*, 27–33.

224. Colin Powell, "Press Briefing," April 5, 1993, Powell Papers.

225. Haulman, "A Country Too Far."

226. Levin and Warner, "Review of the Circumstances Surrounding the Ranger Raid on October 3–4, 1993 in Mogadishu, Somalia."

227. Poole, *The Effort to Save Somalia*, 3.

228. Halberstam, *War in A Time of Peace*, 259.

229. Levin and Warner, "Review of the Circumstances Surrounding the Ranger Raid on October 3–4, 1993 in Mogadishu, Somalia."

230. Clinton, *My Life*, 550.

231. Levin and Warner, "Review of the Circumstances Surrounding the Ranger Raid on October 3–4, 1993 in Mogadishu, Somalia."

232. Powell, *My American Journey*, 584.

233. Levin and Warner, "Review of the Circumstances Surrounding the Ranger Raid on October 3–4, 1993 in Mogadishu, Somalia."

234. Powell, *My American Journey*, 586.

235. Colin Powell, remarks at the "Defense Writers' Group Breakfast Meeting," September 23, 1993, Powell Papers.

236. Levin and Warner, "Review of the Circumstances Surrounding the Ranger Raid on October 3–4, 1993 in Mogadishu, Somalia."

237. Powell, *My American Journey*, 588.

238. Clinton, *My Life*, 550; Haulman, "A Country Too Far."

239. Annan, *Interventions*, 45.

240. Michael Wines, "Mission to Somalia; Bush Declares Goal in Somalia, to 'Save Thousands'" *New York Times*, December 5, 1992.

241. Powell, *It Worked for Me*, 206.

242. Cheney, "Richard B. Cheney Oral History, Secretary of Defense."

243. Bacevich, *The New American Militarism*, 50; Cohen, *Supreme Command*, 194–98.

244. Powell, "Colin Powell Oral History, Chairman of the Joint Chiefs of Staff."

245. Ibid.

246. Bacevich, *The New American Militarism*, 50; Cohen, *Supreme Command*, 194–98.

247. Ibid.

248. Schwarzkopf, *It Doesn't Take A Hero*, 480, 489.

249. Powell, "Colin Powell Oral History, Chairman of the Joint Chiefs of Staff."

250. Schwarzkopf, *It Doesn't Take A Hero*, 489.

251. Cheney, *In My Time*, 226.

252. Puryear, *American Generalship*, 229.

253. Powell, *My American Journey*, 46.

254. Colin L. Powell, author interview; Jay F. Marks, "Leadership Is All About Followership," *The Oklahoman*, March 22, 2006.

255. Eric Schmitt, "Colin Powell, Who Led U.S. Military into a New Era, Resigns," *New York Times*, September 30, 1993.

256. Meacham, *Destiny and Power*, 508; Jeffrey Hart, "Ditch Dan, and Call in Colin Powell for Vice President," *Daily News*, September 12, 1990; Michael Killian, "Both Parties Buzzing about Gen Powell for Vice President," *Chicago Tribune*, February 3, 1991; Richard Mackenzie, "An Officer and a Gentleman," 9.

257. Christopher, *Chances of a Lifetime*, 149.

CHAPTER 6 Presidential Icon (1993–2000)

1. DeYoung, *Soldier*, 250; Moore, "Powell Remains Most Popular Figure in America," Gallup.com, September 30, 2002.

2. Stark, "President Powell?," 22.

3. Powell, *My American Journey*, 561, 602–3.

4. Gordon and Trainor, "Beltway Warrior," 40.

5. DeYoung, *Soldier*, 226.

6. Tom Clancy to Colin Powell, February 10, 1992, Powell Papers.

7. Sarah Lyall, "General Powell to Trade the Sword for the Pen," *New York Times*, August 18, 1993.

8. Girard, *Clinton in Haiti*, 1–3.

9. Pastor, "More and Less Than It Seemed," 514.

10. Powell, "No Substitute for the Soldier on the Ground," 13.

11. Powell, *My American Journey*, 599.

12. DeYoung, *Soldier*, 247.

13. Pastor, "More and Less Than It Seemed," 517.

14. Powell, *My American Journey*, 600.

15. Pastor, "More and Less Than It Seemed," 517; Steve Goldstein, "Talks Barely Beat Invasion U.S. Intervention in Haiti," *Baltimore Sun*, September 20, 1994.

16. Pastor, "More and Less Than It Seemed," 517.

17. Powell, *My American Journey*, 600.

18. Powell, "No Substitute for the Soldier on the Ground," 14.

19. Pastor, "More and Less Than It Seemed," 518.

20. Steve Goldstein, "Talks Barely Beat Invasion U.S. Intervention in Haiti," *Baltimore Sun*, September 20, 1994.

21. DeYoung, *Soldier*, 248; Powell, *My American Journey*, 601.

22. Pastor, "More and Less Than It Seemed," 519; Powell, "No Substitute for the Soldier on the Ground," 14.

23. Pastor, "More and Less Than It Seemed," 519.

24. Clinton, *My Life*, 618; Girard, *Clinton in Haiti*, 6.

25. "The President's News Conference with President Jimmy Carter, General Colin Powell, and Senator Sam Nunn on Haiti," September 19, 1994, The American Presidency Project.

26. DeYoung, *Soldier*, 249–50.

27. Steve Daley, "Powell's Aura Continuing to Brighten," *Chicago Tribune*, September 22, 1994.

28. Fineman, "Powell on the March," 26, 31.

29. Rose DeWolf, "It's Hotter Than a Pistol, But Can't Do It All Losing Candidates Also Penned Tomes" *Philadelphia Daily News*, September 26, 1995.

30. DeYoung, *Soldier*, 262.

31. Powell, *My American Journey*, 608.

32. Ibid., 607.

33. Ibid., 609.

34. Ibid.

35. Christopher, *Chances of a Lifetime*, 149, 175; Stephanopoulos, *All Too Human*, 129; Powell, *My American Journey*, 561, 602–3.

36. Powell, *My American Journey*, 602–3.

37. Colin Powell to Harry Evans, summer 1995, Powell Papers; Murdock, "Powell for President," 9.

38. Gibbs, "General Letdown," 56; DeYoung, *Soldier*, 270.

39. DeYoung, *Soldier*, 271.

40. Ibid., 272.

41. Auster, "Colin Powell Superstar."

42. Klein, "Can Colin Powell Save America," 20.

43. Meacham, "How Colin Powell Plays the Game," 33.

44. *Evans-Novak Political Report* (September 19, 1995): 1–2.

45. Stark, "President Powell?," 22; Allison and Rusher, "Let the Race Begin," 49.

46. Morris, interview, *Frontline*.

47. Stephanopoulos, *All Too Human*, 196, 389.

48. Gates, "Powell and the Black Elite," 66; Gates, *Thirteen Ways of Looking at a Black Man*, 75.

49. Lane, "The Legend of Colin Powell," 21.

50. Gordon and Trainor, "Beltway Warrior," 42.

51. Gordon and Trainor, *The Generals' War*.

52. Gordon and Trainor, "Beltway Warrior," 42.

53. R. W. Apple Jr., "Noncandidate Powell Stirs Waves on Republican Right," *New York Times*, October 3, 1995; Ponnuru, "Powell Cons."

54. Editorial, "The Powell Shake-Up," *New York Times*, October 31, 1995.

55. Laura Ingraham and Stephen P. Vaughn, "Powell Is Bad for the G.O.P.," *New York Times*, September 20, 1995.

56. DeYoung, *Soldier*, 269.

57. Kohn, "Out of Control," 13, 11, 9, 9, 11, 13, 12.

58. Richard L. Berke, "Powell Record is Criticized by Conservatives in GOP," *New York Times*, November 3, 1995.

59. Paul Taylor and Dan Balz, "Conservatives Fire Away at Powell's Possible Bid," *Washington Post*, November, 3, 1995.

60. "Powell's Decision," *NewsHour*, PBS, November 8, 1995.

61. Steven A. Holmes, "A Decision Relieving Some, But Disappointing Others," *New York Times*, November 9, 1995.

62. "The Powell Decision: Excerpts from Powell News Conference on Political Plans," *New York Times*, November 8, 1995.

63. Francis X. Clines, "Powell Rules Out '96 Race; Cites Concerns for Family and His Lack of 'a Calling,'" *New York Times*, November 9, 1995.

64. Maureen Dowd, "The General's Retreat," *New York Times*, November 9, 1995.

65. "Real Reasons Colin Powell Isn't Running," *Top Ten Lists from Late Show with David Letterman*, November 9, 1995, Powell Papers.

66. Woodward, "The Powell Predicament," 12.

67. Matthew Cooper, "Colin's K-Street Crowd," and Orlando Patterson, "The Culture of Caution," *New Republic* (November 27, 1995): 18–26.

68. Colin Powell, "Oral History, Chairman of the Joint Chiefs of Staff."

69. Meacham, "How Colin Powell Plays the Game," 42.

70. Colin Powell to Newt Gingrich, June 19, 1996, Powell Papers.

71. Gibbs, "General Letdown," 57.

72. DeYoung, *Soldier*, 278–79.

73. "General Powell's presentation," Republican National Committee, July 5, 1996, Powell Papers.

74. "Full Text: Gen. Colin Powell's 1996 Speech," ABC News.com, August 12, 1996.

75. Paul West, "'We're a Big Enough Party to Disagree': Fiery Powell Speech Opens Convention," *Baltimore Sun*, August 13, 1996.

76. Powell, *It Worked for Me*, 275.

77. Allison, "The General Volunteers," 51.

78. DeYoung, *Soldier*, 282; Pew Research Center, "Section 4: News Media Credibility," June 8, 1998.

79. Thaddeus Herrick, "Powell Helps Bush Launch Texas-wide Campaign for Volunteers to Help Youths," *Houston Chronicle*, September 24, 1997.

80. DeYoung, *Soldier*, 282, 289.

81. Steven Lee Myers, "Bush's Missile Defenses Could Limit Warhead Cuts, Experts Warn," *New York Times*, May 23, 2000.

82. "Potential Nuclear Initiative," April 26, 2000, Powell Papers; Condoleezza Rice speech draft, May 2, 2000, Powell Papers.

83. DeYoung, *Soldier*, 291.

84. "Transcript of Colin Powell's Speech," ABC News.com, July 31, 2000.

85. Donald Rumsfeld to Colin Powell, August 1, 2000, Powell Papers.

86. "Republican National Convention: Laura Bush, Gen. Colin Powell Address Delegates," CNN.com, July 31, 2000.

87. Ibid.

88. "How Groups Voted in 2000," Cornell University Roper Center, https://ropercenter.cornell.edu/polls/us-elections/how-groups-voted/how-groups-voted-2000/.

89. DeYoung, *Soldier*, 295.

90. Ibid., 296.

91. Cheney, *In My Time*, 298.

92. "President-Elect Bush Nominates General Colin Powell for Secretary of State," CNN.com, December 16, 2000.

93. Ibid.

94. Ibid.

95. Unger, *The Fall of the House of Bush*, 184; Daalder and Destler, *In the Shadow of the Oval Office*, 255.

96. Colin L. Powell, author interview; DeYoung, *Soldier*, 297.

97. Thomas L. Friedman, "The Powell Perplex," *New York Times*, December 19, 2000.

98. Kaplan, "Yesterday's Man," 21.

99. "President-Elect Bush Nominates General Colin Powell for Secretary of State," CNN.com, December 16, 2000.

CHAPTER 7   Leader, Follower, Odd Man Out (2001–2004)

1. "Confirmation Hearing by Secretary-Designate Colin L. Powell," January 17, 2001, Department of State Archive.

2. Ibid.

3. Ibid.

4. Carlucci and Brzezinski, "State Department Reform"; Carlucci, "What State Needs," 20.

5. Moskin, *American Statecraft*, 689.

6. "Colin Powell Addresses State Department Employees on First Day at Work," CNN.com, January 22, 2001.

7. Thomas and Berry, "Colin Powell," 10.

8. "Colin Powell Addresses State Department Employees on First Day at Work," CNN.com, January 22, 2001; "Town Hall Meeting," January 25, 2001, State Department Archive.

9. "Town Hall Meeting," January 25, 2001, State Department Archive.

10. Barber, "The Colin Powell Difference."

11. "Town Hall Meeting," January 25, 2001, State Department Archive.

12. DeYoung, *Soldier*, 309.

13. "Secretary Colin Powell's State Department," *Ambassadors Review* (Spring 2003): 78–99.

14. Hill, *Outpost*, 200; Jones, "The Other Side of Powell's Record," http://www.unc.edu/depts/diplomat/item/2006/0103/jone/jonesc_powell.html.

15. Foreign Affairs Council, "Secretary Colin Powell's State Department," 80, 82.

16. Powell, Personal Emails, Colin Powell to Robert Kaplan, July 5, 2016.

17. Foreign Affairs Council, "Secretary Colin Powell's State Department," 79, 83.

18. Hill, *Outpost*, 199.

19. "Foreign Affairs Council Task Force Report," Richard Lugar, *Congressional Record—Senate,* December 8, 2004.

20. Foreign Affairs Council, "Secretary Colin Powell's State Department," iii, v.

21. Congressional Research Service, "China-U.S. Aircraft Collision Incident of April 2001."

22. David E. Sanger, "Collision with China: The Overview; Bush Is Demanding a 'Prompt' Return of Plane and Crew," *New York Times*, April 3, 2001.

23. DeYoung, *Soldier*, 330.

24. Ibid., 330–31.

25. Rumsfeld, *Known and Unknown*, 312–15.

26. Rice, *No Higher Honor*, 48.

27. Colin Powell, interview with Bob Schieffer, *Face the Nation*, CBS, April 8, 2001.

28. Congressional Research Service, "China–U.S. Aircraft Collision Incident of April 2001."

29. White House Press Release, "President Thanks Secretary Powell," November 15, 2004.

30. Rumsfeld, *Known and Unknown*, 314; Robert Kagan and William Kristol, "We Lost," *Washington Post*, April 13, 2001.

31. Kagan and Kristol, "A National Humiliation," 31.

32. Baker, *Days of Fire*, 100.

33. Colin Powell, interview with Bob Schieffer, *Face the Nation*, CBS, April 8, 2001.

34. DeYoung, *Soldier*, 331.

35. Sheryl Gay Stolberg, "In Global Battle on AIDS, Bush Creates Legacy," *New York Times*, January 5, 2008.

36. Bush, *Decision Points*, 336.

37. Ibid.

38. "Remarks by the President," May 11, 2001, State Department Archive.

39. Annan, *Interventions*, 240.

40. "President Promotes New Mother and Child HIV Prevention Initiative," June 19, 2002, State Department Archive.

41. Annan, *Interventions*, 241.

42. "President Signs HIV/AIDS Act," May 27, 2003, State Department Archive.

43. "Emergency AIDS Relief Officials Talk to Reporters," C-SPAN.org, February 24, 2004.

44. Colin L. Powell, author interview.

45. DeYoung, *Soldier*, 326–27; Colin L. Powell, author interview.

46. Rice, *No Higher Honor*, 41–42; Colin L. Powell, author interview.

47. DeYoung, *Soldier*, 328.

48. Ibid.

49. David E. Sanger, "Leaving for Europe, Bush Draws on Hard Lessons of Diplomacy," *New York Times*, May 22, 2002.

50. DeYoung, *Soldier*, 329.

51. Indyk, *Innocent Abroad*, 14.

52. Suskind, *The Price of Loyalty*, 70–72.

53. Ibid., 72.

54. DeYoung, *Soldier*, 355.

55. Suskind, *The Price of Loyalty*, 71.

56. "President Thanks Secretary Powell," November 15, 2004, White House Press Release.

57. DeYoung, *Soldier*, 355.

58. Ibid., 354–56.

59. Norman Kempster, "Bush Supports the Idea of a Palestinian State," *Los Angeles Times*, October 3, 2001.

60. "U.S. President Bush's Speech to United Nations," CNN.com, November 10, 2001.

61. Ibid.

62. Colin Powell speech, University of Louisville, November 19, 2001, State Department Archive.

63. Ibid.

64. DeYoung, *Soldier*, 359.

65. Clancy, *Battle Ready*, 369.

66. Ibid., 372.

67. Ibid., 369.

68. DeYoung, *Soldier*, 360.

69. Clancy, with Zinni and Koltz, *Battle Ready*, 391–96.

70. Ibid., 397–405; Baker, *Days of Fire*, 196; DeYoung, *Soldier*, 379.

71. "Extracts from Bush's Speech," BBC.com, April 4, 2002.

72. Baker, *Days of Fire*, 196.

73. DeYoung, *Soldier*, 379.

74. Ibid., 380.

75. Annan, *Interventions*, 279.

76. Woodward, *Bush at War*, 325.

77. Cheney, *In My Time*, 381–82.

78. DeYoung, *Soldier*, 383.

79. Bumiller, *Condoleezza Rice*, 177–78; DeYoung, *Soldier*, 384.

80. Cheney, *In My Time*, 381.

81. DeYoung, *Soldier*, 384.

82. "Colin Powell Press Conference," *NewsHour*, PBS, April 17, 2002.

83. Samuels, "A Conversation with Colin Powell."

84. "President Bush Call for New Palestinian Leadership," June 25, 2002, White House Archives.

85. Tenet, *At the Center of the Storm*, 73.

86. Bumiller, *Condoleezza Rice*, 182–83.

87. Bush, *Decision Points*, 404–5; "Bush Promises 'Road Map' For Mideast Peace," CNN.com, March 14, 2003.

88. Rice, *No Higher Honor*, 147.

89. "Remarks by the President at a Multilateral Meeting with Arab Leaders," June 3, 2003, White House Archives.

90. DeYoung, *Soldier*, 472.

91. Gelman, *Angler*, 240, 372–73; Bush, *Decision Points*, 90; Rumsfeld, *Known and Unknown*, 641–42.

92. Steven Mufson, "Bush to Pick Up Clinton Talks on N. Korean Missiles," *Washington Post*, March 7, 2001; Bush, *Decision Points*, 90–91; DeYoung, *Soldier*, 324; Suskind, *The Price of Loyalty*, 114–15.

93. Rice, *No Higher Honor*, 35–36.

94. Bumiller, *Condoleezza Rice*, 145–47.

95. "Remarks by Secretary of State Colin Powell to the Pool," March 7, 2001, White House Archives; Baker, *Days of Fire*, 94–95; DeYoung, *Soldier*, 325.

96. DeYoung, *Soldier*, 325.

97. Ibid., 326.

98. Ibid., 474.

99. Colin L. Powell, author interview; DeYoung, *Soldier*, 391.

100. Burns, *The Missile Defense Systems of George W. Bush*, 99–100.

101. Colin L. Powell, author interview; Dubose and Bernstein, *Vice*, 185–86.

102. Rice, *No Higher Honor*, 162.

103. DeYoung, *Soldier*, 498.

104. Hill, *Outpost*, 200–1.

105. DeYoung, *Soldier*, 500; Colin L. Powell, author interview.

106. Baker, *Days of Fire*, 314.

107. DeYoung, *Soldier*, 508; Hill, *Outpost*, 200.

108. DeYoung, *Soldier*, 509.

109. Ibid., 339.

110. Clarke, *Against All Enemies*, 228.

111. "Day One Transcript: 9/11 Commission Hearing," WashingtonPost.com, March 23, 2004.

112. Ibid.

113. Ibid.

114. Powell, "Interview: Colin Powell"; DeYoung, *Soldier*, 338–41.

115. Colin L. Powell, "Statement at the Special General Assembly," September 11, 2001, State Department Archive.

116. "Text of Bush's Address," CNN.com, September 11, 2001.

117. Rice, *No Higher Honor*, 77.

118. Woodward, *Bush at War*, 31.

119. Ibid., 33.

120. Rumsfeld, *Known and Unknown*, 346; Shelton, *Without Hesitation*, 437.

121. Shelton, *Without Hesitation*, 437.

122. Ibid.

123. Powell, "Interview: Colin Powell."

124. Woodward, *Bush at War*, 32.

125. Shelton, *Without Hesitation*, 439–40.

126. Woodward, *Bush at War*, 43.

127. Ibid.; Cheney, *In My Time*, 330–31.

128. Woodward, *Bush at War*, 43.

129. Clark, *Against All Enemies*, 32; National Commission on Terrorist Attacks upon the United States, *9/11 Commission Report*, 334; Baker, *Days of Fire*, 135.

130. Clark, *Against All Enemies*, 30–31.

131. Ibid., 31.

132. Woodward, *Bush at War*, 43.

133. Ibid., 45; Baker, *Days of Fire*, 134–35.

134. Woodward, *Bush at War*, 58.

135. Tenet, *At the Center of the Storm*, 179–80; Armitage, "Interview: Richard Armitage."

136. Armitage, "Interview: Richard Armitage," *Frontline*.

137. Woodward, *Bush at War*, 48–49.

138. Cheney, *In My Time*, 330–31.

139. Woodward, *Bush at War*, 49.

140. Shelton, *Without Hesitation*, 441–42.

141. Woodward, *Bush at War*, 61.

142. Ibid., 49.

143. Ibid.

144. Ibid., 59.

145. Tenet, *At the Center of the Storm*, 181.

146. Woodward, *Bush at War*, 61.

147. Baker, *Days of Fire*, 136; Tenet, *At the Center of the Storm*, 175–76.

148. Woodward, *Bush at War*, 62–63.

149. Ibid., 65.

150. Woodward, *Bush at War*, 65.

151. Fleischer, *Taking Heat*, 277.

152. Woodward, *Bush at War*, 45.

153. "Bush Tours Ground Zero in Lower Manhattan," CNN.com, September 14, 2001.

154. S.J.Res. 23 (107th): Authorization for Use of Force.

155. Bush, *Decision Points*, 187–88.

156. Ibid., 186–87; Tenet, *At the Center of the Storm*, 177–79.

157. Baker, *Days of Fire*, 144.

158. Bush, *Decision Points*, 189.

159. Woodward, *Bush at War*, 84.

160. Powell, "Interview: Colin Powell."

161. Woodward, *Bush at War*, 84; Bush, *Decision Points*, 189; Baker, *Days of Fire*, 144.

162. Shelton, *Without Hesitation*, 444.

163. Ibid.

164. Ibid.

165. Rumsfeld, *Known and Unknown*, 425; Woodward, *Plan of Attack*, 1–3. Franks, *American Soldier*, 329; Feith, *War and Decision*, 218.

166. Shelton, *Without Hesitation*, 444.

167. Ibid., 444–45.

168. Woodward, *Bush at War*, 87.

169. Baker, *Days of Fire*, 144; Rice, *No Higher Honor*, 87; Woodward, *Bush at War*, 88.

170. Woodward, *Bush at War*, 89; Bush, *Decision Points*, 189.

171. Woodward, *Bush at War*, 90.

172. Ibid., 91; Bush, *Decision Points*, 190; Cheney, *In My Time*, 334; Rice, *No Higher Honor*, 87.

173. Powell, "Interview: Colin Powell."

174. Ibid.

175. Dick Cheney, interview, *Meet the Press*, NBC, September 16, 2001; Baker, *Days of Fire*, 146.

176. "Reluctant Warrior," *Guardian*, September 29, 2001.

177. Powell, "Interview: Colin Powell."

178. Woodward, *Bush at War*, 99; Bob Woodward and Dan Balz, "Combating Terrorism: It Starts Today," *Washington Post*, February 1, 2002.

179. Woodward, *Bush at War*, 98.

180. Bob Woodward and Dan Balz, "Combating Terrorism: It Starts Today," *Washington Post*, February 1, 2002; Woodward, *Bush at War*, 98.

181. "President Bush Addresses the Nation," *Washington Post*, September 20, 2001.

182. "Executive Order Freezing Terrorist Assets," *Washington Post*, September 24, 2001.

183. Woodward, *Bush at War*, 113.

184. Armitage, "Interview: Richard Armitage."

185. Bush, *Decision Points*, 196–97.

186. Powell, "Interview: Colin Powell."

187. Rumsfeld, *Known and Unknown*, 374.

188. Woodward, *Bush at War*, 177.

189. Ibid., 176.

190. "Blair: Bin Laden behind the Attacks," CNN.com, October 4, 2004.

191. Woodward, *Bush at War*, 124; William Kristol, "Bush vs. Powell, *Washington Post*, September 25, 2001.

192. Woodward, *Bush at War*, 122.

193. Ibid., 123.

194. Ibid., 130.

195. Ibid., 192.

196. Tenet, *At the Center of the Storm*, 208–13.

197. Armitage, "Interview: Richard Armitage."

198. Bush, *Decision Points*, 194–95, 197.

199. "Presidential Address to the Nation," October 7, 2001, White House Archives.

200. Woodward, *Bush at War*, 219, 231.

201. Ibid., 237.

202. Annan, *Interventions*, 337

203. Colin L. Powell, "Press Briefing on Board Plane," October 15, 2001, State Department Archive.

204. Rumsfeld, *Known and Unknown*, 392.

205. Ibid.

206. Woodward, *Bush at War*, 243.

207. Ibid., 243–44; Baker, *Days of Fire*, 168.

208. Woodward, *Bush at War*, 244; Baker, *Days of Fire*, 168.

209. R. W. Apple Jr., "A Military Quagmire Remembered: Afghanistan as Vietnam," *New York Times*, October 31, 2001; "The Quagmire Issue," editorial, *Dallas Morning News*, October 26, 2001; Maureen Dowd, "Liberties, Can Bush Bushkazi?," *New York Times*, October 28, 2001.

210. Woodward, *Bush at War*, 223.

211. Ibid., 275.

212. Ibid., 291.

213. Ibid., 291.

214. Powell, "Interview: Colin Powell."

215. Tenet, *At the Center of the Storm*, 217.

216. Bolger, *Why We Lost*, 50–51; Woodward, *Bush at War*, 312.

217. Rumsfeld, *Known and Unknown*, 400.

218. Khalilzad, *The Envoy*, 119–27.

219. Annan, *Interventions*, 341.

220. Bush, *Decision Points*, 204–9; Rice, *No Higher Honor*, 108–10.

221. Unger, *The Fall of the House of Bush*, 222–23; Barton Gellman and Jo Becker, "A Different Understanding with the President," *Washington Post*, June 24, 2007.

222. Goldsmith, *The Terror Presidency*, 106–9; Rumsfeld, *Known and Unknown*, 556, 588; Cheney, *In My Time*, 356–67; Bush, *Decision Points*, 164–68; Rice, *No Higher Honor*, 104–6.

223. Rumsfeld, *Known and Unknown*, 556, 588.

224. Mayer, *The Dark Side*, 80; Barton Gellman and Jo Becker, "A Different Understanding with the President," *Washington Post*, June 24, 2007.

225. Gellman, *Angler*, 168.

226. Rice, *No Higher Honor*, 105–6.

227. Rumsfeld, *Known and Unknown*, 601.

228. Goldsmith, *The Terror Presidency*, 134; Baker, *Days of Fire*, 173–75; Gellman, *Angler*, 162–68; Pfiffner, *Torture as Public Policy*, 14–17.

229. Katharine Q. Seelye, "First 'Unlawful Combatants' Seized in Afghanistan Arrive at U.S. Base in Cuba," *New York Times*, January 12, 2002; Eichenwald, *500 Days*, 217–18; Greenberg, *The Least Worst Place*, 121.

230. DeYoung, *Soldier*, 365; Rice, *No Higher Honor*, 107.

231. Rice, *No Higher Honor*, 107.

232. Yoo and Delahunty memorandum for Haynes, January 9, 2002, in Greenberg and Dratel, *The Torture Papers*, 38–79.

233. Taft, "Unclassified Memorandum To: John C. Yoo."

234. Greenberg, *The Least Worst Place*, 51–54.

235. Linda Greenhouse, "Supreme Court Blocks Guantanamo Tribunals," *New York Times*, June 29, 2006; Goldsmith, *The Terror Presidency*, 134; Baker, *Days of Fire*, 173–75; Gellman, *Angler*, 162–68; Pfiffner, *Torture As Public Policy*, 14–17.

236. DeYoung, *Soldier*, 369; Gellman, *Angler*, 170.

237. Rowan Scarborough, "Powell Wants Detainees to Be Declared POWs; Memo Shows Differences with White House," *Washington Times*, January 26, 2002.

238. DeYoung, *Soldier*, 370.

239. Katherine Q. Seelye, "Powell Asks Bush to Review Stand on War Captives," *New York Times*, January 27, 2002; Katherine Q. Seelye and David Sanger, "Captives; Bush Reconsiders Stand on Treating Captives of War," *New York Times*, January 29, 2002.

240. DeYoung, *Soldier*, 370.

241. Powell to Counsel to the President, "Draft Decision Memorandum," January 26, 2002, in Greenberg and Dratel, *The Torture Papers*, 122–25.

242. Powell to Counsel to the President, "Draft Decision Memorandum," January 26, 2002, in Greenberg and Dratel, *The Torture Papers*, 122–25.

243. Taft to Counsel to the President, "Comments on Your Paper," February 2, 2002, in Greenberg and Dratel, *The Torture Papers*, 129–33.

244. Taft to Counsel to the President, "Comments on Your Paper," February 2, 2002, in Greenberg and Dratel, *The Torture Papers*, 129–33.

245. Goldsmith, *The Terror Presidency*, 113–15.

246. Myers, *Eyes On the Horizon*, 205.

247. Baker, *Days of Fire*, 185.

248. Eichenwald, *500 Days*, 229–30.

249. Bush Memorandum, "Humane Treatment of al Qaeda and Taliban," February 7, 2002, in Greenberg and Dratel, *The Torture Papers*, 134–35; Goldsmith, *The Terror Presidency*, 109–10.

250. Bolger, *Why We Lost*, 66.

251. Senate Armed Services Committee, "Inquiry into the Treatment of Detainees," November 20, 2008, https://www.armed-services.senate.gov/imo/media/doc/Detainee-Report-Final_April-22-2009.pdf.

252. Felice, *How Do I Save My Honor?*, 68.

253. Powell, *It Worked for Me*, 10; Powell, *My American Journey*, 320.

254. Baker, "James A. Baker III, Oral History, White House Chief of Staff; Secretary of State."

255. Powell, "Colin Powell Oral History, Chairman of the Joint Chiefs of Staff."

CHAPTER 8 Adviser (2002–2003)

1. Powell, Personal Emails, Colin Powell to Lawrence Wilkerson, August 7, 2015, and Colin Powell to Marybel Batjer, August, 10, 2015.

2. Cheney, *In My Time*, 367.

3. Clarke, *Against All Enemies*, 32.

4. Rumsfeld, *Known and Unknown*, 425.

5. Bush, *Decision Points*, 235; Myers, *Eyes On the Horizon*, 222–23; Tommy Franks, *American Soldier*, 346–56.

6. "Bush State of the Union Address," CNN.com, January 29, 2002.

7. Tenet, *At the Center of the Storm*, 307.

8. Woodward, *Plan of Attack*, 91.

9. "Patrick E. Tyler and David E. Sanger, "U.S. to Press Iraq to Let U.N. Search for Banned Arms," *New York Times*, December 1, 2001.

10. Woodward, *Plan of Attack*, 39.

11. Ibid., 103.

12. Khalilzad, *The Envoy*, 98–99.

13. Ibid., 22.

14. Bush, *Decision Points*, 230; Rice, *No Higher Honor*, 172.

15. DeYoung, *Soldier*, 377; Woodward, *Plan of Attack*, 103.

16. Richard Wolffe and Gerard Baker, "Powell's New Doctrine," *Financial Times*, February 14, 2002.

17. "Text of Bush's Speech at West Point," *New York Times*, June 1, 2002.

18. Ibid.

19. Rumsfeld, *Known and Unknown*, 423; "The National Security Strategy," White House Archives, September 20, 2002.

20. Bush, *Decision Points*, 236–37; Rice, *No Higher Honor*, 177–78.

21. Zenko, "Forgoing Limited Force," 628.

22. Bush, *Decision Points*, 237.

23. Rice, *No Higher Honor*, 177–78.

24. Straw, *Last Man Standing*, 332; Meyer, *DC Confidential*, 161–62.

25. Haass, *War of Necessity*, 213–14.

26. "The Downing Street Memo," July 23, 2002, National Security Archive, https://nsarchive2.gwu.edu/NSAEBB/NSAEBB328/II-Doc14.pdf; Tenet, *At the Center of the Storm*, 310.

27. "The Downing Street Memo," July 23, 2002, National Security Archive, https://nsarchive2.gwu.edu/NSAEBB/NSAEBB328/II-Doc14.pdf.

28. Hill, *Outpost*, 201.

29. Baker, *Days of Fire*, 207; Woodward, *Plan of Attack*, 148–53.

30. Bush, *Decision Points*, 235; Franks, *American Soldier*, 385; Colin Powell to author (email), March 27, 2017.

31. Colin Powell to author (email), March 27, 2017.

32. Powell, *It Worked for Me*, 211.

33. Baker, *Days of Fire*, 208.

34. Colin Powell to author (email), March 27, 2017.

35. DeYoung, *Soldier*, 401–2.

36. "Aspen Ideas Festival Conversation with Colin Powell," Aspen Institute, July 8, 2007, https://www.aspenideas.org/sites/default/files/transcripts/Powell-Lehrer_transcript.pdf.

37. Bush, *Decision Points*, 251.

38. Ibid., 238.

39. Woodward, *Plan of Attack*, 151.

40. Powell, *It Worked for Me*, 211.

41. Woodward, *Plan of Attack*, 151; DeYoung, *Soldier*, 402.

42. Woodward, *Plan of Attack*, 152.

43. Breslow, "Colin Powell: U.N. Speech 'Was a Great Intelligence Failure.'"

44. Haass, *War of Necessity*, 216.

45. Chuck Hagel, interview, *Face the Nation*, CBS, August 4, 2002.

46. Brent Scowcroft, interview, *Face the Nation*, CBS, August 4, 2002.

47. Sparrow, *The Strategist*, 525.

48. Cheney, *In My Time*, 388.

49. Chuck Hagel, interview, *Hardball with Chris Matthews*, MSNBC, August 26, 2002.

50. Brent Scowcroft, "Don't Attack Saddam," *Wall Street Journal*, August 15, 2002.

51. James A. Baker III, "The Right to Change a Regime," *New York Times*, August 25, 2002.

52. Sparrow, *The Strategist*, 525.

53. Goldberg, "Breaking Ranks."

54. Cheney, *In My Time*, 389.

55. Ibid., 383, 389–90.

56. Dick Cheney, "In Cheney's Words: The Administration Case for Removing Saddam Hussein," *New York Times*, August 27, 2002.

57. Baker, *Days of Fire*, 211; Dubose and Bernstein, *Vice*, 176.

58. Tenet, *At the Center of the Storm*, 315–17.

59. Baker, *Days of Fire*, 213.

60. Ibid., 211; Bumiller, *Condoleezza Rice*, 189–90.

61. "Vice President Honors Veterans of Korean War," August 29, 2002, White House Archives.

62. Woodward, *Plan of Attack*, 167.

63. Colin L. Powell, "Interview on BBC *Breakfast with Sir David Frost*," August 29, 2002, State Department Archive.

64. Bush, *Decision Points*, 239.

65. Rice, *No Higher Honor*, 180.

66. Tenet, *At the Center of the Storm*, 319.

67. Naughtie, *The Accidental American*, 120.

68. Ibid., 121.

69. Cheney, *In My Time*, 373–74; Bush, *Decision Points*, 238–39; Meyer, *DC Confidential*, 252.

70. Baker, *Days of Fire*, 216.

71. "President Bush's Address to the United Nations," CNN.com, September 12, 2002.

72. Baker, *Days of Fire*, 215; Isikoff and Corn, *Hubris*, 24–25.

73. "President Discusses Foreign Policy with Congressional Leaders," September 4, 2002, White House Archives.

74. Gellman, *Angler*, 215.

75. Bush, *Decision Points*, 251.

76. Smith, *Bush*, 316.

77. Ricks, *Fiasco*, 60.

78. Baker, *Days of Fire*, 220; Isikoff and Corn, *Hubris*, 124–25; Gellman, *Angler*, 215–220; Draper, *Dead Certain*, 178.

79. Baker, *Days of Fire*, 221; Gellman, *Angler*, 219–20.

80. "President Bush Discusses Iraq with Congressional Leaders," September 26, 2002, White House Archives.

81. Eric Schmitt, "Rumsfeld Says U.S. Has 'Bulletproof' Evidence of Iraq's Links to Al Qaeda," *New York Times*, September 28, 2002.

82. National Intelligence Council, "Key Judgments from 'Iraq's Continuing Programs for Weapons of Mass Destruction,'" October 2002; Tenet, *At the Center of the Storm*, 321–39; Morell, *The Great War of Our Time*, 86–91.

83. "Authorization for Use of Military Force against Iraq Resolution of 2002," October 10, 2002.

84. "Aspen Ideas Festival Conversation with Colin Powell," Aspen Institute, July 8, 2007, https://www.aspenideas.org/sites/default/files/transcripts/Powell-Lehrer_transcript.pdf.

85. Woodward, *Plan of Attack*, 220–21.

86. Colin L. Powell, "Interview on CNN's 'Larry King Live,'" State Department Archive, October 9, 2002.

87. Karen DeYoung, "For Powell, a Long Road to Victory," *Washington Post*, November 10, 2002.

88. Straw, *Last Man Standing*, 379.

89. United Nations Security Council Resolution 1441, November 8, 2002.

90. Straw, *Last Man Standing*, 381.

91. Colin L. Powell, "Interview On CNN's 'Larry King Live,'" October 9, 2002, State Department Archive.

92. Colin L. Powell, "Secretary's Interview on *Oprah Winfrey Show*," State Department Archive, October 22, 2002.

93. "Interview by Ellen Ratner of Talk Radio News," State Department Archive, October 30, 2002.

94. Annan, *Interventions*, 348.

95. Colin Powell to author (email), March 27, 2017.

96. Bush, *Decision Points*, 241.

97. Rice, *No Higher Honor*, 184.

98. Woodward, *Plan of Attack*, 227.

99. "President Pleased with U.N. Vote," November 8, 2002, White House Archives.

100. Karen DeYoung, "For Powell, a Long Road to Victory," *Washington Post*, November 10, 2002.

101. Annan, *Interventions*, 349.

102. Baker, *Days of Fire*, 239.

103. Colin Powell, "Press Conference on Iraqi Declaration," December 19, 2002, State Department Archive.

104. DeYoung, *Soldier*, 428.

105. Ibid.

106. Blix, *Disarming Iraq*, 111.

107. Baker, *Days of Fire*, 240.

108. *Hubris: Selling the Iraq War*, MSNBC, February 18, 2013.

109. Rumsfeld, *Known and Unknown*, 450.

110. DeYoung, *Soldier*, 429.

111. Woodward, *Plan of Attack*, 271.

112. DeYoung, *Soldier*, 430; Woodward, *Plan of Attack*, 271–72.

113. Bush, *Decision Points*, 244.

114. Breslow, "Colin Powell: U.N. Speech 'Was a Great Intelligence Failure'"; Colin L. Powell, interview, *NewsNight*, BBC, February 20, 2003.

115. DeYoung, *Soldier*, 432.

116. Ibid., 433.

117. Julia Preston, "An Attack on Iraq Not Yet Justified, France Warns U.S.," *New York Times*, January 21, 2003.

118. Powell, *It Worked for Me*, 6–7; DeYoung, *Soldier*, 433–34.

119. Colin L. Powell, "Remarks at the World Economic Forum," January 26, 2003, State Department Archive.

120. Ibid.

121. Haass, *War of Necessity*, 240.

122. "No 'Genuine Acceptance' of Disarmament, Blix Says," *Washington Post*, January 28, 2003; Blix, *Disarming Iraq*, 138–41.

123. Meyer, *DC Confidential*, 259.

124. Colin L. Powell, "Briefing on the Iraq Weapons Inspectors' 60-Day Report: Iraq Non-cooperation and Defiance of the UN," January 27, 2003, State Department Archive.

125. Don Van Natta Jr, "Bush Was Set on Path to War, British Memo Says," *New York Times*, March 27, 2006.

126. David W. Moore, "Powell Remains Most Popular Political Figure in America," Gallup.com, September 30, 2002.

127. Lawrence Wilkerson, interview with Amy Goodman, *Democracy Now!*, August 30, 2011.

128. Bush, *Decision Points*, 244–45.

129. Baker, *Days of Fire*, 242.

130. DeYoung, *Soldier*, 441.

131. Ibid.

132. Tenet, *At the Center of the Storm*, 360–62.

133. Ibid., 361–62; Baker, *Days of Fire*, 239–40.

134. Cheney, *In My Time*, 395.

135. DeYoung, *Soldier*, 436.

136. Tenet, *At the Center of the Storm*, 371–72; Woodward, *Plan of Attack*, 291.

137. Powell, *It Worked for Me*, 217–24.

138. Ibid., 220.

139. Haass, *War of Necessity*, 240–41.

140. Cheney, *In My Time*, 396.

141. Morell, *The Great War of Our Time*, 94; Tenet, *At the Center of the Storm*, 372–73.

142. Tenet, *At the Center of the Storm*, 374; Powell, *It Worked for Me*, 219.

143. Morell, *The Great War of Our Time*, 95.

144. Nigel Farndale, "Colin Powell on Why He Doesn't Regret a Thing," *Telegraph*, October 29, 2012.

145. Marie Brenner, "PlameGate. Lies and Consequences: Sixteen Words That Changed the World," VanityFair.com, October 17, 2006.

146. Karen DeYoung, "Post Magazine: Colin Powell," *Washington Post*, October 2, 2006.

147. Morell, *The Great War of Our Time*, 95–96.

148. Tenet, *At the Center of the Storm*, 342–56, 372–74.

149. Morell, *The Great War of Our Time*, 95; Tenet, *At the Center of the Storm*, 373.

150. Powell, *It Worked for Me,* 220; Lawrence Wilkerson, interview, "The Dark Side," *Frontline,* PBS, December 13, 2005.

151. Morell, *The Great War of Our Time*, 97; Tenet, *At the Center of the Storm*, 374.

152. Richard Haass, "Q&A: Richard Haass on Colin Powell," *New York Times*, November 15, 2004.

153. Tenet, *At the Center of the Storm*, 374.

154. Lawrence Wilkerson, interview, "The Dark Side," *Frontline,* PBS, December 13, 2005.

155. Rice, *No Higher Honor*, 200.

156. Myers, *Eyes On the Horizon*, 233.

157. DeYoung, *Soldier*, 446.

158. Colin L. Powell, "U.S. Policy on Iraq: "We Will Not Shrink from War," *Wall Street Journal*, February 3, 2003.

159. DeYoung, *Soldier*, 448.

160. Tenet, *At the Center of the Storm*, 369.

161. Colin L. Powell, "Remarks to the United Nations Security Council," February 5, 2003, State Department Archive.

162. Ibid.

163. Ibid.

164. Warrick, *Black Flags*, 95–98.

165. Ibid.

166. Ibid.

167. Powell, *It Worked for Me*, 220.

168. Tenet, *At the Center of the Storm*, 375.

169. Rice, *No Higher Honor*, 200.

170. Bush, *Decision Points*, 245.

171. Rove, *Courage and Consequence*, 303.

172. Annan, *Interventions*, 351.

173. Ibid., 351.

174. Ibid., 352.

175. Wolffe and Klaidman, "Judging the Case"; "Powell Reversed the Trend But Not the Tenor of Public Opinion," Pew Research Center, February 14, 2003.

176. George Will, "Disregarding the Deniers," *Washington Post*, February 6, 2003.

177. "Nick Anderson, "Much of the Skepticism among Lawmakers Appears to Buckle," *Los Angeles Times*, February 5, 2003.

178. "Irrefutable," *Washington Post*, February 6, 2003; "The Case Against Iraq," *New York Times*, February 6, 2003.

179. Mary McGrory, "I'm Persuaded," *Washington Post*, February 6, 2003.

180. Jim Hoagland, "An Old Trooper's Smoking Gun," *Washington Post*, February 6, 2003.

181. Senate Foreign Relations Committee, February 6, 2003.

182. Bush, *Decision Points*, 245.

183. Powell, *It Worked for Me*, 222.

184. Baker, *Days of Fire*, 252.

185. Colin L. Powell, "Briefing on Situation with Iraq," March 17, 2003, State Department Archive.

186. "President Bush Says Saddam Hussein Must Leave Iraq within 48 Hours," March 17, 2003, White House Archives.

187. Bush, *Decision Points*, 223; Franks, *American Soldier*, 431.

188. Bush, *Decision Points*, 223.

189. Purdum, *Time of Our Choosing*, 106.

190. "Transcript: David Kay at Senate Hearing," CNN.com, January 28, 2004.

191. Dana Priest and Walter Pincus, "U.S. 'Almost All Wrong' on Weapons," *Washington Post*, October 7, 2004.

192. "Report on the U.S. Intelligence Community's Prewar Intelligence Assessments on Iraq," U.S. Senate Select Committee on Intelligence, July 9, 2004, National Security Archive, https://nsarchive2.gwu.edu/NSAEBB /NSAEBB254/doc12.pdf.

193. Powell, *It Worked for Me*, 223.

194. Felice, *How Do I Save My Honor?*, 65–95.

195. Hill, *Outpost*, 201.

196. Annan, *Interventions*, 1.

197. Leung, "The Man Who Knew."

198. Colin Powell, interview, *The Daily Show with Jon Stewart*, Comedy Central, June 8, 2005.

199. "Colin Powell on Iraq, Race, and Hurricane Relief," ABCNews.com, September 8, 2005.

200. Nigel Farndale, "Colin Powell on Why He Doesn't Regret a Thing," *Telegraph*, October 29, 2012.

201. Steven R. Weisman, "Powell Calls His U.N. Speech a Lasting Blot on His Record," *New York Times*, September 9, 2005.

202. Karen DeYoung, "Falling on His Sword: Colin Powell's Most Significant Moment Turned Out to Be His Lowest," *Washington Post*, October 1, 2006.

203. National Intelligence Council, "National Intelligence Estimate: 'Iraq's Continuing Programs for Weapons of Mass Destruction,'" 36, 41, 46, 28, 33, 28.

204. Ibid., 13, 14, 8–9, 9.

205. Ibid., 67, 67, 66, 68, 68, 68, 68, 68.

206. Ibid., 68, 8, 8, 66, 67, 67.

207. Powell, *It Worked for Me*, 219.

208. Senate Intelligence Committee, "Report on the U.S. Intelligence Community's Prewar Assessment on Iraq"; "The Man Who Knew: Ex-Powell Aide Says Saddam-Weapons Threat Was Overstated," *60 Minutes*, CBS, October 14, 2003.

209. "The Man Who Knew: Ex-Powell Aide Says Saddam-Weapons Threat Was Overstated," *60 Minutes*, CBS, October 14, 2003; Isikoff and Corn, *Hubris*, 39–40.

210. Lawrence Wilkerson, interview with Amy Goodman, *Democracy Now!*, August 30, 2011; *Hubris: Selling the Iraq War*, MSNBC, February 18, 2013; Mayer, *The Dark Side*, 136–37; Douglas Jehl, "Qaeda-Iraq Link U.S. Cited Is Tied to Coercion Claim," *New York Times*, December 9, 2005.

211. Douglas Jehl and David E. Sanger, "Powell's Case, a Year Later: Gaps in Picture of Iraq Arms," *New York Times*, February 1, 2004; Mayer, *The Dark Side*, 136–37.

212. Drumheller, *On the Brink*, 83; Drogin, *Curveball*.

213. Drumheller, *On the Brink*, 83.

214. U.S. Army, "Evaluations," *Army Leadership Development Strategy 2013*, http://data.cape.army.mil/web/character-development-project/repository/alds-2013.pdf.

215. Powell, *It Worked for Me*, 219.

216. Nickerson, "Confirmation Bias," 175–220.

217. Colin Powell, interview, *The Daily Show with Jon Stewart*, Comedy Central, June 12, 2012.

218. Powell, *It Worked for Me*, 223.

219. *Hubris: Selling the Iraq War*, MSNBC, February 18, 2013.

220. Philip Bump, "15 Years After the Iraq War Began, the Death Toll is Still Murky," *Washington Post*, March 20, 2018; Stiglitz and Bilmes, *The Three Trillion Dollar War*; Watson Institute, Cost of War Project.

221. Powell, *It Worked for Me*, 223.

222. DeYoung, *Soldier*, 458.

223. Ibid., 469.

224. "U.S. Diplomat's Letter of Resignation," *New York Times*, February 27, 2003.

225. Ibid.

226. DeYoung, *Soldier*, 469.

CHAPTER 9   Defender in Chief (2003–2004)

1. Myers, *Eyes On the Horizon*, 242–45, 248.

2. Gordon and Trainor, *Cobra II*, 36, 116–19.

3. Battle and Blanton, "Top Secret Polo Step," National Security Archive, https://nsarchive2.gwu.edu/NSAEBB/NSAEBB214/index.htm.

4. Franks, *American Soldier*, 393–94.

5. Ibid., 394.

6. Ibid.

7. Donald H. Rumsfeld, "A New Kind of War," *New York Times*, September 27, 2001.

8. Ibid.

9. Rumsfeld, *Known and Unknown*, 437–38.

10. Franks, *American Soldier*, 395.

11. Ibid., 395–97.

12. Thomas E. Ricks, "Projection on Fall of Hussein Disputed; Ground Forces Chiefs, Pentagon at Odds," *Washington Post*, December 18, 2002. For Shinseki and Jones's strong disagreements with Rumsfeld, see Perry, *The Pentagon's Wars*, 152–58; Marine Corps Lieutenant General Greg Newbold, Jones's director of operations on the Joint Staff, had also expressed his opposition to Rumsfeld's plan to deploy a relatively small ground force. He resigned in November 2002; see Margolick, "The Night of the Generals."

13. Baker, *Days of Fire*, 243; Perry, *The Pentagon's Wars*, 149.

14. Rudd, *Reconstruction Iraq*, 140.

15. Testimony of Eric Shinseki, "The Fiscal Year 2004 Defense Budget," Hearing of the U.S. Senate Armed Services Committee, February 25, 2003.

16. Thomas E. White, interview, "Rumsfeld's War," *Frontline*, PBS, August 12, 2004; Gordon and Trainor, *Cobra II*, 117–18.

17. Murphy and Purdum, "Farewell to All That."

18. Testimony of Paul Wolfowitz, "The Fiscal Year 2004 Defense Budget," Hearing of the House Budget Committee, February 27, 2003.

19. Transcript, Department of Defense News Briefing, Donald Rumsfeld and Richard Myers, February 28, 2003, Department of Defense, http://archive .defense.gov/Transcripts/Transcript.aspx?TranscriptID=1976.

20. Dick Cheney, interview with Tim Russert, *Meet the Press*, NBC, March 16, 2003.

21. Bush, *Decision Points*, 251.

22. Ibid., 251.

23. Powell, *It Worked for Me*, 10.

24. Tenet, *At the Center of the Storm*, 419; Rice, *No Higher Honor*, 191; Bush, *Decision Points*, 249.

25. Rice, *No Higher Honor*, 191; Colin Powell, "Interview with the *USA/Today* Editorial Board," October 18, 2004, State Department Archive.

26. Haass, *War of Necessity*, 251.

27. Bumiller, *Condoleezza Rice*, 195.

28. Powell, Personal Emails, Condoleezza Rice to Colin Powell, June 9, 2015.

29. Rudd, *Reconstructing Iraq*, 29–151.

30. "The Future of Iraq Project," State Department, National Security Archive, https://nsarchive2.gwu.edu/NSAEBB/NSAEBB198/index.htm; Eric Schmitt and Joel Brinkley, "State Dept. Study Foresaw Trouble Now Plaguing Iraq," *New York Times*, October 19, 2003; DeYoung, *Soldier*, 397–98.

31. "The Future of Iraq Project," State Department; Eric Schmitt and Joel Brinkley, "State Dept. Study Foresaw Trouble Now Plaguing Iraq," *New York Times*, October 19, 2003; DeYoung, *Soldier*, 459.

32. Rudd, *Reconstruction Iraq*, 68–77.

33. Rumsfeld, *Known and Unknown*, 486.

34. Rudd, *Reconstruction Iraq*, 131.

35. Michael R. Gordon, "Diplomat Who Led Secret Talks with Iran Plans to Retire," *New York Times*, April 11, 2014.

36. Richard N. Haass to Colin Powell, "Reconstruction in Iraq—Lessons from the Past," September 26, 2002, in Haass, *War of Necessity*, 279–93.

37. Haass, *War of Necessity*, 281.

38. DeYoung, *Soldier*, 459.

39. Glasser, "You Can't Bomb It Away."

40. Tenet, *At the Center of the Storm*, 317–18.

41. Murphy and Purdum, "Farewell to All That."

42. Feith, *War and Decision*, 422; Rumsfeld, *Known and Unknown*, 486, 490–91.

43. Rumsfeld, *Known and Unknown*, 484; Bonin, *Arrows of the Night*, 172–224.

44. Tenet, *At the Center of the Storm*, 397; Rumsfeld, *Known and Unknown*, 488–89.

45. DeYoung, *Soldier*, 462.

46. Powell, Personal Emails, Colin Powell to Condoleezza Rice, June 9, 2015.

47. Bush, *Decision Points*, 249; Rice, *No Higher Honor*, 193; Haass, *War of Necessity*, 255.

48. Powell, Personal Emails, Colin Powell to Condoleezza Rice, June 9, 2015.

49. Rumsfeld, *Known and Unknown*, 493–94.

50. DeYoung, *Soldier*, 463.

51. Rumsfeld, *Known and Unknown*, 489–94.

52. Tenet, *At the Center of the Storm*, 398–99; Baker, *Days of Fire*, 264.

53. Gingrich, "Transforming the State Department." Gingrich continued his broadside in June 2003; see Gingrich, "Rogue State Department."

54. Barbara Slavin, "Gingrich Takes Swipe at State Department," *USA Today*, April 23, 2003; DeYoung, *Soldier*, 468.

55. Colin L. Powell, "Testimony before the Senate Appropriations Subcommittee on Foreign Operations," April 30, 2003, State Department Archive.

56. Franks, *American Soldier*, 523; Myers, *Eyes On the Horizon*, 249.

57. Franks, *American Soldier*, 530–31.

58. Tenet, *At the Center of the Storm*, 399.

59. Haass, *War of Necessity*, 252–53.

60. Rudd, *Reconstruction Iraq*, 133.

61. Ibid., 129–30.

62. Rice, *No Higher Honor*, 208.

63. Rudd, *Reconstruction Iraq*, 146, 200.

64. Baker, *Days of Fire*, 271; Rudd, *Reconstruction Iraq*, 146.

65. Woodward, *Plan of Attack*, 284; Baker, *Days of Fire*, 271.

66. Feith, *War and Decision*, 387–88.

67. Rice, *No Higher Honor*, 210.

68. Feith, *War and Decision*, 422; Rice, *Democracy*, 281.

69. Rice, *No Higher Honor*, 211.

70. Bremer, *My Year in Iraq*, 76.

71. Feith, *War and Decision*, 433; Jason. M Breslow, "Colin Powell: U.N. Speech 'Was a Great Intelligence Failure.'"

72. Rudd, *Reconstruction Iraq*, 308.

73. Breslow, "Colin Powell: U.N. Speech 'Was a Great Intelligence Failure'"; Rice, *Democracy*, 291–92.

74. Khalilzad, *The Envoy*, 174.

75. Bush, *Decision Points*, 259; Rumsfeld, *Known and Unknown*, 487.

76. Tenet, *At the Center of the Storm*, 403; Woodward, *State of Denial*, 218.

77. Annan, *Interventions*, 1.

78. Colin L. Powell, "Press Gaggle," May 30, 2003, State Department Archive.

79. DeYoung, *Soldier*, 481; Tenet, *At the Center of the Storm*, 380–81.

80. Nicholas D. Kristof, "Missing in Action: Truth," *New York Times*, May 6, 2003; Wolffe, "(Overselling) the World on War."

81. Duffy, "Weapons of Mass Disappearance."

82. Walter Pincus, "CIA Did Not Share Doubt on Iraq Data; Bush Used Report of Uranium Bid," *Washington Post*, June 12, 2003.

83. Ackerman and Judis, "The First Casualty."

84. Cheney, *In My Time*, 402–3; Baker, *Days of Fire*, 191–92.

85. Wolffe, "(Overselling) the World on War," 24; Tenet, *At the Center of the Storm*, 453–54; Walter Pincus, "Cheney's Recall is Selective with 'In My Time,'" *Washington Post*, September 5, 2011.

86. Joseph Wilson, "What I Didn't Find in Africa, *New York Times*, July 7, 2003.

87. Comey, *A Higher Loyalty*, 72–73; McClellan, *What Happened*, 2, 8–9, 165, 171, 178, 229, 305; Isikoff and Corn, *Hubris*, 236–67.

88. "Statement by George J. Tenet Director of Central Intelligence," press release, CIA.gov, July 11, 2003; Tenet, *At the Center of the Storm*, 449–75.

89. Robert D. Novak, "Mission to Niger," *Washington Post*, July 14, 2003.

90. Cheney, *In My Time*, 403; Walter Pincus, "Cheney's Recall is Selective with 'In My Time,'" *Washington Post*, September 5, 2011.

91. Isikoff and Corn, *Hubris*, 277; Brenner, "PlameGate."

92. "Transcript of Bob Woodward's Taped Interview Excerpt with Richard Armitage," June 13, 2003, National Security Archive, https://nsarchive2.gwu.edu/NSAEBB/NSAEBB215/def_ex/DX511.pdf.

93. Novak, *The Prince of Darkness*, 5; Bob Woodward, "Testifying in the CIA Leak Case," *Washington Post*, November 16, 2005; Howard Kurtz, "Woodward Apologizes to Post for Silence in Role in Leak Case," *Washington Post*, November 17, 2005.

94. Novak, "The CIA Leak."

95. Isikoff and Corn, *Hubris*, 264.

96. Stewart, *Tangled Webs*, 157–58.

97. "Transcript Colin Powell interview," CBS's *Face the Nation*, August 28, 2011; Stewart, *Tangled Webs*, 17–159; Baker, *Days of Fire*, 287; Isikoff and Corn, *Hubris*, 263–64, 326.

98. Stewart, *Tangled Webs*, 157–59, 227–31.

99. "Grand Jury Hears Testimony from Powell in CIA Case," *USAToday*, August 1, 2004.

100. "Armitage Admits Leaking Plame Identity," CNN.com, September 8, 2006.

101. Carol D. Leonning and Amy Goldstein, "Libby Told 'a dumb lie' Prosecutor Says in Closing Argument," *Washington Post*, February 21, 2007; Carol D. Leonning and Amy Goldstein, "Libby Found Guilty in CIA Leak Case," *Washington Post*, March 7, 2007.

102. "Text of David Kay's Unclassified Statement," CNN.com, October 2, 2003.

103. James Risen and Judith Miller, "No Illicit Arms Found in Iraq, US Inspector Tells Congress," *New York Times*, October 3, 2003.

104. Ibid.

105. Dana Priest and Walter Pincus, "Search in Iraq Finds No Banned Weapons," *Washington Post*, October 3, 2003.

106. Bush, *Decision Points*, 262.

107. Colin Powell, "What Kay Found," *Washington Post*, October 7, 2003.

108. Ibid.

109. Ibid.

110. Tenet, *At the Center of the Storm*, 404–5.

111. David E. Sanger, "White House to Overhaul Iraq and Afghan Missions," *New York Times*, October 6, 2003.

112. Breslow, "Colin Powell: U.N. Speech 'Was a Great Intelligence Failure.'"

113. Rice, *No Higher Honor*, 242–43.

114. Bremer, *My Year in Iraq*, 143.

115. Rumsfeld, *Known and Unknown*, 506; Feith, *War and Decision*, 469–70.

116. Powell, Personal Emails, Colin Powell to Condoleezza Rice, August 29, 2016.

117. Bremer, *My Year in Iraq*, 12.

118. Bumiller, *Condoleezza Rice*, 226–28.

119. Bremer, *My Year in Iraq*, 207, 226–27.

120. Tenet, *At the Center of the Storm*, 437.

121. Ibid., 437–38; Rice, *No Higher Honor*, 246.

122. Baker, *Days of Fire*, 288–92; Gordon and Trainor, *The Endgame*, 27–35.

123. "Interview on the Michael Reagan Radio Show," December 23, 2003, State Department Archive; Steven R. Weisman, "Powell Defends Diplomatic Role," *New York Times*, December 23, 2003.

124. "Secretary Powell's Press Conference," January 8, 2004, State Department Archive.

125. Ibid.

126. "Former U.N. Inspector to Head WMD Hunt in Iraq; Kay: No WMD Stockpiles Found in Iraq," CNN.com, January 23, 2004; James Risen, "Ex-Inspector Says C.I.A. Missed Disarray in Iraqi Arms Program," *New York Times*, January 26, 2004.

127. "Press Briefing en Route to Georgia," January 24, 2004, State Department Archive.

128. Peter Slevin, "Powell Concedes Iraq May No Longer Have Had WMD," *Washington Post*, January 25, 2004.

129. DeYoung, *Soldier*, 488.

130. "Transcript: David Kay at Senate Hearing," CNN.com, January 28, 2004.

131. Bush, *Decision Points*, 261–62.

132. "Interview by the *Washington Post* Editorial Board," February 2, 2004, State Department Archive.

133. Ibid.

134. Ibid.

135. Ibid.

136. Ibid.

137. Ibid.

138. Glen Kessler, "Powell Says New Data May Have Affected War Decision," *Washington Post*, February 3, 2004; "Powell Says Doubts May Have Changed Decision on War," Reuters, February 3, 2004; Barry Schweid, "Colin Powell Defends Decision on Iraq War," Associated Press, February 3, 2004.

139. DeYoung, *Soldier*, 490.

140. "Interview by the *Washington Post* Editorial Board," February 2, 2004, State Department Archive.

141. "Colin Powell Makes Statement in Front of State Department," CNN.com, February 3, 2004.

142. Richard W. Stevenson, "Powell and White House Get Together on Iraq War," *New York Times*, February 4, 2004.

143. Tenet, "Iraq and Weapons of Mass Destruction."

144. "Transcript of February 8, 2004," *Meet the Press*, NBC.

145. "Interview on the *Sean Hannity Show*," February 6, 2004, State Department Archive.

146. "Testimony before the House International Relations Committee," February 11, 2004, State Department Archive.

147. "Interview with *Paula Zahn Now*," February 27, 2004, State Department Archive.

148. Ibid.

149. "Interview on Cox Broadcasting," February 18, 2004, State Department Archive.

150. Allawi, *The Occupation of Iraq*, 219–32; Bremer, *My Year in Iraq*, 286–308.

151. Colin L. Powell, "Counterterrorism Policy," March 23, 2004, "Written Remarks Submitted to: The National Commission on Terrorist Attacks Upon the United States," State Department Archive.

152. "Interview with *Paula Zahn Now*," February 27, 2004, State Department Archive.

153. Allawi, *The Occupation of Iraq*, 266–79; Baker, *Days of Fire*, 321–22; Bremer, *My Year in Iraq*, 326–38.

154. Woodward, *Plan of Attack*, 249, 422, 440.

155. Ibid., 150.

156. Douglas Jehl, "Powell Said to Have Warned Bush before the War, a New Book Says," *New York Times*, April 17, 2004.

157. Steven R. Weisman, "Airing of Powell's Misgivings Tests Cabinet Ties," *New York Times*, April 19, 2004.

158. "Interview on APTV with Barry Schweid and George Gedda," April 19, 2004, State Department Archive.

159. "Interview on CNN's *Larry King Live*," May 4, 2004, State Department Archive.

160. Maureen Dowd, "House of Broken Toys," *New York Times*, April 18, 2004.

161. Clarence Page, "Did Loyalty Finally Trip Up Colin Powell," *Chicago Tribune*, April 21, 2004.

162. Sidney Blumenthal, "What Colin Powell Saw But Didn't Say," *Guardian*, April 22, 2004.

163. "Which Powell Is Which," editorial, *New York Times*, April 20, 2004.

164. Greenberg and Dratel, *The Torture Papers*, 926; Myers, *Eyes On the Horizon*, 260–61.

165. Gourevitch and Morris, *The Ballad of Abu Ghraib*, 250–51.

166. James, *Fixing Hell*, 272.

167. Julie Hirschfeld Davis, "General Testifies That He Didn't See Red Cross Report for 3 Months," *Baltimore Sun*, May 20, 2004.

168. Greenberg and Dratel, *The Torture Papers*, 416.

169. Bush, *Decision Points*, 88–89; DeYoung, *Soldier*, 502.

170. Myers, *Eyes On the Horizon*, 260–61.

171. Ibid., 261.

172. Bush, *Decision Points*, 88–89.

173. "Interview on CNN's *Larry King Live*," May 4, 2004, State Department Archive.

174. DeYoung, *Soldier*, 502.

175. Rumsfeld, *Knowns and Unknowns*, 545–46.

176. Greenberg and Dratel, *The Torture Papers*, 909.

177. Ibid., 172–217; Goldsmith, *The Terror Presidency*, 142, 148.

178. Baker, *Days of Fire*, 193–95; Sands, *Torture Team*, 2–6; Pryer, *The Fight for the High Ground*, 11, 24.

179. "Military Lawyers Objected to Harsh Interrogation Techniques," CNN.com, June 17, 2008; U.S. Senate Armed Services Committee, "Inquiry into the Treatment of Detainees in U.S. Custody," xiii.

180. Goldsmith, *The Terror Presidency*, 166–67.

181. Peter Baker, "Bush Team Approved CIA Tactics, But Was Kept in the Dark about Details, Says Report," *New York Times*, December 9, 2014.

182. Barton Gellman and Jo Becker, "The Unseen Path to Cruelty," *Washington Post*, June 25, 2007; DeYoung, *Soldier*, 503–5.

183. Dana Priest and Barton Gellman, "U.S. Decries Abuse But Defends Interrogations," *Washington Post*, December 26, 2002.

184. Muller, "Memorandum for Record, Humane Treatment of CIA Detainees."; Gordon, *American Nuremburg*, 111.

185. Jan Crawford Greenburg, Howard L. Rosenberg, and Ariane de Vogue, "Top Bush Advisors Approved 'Enhanced Interrogations,'" ABCNews .go.com, April 9, 2008.

186. Central Intelligence Agency Inspector General, "Counterterrorism Detention and Interrogation Activities (September 2001–October 2003)," May 7, 2004, https://www.cia.gov/library/readingroom/document/5856717.

187. Rizzo, *Company Man*, 196–97.

188. "Interview on *Fox News Sunday* with Chris Wallace," May 16, 2004, State Department Archive.

189. "Interview on NBC's *Meet the Press* with Tim Russert," May 16, 2004, State Department Archive.

190. "Interview on ABC's *This Week with George Stephanopoulos*," May 16, 2004, State Department Archive.

191. Rumsfeld, *Known and Unknown*, 545–46.

192. Baker, *Days of Fire*, 327–28.

193. Warren Strobel, "General Who Probed Abu Ghraib Says Bush Officials Committed War Crimes," McClatchydc.com, June 18, 2008.

194. Rizzo, *Company Man*, 215.

195. "Dead Wrong: Inside an Intelligence Meltdown," *CNN Presents*, CNN, August 21, 2005.

196. Rizzo, *Company Man*, 206.

197. Tenet, *At the Center of the Storm*, 479.

198. Morell, *The Great War of Our Time*, 98.

199. Colin L. Powell, author interview.

200. Glenn Kessler, "State Dept. Changes Seen If Bush Reelected," *Washington Post*, August 4, 2003.

201. DeYoung, *Soldier*, 476–79; Bumiller, *Condoleezza Rice*, 249.

202. Hylton, "Casualty of War," 226.

203. Ibid.

204. Annan, *Interventions*, 3.

205. Baker, *Days of Fire*, 330–31.

206. Ibid.

207. Bush, *Decision Points*, 90.

208. Allawi, *The Occupation of Iraq*, 216–32.

209. Bremer, *My Year in Iraq*, 356–58; Rumsfeld, *Known and Unknown*, 661–63; Perry, *The Pentagon's Wars*, 190–91.

210. Gordon and Trainor, *Endgame*, 53–54.

211. Allawi, *The Occupation of Iraq*, 283–88.

212. Bremer, *My Year in Iraq*, 378.

213. Robin Wright, "GOP Star to Skip Convention," *Washington Post*, August 7, 2004.

214. Ibid.

215. Bumiller, *Condoleezza Rice*, 244–45.

216. Elisabeth Bumiller, "White House Letter; No Speeches from Powell or Rice, but a Miss America Will Have Her Say," *New York Times*, August 30, 2004.

217. Dana Priest and Walter Pincus, "U.S. 'Almost All Wrong' on Weapons," *Washington Post*, October 7, 2004.

218. Ibid.

219. "The Verdict Is In," editorial, *New York Times*, October 7, 2004.

220. "Interview on NBC's *Today Show with Matt Lauer*," September 8, 2004, State Department Archive.

221. "Interview by Hubert Wetzel and Guy Dinmore of *Financial Times*," November 8, 2004, State Department Archive.

222. Allawi, *The Occupation of Iraq*, 322–39.

223. "Interview by Hubert Wetzel and Guy Dinmore of *Financial Times*," November 8, 2004, State Department Archive.

224. Bush, *Decision Points*, 89–90.

225. McClellan, *What Happened*, 242–43.

226. Baker, *Days of Fire*, 365.

227. Woodward, *State of Denial*, 361.

228. Bush, *Decision Points*, 91.

229. "Secretary Powell's Letter of Resignation," November 12, 2004, State Department Archive.

230. "President Thanks Secretary Powell," November 15, 2004, State Department Archive.

231. Bush to Powell, November 15, 2004, Powell Papers.

232. "On-the-Record Briefing," November 15, 2004, State Department Archive.

233. "Good Soldier Powell," editorial, *New York Times*, November 16, 2004.

234. Richard Cohen, "Powell's Flawed Exit Strategy," *Washington Post*, November 16, 2004.

235. "Mr. Powell Departs," editorial, *Washington Post*, November 16, 2004.

236. "One of the Few Voices of Sanity," *Guardian*, November 16, 2004.

237. Walter Isaacson, "Colin Powell's Redeeming Failures," *New York Times*, November 16, 2004.

238. Colin Powell to author (email), March 27, 2017.

239. Powell, *It Worked for Me*, 222.

240. Hammond, *Beyond Rationality*, 67.

241. Powell, *My American Journey*, 109, 242; Colin Powell, "A Leadership Primer."

242. Powell, *It Worked for Me*, 223.

243. Ibid., 219.

244. Colin Powell to author (email), August 5, 2017.

245. Bush Memorandum, "Humane Treatment of al Qaeda and Taliban," February 7, 2002, in Greenberg and Dratel, *The Torture Papers*, 134–35.

EPILOGUE

1. Means, *Colin Powell*, 181.

2. Rudy Abramson and John Broder, "Four-Star Power: Colin Powell's Career Has Proceeded with the Certainty of a Laser-Guided Missile. How Much Higher Will He Go?" *Los Angeles Times*, April 7, 1991.

3. Woodward, *The Commanders*, 108.

4. Roth, *Sacred Honor*, 103.

5. Rothkopf, *Running the World*, 255, 210.

6. Hylton, "Casualty of War," 5.

7. Powell, *It Worked for Me*, 223.

8. Powell, *My American Journey*, 57, 142–43.

9. Colin L. Powell, author interview; Powell, *My American Journey*, 342–43.

10. Gates, *A Passion for Leadership*, 163–64.

11. Adam Goldman, "Gina Haspel, Trump's Choice for C.I.A., Played Role in Torture Program," *New York Times*, March 13, 2018.

12. "Interview on *Fox News Sunday with Chris Wallace*," May 16, 2004, State Department Archive.

13. "Full Transcript: Colin Powell talks with Rachel Maddow," NBC News.com, April 1, 2009.

14. "Interview on CBS's *Face the Nation*," CBSNews.com, May 24, 2009.

15. Ibid.

BIBLIOGRAPHY

Ackerman, Spencer, and John D. Judis. "The First Casualty." *New Republic* (June 19, 2003): 14–25.

Adelman, Ken. "Ground Zero: Colin Powell on War, Peace, and Balancing at the Center of Power." *Washingtonian* (May 1990): 71.

Adler, Bill. *The Generals: The New American Heroes.* New York: Avon Books, 1991.

Albright, Madeleine. *Madam Secretary.* New York: Harper Perennial, 2013.

Allawi, Ali A. *The Occupation of Iraq: Winning the War, Losing the Peace.* New Haven, CT: Yale University Press, 2007.

Allison, Sue. "The General Volunteers: Still Helping Uncle Sam, Colin Powell Enlists His Countrymen to Serve One Another." *Life* (May 1997): 51.

Allison, Wick, and William A. Rusher. "Let the Race Begin." *National Review* (April 4, 1994): 46–50.

Annan, Kofi. *Interventions: A Life in War and Peace.* With Nader Mousa-vizadeh. New York: Penguin Books, 2012.

Armitage, Richard. "Interview: Richard Armitage." "Campaign against Terror." *Frontline.* PBS. April 19, 2002.

Aoi, Chiyuki. *Legitimacy and the Use of Armed Force: Stability Missions in the Post–Cold War Era.* London: Routledge, 2011.

Atkinson, Rick. *Crusade: The Untold Story of the Persian Gulf War.* New York: Houghton Mifflin, 1993.

Auster, Bruce B. "Colin Powell Superstar: From the Pentagon to the White House?" *U.S. News & World Report* (September 20, 1993): 48–59.

Bacevich, Andrew J. *The New American Militarism: How Americans are Seduced by War.* Oxford: Oxford University Press, 2005.

Baker, James A. "James A. Baker III, Oral History, White House Chief of Staff; Secretary of State," Presidential Oral Histories. Miller Center, University of Virginia. March 17, 2011. https://millercenter.org/the-presidency /presidential-oral-histories/james-baker-iii-oral-history-2011-white -house-chief.

————. *The Politics of Diplomacy: Revolution, War and Peace, 1989–1992*. New York: G. P. Putnam's Sons, 1995.

Baker, Peter. *Days of Fire: Bush and Cheney in the White House*. New York: Doubleday, 2013.

Baker, Susan D. "Followership: The Theoretical Foundation of a Contemporary Construct." *Journal of Leadership & Organizational Studies* 14, no. 1 (August 2007): 50–60.

Barber, Ben. "The Colin Powell Difference: Foreign Service Veterans, the New Secretary of State's Openness is a Welcome Change from Madeleine Albright's Snobbery." Salon.com. May 19, 2001. https://www.salon.com/2001/05/19/state_department/.

Barry, John. "The Day We Stopped the War." *Newsweek* (January 19, 1992): 16–25.

Battle, Joyce, and Thomas Blanton. "Top Secret Polo Step: Iraq War Plan Assumed Only 5,000 U.S. Troops Still There by December 2006." National Security Archive. https://nsarchive2.gwu.edu/NSAEBB/NSAEBB214/.

Baxter, Peter. *Somalia: US Intervention, 1992–1994*. West Midlands, England: Helion & Company, 2013.

Becton, Julius W., Jr. *Becton: Autobiography of a Soldier and Public Servant*. Annapolis, MD: Naval Institute Press, 2008.

Beinart, Peter. *The Icarus Syndrome: A History of American Hubris*. New York: Harper, 2010.

Belknap, Michal R. *The Vietnam War on Trial: The My Lai Massacre and the Court-Martial of Lieutenant Calley*. Lawrence: University Press of Kansas, 2002.

Bilton, Michael, and Kevin Sim. *Four Hours in My Lai*. New York: Penguin Books, 1992.

Blix, Hans. *Disarming Iraq*. London: Bloomsbury, 2004.

Bolger, Daniel. *Why We Lost: A General's Inside Account of the Iraq and Afghanistan Wars*. New York: First Mariner Books, 2015.

Bonin, Richard. *Arrows of the Night: Ahmad Chalabi and the Selling of the Iraq War*. New York: Anchor Books, 2011.

Bremer, L. Paul. *My Year in Iraq: The Struggle to Build a Future of Hope*. New York: Simon & Schuster, 2005.

Brenner, Marie. "PlameGate. Lies and Consequences: Sixteen Words that Changed the World." *Vanity Fair* (October 17, 2006): 204–64, https://www.vanityfair.com/news/2006/04/brenner200604.

Breslow, Jason M. "Colin Powell: U.N. Speech 'Was a Great Intelligence Failure.'" *Frontline*. PBS. May 17, 2016. http://www.pbs.org/wgbh/frontline/article/colin-powell-u-n-speech-was-a-great-intelligence-failure/.

Brinkley, Douglas, ed. *The Reagan Diaries*. New York: HarperCollins, 2007.

Bumiller, Elisabeth. *Condoleezza Rice: An American Life*. New York: Random House, 2007.

Burns, James MacGregor. *Transforming Leadership: A New Pursuit of Happiness*. New York: Grove Press, 2003.

Burns, Richard Dean. *The Missile Defense Systems of George W. Bush*. Santa Barbara, CA: Praeger, 2010.

Bush, George H. W., and Brent Scowcroft. *A World Transformed*. New York: Vintage Books, 1998.

Bush, George W. *Decision Points*. New York: Crown, 2010.

Byrne, Malcolm. *Iran-Contra: Reagan's Scandal and the Unchecked Abuse of Presidential Power*. Lawrence: University Press of Kansas, 2014.

Carlucci, Frank. "Frank Carlucci Oral History, Assistant to the President for National Security Affairs; Secretary of Defense." Presidential Oral Histories. Miller Center, University of Virginia. August 28, 2001. https://miller center.org/the-presidency/presidential-oral-histories/frank-carlucci -oral-history-assistant-president-national.

———. "What State Needs: Resources for Reform." *Foreign Service Journal* 78, no. 5 (May 2001): 17–20.

Carlucci, Frank C., and Ian J. Brzezinski. "State Department Reform." Council on Foreign Relations and Center from Strategic and International Studies, 2001. https://cfrd8-files.cfr.org/sites/default/files/pdf/2005/10/state _department.pdf.

Chaleff, Ira. *The Courageous Follower: Standing Up To and For Our Leaders*. San Francisco: Berrett-Koehler, 2009.

Cheney, Dick. *In My Time: A Personal and Political Memoir*. With Liz Cheney. New York: Threshold Editions, 2011.

———. "Richard B. Cheney Oral History, Secretary of Defense." Presidential Oral Histories. Miller Center, University of Virginia. March 16–17, 2000. https://millercenter.org/the-presidency/presidential-oral-histories /richard-b-cheney-oral-history-secretary-defense.

Christopher, Warren. *Chances of a Lifetime*. New York: Scribner, 2001.

Clancy, Tom, with Tony Zinni and Tony Koltz. *Battle Ready*. New York: Berkley Books, 2004.

Clancy, Tom, with Carl Stiner and Tony Koltz. *Shadow Warriors: Inside the Special Forces*. New York: Berkley Books, 2003.

Clarke, Richard A. *Against All Enemies: Inside America's War on Terror*. New York: Free Press, 2004.

Clinton, Bill. *My Life*. New York: Knopf, 2004.

Cohen, Eliot A. *Supreme Command: Soldiers, Statesmen, and Leadership in Wartime*. New York: Anchor Books, 2002.

Cohen, Herman. *Intervening in Africa: Superpower Peacemaking in a Troubled Continent*. New York: St. Martin's Press, 2000.

Cole, Ronald H. *Operation Just Cause: The Planning and Execution of Joint Operations in Panama*. Washington, DC: Joint History Office, Office of the Chairman of the Joint Chiefs of Staff, 1995.

Comey, James. *A Higher Loyalty: Truth, Lies, and Leadership*. New York: Flatiron Books, 2018.

Congressional Research Service. "China–U.S. Aircraft Collision Incident of April 2001: Assessments and Policy Implications," October 10, 2001. Federation of American Scientists. https://fas.org/sgp/crs/row/RL30946.pdf.

Cooper, Matthew. "Colin's K-Street Crowd." *New Republic* (November 27, 1995): 18–21.

Crandall, Russell. *Gunboat Democracy: U.S. Interventions in the Dominican Republic, Grenada, and Panama*. Lanham, MD: Rowman & Littlefield, 2006.

Crisis Magazine. "Pat Schroeder v. Colin Powell: Congresswoman Taunts, the General Replies." (July 1, 1992). https://www.crisismagazine.com/1992/pat-schroeder-v-colin-powell-the-congresswoman-taunts-the-general-replies.

Crowe, William J., Jr. *The Line of Fire: From Washington to the Gulf, the Politics and Battles of the New Military*. With David Chanoff. New York: Simon & Schuster, 1993.

Daalder, Ivo H., and I. M. Destler. *In the Shadow of the Oval Office: Profiles of the National Security Advisers and the Presidents They Served—From JFK to George W. Bush*. New York: Simon & Schuster, 2009.

———. "The National Security Council Project, Oral History Roundtables: The Role of the National Security Adviser." October 25, 1999. http://docplayer.net/63309171-The-national-security-council-project.html.

DeYoung, Karen. *Soldier: The Life of Colin Powell*. New York: Alfred A. Knopf, 2006.

Donnelly, Thomas, Margaret Roth, and Caleb Baker. *Operation Just Cause: The Storming of Panama*. New York: Random House, 1991.

Draper, Robert. *Dead Certain: The Presidency of George W. Bush*. New York: Free Press, 2007.

Draper, Theodore. *A Very Thin Line: The Iran-Contra Affairs*. New York: Hill and Wang, 1991.

Drogin, Bob. *Curveball: Spies, Lies, and the Con Man Who Caused a War*. New York: Random House, 2007.

Drumheller, Tyler. *On the Brink: An Insider's Account of How the White House Compromised American Intelligence*. With Elaine Monaghan. New York: Carol & Graff, 2006.

Dubose, Lou, and Jake Bernstein. *Vice: Dick Cheney and the Hijacking of the American Presidency*. New York: Random House, 2006.

Duffy, Michael. "Weapons of Mass Disappearance." *Time* (June 1, 2003): 28.

Eichenwald, Kurt. *500 Days: Secrets and Lies in the Terror Wars*. New York: Touchstone, 2012.

Feith, Douglas J. *War and Decision: Inside the Pentagon at the Dawn of the War on Terrorism*. New York: Harper, 2008.

Felice, William F. *How Do I Save My Honor? War, Moral Integrity, and Principled Resignation*. Lanham, MD: Rowman & Littlefield, 2009.

Felix, Antonia. *Wesley Clark: A Biography*. New York: Newmarket Press, 2004.

Fineman, Howard. "Powell on the March." *Newsweek* (September 11, 1995): 26–31.

Fleischer, Ari. *Taking Heat: The President, the Press, and My Years in the White House*. New York: HarperCollins, 2005.

Foreign Affairs Council. "Secretary Colin Powell's State Department." *Ambassadors Review* (Spring 2003): 78–99.

Frank, Nathaniel. *Under Friendly Fire: How the Gay Ban Undermines the Military and Weakens America*. New York: Thomas Dunne Books, 2009.

Franks, Tommy. *American Soldier*. New York: ReganBooks, 2004.

Friedman, Saul. "Four Star Warrior." *Newsday Magazine* (February 11, 1990): 10.

Gates, Henry Louis, Jr. "Powell and the Black Elite." *New Yorker* (September 25, 1995): 64–80.

———. *Thirteen Ways of Looking at a Black Man*. New York: Vintage Books, 1997.

Gates, Robert M. *From the Shadows: The Ultimate Insider's Story of Five Presidents and How They Won the Cold War*. New York: Simon & Schuster, 1996.

———. *A Passion for Leadership: Lessons on Change and Reform from Fifty Years of Public Service*. New York: Alfred A. Knopf, 2016.

Gelman, Barton. *Angler: The Cheney Vice Presidency*. New York: Penguin, 2008.

Gibbs, Nancy. "General Letdown." *Time* (November 20, 1995): 48.

Gingrich, Newt. "Rogue State Department." *Foreign Policy* 137 (July/August 2003): 42–48.

———. "Transforming the State Department: The Next Challenge for the Bush Administration." American Enterprise Institute. April 22, 2003. https://www.aei.org/publication/transforming-the-state-department/.

Girard, Philippe R. *Clinton in Haiti: The 1994 U.S. Invasion of Haiti*. New York: Palgrave Macmillan, 2004.

Glasser, Susan B. "You Can't Bomb It Away." Politico.com. March 15, 2015. http://www.politico.com/magazine/story/2015/03/bill-burns-interview-iran-talks-116078.

Goldberg, Jeffrey. "Breaking Ranks: What Turned Brent Scowcroft against the Bush Administration." *New Yorker* (October 21, 2005): 54–65.

Goldsmith, Jack. *The Terror Presidency: Law and Judgment inside the Bush Administration.* New York: W.W. Norton, 2009.

Gole, Henry G. *General William E. DePuy: Preparing the Army for Modern War.* Lexington: University Press of Kentucky, 2008.

Gordon, Michael R., and Bernard E. Trainor. "Beltway Warrior." *New York Times Magazine* (August 27, 1995): 40–43.

———. *Cobra II: The Inside Story of the Invasion and Occupation of Iraq.* New York: Pantheon, 2006.

———. *The Endgame: The Inside Story of the Struggle for Iraq, from George W. Bush to Barack Obama.* New York: Pantheon Books, 2012.

———. *The Generals' War: The Inside Story of the Conflict in the Gulf.* New York: Little, Brown, 1995.

Gordon, Rebecca. *American Nuremburg: The U.S. Officials Who Should Stand Trial for Post-9/11 War Crimes.* New York: Hot Books, 2016.

Gourevitch, Philip, and Errol Morris. *The Ballad of Abu Ghraib.* New York: Penguin Books, 2009.

Greenberg, Karen. *The Least Worst Place: Guantanamo's First 100 Days.* Oxford: Oxford University Press, 2009.

Greenberg, Karen, and Joshua L. Dratel, eds. *The Torture Papers: The Road to Abu Ghraib* Cambridge: Cambridge University Press, 2005.

Haass, Richard N. *War of Necessity, War of Choice: A Memoir of Two Iraq Wars.* New York: Simon & Schuster, 2009.

Halberstam, David. *War in a Time of Peace: Bush, Clinton, and the Generals.* New York: Simon & Schuster, 2001.

Hamilton, Lee H., and Daniel K. Inouye. *Report of the Congressional Committees Investigating the Iran-Contra Affair, with Supplemental, Minority, and Additional Views.* Washington, DC: Government Printing Office, 1987. https://archive.org/details/reportofcongress87unit.

Hammond, Kenneth R. *Beyond Rationality: The Search for Wisdom in a Troubled Time.* Oxford: Oxford University, 2007.

Harari, Oren. *The Leadership Secrets of Colin Powell.* New York: McGraw-Hill, 2002.

Haulman, Daniel L. "A Country Too Far: U.S. Military Operations In Somalia, 1992–94." Air Force Historical Research Agency, May 6, 2004. www.afhra.af.mil/Portals/16/documents/Studies/AFD-070912-041.pdf.

Henke, Holger. *The West Indian Americans.* Westport, CT: Greenwood Press, 2001.

Hill, Christopher R. *Outpost: Life on the Frontlines of American Diplomacy, A Memoir.* New York: Simon & Schuster, 2014.

Hollander, E. P. "Leadership, Followership, Self, and Others." *Leadership Quarterly* 3, no. 1 (1992): 43–54.

Hughes, Libby. *Colin Powell: A Man of Quality*. Parsippany, NJ: Dillon Press, 1996.

Hylton, Wil S., "Casualty of War," *GQ* (June 2004): 226–32, 235–36.

Indyk, Martin. *Innocent Abroad: An Intimate Account of American Peace Diplomacy in the Middle East*. New York: Simon & Schuster, 2009.

Isikoff, Michael, and David Corn. *Hubris: The Inside Story of Spin, Scandal, and the Selling of the Iraq War*. New York: Crown, 2006.

Jaffe, Lorna S. *The Development of the Base Force, 1989–1992*. Washington, DC: Joint History Office, Office of the Joint Chiefs of Staff, July 1993.

James, Larry C. *Fixing Hell: An Army Psychologist Confronts Abu Ghraib*. New York: Grand Central, 2008.

Jones, Christopher M. "The Other Side of Powell's Record." *American Diplomacy* (March 2006). http://www.unc.edu/depts/diplomat/item/2006/0103/jone/jonesc_powell.html.

Jones, Howard. *My Lai: Vietnam, 1968, and the Descent into Darkness*. Oxford: Oxford University Press, 2017.

Kagan, Robert, and William Kristol. "A National Humiliation." *Weekly Standard* (April 15, 2001): 16–23.

Kaplan, Lawrence F. "Yesterday's Man: Colin Powell's Out-of-Date Foreign Policy." *New Republic* (January 1, 2001): 17–21.

Keller, Bill. "The World According to Powell." *New York Times Magazine* (November 25, 2001): 60–67, 74–76.

Kellerman, Barbara. *Followership: How Followers Are Creating Change and Changing Leaders*. Boston: Harvard Business Press, 2008.

Kelley, Robert E. *How to Be A Star at Work: Nine Breakthrough Strategies You Need to Succeed*. New York: Times Business/Random House, 1998.

———. "In Praise of Followers." *Harvard Business Review* (November–December, 1988): 142–48.

———. *The Power of Followership: How to Create Leaders People Want to Follow and Followers Who Lead Themselves*. New York: Doubleday/Currency, 1992.

Khalilzad, Zalmay. *The Envoy: From Kabul to the White House, My Journey Through a Turbulent World*. New York: St. Martin's Press, 2016.

Kitfield, James. *Prodigal Soldiers: How the Generation of Officers Born of Vietnam Revolutionized the American Style of War*. Washington, DC: Potomac Books, 1995.

Klein, Joe. "Can Colin Powell Save America." *Newsweek* (October 9, 1994): 20–24.

Kohn, Richard H. "Out of Control: The Crisis in Civil–Military Relations." *National Interest* (Spring 1994): 3–17.

Lacayo, Richard. "The Rebellious Soldier." *Time* (February 15, 1993): 32.

Lane, Charles. "The Legend of Colin Powell." *New Republic* (April 17, 1995): 20–32.

Leung, Rebecca. "The Man Who Knew: Ex-Powell Aide Says Saddam-Weapons Threat Was Overstated." *60 Minutes*, CBS, October 14, 2003. http://www.cbsnews.com/news/the-man-who-knew-14-10-2003/.

Levin, Carl, and John Warner. "Review of the Circumstances Surrounding the Ranger Raid on October 3–4, 1993 in Mogadishu, Somalia." September 29, 1995. Federation of American Scientists. https://fas.org/irp/congress/1995_rpt/mogadishu.pdf.

Liman, Arthur L. *Lawyer: A Life of Counsel and Controversy*. With Peter Israel. New York: PublicAffairs, 1998.

Lipman-Blumen, Jean. *The Allure of Toxic Leaders*. Oxford: Oxford University Press, 2005.

Locher, James R. *Victory on the Potomac: The Goldwater–Nichols Act Unifies the Pentagon*. College Station: Texas A & M University Press, 2004.

Mackenzie, Richard. "An Officer and a Gentleman." *Insight* (October 8, 1990): 9.

Margolick, David. "The Night of the Generals." *Vanity Fair* (March 5, 2007): 246–80.

Mayer, Jane. *The Dark Side: The Inside Story of How the War on Terror Turned into a War on American Ideals*. New York: Doubleday, 2008.

McClellan, Scott. *What Happened: Inside the Bush White House and Washington's Culture of Deception*. New York: PublicAffairs, 2008.

McFarlane, Robert C. *Special Trust*. With Zofia Smardz. New York: Cadell & Davies, 1994.

Meacham, Jon. *Destiny and Power: The American Odyssey of George Herbert Walker Bush*. New York: Random House, 2015.

———. "How Colin Powell Plays the Game." *Washington Monthly* (December 1994): 33–42.

Means, Howard. *Colin Powell: Soldier/Statesman—Statesman/Soldier*. New York: Donald I. Fine, 1992.

Meyer, Christopher. *DC Confidential: The Controversial Memoirs of Britain's Ambassador to the U.S. at the Time of 9/11 and the Run-up to the Iraq War*. London: Phoenix, 2005.

Morell, Michael. *The Great War of Our Time: The CIA's Fight against Terrorism—From al Qa'ida to ISIS*. New York: Twelve, 2015.

Morris, Dick. Interview with Chris Bury. "The Clinton Years." *Frontline*. PBS. June 2000. https://www.pbs.org/wgbh/pages/frontline/shows/clinton/interviews/morris.html.

Moskin, J. Robert. *American Statecraft: The Story of the U.S. Foreign Service*. New York: St. Martin's Press, 2013.

Muller, Scott W. "Memorandum for Record, Humane Treatment of CIA Detainees." February 12, 2003. https://ciasavedlives.com/resources.html.

Murdock, Deroy. "Powell for President: Americans Try to Solve a Four-Star Mystery." *National Minority Politics* (December 1994): 6.

Murphy, Cullen, and Todd S. Purdum. "Farewell to All That: An Oral History of the Bush White House." *Vanity Fair* (December 28, 2008): 88–160, https://www.vanityfair.com/news/2009/02/bush-oral-history200902.

Myers, General Richard B. *Eyes On the Horizon: Serving on the Front Lines of National Security*. New York: Threshold Editions, 2009.

National Commission on Terrorist Attacks upon the United States. *9/11 Commission Report: Final Report of the National Commission on Terrorist Attacks upon the United* States. New York: W.W. Norton, 2004.

National Intelligence Council. "National Intelligence Estimate: 'Iraq's Continuing Programs for Weapons of Mass Destruction.'" October 2002. https://www.scribd.com/doc/259216899/Iraq-October-2002-NIE-on -WMDs-unedacted-version.

National Journal, "Managing the Departments: Grades for Bush's Cabinet Secretaries," *Government Executive,* January 27, 2003. https://www.gov exec.com/management/2003/01/managing-the-departments-grades -for-bushs-cabinet-secretaries/13317/.

Naughtie, James. *The Accidental American: Tony Blair and the Presidency*. New York: PublicAffairs, 2004.

Nickerson, Raymond S. *Conditional Reasoning: The Unruly Syntactics, Semantics, Thematics, and Pragmatics of "IF."* Oxford: Oxford University Press, 2015.

———. "Confirmation Bias: A Ubiquitous Phenomenon in Many Guises." *Review of General Psychology* 2, no. 2 (1998): 175–220.

Njoku, Raphael Chijioke. *The History of Somalia*. Santa Barbara, CA: Greenwood, 2013.

Novak, Robert D. *The Prince of Darkness: 50 Years Reporting in Washington*. New York: Crown Forum, 2008.

Pardew, James W. *Peacemakers: American Leadership and the End of Genocide in the Balkans*. Lexington: University of Kentucky Press, 2018.

Parry, Robert. *America's Stolen Narrative: From Washington and Madison to Nixon, Reagan and the Bushes to Barack Obama*. Arlington, VA: Media Consortium, 2012.

Parry, Robert, Sam Parry, and Nat Parry. *Neck Deep: The Disastrous Presidency of George W. Bush*. Arlington, VA: Media Consortium, 2007.

Pastor, Robert A. "More and Less Than It Seemed: The Carter-Nunn-Powell Mediation in Haiti, 1994." In *Herding Cats: Multiparty Mediation in a Complex World*, edited by Chester A. Crocker, Fen Osler Hampson, and

Pamela Aall, 505–26. Washington, DC: United States Institute of Peace Press, 1999.

Patterson, Orlando. "The Culture of Caution." *New Republic* (November 27, 1995): 22–26.

Peers, W. R. *The My Lai Inquiry*. New York: W.W. Norton, 1979.

Perry, Mark. *The Pentagon's Wars: The Military's Undeclared War against America's Presidents*. New York: Basic Books, 2017.

Pfiffner, James P. *Torture as Public Policy: Restoring U.S. Credibility on the World Stage*. Boulder, CO: Paradigm, 2010.

Ponnuru, Ramesh. "Powell Cons." *National Review* (October 23, 1995): 20–21.

Poole, Walter S. *The Effort to Save Somalia: August 1992–March 1994*. Washington, DC: Joint History Office, Office of the Chairman of the Joint Chiefs of Staff, 2005.

Powell, Colin L. "Colin Powell Oral History, Chairman of the Joint Chiefs of Staff." Presidential Oral Histories. Miller Center, University of Virginia. December 16, 2011. https://millercenter.org/the-presidency/presidential-oral-histories/colin-powell-oral-history-chairman-joint-chiefs-staff.

———. "Interview: Colin Powell." "Campaign against Terror." *Frontline*. PBS. June 7, 2002.

———. *It Worked for Me: In Life and Leadership*. With Tony Koltz. New York: Harper, 2012.

———. "A Leadership Primer" (PowerPoint). Briefing presented by Gen Powell to the Outreach to America Program, Sears Corporate Headquarters, Chicago, IL. Air University: U.S. Air Force. http://www.au.af.mil/au/afri/aspj/apjinternational/apj-s/2011/2011-4/2011_4_02_powell_s_eng.pdf.

———. *My American Journey*. With Joseph E. Persico. New York: Random House, 1995.

———. "No Substitute for the Soldier on the Ground." *Army* (December 1994): 13–16.

———. "Oral History: Colin Powell." "The Gulf War." *Frontline*. PBS. n.d. www.pbs.org/wgbh/pages/frontline/gulf/oral/powell/1.html.

———. Papers of General Colin L. Powell (Ret.). Special Collections, National Defense University Library, Fort Lesley J. McNair, Washington, DC.

———. Personal Emails. June 2014–August 2016. https://web.archive.org/web/20170308121623/http://dcleaks.com/index.php/portfolio_page/colin-luther-powell/.

———. Speeches and Remarks as Secretary of State, 2001–2005. State Department Archive. https://2001-2009.state.gov/secretary/former/powell/remarks/index.htm.

———. "U.S. Forces: Challenges Ahead." *Foreign Affairs* (Winter 1992/1993): 32–45.

Power, Samantha. *"A Problem from Hell": America and the Age of Genocide.* New York: Basic Books, 2013.

Pryer, Douglas A. *The Fight for the High Ground: The U.S. Army and Interrogation during Operation Iraqi Freedom I, May 2003–April 2004.* Fort Leavenworth, KS: CGSC Foundation Press, 2009.

Purdum, Todd S. *Time of Our Choosing: America's War in Iraq.* New York: Times Books, 2003.

Puryear, Edgar F., Jr. *American Generalship, Character is Everything: The Art of Command.* New York: Presidio, 2000.

Reagan, Ronald. *An American Life: Ronald Reagan, the Autobiography.* New York: Simon and Schuster, 1990.

Rice, Condoleezza. *Democracy: Stories from the Long Road to Freedom.* New York: Twelve, 2017.

———. *No Higher Honor: A Memoir of My Years in Washington.* New York: Crown, 2011.

Ricks, Thomas E. *Fiasco: The American Military Adventure in Iraq.* New York: Penguin Books, 2007.

———. *The Generals: American Military Command from World War II to Today.* New York: Penguin Books, 2012.

Riggio, Ronald E., Ira Chaleff, and Jean Lipman-Blumen, eds. *The Art of Followership: How Followers Create Great Leaders and Great Organizations.* San Francisco: Jossey-Bass, 2008.

Rizzo, John. *Company Man: Thirty Years of Controversy and Crisis in the CIA.* New York: Scribner, 2014.

Roth, David. *Sacred Honor: Colin Powell, the Inside Account of His Life and Triumphs.* Grand Rapids, MI: Zondervan, 1993.

Rothkopf, David J. *Running the World: The Inside History of the National Security Council and the Architects of American Power.* New York: Public Affairs, 2005.

Rove, Karl. *Courage and Consequence: My Life as a Conservative in the Fight.* New York: Threshold Editions, 2010.

Rudd, Gordon W. *Reconstruction Iraq: Regime Change, Jay Garner, and the ORHA Story.* Lawrence: University Press of Kansas, 2011.

Rumsfeld, Donald. *Known and Unknown: A Memoir.* New York: Sentinel, 2011.

Samuels, David. "A Conversation with Colin Powell." *Atlantic* (April 2007). https://www.theatlantic.com/magazine/archive/2007/04/a-conversation-with-colin-powell/305873/.

Sands, Philippe. *Torture Team: Rumsfeld's Memo and the Betrayal of American Values.* New York: Palgrave Macmillan, 2008.

Schwarzkopf, H. Norman. *It Doesn't Take A Hero.* With Peter Petre. New York: Bantam Books, 1992.

Senate Armed Services Committee Report. "Inquiry into the Treatment of Detainees in U.S. Custody." November 20, 2008. U.S. Senate. https://www.armed-services.senate.gov/download/inquiry-into-the-treatment-of-detainees-in-us-custody.

Senate Foreign Relations Committee, February 6, 2003, *Congressional Record,* V149 part 2, January 21–February 11, 2003.

Senate Intelligence Committee. "Report on the U.S. Intelligence Community's Prewar Assessment on Iraq." July 7, 2004. Federation of American Scientists. https://fas.org/irp/congress/2004_rpt/.

Shelton, Hugh. *Without Hesitation: The Odyssey of an American Warrior.* New York: St. Martin's Press, 2010.

Shultz, George P. *Turmoil and Triumph: My Years as Secretary of State.* New York: Charles Scribner's Sons, 1993.

Smith, Jean Edward. *Bush.* New York: Simon & Schuster, 2016.

Sparrow, Bartholomew. *The Strategist: Brent Scowcroft and the Call of National Security.* New York: Public Affairs, 2015.

Stark, Steven. "President Powell?" *Atlantic* (October 1993): 22–29.

Stephanopoulos, George. *All Too Human: A Political Education.* New York: Little, Brown, 1999.

Stewart, James B. *Tangled Webs: How False Statements Are Undermining America.* New York: Penguin Books, 2011.

Stiglitz, Joseph E., and Linda J. Bilmes. *The Three Trillion Dollar War: The True Cost of the Iraq Conflict.* New York: W. W. Norton, 2008.

Straw, Jack. *Last Man Standing: Memoirs of a Political Survivor.* London: Macmillan, 2012.

Sununu, John H. *The Quiet Man: The Indispensable Presidency of George H. W. Bush.* New York: Broadside Books, 2015.

Suskind, Ron. *The Price of Loyalty: George Bush, the White House, and the Education of Paul O'Neill.* New York: Simon & Schuster, 2004.

Taft, William H., IV. "Unclassified Memorandum To: John C. Yoo." January 11, 2002. National Security Archive. https://nsarchive2.gwu.edu/torturing democracy/documents/20020111.pdf.

Tenet, George J. *At the Center of the Storm: My Years at the CIA.* New York: HarperCollins, 2007.

———. "Iraq and Weapons of Mass Destruction." Speech at Georgetown University, February 5, 2004. Central Intelligence Agency. https://www.cia.gov/news-information/speeches-testimony/2004/tenet_georgetown speech_02052004.html.

Thomas, Evan. "The Reluctant Warrior." *Newsweek* (May 12, 1992): 18.

Thomas, Evan, and John Berry. "Colin Powell: Behind The Myth." *Newsweek* (March 4, 2001): 10–14.

Timberg, Robert. *The Nightingale's Song.* New York: Simon & Schuster, 1995.

Torreon, Barbara Salazar. "A Guide to Major Congressional and Presidential Awards." March 31, 2004. Air University: U.S. Air Force. www.au.af.mil /au/awc/awcgate/crs/rs20884.pdf.

Turse, Nick. *Kill Anything That Moves: The Real American War in Vietnam.* New York: Henry Holt, 2013.

Unger, Craig. *The Fall of the House of Bush: The Untold Story of How a Band of True Believers Seized the Executive Branch, Started the Iraq War, and Still Imperils America's Future.* New York: Scribner, 2007.

Waas, Murray, ed. *The United States v. I. Lewis Libby.* New York: Union Square Press, 2007.

Walsh, Lawrence E. *Final Report of the Independent Counsel for Iran/Contra Matters.* 3 vols. Washington, DC: U.S. Court of Appeals for the District of Columbia Circuit, 1993.

———. *Firewall: The Iran-Contra Conspiracy and Cover-up.* New York: W.W. Norton, 1997.

Warrick, Joby. *Black Flags: The Rise of ISIS.* New York: Anchor Books, 2015.

Watson Institute for International & Public Affairs, Brown University. Cost of War Project. http://watson.brown.edu/costsofwar/.

Weinberger, Caspar W. "Caspar Weinberger Oral History, Secretary of Defense." November 19, 2002. Presidential Oral Histories. Miller Center, University of Virginia. https://millercenter.org/the-presidency/presidential -oral-histories/caspar-weinberger-oral-history-secretary-defense.

———. *Fighting for Peace: Seven Critical Years in the Pentagon.* New York: Warner Books, 1990.

———. *In the Arena: A Memoir of the 20th Century.* With Gretchen Roberts. Washington, DC: Regnery, 2001.

———. "The Uses of Military Power." National Press Club. *Frontline.* PBS. November 28, 1984. http://www.pbs.org/wgbh/pages/frontline/shows /military/force/weinberger.html.

Western, Jon. *Selling Intervention and War: The Presidency, the Media, and the American Public.* Baltimore, MD: Johns Hopkins University Press, 2005.

Wolffe, Richard. "(Over)selling the World on War." *Newsweek* (June 9, 2003): 24.

Wolffe, Richard, and Daniel Klaidman. "Judging the Case." *Newsweek* (February 17, 2003): 16.

Woodward, Bob. *Bush at War.* New York: Simon & Schuster, 2002.

———. *The Commanders.* New York: Simon & Schuster, 1991.

———. *Plan of Attack.* New York: Simon & Schuster, 2004.

———. "The Powell Predicament." *Washington Post Magazine* (September 24, 1995): 9–17.

———. *Veil: The Secret Wars of the CIA, 1981–1987.* New York: Simon and Schuster, 1987.

Yant, Martin. *Desert Mirage: The True Story of the Gulf War.* Buffalo, NY: Prometheus Books, 1991.

Zenko, Micah. "Forgoing Limited Force: The Bush Administration's Decision Not to Attack Ansar al-Islam." *Journal of Strategic Studies* (August 2009): 615–49.

Zinni, Tony. *The Battle for Peace: A Frontline Vision of America's Power and Purpose.* With Tony Koltz. New York: Palgrave Macmillan, 2006.

INDEX

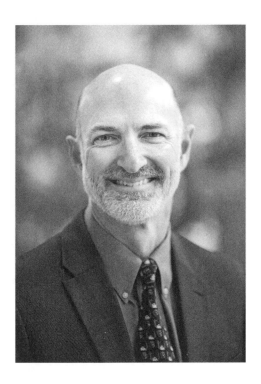

JEFFREY J. MATTHEWS is the George Frederick Jewett Distinguished Professor at the University of Puget Sound in Tacoma, Washington. He teaches American history and leadership and has written or edited three previous books, including *Blacksheep Leadership* and *The Art of Command: Military Leadership from George Washington to Colin Powell*.